Organization Design

SAGE PUBLISHING: OUR STORY

We believe in creating fresh, cutting-edge content that helps you prepare your students to make an impact in today's ever-changing business world. Founded in 1965 by 24-year-old entrepreneur Sara Miller McCune, SAGE continues its legacy of equipping instructors with the tools and resources necessary to develop the next generation of business leaders.

- We invest in the right authors who distill the best available research into practical applications
- We offer intuitive digital solutions at student-friendly prices
- We remain permanently independent and fiercely committed to quality, innovation, and learning.

Organization Design

Creating Strategic & Agile Organizations

Donald L. Anderson

University of Denver

Los Angeles | London | New Delhi
Singapore | Washington DC | Melbourne

FOR INFORMATION:

SAGE Publications, Inc.
2455 Teller Road
Thousand Oaks, California 91320
E-mail: order@sagepub.com

SAGE Publications Ltd.
1 Oliver's Yard
55 City Road
London, EC1Y 1SP
United Kingdom

SAGE Publications India Pvt. Ltd.
B 1/I 1 Mohan Cooperative Industrial Area
Mathura Road, New Delhi 110 044
India

SAGE Publications Asia-Pacific Pte. Ltd.
3 Church Street
#10-04 Samsung Hub
Singapore 049483

Acquisitions Editor: Maggie Stanley
Editorial Assistant: Alissa Nance
Marketing Manager: Amy Lammers
Production Editor: Veronica Stapleton Hooper
Copy Editor: Diane DiMura
Typesetter: Hurix Digital
Proofreader: Barbara Coster
Indexer: Karen Wiley
Cover Designer: Gail Buschman

Printed in the United States of America.

Library of Congress Cataloging-in-Publication Data

Names: Anderson, Donald L., 1971- author.

Title: Organization design : creating strategic & agile organizations / Donald L. Anderson, University of Denver.

Description: Thousand Oaks, Calif. : SAGE, [2019] | Includes bibliographical references and index.

Identifiers: LCCN 2018009388 | ISBN 9781506349275 (pbk. : alk. paper)

Subjects: LCSH: Organizational change. | Organizational behavior. | Organizational effectiveness.

Classification: LCC HD58.8 .A68146 2019 | DDC 658.4/06—dc23 LC record available at https://lccn.loc.gov/2018009388

This book is printed on acid-free paper.

SFI label applies to text stock

18 19 20 21 22 10 9 8 7 6 5 4 3 2 1

BRIEF CONTENTS

DETAILED CONTENTS

Sara Miller McCune founded SAGE Publishing in 1965 to support the dissemination of usable knowledge and educate a global community. SAGE publishes more than 1000 journals and over 800 new books each year, spanning a wide range of subject areas. Our growing selection of library products includes archives, data, case studies and video. SAGE remains majority owned by our founder and after her lifetime will become owned by a charitable trust that secures the company's continued independence.

Los Angeles | London | New Delhi | Singapore | Washington DC | Melbourne

PREFACE

Observers of contemporary organizations continue to enumerate the enormous challenges facing leaders today. Leaders are required to operate with global teams to serve global customers; to cope with increased competitive pressures from rivals large, small, new, and unexpected; to innovate in agile ways to secure even a short-term competitive advantage; and to do all of this with fewer resources than ever before. Organizations are developing increasingly complex designs to account for the collaboration required in today's rapidly changing, global, dynamic environment. In many ways, organization design is a core leadership competency to address these challenges. Yet while dozens of publications introduce students and business leaders to the foundations of strategy or talent management, there are few introductory publications in the field of organization design.

Organization design is a complex subject that can be intimidating to newcomers. Students who come to the field of organization design through strategy find themselves quickly mired in complex discussions of four-sided matrix designs or virtual organizations. These frameworks seem to forget that people design organizations and execute on their strategies. Other students who come to design from the people side or human resources discipline tend to become lost in discussions of strategy and complex global operating models. Practicing organization design requires an understanding of industry trends and strategic positioning as well as an understanding of organizational behavior, organizational change, and even psychology.

Organization design is an interdisciplinary field of theory and practice. Students and managers who apply design concepts need to not only understand design theory, but how to translate that theory into practice. These topics can be difficult to understand, much less to apply in an ever changing contemporary environment and adapt to the unique needs of any given organization.

The purpose of this book is to expose you to not only classic and traditional but also contemporary and innovative organization design concepts, and to do so in a way that is accessible to a novice. Design practitioners come in many forms: You might be a leader looking to enhance your knowledge of organization design so that you can create a department or team that is aligned with the organization's strategy and removes barriers to performance. You might be a human resources (HR) professional or organization development consultant whose role is to work with leaders in your organization on their organization design challenges and to facilitate them through a design process. In any case, the concepts, theories, and approaches in this book are intended to provide an introduction to the field of organization design and the choices that must be weighed. You will find the term *organization designer* throughout the book to emphasize these different roles, from leader to consultant to HR practitioner.

Consistent with the view that there is no one right organization design, you will not find any particular design advocated or an attempt to push the latest fad designs. Instead, it is important that as managers, students, and practitioners we have an appreciation for the thought process involved in organization design.

It is more helpful to develop an understanding of the choice points, trade-offs, considerations, and consequences of any design alternative than to adopt a design just because it is popular. By learning more about organization design in this way, you will be a better observer of organization design challenges and a better critic of proposed designs and their consequences. You will also be in a position to recommend alternatives that are more likely to result in the objectives you are trying to reach.

OVERVIEW OF THE BOOK

We will begin in Chapter 1 by defining organization design and outlining its history. We will explore why organization design is a relevant field of study for today's managers. Chapter 2 will expose you to key concepts of organization design, including the STAR model that we will use as the foundation of the book. We will learn the organization design process of understanding the scope of the design effort, conducting design assessments to evaluate strengths and weaknesses in an existing design, testing a design, and developing design criteria.

Chapters 3 through 7 will address the five components of the STAR model of organization design. We will begin with an exploration of the concept of strategy in Chapter 3 where our goal will be to assess whether the organization has a consistent or defined strategy and where we will understand foundational concepts in the field of strategy. In Chapter 4, we will examine different kinds of organizational structures and the advantages and disadvantages of each. We will look at matrix organizations in depth to understand their unique benefits and challenges. In Chapter 5, we examine the lateral capability of an organization's design to understand the information and decision-making processes that cross the structural units of the organization. Here we will also delve specifically into global operating models as a central concept. In Chapter 6 we will focus on the people issues of the design. We will consider the relationship between organizational capabilities and individual capabilities and how to manage talent practices in a way that support the strategy. Chapter 7 will consider rewards and how to develop effective reward and recognition programs that motivate employees in a way that is consistent with the other aspects of the design.

In Chapter 8, we will discuss reorganizing, that is, how to implement organization design changes and manage transitions between current and new designs. We will also examine a leader's role in organization design and how organizational culture relates to design. Chapter 9 will expand on the contemporary challenge of agility. Organizations today are faced with developing designs that can respond quickly to market changes, and becoming an agile organization means changes at each point of the design. To conclude, in Chapter 10, we will examine future issues of organization design and some of the capabilities that managers need to have to be successful designers.

EXERCISES, ACTIVITIES, AND THE ORGANIZATION DESIGN SIMULATION

Throughout the book, you will find discussion questions, exercises, and case studies intended to bring design concepts to life. Many of these case studies will invite you to put yourself in the shoes of the leader and consider the real life choices that they face, as leaders must be conscious of the trade-offs they make. What are the advantages of choosing option A over B, and what are the consequences of that choice? What problems does that choice solve, and what additional problems might that choice create? Are there ways of mitigating the new problems that get created? As you learn the principles and concepts of organization design and you are able to debate these issues with others, your answers to these questions will become clearer.

A unique organization design simulation activity in the Appendix will also allow you to practice designing your own fictional organization. You will find instructions guiding you to this simulation exercise following Chapters 3, 5, 7, and 8. The activity will invite you to roll the dice and invent an imaginary organization of your choosing. Whether you design a global manufacturer of virtual reality headsets, a national franchise of yoga studios, a citywide bakery serving local restaurants, or something else entirely, the organization design principles you learn in the text will guide you through the very real thought process of design as you create your company.

INSTRUCTOR TEACHING SITE

A password-protected instructor's manual is available at **study.sagepub.com/andersonorgdesign** to help instructors plan and teach their courses. These resources have been designed to help instructors make the classes as practical and interesting as possible for students.

PowerPoint Slides capture key concepts and terms for each chapter for use in lectures and review.

A Test Bank includes multiple-choice, short-answer, and essay exam questions for each chapter.

Video Resources for each chapter help launch class discussion.

SAGE Journal Content ties important research and scholarship to chapter concepts to strengthen learning.

SAGE Business Cases give students insight into real-world applications.

Instructor's Manual contains discussion questions, exercises, and case notes to further spark class dialogue.

* * *

I would like to thank the staff at SAGE and the reviewers, clients, colleagues, students, friends, and family who have shaped the development of this book, especially my wife Jennifer, who supported the project and encouraged me to write it from the very beginning.

—Donald L. Anderson

ACKNOWLEDGMENTS

SAGE would like to thank the following reviewers:

Henry Adobor, Quinnipiac University

Deborah Armstrong, University of New Brunswick Saint John

Thomas E. Butkiewicz, Chapman University

Jeffrey J. Darville, La Roche College

Robert Dibie, Indiana University Kokomo

Pat Driscoll, Texas Woman's University

Issam Ghazzawi, University of La Verne

Doris Gomez, Regent University

Bruce Hanson, Concordia University Irvine

Ralph Haug, Roosevelt University

Andrew T. Hinrichs, California State University, Stanislaus

Katherine Hyatt, Reinhardt University

Lisa Knowles, St. Thomas University

Michael Kramer, Lewis University

Barbara J. Limbach, Chadron State College

Ann Membel, Regis University

Stephen Mumford, Gwynedd Mercy University

Mary Jo Shane, California Lutheran University

Rumaisa Shaukat, University of Ottawa

Ann Snell, Tulane University

Denise M. Tanguay, Eastern Michigan University

Joseph W. Weiss, Bentley University

Debra K. Westerfelt, Ashland University

Bruce Winston, Regent University

ABOUT THE AUTHOR

Donald L. Anderson, PhD, University of Colorado, teaches organization development and organization design at the University of Denver. He is the author of the text *Organization Development* (4th ed., Sage, 2017) and editor of *Cases and Exercises in Organization Development & Change* (2nd ed., Sage, 2017). He is a practicing organization development consultant and has consulted internally and externally with a wide variety of organizations, including Fortune 500 corporations, small businesses, nonprofit organizations, and educational institutions. Dr. Anderson's research interest is in discourse in organizational and institutional settings, and his studies of organizational discourse and change have been published in journals such as the *Journal of Organizational Change Management*, *Gestion*, and the *Journal of Business and Technical Communication*. Dr. Anderson is a member of the Academy of Management and serves on the editorial boards of the journal *Management Communication Quarterly*, SAGE Business Cases, and SAGE's Business and Management Advisory Board.

CHAPTER 1

INTRODUCTION TO ORGANIZATION DESIGN

On July 22, 2014, a full-page ad appeared in the *New York Times* (Figure 1.1).

The ad featured a dizzying array of organizational boxes and lines depicting the complex interfaces required to manage the U.S. Department of Homeland Security (DHS). Just over one year after the attacks of September 11, 2001, Congress established the DHS as a new department formed from all or some of 22 different government agencies. The intent was to bring together disparate practices and groups to remedy "the current confusing patchwork of government activities into a single department whose primary mission is to protect our homeland" (Proposal to Create the Department of Homeland Security, 2002, p. 1). The initial proposal promised a "clear and efficient organizational structure" (p. 2). This was no small achievement, as the U.S. federal government is a very large and complex organization comprising more than 2.7 million workers in addition to almost 1.5 million military personnel, according to the U.S. Office of Personnel Management. More than 240,000 of these employees work in the DHS.

A report that was subsequently produced more than 10 years after the establishment of the new department lamented the complexity of this new model. It noted that the DHS was required to report to almost 100 different congressional committees and subcommittees. Whereas a government agency such as the Department of State might report predominantly to the Foreign Affairs committees in the House and Senate, DHS was faced with oversight from dozens of committees that had overlapping and perhaps even competing authority and jurisdictions. On the one hand, one could argue that this complexity created too many interactions that resulted in duplicative, wasted effort. Are employees spending time producing similar presentations and reports and sitting in meetings that may not be the best use of their time? On the other hand, this might be exactly the model required to manage the complex threats in areas as diverse as cybersecurity and bioterrorism. Perhaps these multiple connections create

Learning Objectives

In this chapter you will learn

- What organization design is and how it is defined.
- The history and development of the field of organization design.
- Why organization design is relevant as a subject of study and practice today.

Figure 1.1

THE 9/11 COMMISSION URGED CONGRESS TO SIMPLIFY THE OVERSIGHT OF HOMELAND SECURITY.

INSTEAD, WE HAVE THIS.

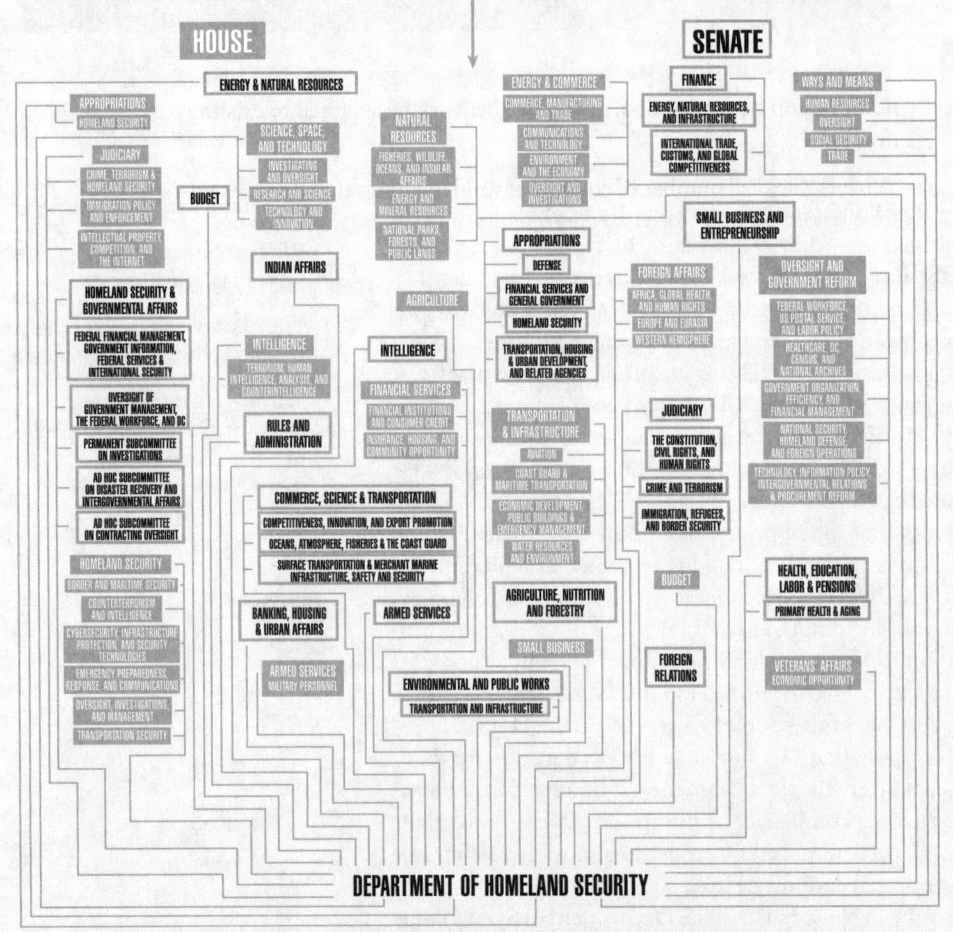

"THINK OF HAVING A HUNDRED BOSSES. THINK OF REPORTING TO A HUNDRED PEOPLE. IT MAKES NO SENSE. YOU COULD NOT DO YOUR JOB UNDER THOSE CIRCUMSTANCES."[1]

9/11 COMMISSION CHAIRMAN THOMAS H. KEAN

Congress's confused oversight of the Department of Homeland Security has left our nation vulnerable to cyberthreats, biohazards, and small planes and boats carrying unknown cargo.[2] The 9/11 Commission recommended streamlining oversight of the Department of Homeland Security. Instead, Congress made matters worse. In 2004, DHS answered to 88 Congressional committees and subcommittees. In the last Congress, that number had grown to 92 – along with 27 other caucuses, commissions and groups. It's been 10 years since the 9/11 Commission urged Congress to act.

WHAT IS CONGRESS WAITING FOR?

THE ANNENBERG PUBLIC POLICY CENTER OF THE UNIVERSITY OF PENNSYLVANIA

To read the Sunnylands-Aspen report and see the video "Homeland Confusion"
Visit: www.annenbergpublicpolicycenter.org/security

1, 2. Sunnylands Aspen Institute Task Force Report, 9/11/2013.

Source: Annenberg Public Policy Center of the University of Pennsylvania. (2014, July 22). Instead, we have this. *The New York Times*.

opportunities for collaboration and information sharing that otherwise would not exist? Whether this is the right model or not for this organization, the ad brought issues of organization design to national attention in a way that most Americans had probably never considered about the federal government. It introduced issues in a way that most people could relate to and begin to debate.

For example, consider these common questions that organizational leaders must address:

- How much complexity in an organization is necessary and helpful to respond to a complex and rapidly changing environment?
- When a new set of activities is introduced to an organization, should a new division be established, or should the work be assigned to existing divisions?
- What is the ideal number of committees and meetings that does not waste time but encourages the right coordination and information sharing?

Despite the number of organizations we interact with on a regular basis, including schools, churches, hospitals, and businesses large and small, most of us rarely consider their designs consciously until something is not working effectively. You might be a frustrated customer at the mercy of a poor organization design when you had a problem with a company and heard from every employee that your problem was not the responsibility of that department. You might wonder why the same insurance company you have for auto insurance and life insurance cannot seem to share information between the different divisions or why two doctors in the same office do not have similar billing practices. In addition, consider your place of employment. You may have noticed inefficiencies in how your department operates, or you might have seen what happens when work falls through the cracks because it was no one's responsibility. You may have been part of a merger with or acquisition by another company, or you might have experienced the confusion that resulted from your own department being divided or integrated with another internally.

All of this is to say that you have certainly experienced organization design even if you have never before considered the issues and decision points in an organization's design. The purpose of this book is to introduce you to the field of organization design, an area of academic research and professional practice devoted to the conscious design of organizations of all forms, from nonprofit organizations to for-profit companies and local, state, and national governments.

ORGANIZATION DESIGN DEFINED

Over the decades of its history, organization design has been defined in different ways. Let's look at three widely respected definitions of organization design:

- "Organization design is conceived to be a decision process to bring about a coherence between the goals or purposes for which the organization exists, the patterns of division of labor and interunit coordination and the people who will do the work" (Galbraith, 1977, p. 5).

- "Organization design is the making of decisions about the formal organizational arrangements, including the formal structures and the formal processes that make up an organization" (Nadler & Tushman, 1988, p. 40).
- "Organization design is the deliberate process of configuring structures, processes, reward systems, and people practices and policies to create an effective organization capable of achieving the business strategy" (Galbraith, Downey, & Kates, 2002, p. 2).

You may have noticed a number of consistent themes included in each of these definitions.

Organization Design Is a Set of Deliberate Decisions

All organizations are designed (or have a design), even if they were not designed that way intentionally. In addition, all organizations evolve and change, and as they do, the design usually changes as well. Sometimes these changes are thoughtfully considered. An executive leaves the company and two existing units with complementary capabilities get combined. The company decides to enter into a new market and establishes a separate division to manage the product development, marketing, and sales of the new products for that market. At other times, the organization may be changing without conscious attention. Customer demands may grow to the point that the existing customer service organization cannot effectively manage the number of new contracts being generated. A failed product line may result in expensive manufacturing capacity that is no longer needed. An organization design approach helps to purposefully evaluate how and why the organization is designed as it is. Kates (2009) calls organization design a "decision science that focuses on setting frameworks and making sound choices among competing alternatives" (p. 447). What distinguishes organization design is the intentionality of decisions. As Galbraith (1977) puts it, "Design efforts can result in organizations which perform better than those which arise naturally" (p. 4). Without conscious attention to design, many organizations will evolve haphazardly and ineffectively.

Organization Design Is a Process

In addition, organization design is a process, not an activity or event. Since the organization is always in a fluid and dynamic process of evolution, growth, adaptation, and change, the design is as well. Companies decide to enter into new markets, discontinue product lines, or enhance or reduce services. Each of these changes has a design implication. "To some extent, managers are making design decisions all the time. Every time a specific job is assigned, a procedure created, a method altered, or a job moved, the organization design is being tinkered with" (Nadler & Tushman, 1988, p. 41). A design perspective can provide a thought process to managers to make these daily decisions with a rational lens.

It is tempting to think of organization design as a noun, as something an organization is or has. Indeed, among both managers and design theorists it is not uncommon to think of an organization design as an architect would think about design ("organizational architecture," Brickley, Smith, Jr., Zimmerman, & Willett, 2003; Nadler & Tushman, 1997). By adopting this metaphor, "when people in organizations talk about the design of an organization, they tend to equate it with things like organization charts, written procedures, and job specifications. . . . As a result, organizational designs tend to focus on structures rather than processes" (Weick, 1993, p. 348). Instead, Weick reminds us that organization design is often more continuous, emergent, and fluid than it appears if we assume that design is like a skyscraper. Design from this perspective is not a recipe, blueprint, organizational chart, or any other static and solid entity. As designs are infused with life by people, they grow, develop, and adapt, often in ways that were never imagined. The process of design, then, is an ongoing activity. In this respect, organization design might be better described as organization *designing*, a verb reminding managers that it is a process that is never complete (Yoo, Boland, & Lyytinen, 2006). Put succinctly, "A well designed organization is not a stable solution to achieve, but a developmental process to keep active" (Starbuck & Nystrom, 1981, p. xx).

Organization Design Assumes a Systems Approach to Organization

The definitions above use words such as *units*, *arrangements*, *patterns*, and *configurations* to describe the idea that organizations are considered to be a combination of intersecting parts that work together to achieve a goal. We refer to this as a systems approach to organization. "All social systems, including organizations, consist of the patterned activities of a number of individuals" (D. Katz & Kahn, 1966, p. 17). Open systems (natural and organizational) display common characteristics, such as the importation of energy or inputs, a throughput or transformation process, an output, feedback, and homeostasis or equilibrium. Systems theorists refer to organizational systems as "open" versus "closed" because the system is interconnected with its environment (Kast & Rosenzweig, 1972). As the environment changes (due to competitive threats, changes in customer preferences, government regulations, etc.), the organization must change and adapt in response. Open systems thinking is the process of considering how people, processes, structures, and policies all exist in an interconnected web of relationships. For example, a hospital has doctors and nurses that collaborate with other departments (e.g., cardiology, radiology, and physical therapy) to achieve the best care for patients. Each of these departments must work interdependently with the information technology department for patient records and the finance department for patient billing. The external environment outside the hospital itself includes government regulatory agencies that place new demands and requirements on the organization.

An organization design process places attention on the interdependencies between the different units of the organization to ensure effective coordination between them. This is important because the design of the system will often cause different individuals to behave in similar patterned ways. In other words, "When placed in the same system, people, however different, tend to produce similar results" (Senge, 1990, p. 42). Organization designers therefore pay more attention to definitions of roles and structures than individual idiosyncrasies or personalities. Instead of explaining outcomes as the result of a single individual or department, a design perspective based on systems thinking may help us see how the design encourages certain behavior patterns, often subtly and without conscious decision. If the radiology department outsources the interpretation of x-rays, that decision may result in an impact to the billing department as well as to the timeliness, format, and content of the reports to physicians. A systems approach to design reminds us that changes in one part of the organization affect other parts of the organization as well. Thus the different departments must be in alignment and designed to be in coherence with one another, a point that we will cover in more detail later.

Organization Design Is Based on the Organization's Strategy

Organizations are a means to an end, that is, they are designed to accomplish goals and objectives based on a business strategy. This implies that "successful design of an organization requires deeply understanding the context for which the organization is being designed—the environment in which the firm competes, the business strategies and models it will use to compete, and the capabilities it needs to compete" (Beckman, 2009, p. 6). Organization design is sometimes called *strategic organization design* to emphasize both the idea that (1) organization designs must be based on the business strategy; and (2) the organization should be designed strategically, that is, intentionally, a point covered above. This implies that organizations that have different strategies will have different designs. A technology organization that requires constant innovation and sophisticated new products will be designed very differently from a low-cost manufacturer. "Design drives the way strategies are formulated or formed, and determines whether and how they can be implemented. It is the vehicle by which firms recognize the need for adaptation, determine its course, and put change into effect. It is the framework that enables and allows collective behavior to occur" (Greenwood & Miller, 2010, p. 79). The strategic choices that the company makes will affect all aspects of the system and the design choices that need to be made, including the numbers of people in different divisions and how they are rewarded and skilled.

Organization Design Encompasses Multiple Levels of Analysis

Organization design can be seen as a field that has big picture, strategic, holistic, and top-down aspects, as well as more specific, detailed, and focused decisions. An organization designer must be concerned with "relatively macro issues such as the number of individuals reporting directly to the CEO and the types of activities for which each of them is responsible as well as relatively micro issues such as the nature of the training the organization is prepared to provide to entry-level managerial personnel" (Kimberly, 1984, pp. 121–122). The goals of the organization will drive design decisions at multiple levels of analysis. "An appreciation of organization design and behavior requires a multidisciplinary perspective across many levels of analysis: the individual, group, organization, industry or population of organizations, and macrosocial movements" (Van de Ven & Joyce, 1981, p. 3). Organization designers must be comfortable with the forest and the trees to see not only the parts of the organization but also how they fit together.

Organization Design Is More Than Organizational Structure

The definitions above mention organizational structure as an aspect of design, but they also note that design goes beyond structure. If you have ever been part of a restructuring at work, you might have had the common experience that while reporting relationships may have changed and a new organizational chart was published, little else changed after the dust settled. Challenges remain, such as the following:

- Priorities are unclear.
- Decision making is slow.
- People still aren't clear about what they are responsible for.

- The same gaps between departments exist or duplication of work has not been addressed.
- Changes in one department now cause difficulties in another.
- Employees aren't empowered to manage their own work.
- Goals and metrics reward one thing but expect another.
- Employees are given new expectations for their work but have not received the right training.
- Acquisitions have not been effectively integrated.

These challenges often remain because changes were made at the level of organization structure but other aspects of the design were not considered. Organizational structure is visible and easily grasped and interpreted by managers and employees, and it can often be an easier aspect of the design to change quickly. Ask managers to describe their organizations and many will begin by drawing an organizational chart. But "structure change is often overly relied on or is misguided because the business problem is not well defined. Organization structure is a powerful but blunt instrument for change. Changes in processes, people, rewards, and measures are nearly always critical complements to realignments in structure" (Kesler & Kates, 2011, p. 6). Three manufacturing divisions might be integrated into one central unit in an attempt to speed up manufacturing cycle times, but without attention to the fundamental reasons behind why cycle times are too slow, lasting change is unlikely to result from structure change alone. As Kimberly (1984) puts it, "[A]t their worst, ill-conceived, poorly managed design efforts generate organizational charades: the illusion of change is created while existing relationships are unchanged" (p. 122). Knee-jerk structure changes as reactions to organizational performance issues are rarely successful. "Most design efforts invest far too much time drawing the organization chart," Galbraith (2002, p. 14) concludes. Design changes may include structure changes but must go beyond them to be successful.

Organization Design Is an Interdisciplinary Field of Research and Practice

As you may be able to tell from these definitions and the concepts addressed in organization design addressed above, this is an interdisciplinary field of both research and practice. The field draws insights from a number of other disciplines. Snow, Miles, and Miles (2006) note that "the relevant knowledge base is very diverse, including concepts, approaches, and research findings from fields such as psychology, economics, logistics, information technology, and change management. . . . Thus, organization design can be thought of as 'scientific art' and its best practitioners have a deep understanding of how organizations work as well as how they can and must be changed" (pp. 3–4). Galbraith (2008) points out that organization design includes knowledge from "sociology, organization theory, applied psychology, consulting practice, or anywhere there is useful information. It is a very eclectic field" (p. 325). Simons (2005) argues that "to design an organization effectively, you need to understand business strategy, marketing, organization behavior, information technology, accounting, and leadership" (p. vii). It is likely that most managers lack a deep background in one or more of these areas and may have made design decisions based on intuition or personal experience. Today many leaders are finding organization design decisions to be more relevant than ever based on pressures in the contemporary environment and the critical relationship that organization design has on organizational performance.

HISTORY OF ORGANIZATION DESIGN

While the term *organization design* may only date to the 1960s (Kimberly, 1984), the issues and problems of organization design can in many ways be traced back to the beginnings of modern organizations. Many of the questions that leaders struggle with today are also found in the history of organizations, as this brief history lesson will illustrate.

1850s to Early 20th Century

To be sure, before the 1850s, there were few organizations that were so large that they needed an extensive bureaucratic structure to manage them (Chandler, 1962), so there would have been no need for organization design as we know it. Small, family-owned businesses of the day were typically managed by the business owners themselves. The roles of president, financial officer, shipping clerk, store manager, and customer service agent would have been filled by the same person or perhaps shared by two or three people. Collaboration would have been relatively simple and decisions quickly coordinated without the need for a formal definition of authority or division of labor. Even in the early days of the railroads, where the lengths of most tracks were relatively short, a minimal number of people would have been needed to manage them. As Chandler (1962) discovered in an 1855 quote from a railroad executive,

> A superintendent of a road fifty miles in length can give its business his [*sic*] personal attention and may be constantly on the line engaged in the direction of its details; each person is personally known to him, and all questions in relation to its business are at once presented and acted upon. (p. 21)

Consider what happened, however, when the following years saw the expansion of the railroads from coast to coast. The railroad companies now found that it was more difficult to manage with a single superintendent who could conduct all management activities alone. A headquarters staff and field units began to develop. Functional structures were created that segregated different duties by type of work performed. Departments were organized to handle different activities such as accounting, passengers, railroad schedules, and freight. The Pennsylvania Railroad, for example, may have been the first to create a detailed description of an organizational structure. A document described lines of communication and decision-making authority internally within the transportation department, and it outlined cross-functional relationships with other departments such as accounting. These departments themselves were now led by managers who had functional expertise and day-to-day decision authority. This also allowed for the development of a new type of executive who would have a strategic thinking capacity and future orientation in contrast to the day-to-day work of a department manager. A key design problem during this era was to determine which decisions should be made by a centralized headquarters group and which decisions should be delegated to the decentralized field units (a design decision that continues today; Galbraith, 2008).

The expansion of the railroads also held implications for other businesses. New and expanded markets now existed for other companies as it was now possible to ship goods long distances to the growing U.S. urban population. This meant growth opportunities for mining companies and American factories. Snow (2015) calls this the "age of competition" as companies struggled with the challenges of building their organizations to address the growing need for mass production, understanding their different markets, and managing the dual goals of maintaining the existing organization while expanding into new diversified businesses. As companies grew, they were challenged not only to manage greater production volumes but to deal with new and different functions. Operating activities became more specialized, which required coordination and planning between them. For example, Andrew Carnegie built the modern steel business in the United States (Carnegie Steel, which eventually became U.S. Steel). Key to its organization was vertically integrated ownership of both raw materials as well as manufacturing, and centralized management structures (Snow, 2015). Snow (2015) writes that "the success of the functional organization depended on the contributions of specialized departments (manufacturing, sales, accounting, etc.), coordinated and controlled by centrally determined plans, budgets, and schedules" (p. 436), noting that the functional structure was the prevailing structure choice of most organizations in this period.

1910s to World War II

In the 1910s, the problem of factory efficiency, output, and division of labor began to interest management theorists, articulated most notably in the work of Frederick Taylor (1911). If making a pair of shoes requires five steps, instead of having each worker complete all five, why not specialize the tasks so that step 1 is performed by one worker, step 2 by another worker, and so on? Each worker becomes an expert in the given step, whether it is cutting, assembly, or polishing (Galbraith, 1977). This created problems of motivation among workers who now only managed minor steps and did not experience the satisfaction of having created an entire finished product.

In addition, coordination° is now required among the workers leading to the need for a boss ("foreman," in Taylor's words). If workers can divide labor into subspecialties, then perhaps such a concept could apply to management as well, so Taylor argued that different kinds of foremen could manage different types of work (e.g., maintenance, inspection, scheduling). Thus a single worker could have eight different bosses depending on the content area. Most observers at the time agreed that this was too complicated to work out in practice, and argued for the principle of "unity of command . . . [meaning] that authority should pass in an unbroken chain of command from the top management to the worker" (Galbraith, 2008, p. 326). Today, these questions remain central to organization design—how jobs should be divided, how to motivate employees, how departments should be formed, how many employees one manager can supervise, how many managers are needed, and how multiple managers in matrix organizations should influence the work of individual employees.

After World War I, many companies expanded into new product areas (Chandler, 1962). For example, General Electric and Westinghouse began as producers of light bulbs and generators, respectively, but by the 1920s had begun building aircraft engines and consumer goods such as washing machines, vacuum cleaners, and refrigerators. Thus many organizations that had a single product line and a functional structure were now challenged with using the same organizational structure to manage multiple and diverse types of products. Departments such as finance, procurement, shipping, and manufacturing that may have had standard practices for dealing with a single product struggled to deal with this additional complexity. A divisional structure was created out of these challenges, where each product line or category would have its own division. An administrative structure was set up to oversee the different operating divisions. This divisional structure is credited with the success of General Motors in the post–Depression era (Snow, 2015). It may have taken some time for this new type of design to catch on, as most Fortune 500 companies still had functional structures in 1950, but 20 years later, the multidivisional structure was the choice of 90 percent of organizations (Galbraith, 2008). Some argue that the divisional structure facilitated global expansion since international offices could be added as new divisions that would create products for new markets (Galbraith, 2008; Snow, 2015).

Post–World War II to 1960s

In the expansion of the social sciences following World War II, the 1960s saw the publication of three studies that had a lasting impact on the field of organization design.

Burns and Stalker (1961). Burns and Stalker studied 20 British and Scottish firms in a variety of industries (textiles and electronics among them) and found that each firm tended to display characteristics of one of two types—it was either organic or mechanistic (see Figure 1.2). Table 1.1 describes several of the characteristics of mechanistic and organic organizations.

What made the Burns and Stalker study notable at the time was that they argued that neither approach was naturally better, despite arguments of the era that an organic system was generally preferable. They wrote,

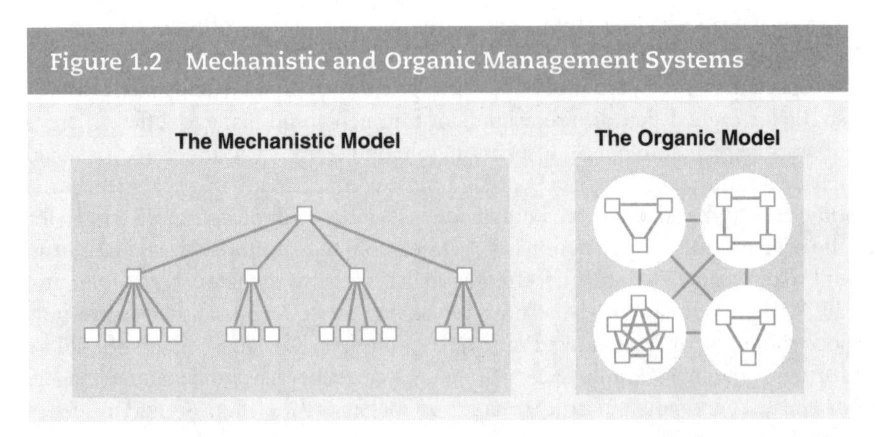

Figure 1.2 Mechanistic and Organic Management Systems

Source: Robbins, Stephen P. (2005). *Organizational behavior. 11th ed.* Upper Saddle River, NJ: Pearson.

Table 1.1 Comparison of Mechanistic and Organic Systems	
Characteristics of Mechanistic Systems	**Characteristics of Organic Systems**
Specialized differentiation of functional tasks	Individual job broadly defined, not self-contained
A hierarchical structure of control, authority, and communication	A network structure of control, authority, and communication
A tendency for interaction between members to be vertical (i.e., between superior and subordinate)	A lateral rather than vertical direction of communication through the organization, communication between people of different rank, resembling consultation rather than command
A tendency for operations and working behavior to be governed by instructions and decisions issued by superiors	Content of communication consists of information and advice rather than instructions and decisions
Negotiation of tasks done by immediate superiors	Adjustment and continual redefinition of individual tasks through interaction with others
Authority dictated by hierarchical position	Authority decided by whoever is most informed and capable

Source: Adapted from Burns, T., & Stalker, G. M. (1961). *The manangement of innovation*. London, England: Tavistock, pp. 120–122.

> We desire to avoid the suggestion that either system is superior under all circumstances to the other. In particular, nothing in our experience justifies the assumption that mechanistic systems should be superseded by organic in conditions of stability. The beginning of administrative wisdom is the awareness that there is no one optimum type of management system. (p. 125)

Both designs were effective in their given context—organic firms worked for organizations that experienced rapidly changing environments whereas mechanistic firms worked best in relatively stable industries, with predictable and regularly patterned activities. This finding marks the beginning of a contingency theory of organization design (reviewed in more detail in the next chapter) that suggests that there is no one ideal type of organization design, but that the selection of a design will vary according to the organization's environment. By refusing to come down on the side of the mechanistic approach prescribed by classical management theorists or the organic approach to design preferred by the neo-human relations theorists, the Burns and Stalker study endorsed both in different contexts. In doing so, the Burns and Stalker model has been called "the most widely known contingency theory of organizational structure" (Donaldson, 2001, p. 38).

Chandler (1962). Chandler's study began as a comparative analysis of four companies: du Pont, General Motors, Jersey Standard, and Sears. Each of these companies independently (and without imitation of the others) implemented what Chandler called a "decentralized" structure shortly after World War I. By "decentralized," Chandler means that as each company expanded its capabilities, it created a new division for a product line. Product lines contained each major function (sales, engineering, manufacturing, finance, etc.), and each of those functional units was typically made up of different field units (field sales offices, manufacturing plants, or accounting units). While this structure might be commonplace today, remember that Chandler was investigating organization designs in the 1920s, and such designs were innovative and uncommon among large organizations. Chandler was interested in what prompted these four organizations to evolve in a similar pattern even though they were not connected with one another and were not part of the same industry.

Chandler found a pattern in how each organization responded to growth. First, the company expanded in volume, which led to the need to establish new administrative offices to handle the workload. Next, geographical growth led to field units to handle local needs, and an overarching central office to handle different types of functions. National expansion into new product lines meant that a general office was needed to allocate resources across the different product lines. Thus, Chandler found that the evolution of organizational structures could be explained by the needs that the companies had for dealing with the complexity of operations that came from growth.

> The thesis that different organizational forms result from different types of growth can be stated more precisely if the planning and carrying out of such growth is considered a *strategy*, and the organization devised to administer these enlarged activities and resources, a *structure*. (p. 13)

Chandler's thesis—that structure follows strategy—has been one of the most influential concepts in the field of organization design. Galbraith (2012) has extended Chandler's discussion of portfolio strategies and structures to trace the evolution of design to today's multidimensional structures.

Lawrence and Lorsch (1967b). As we saw in the Burns and Stalker (1961) study, Lawrence and Lorsch (1967b) began their landmark study with the observation that classical management theory traditionally sought to make prescriptive recommendations to managers about ideal ways to manage and organize. They noted that at the time, "most organizational research and theory has implicitly, if not explicitly, focused on the one best way to organize in all situations." They proposed that a more appropriate question is to ask "what kind of organization does it take to deal with different environmental conditions?" (p. 3). Like the Burns and Stalker study, theirs was a comparative study, in this case of six different organizations in three different industries (plastics, container, and food).

Two key concepts in the Lawrence and Lorsch study are differentiation and integration. Differentiation describes the separation of the organization into different subunits or departments, based on the needs of the environment. If different customer segments require different marketing approaches, or if different products require different manufacturing strategies, then these organizations will need to be more internally differentiated, that is, each division will have its own unique processes or approaches. In addition, differentiation describes the cultural and behavioral differences of the subunits, including attitudes and way of thinking and operating. Integration refers to the degree of interdependence and the need for coordination among the different units. Product lines that have similar manufacturing components, for example, are likely to find the need to be more integrated.

Groups that are highly differentiated and require little interaction with one another can operate independently with little effect on performance. However, most organizations require some level of connection between departments to accomplish their goals. The more similar two departments were in their study, the more effective the integration, and the more different the departments, the more difficulties they had with integration. "As a result, when groups in an organization need to be highly differentiated, but also require tight integration, it is necessary for the organization to develop more complicated integrating mechanisms" (Lawrence & Lorsch, 1969, p. 13). They note that the most fundamental of integrating mechanisms is the simple management hierarchy, where managers can coordinate the activities of multiple groups. When the requirements for coordination become more complex, however, members of the organization will need to develop more sophisticated practices of integration, such as cross-functional teams. The best performing departments in their study achieved the required degree of differentiation to meet environmental demands and found ways for those departments to work well together. Cross-functional department coordination remains a central issue in organization design today.

1970s and 1980s

Throughout the post–World War II period, as we have seen, organizations gradually moved toward a multidivisional structure. Beginning largely in the 1960s in aerospace organizations, matrix organizations (Davis & Lawrence, 1977) grew in popularity and expanded into other industries widely in the 1970s. For these companies it was cost prohibitive to hire new employees for each new project when there were available employees who were underutilized in other departments. The matrix organization addressed the need for the efficiency that existed in the functional structure as well as the market focus and flexibility of the divisional structure. Matrix organizations solved the problems of the need for dual focus (e.g., the need to focus on functions, products, services, and markets), a high need for information-processing capacity due to uncertainty, and the economic pressure for shared resources (Davis & Lawrence, 1977). Over the next decades, it would be observed that "virtually all large multinational corporations employ some form of matrix organizing" (Snow, 2015, p. 437).

In the 1970s, a popular notion surfaced that "organizations could be usefully conceptualized as configurations of resources" (called a "configurational approach," Snow, Miles, & Miles, 2006, p. 5) or patterns of strategy, structures, management processes, and people. Frameworks, models, and typologies of design concepts began to appear, notably the STAR model, which we will review in Chapter 2. Some of the first books to explicitly discuss organization design as a field were published in this era, led by the pioneering work of Jay Galbraith (1973). Most writers arrived at a similar conclusion: that "high-performing configurations are those with internal and external congruence, alignment, or fit" (Snow, Miles, & Miles, 2006, p. 6).

The 1980s saw a new form of design called a dynamic network or multifirm network organization (Miles & Snow, 1986; Snow, 2015). Instead of all activities to produce a product or service occurring inside a single organization, many organizations elected to partner or outsource some of their functions to specialist organizations. This network organization had four characteristics, according to Miles and Snow (1986):

- Vertical disaggregation: the separation of product development, manufacturing, shipping, and logistics into unique activities performed by different organizations.
- Brokers: a hub-and-spoke model where one or more parties brings the network together.
- Market mechanisms: market needs and contracts for services hold the network together.
- Full-disclosure information systems: "Broad-access computerized information systems are used as substitutes for lengthy trust-building processes based on experience" (p. 65).

"A properly constructed network can display the technical specialization of the functional structure, the market responsiveness of the divisional structure, and the balanced orientation of the matrix" (Miles & Snow, 1986, p. 65). Because each organization specializes in a core competency, the dynamic network organization brings together the strengths of each organization in a way that maximizes scale and flexibility.

1990s and 2000s

Galbraith (1991) observed that "the primary force in today's business environment is global competition" (p. 51), noting that this was a continuation of a trend that had begun more than a decade earlier. Slower growth rates from the 1980s prompted businesses to look for new customers in new geographies. In addition, cost pressures forced them to look to cut unnecessary expenses. Galbraith noted that "there are hidden costs in the interfaces between business functions like engineering and manufacturing" (p. 58). Galbraith wrote that business strategies at the time involved recovery moves such as automation and cost containment, increasing productivity through outsourcing, global expansion, and development of new services or technologies.

Supporting this thinking, Zeffane (1992) noted that the rise of service economies and the pace of socioeconomic change had resulted in "a fundamental shift in the way organizations in different nations are conducting their operations" and that "massive organizational restructuring is being undertaken in various countries" (p. 18). Structural questions such as span of control, centralization versus decentralization, and the choice of organic over mechanistic designs were identified as important considerations in the early 1990s. Zeffane observed a trend toward increased decentralization and removal of layers of management, taking advantage of the ability of new information technologies to speed information flow, resulting in a more fluid and flexible organizational structure. "Survival is increasingly dependent on the development of a lean, focused organization" where teams substituted for traditional authoritative management (p. 22).

Similarly, Hammer and Champy's (1993) book *Reengineering the Corporation* pointed out that in most organizations, there exist tremendous inefficiencies caused by organizational structures that segment research and development, engineering, manufacturing, shipping, customer service, and more into distinct divisions that may each be successful but at the expense of another department. Rather than make small incremental changes to existing processes (e.g., small technology improvements that could save a few hours or dollars in manufacturing or shipping), companies could save more time and money by rethinking and restructuring entire operations.

At the end of the 1990s, Galbraith and Lawler (1998) observed that organization design choices were increasingly relevant to business leaders. They wrote that

> the search is on for new, more effective approaches to organizing. . . . It is increasingly apparent that corporations, in order to be competitive, must continuously improve—indeed, at times dramatically improve—the way they organize their management. How organizations are structured, how people are paid, how performance is measured, how individuals are trained and developed: increasingly, these are proving to be areas in which successful innovation can lead to improved performance and to sustainable competitive advantage. (p. 1)

The practical implications of design decisions gained currency among a wider audience of leaders and managers.

Today's trends in organization design concern many of the above issues and more. Big data, socially responsible and sustainable organizations, holacracy and alternative structures, and self-organizing and design thinking principles are all impacting the field of design today. In the last chapter of the book, we will address these and other future trends in organization design.

THE CASE FOR ORGANIZATION DESIGN TODAY

As you can see from this brief examination of its history, organization design has evolved as a field of study with growing interest. It is especially relevant to today's leaders and organizations, for four reasons. First, design choices impact an organization's ability to get the outcomes it seeks. Second, leaders have influential and lasting design decisions to make, but design is a neglected competency of leadership. Third, the challenges that today's organizations are experiencing have important design implications. Finally, a focus on agility is a critical design issue today.

Design Affects Performance

Organization design is important as a field of research and practice because design affects an organization's performance. Eriksen (2006) has noted that the "design of the organization is crucial for organizational performance since it influences the organization's ability to act and react effectively" (p. 165). The influence of design can have both positive and negative effects on organizational performance. Design can facilitate the achievement of goals but it can also inhibit success by providing barriers and obstacles such as role confusion or poorly defined processes. (See box on next page for examples.)

INFLUENCES OF ORGANIZATION DESIGN ON PERFORMANCE

- When Tyco Flow Control's Values and Controls unit was redesigned, the goal was to create a global division that could work with global customers. Previously, they worked with customers in isolated regional divisions, which meant that no single division had an overarching view of a global customer's needs. Customers wanted not only a global solution but solutions that worked regionally and even at a local level. Redesigning by global industry segments thus meant that a new kind of coordination would be required across regions. After a multiyear design effort, the company could now produce global customer agreements and a consistent global product roadmap that had never existed previously (Rice & Nash, 2011).
- At the $14 billion industrial cleaning products company Ecolab, rapid growth had created a bureaucratic organization with siloed and isolated units where managers spent less and less time with customers. Frontline employees lacked the authority needed to solve customer problems without management approval, and the organization did not provide the necessary training on products and solutions to allow employees to solve customer problems on their own. With conscious attention to revising policies and processes, changing reward systems, and providing employee training, Ecolab began to address the design issues that were hindering employees from supporting customers (Lorsch & McTague, 2016).
- A hallmark of Toyota's manufacturing capabilities has been its lean production system (documented in Womack, Jones, and Roos, 1990) that enabled Toyota to build high-quality cars worldwide. Several aspects of the organization design of the manufacturing line supported production of a high-quality product. These included the ability for line workers to pull a cord that stopped the line if they noticed a quality defect, standardized manufacturing processes, and a small span of control of team leaders enabling them to help employees who needed it. Job rotations and training programs were prevalent, which provided employees with cross-functional knowledge about the production process in other teams. Suppliers were provided detailed quality training. In the early 2000s, Toyota expanded rapidly, opening 18 new manufacturing plants globally. Some of the new plants did not adopt these same design practices such as line stoppage authority or supplier partnership programs. Turnover increased, and temporary employees were hired to fill staffing gaps, but without the same levels of training. Quality defects grew dramatically, and in 2009 Toyota recalled more than nine million cars worldwide (Camuffo & Wilhelm, 2016).

On the positive side, organization design can provide an organization with a competitive advantage. As Simons (2005) put it, "[O]rganization design is the most important determinant of success for implementing strategy in a large organization" (p. vii). A company can find an advantage if it can successfully achieve an evolution of its organization design as its strategy evolves. "Organization designers seek to differentiate the organization by creating unique, hard-to-replicate capabilities that can produce lasting and sustainable competitive advantage" (Kesler & Kates, 2016, p. 104). Pioneering organizations can experiment with new organization designs to find new ways to design and develop products or provide service to customers. If they can master a new design before a competitor can, they may be able to speed their time to market in the launch of a new product or save costs in creative ways to enhance their financial performance. Some authors go so far as to say that "most CEOs will find that they will gain more leverage from focusing on organizational design than they will gain from nearly anything else they can do" (Bryan & Joyce, 2007, p. 17). Organization design influences the distribution of people, budgets, and other resources, focusing organizational members' attention on what is important. Design can provide a lens on decision making so that managers make choices that are consistent with the organization's direction and strategy, ultimately impacting its effectiveness.

On the negative side, a poor organization design can inhibit the effective accomplishment of work, and while "smart people figure out how to work around the barriers they encounter . . . they waste time and energy" (Kates & Galbraith, 2007, p. 2) in doing so. Most of us have experienced the familiar bureaucratic red tape that burdens organizations with what seem to be unnecessary requirements, process steps, and policies. When the organization's design contains barriers, it slows employees down and it can hamper organizational performance.

> People do make a misaligned organization work, but at a price. The people in an organization that is misaligned with its strategy and stakeholder environment cannot serve its customers and work around the system at the same time. They can perform much more effectively when the system supports them in doing their work. (Galbraith, 2014a, p. 2)

When the design works with the company's strategy and stakeholders, employees and customers encounter less frustration.

Design Is a Leadership Competency

Organization design continues to grow as a field in popularity and interest among both academics and practitioners. It has been written that organization design is one of three key levers of performance (along with strategy and talent) that a business leader can influence (Kesler & Kates, 2011). Managers may not think of themselves as organization designers, but all managers are involved in some respect in design decisions. "Anyone who is responsible for achieving goals through other people must assign resources and decide how subordinates will work together. To be fully effective, all managers must understand the implications of design choices on the units they lead" (Simons, 2005, p. 2). Many leaders have not always had the opportunity to learn about the thought processes involved in designing their organizations. "Very few business schools teach students how to design organizations effectively," Simons (2005, p. vii) observed. While dozens of publications introduce students and business leaders to the foundations of strategy or talent management, there are few introductory publications in the field of organization design. As a result, many leaders who are not familiar with organizational theory make design decisions based on political issues or people's capabilities. Design is worth studying because the concepts and practices of the field of organization design help leaders see the many consequences (intended and unintended) of design decisions. They can then make more conscious decisions in ways that will improve organizational performance. Some managers are called upon to implement designs that their bosses have decided to implement. As Nadler and Tushman (1997) put it,

"[T]he truth is that continuous design, at one level or another, will become a fact of life, and the successful managers will be those who can understand it, embrace it, explain it to others, and help make it happen" (p. 6). For these managers it is important to understand the logic behind the design, to ascertain what message the design choices are trying to send, to be able to communicate the design's rationale to others, and to address inevitable flaws in the design.

Today's Organizations Experience Significant Design Challenges

Observers of contemporary organizations continue to enumerate the enormous challenges facing leaders today, all of which hold significant implications for organization design. "The interest in organization design has been increasing over the past couple of decades. One of the reasons is that our organizations have been increasing in complexity over that time" (Galbraith, 2014a, p. 2). These are just a few of the numerous and complex issues that leaders must address today:

- globalization;
- a rapidly changing competitive environment, with new or more agile competitors;
- more frequent strategic shifts;
- technology that changes internal processes and external customer relationships;
- a requirement to innovate in agile ways to secure even a short-term competitive advantage;
- to do all of this with fewer resources than ever before.

These challenges have design implications. Companies must confront the difficulty of coping with increased competitive pressures from rivals large, small, new, and unexpected, many of whom might be able to respond more quickly to customer demands. Time horizons are decreasing, with expectations of faster times to market, new product innovation, and decreased shelf life of existing product lines.

Here in detail are just three ways that today's trends in organizations prompt design challenges: changes in the nature of work, globalization, and technology.

Changing Nature of Work

- More people are making the choice to work part time, work flexible hours, or telecommute. About 24 percent of all full-time employees did some work at home according to a recent report (Noonan & Glass, 2012), and more than 33 million employees telecommute at least once a month (Hodges, 2009). Technology changes now allow some employees to work from anywhere, making the term *telecommuting* somewhat outdated (Regenold, 2009). According to Lawler (2011), "IBM is among an increasing number of companies where close to 50 percent of employees have no regular office space; instead, they telecommute and use hoteling offices, depending upon where they are at a particular time" (p. 304). There is evidence that this increase in flexibility comes at a cost as well, as the availability of work-from-anywhere scenarios may add hours to the workday, and "the ability of employees to work at home may actually allow employers to raise expectations for work availability during evenings and weekends and foster longer workdays and workweeks" (Noonan & Glass, 2012, p. 45).

- In some organizations, the fixed job description with a set of meticulously itemized work tasks has become obsolete. These organizations encourage "individuals to design a career that meets their needs" (Lawler, 2011, p. 305) by creating a flexible role that matches their skills and interests. One example of this trend can be found at W. L. Gore, where the company "has allowed individuals to create their own jobs by creating projects and building work groups" (Lawler, 2011, p. 304). These approaches take individual differences, skills, and interests into account by allowing employees to take a significant amount of responsibility to select how their career direction changes (and how often) and how their roles can best match their talents.
- As more employees work at a distance from one another, team dynamics change. In fact, global and virtual teaming has already become the norm: Virtual teams exist in more than half of all large companies (Martins, Gilson, & Maynard, 2004). Tammy Johns and Lynda Gratton (2013) report that "experts project that within a few years, more than 1.3 billion people will work virtually" (p. 68), forcing employers to rethink the structure of jobs and physical offices, and that this rise in virtual work requires us to learn how to ensure "that the value gained by tapping world-class talent sources is not lost in clumsy handoffs" (p. 72). Indeed, as Gratton (2011) puts it, "[O]ne of the overwhelming aspects of the future of work is the need to work collaboratively across boundaries" (p. 253).

Globalization

As organizations move toward offshoring parts of their operations or opening subsidiaries in other countries, more people are facing being a member of a team or otherwise working with someone residing on another continent. In many organizations, global customers require global teams to support them. As Friedman (2007) writes in his book *The World Is Flat*,

> [I]t is now possible for more people than ever to collaborate and compete in real time with more people on more different kinds of work from more different corners of the planet and on a more equal footing than at any previous time in the history of the world. (p. 8)

He goes on to emphasize the importance of jobs in the future that "will involve collaborating with others or orchestrating collaboration within and between companies, especially those employing diverse workforces from around the world" (p. 285). Now, more than a decade after Friedman made this observation, globalization is less a trend than it is a basic truism about organizational life.

Technology

For organizations and their customers, rapid technology changes impact everything from internal organizational processes to how customers purchase products or services and interact with the organization. Today's digital technologies enable and change organization design choices unlike ever before. As Bryan and Joyce (2007) put it, "[I]t is large-scale collaboration, across the entire enterprise, enabled by digital technology that is the new element that opens the 21st-century corporation to a greater potential to create wealth" (p. x). Digital technologies can cut across hierarchical silos and improve cross-functional teams, but this collaboration can come at a price. Technologies such as predictive analytics and big data provide organization design opportunities and challenges as well (Galbraith, 2014b).

Organization Designs Today

It is clear that the challenge and opportunity for today's organization designs involves collaboration. Yet today's organizations may not be ready to address these challenges with their old designs. Indeed, not much has changed since Pasmore (1988) articulated the nine "design ills" from which most organizations suffer.

1. An overspecialization of most jobs
2. An overreliance on the ability of supervisors to control employee behavior
3. Too great an investment in maintaining the status quo
4. The breakdown of interdependent systems and activities
5. An overcentralization of information and authority
6. An overreliance on individual monetary rewards
7. The undervaluing of human resources
8. An overreliance on technology as a solution to organizational problems
9. Underattention to the external environment (Pasmore, 1988, pp. 90–93)

Many observers echo Miles, Snow, Fjeldstad, Miles, and Lettl (2010), who observe that "traditional organizational designs . . . will not be able to respond effectively to the opportunities and challenges faced by 21st-century firms and nations. New organizational designs that can mobilize large sets of actors who have the ability to self-organize and collaborate are needed" (p. 101). In many organizations this requires new approaches to design that allow for increased coordination instead of hierarchy, and shared collaborative decision making and governance processes instead of hierarchy and management control. Recent years have witnessed organizations implementing ever more complex designs including multisided matrix organizations, networked organizations and strategic alliances, outsourcing arrangements, and virtual organizations, all designed to address competitive pressures and secure a strategic advantage.

Today's Focus on Agility Is a Design Issue

As we have seen, in past years, organization design might have been an activity for leaders to accomplish, implement, wait to see how the new organization performed, and then to implement another design change after a period of stability. Traditional theories of change emphasize this kind of episodic over continuous change (Weick & Quinn, 1999). *Episodic change* is defined as distinct periods of change, usually infrequent and explicitly defined. Episodic change is usually framed as a response to a stable condition in which adverse conditions are present that force a change. In the world of episodic change, an organization keeps itself stable and constant until a competitor comes out with an innovative new product that threatens the organization's market leadership, or government regulations are implemented that require new processes.

Continuous change, on the other hand, reflects the idea that the organization is never truly out of a state of change and that even in minute ways, change is always occurring. This perspective has become a popular alternative to common military and machine metaphors of organization (Pasmore, 1988; Weick, 2004). The latter assume specialized, repetitive, predictable, and routine tasks and job designs. The metaphors promote a model of management that assumes that supervisors exert control over followers and direct all of their activities, and that followers robotically adhere to this direction. These assumptions fail to resonate for today's organizations that are experiencing a tremendous amount of change and thus cannot rest on past designs. Some argue that the popular concept of organizational fit is too static for today's organizations that require an organization to be regularly redesigning as a matter of routine. As a result, one of today's central design challenges is that of agility. Nadler and Tushman (1997) write that "as continual design becomes a fact of life, successful organizations will learn to create flexible architectures that can accommodate constant change" (p. 16).

SUMMARY

Organization design is a leadership competency that continues to grow in importance. The history of organization design demonstrates that as organizations and their strategies have developed and evolved, so have their designs. Today it is widely recognized that design is worth studying because design affects performance. A good design can remove barriers to collaboration required to achieve the strategy, whereas a poor design can communicate mixed messages that cause confusion. Organization design remains relevant today because contemporary design challenges include changes in the nature of work, globalization, and technology.

QUESTIONS FOR DISCUSSION

1. Have you ever been through a reorganization? What were the reasons for the change? What were the results? Reflect on what organization design means to you. Why do many managers equate organization design with structure?
2. Think about an organization with a history that you know well. How has its design evolved and changed? From what you know of its past, how has it mirrored the history of design described in this chapter?
3. What do you see as some of the most significant design challenges facing organizations today?

FOR FURTHER READING

Galbraith, J. R. (2008). Organization design. In T. G. Cummings (Ed.), *Handbook of organization development* (pp. 325–352). Thousand Oaks, CA: Sage.

Kates, A. (2009). Organization design. In W. J. Rothwell, J. M. Stavros, R. L. Sullivan, & A. Sullivan (Eds.), *Practicing organization development* (pp. 446–456). Hoboken, NJ: Wiley.

Snow, C. C. (2015). Organizing in the age of competition, cooperation, and collaboration. *Journal of Leadership & Organizational Studies, 22*, 433–442.

CHAPTER 2

KEY CONCEPTS AND THE ORGANIZATION DESIGN PROCESS

In Chapter 1, you learned what organization design is, and why it is an important subject of study today. In this chapter, we will delve more deeply into the key concepts with which most managers ought to be familiar. We will also discuss when it is appropriate to begin a design project and how it gets started. We will explore the organization design process that begins with understanding the scope and purpose of the project, deciding who will be involved, and conducting a design assessment. We conclude with an introduction to design criteria and organizational capabilities that provide the practitioner with a set of principles on which to base the design.

Learning Objectives

In this chapter you will learn

- Key concepts of organization design.
- What situations prompt an organization design change.
- Why following a design process is beneficial and the key activities in the design process.
- How to conduct a design assessment and environmental scan, and then to evaluate the current design.
- How and why to begin the design process by creating design criteria.

KEY CONCEPTS OF ORGANIZATION DESIGN

There are several foundational concepts of organization design that will appear throughout the following chapters. First, we will review the STAR model of organization design that has become widespread among writers and practitioners. Next, we review the principles of alignment, congruence, fit, contingency theory, and trade-offs that offer prescriptive guidelines in the design process.

The STAR Model of Organization Design

The STAR model of organization design is arguably the most commonly accepted, used, and referenced by practitioners and theorists, with more than four decades of research and practice to support it. Developed by Jay Galbraith, he explains (in Kates, 2011) that the model evolved from an examination of the common solutions to business problems advocated by researchers and consulting companies. He observed that some consultants advise a reexamination of an organization's strategy, whereas others recommend structural changes, task redesign, or changes in decision-making practices. Still others see the best organizational solutions coming from changes in people, skills, and relationships. Galbraith saw that none of these answers was right or wrong alone, but that each of the approaches needed to work together for an organization to achieve lasting performance change. The three areas—strategy, organization, and people—must work together to achieve high performance, a point that had been made by Lawrence and Lorsch (1967b) in their classic study.

Expanding the organization category to the three areas of structure, processes and lateral capability, and rewards resulted in the STAR model (Figure 2.1), described as follows:

Strategy

- The "company's formula for winning" (Galbraith, 2002, p. 10) that gives it a competitive advantage in the marketplace
- The organization's direction and long-term vision
- Includes which products and services it will create, and markets and customers it will pursue
- Is typically the starting point for the design effort because it "dictates which activities are the most necessary, thereby providing the basis for making the best trade-offs in the organization design" (Galbraith, 2002, p. 11)

Structure

- Distribution of resources, power, and authority
- Role definition, responsibilities, and relationships among departments

Figure 2.1 STAR Model

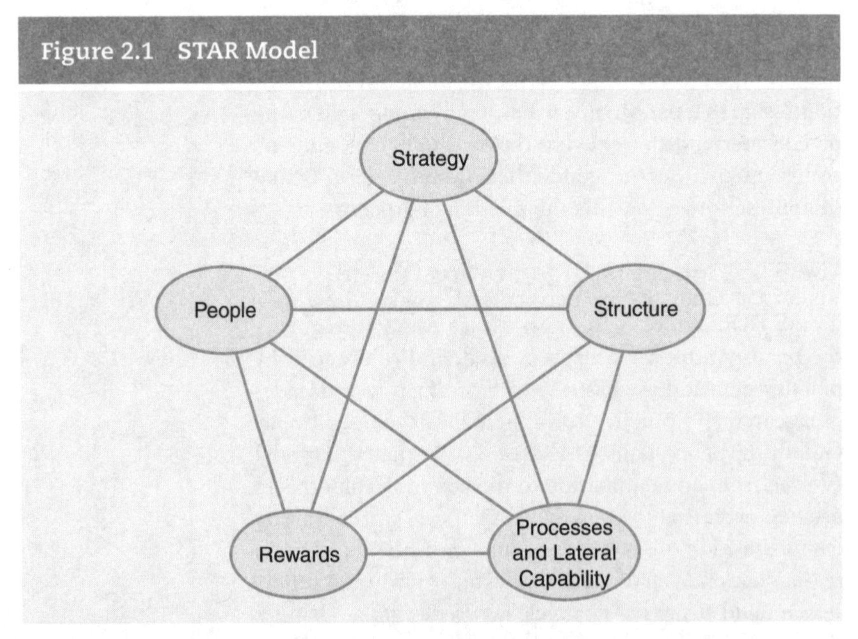

Source: Galbraith, J. R. (2002). *Designing organizations: An executive guide to strategy, structure, and process.* San Francisco, CA: Jossey Bass. Reprinted with permission of John Wiley.

- Includes concepts such as span of control, centralization and decentralization, and department organizing principles such as functions, products, geographies, or markets

Processes and Lateral Capability

- The flow of information that cuts across the structural hierarchy to enable effective collaboration and information sharing
- Decision-making processes and cross-functional collaboration mechanisms
- Includes concepts such as networks, shared processes and goals, teams, integrative roles, and matrix structures

Rewards

- Motivation and incentives for achievement of goals
- Compensation, bonuses, and promotions, plus nonmonetary recognition programs
- Goals and measurement systems such as scorecards and dashboards

People

- Human resources practices related to talent
- Hiring, managing performance, learning and development, and programs to grow talent such as rotations and succession plans
- Includes the skills and competencies required of individuals to enable the design

Galbraith writes that the policies and practices designed at each point of the star will reinforce certain behaviors, which contribute to organizational performance and a coherent organizational culture. Thus culture is an output of the model rather than an aspect of it to change. When leaders try to change culture they end up changing one or more of the elements of the STAR model (Galbraith, 2014a). A leader who wishes to create a culture of innovation to support a "first to market" strategy will likely design product groups around new technology areas, invest in innovation-supporting processes, reward people who innovate, and provide employee training on new technologies. Making those changes will result in innovative behaviors and performance, and a culture to match. We will elaborate on the relationship of culture to design in Chapter 8.

Alignment, Congruence, and Fit

It is not enough to design the points of these models with perfect decisions in each isolated point. The lines that connect the points are also critical. On the STAR model, Galbraith explains, each of the five components supports and must be in alignment with the other four. When any aspect of the STAR model is out of alignment with the rest of the model, the organization's performance suffers. "For an organization to be effective, all the policies must be aligned, interacting harmoniously with one another" (Galbraith, 2002, p. 14). If the strategy is not clear to employees, for example, individuals and teams will be confused about their purposes and overarching objectives. If reward systems do not explicitly articulate tangible and intangible recognition in support of the stated goals and objectives, the organization may be rewarding the wrong activities. If processes and lateral capabilities are not effectively developed to address the disadvantages of the structure, work may get lost in the shuffle as employees are not sure how to work with one another, or the organization may be burdened with conflicts without a way to resolve them.

Similar to the idea of alignment, the concepts of congruence and fit argue that the more congruence among the various components of an organization, the more effective the organization will be. Nadler and Tushman (1983) believe that there must be consistency among interrelated components such as work tasks, individual characteristics such as knowledge and skills, formal organizational arrangements such as structures and processes, and informal arrangements such as norms, values, climate and politics. They write,

> These components exist in states of relative balance, consistency, or "fit" with each other. The different parts of an organization can fit well together and thus function effectively, or fit poorly, thus leading to problems, dysfunctions, or performance below potential. Given the central nature of these "fits" among components in the model, we will talk about it as a *congruence model of organizational behavior*, since effectiveness is a function of the congruence among the various components. (Nadler & Tushman, 1983, p. 114)

Donaldson and Joffe (2014) note three important factors in fit, which they note is a concept that "is central to modern organizational design" (p. 38). First, they note that structure must fit with competitive strategy. A functional structure works best with single businesses, but multiple businesses fit best with a divisional structure. Next, the structure must fit the organization's size so that each division is not too unwieldy. Finally, structure must fit task uncertainty so that the organization can respond to unique tasks in adaptable ways or consistent tasks with standard procedures. Importantly, they note that fit is a dynamic concept so that managers must be aware of the potential for misfit and respond accordingly. As Nissen (2014) put it, "Most approaches to organization design have an equilibrating orientation. As such, the organization is (re)designed to fit its multiple contingencies and then left in that configuration until enough misfits accumulate to warrant re-equilibration through subsequent redesign" (p. 31).

Snow, Miles, and Miles (2006, pp. 6–7) summarize these central principles of congruence:

- The broad framework is that of strategy-structure-environment fit or congruence.
- The organization is conceptualized as a system or configuration whose major components include strategy, people, structure, and management processes.
- Overall organizational performance is heavily dependent on the quality of the internal alignment of the organization's components as well as the external fit between the organization and its environment.
- The process of achieving fit is dynamic, and both the organization's internal and external alignment must be continually monitored and adjusted.

- All of the basic organizational configurations, from the older hierarchical forms to the modern multifirm network organization, have particular strengths and limitations; there is no all-purpose organization design.

Contingency Theory and Complementarity

Since the Burns and Stalker (1961) and Lawrence and Lorsch (1967b) studies (described in Chapter 1), contingency theory has been widely accepted in organization design (for reviews, see Child, 1977; Donaldson, 2001; Tosi & Slocum, 1984). Contingency theory proposes that the organization's fit with its environment affects design choices such as structure and management processes. An organization undertakes a design effort when one or more aspects of the organization appear to be out of alignment with the environment. Market trends and forces, for example, might mean that a certain product line is poised to grow significantly or shrink in importance, and the organization must be prepared to respond in kind.

As described by Galbraith (1973), this line of research has led to two conclusions:

1. There is no one best way to organize.
2. Not all the ways to organize are equally effective (p. 28).

The complexity of the environment requires an equal degree of complexity in the organization (a concept borrowed from the open systems idea of requisite variety or requisite complexity; Ashby, 1956). An organization with a rapidly changing environment will need to change internally in proportion to match (Kates, 2009), and complex business environments will require a complex organization to serve them. As Tushman and Nadler (1978) argued, when organizations face an uncertain environment, they will need to respond by creating "order out of uncertainty" (p. 619) with greater information processing (e.g., monitoring market conditions, and sharing information internally about plans and performance).

In addition, it is important to note that design choices work together as a complementary system (Kates & Galbraith, 2007; the notion of "complementarity" in design is adapted from economics, see Milgrom & Roberts, 1995). Leaders who read the latest *Harvard Business Review* or an industry trade publication or who attend a professional conference will often find other organizations touting their success with a popular new structure, process, or technology. Unfortunately, "piecemeal adoption of management practices has little impact on business performance" (Kates & Galbraith, 2007, p. 4), making isolated implementation of a single practice ineffective. As Whittington, Pettigrew, Peck, Fenton, and Conyon (1999) found, "[H]igh-performing firms are likely to be combining a number of practices at the same time and that the payoffs to a full system of practices are greater than the sum of its parts, some of which taken on their own might even have negative effects" (p. 585).

Applying the STAR model to this thinking, for example, suggests that implementing a new quality management practice such as Six Sigma would be ineffective unless supported by appropriate training and rewards practices. A strategy that depends on quickly solving customer problems across divisions means that a good design decision would be to implement formal cross-functional teams instead of leaving this integration to chance, and to reinforce this practice with supporting technology and performance metrics. Multiple complementary practices are required to make design choices work.

Trade-offs and Competing Choices

A leader in a global company may decide to organize by geographic region instead of by product line, making the trade-off to provide local instead of centralized resources. Or the leader may decide that both geography and functional organization are important and elects to implement a matrix organization, making the trade-off of a more complex structure for a simpler one. None of these decisions is right or wrong in the abstract. "Design decisions are trade-offs. Theoretical models can be used to think through issues and identify possible solutions, but do not offer a 'one size fits all'" (S. Mohrman & Pillans, 2013, p. 11). This means that design choices each have advantages and disadvantages, and that the leader should be conscious of these choice points to make the best possible decision among what may be several appropriate alternatives. Also, design choices each have consequences, so leaders must also be conscious of the potential negative outcomes that are being intentionally chosen, since no design choice is perfect or flawless. Thus, the designer must be aware of unintended negative consequences. As Kates (2009) put it, "A decision that is made early in a process will constrain the choices that can be made later, foreclose avenues of exploration, and eliminate alternatives" (p. 449). One potential application of the STAR model is that "if management can identify the negatives of its preferred option, the other policies around the star model can be designed to counter the negatives while achieving the positives" (Galbraith, 2002, p. 15).

REASONS TO BEGIN A DESIGN PROJECT

With these key concepts as the foundation of organization design, let us turn our attention to why organizations might begin a design project at all. Broadly speaking, an organization turns to a new design "because of the problems and limitations of existing designs, . . . to help preserve and extend the strengths of existing designs while bypassing their limitations" (Miles, Snow, Fjeldstad, Miles, & Lettl, 2010, p. 94). The following are several scenarios that are likely to prompt an organization to consider the need to redesign.

REASONS TO BEGIN A DESIGN PROJECT

- Performance is suffering because of misalignment.
- The strategy changes.
- There is a shift in environment or external context.
- There are internal changes to structures, functions, or jobs.
- The organization has made one or more acquisitions.
- The organization expands globally.
- There are cost pressures.
- There is a leadership change.
- Leaders want to communicate a shift in priorities.

Performance Is Suffering Because of Misalignment

As you might expect from the discussion of alignment above, when any of an organization's practices, policies, and systems are working in opposition to others, the organization's results are likely to suffer. Thus the first reason to undertake a design effort is to correct the aspects of the organization that are misaligned with others. For example, the restructuring of Microsoft in 2013 into functional groups was intended to correct years of destructive internal competition between product groups that had evolved to the point that Microsoft's own products were not compatible with one another (Dhillon & Gupta, 2015). Misaligned product groups that resulted in a decrease in performance suggested an examination of alternative designs.

Caution should be advised here, however, because often action-oriented or reactive leaders will redesign at the first sign of a performance problem without a clear understanding of the reason which may or may not be a design problem. As Snow, Miles, and Miles (2006) put it, "Multiple performance indicators, linked to the organization's various stakeholders, must be examined over time in order to get a clear picture of performance trends as well as a complete assessment of the firm's present condition" (p. 13). A single breakdown in the productivity of the manufacturing line or an isolated example of a delay in responding to a customer's service request might suggest areas for further investigation but do not necessarily require a redesign effort. When these problems become regular and systemic, it may be time to investigate design issues.

The Strategy Changes

When a strategic change is made for any number of reasons—to enter a new market, invest in or divest of an organization's offerings, or to create or discontinue a major product line—an organization design effort is likely called for. These strategy changes influence where to alter, build, or reduce different structures, jobs and skills, key processes, and goals and objectives. In short, strategic change influences every area of the STAR model.

Strategic changes can also accompany the adoption of a new business model. For example, one of India's top telecommunication companies, Bharti Airtel, wanted to increase its focus on customer relationships, acquiring and retaining customers, and expanding existing customer accounts into new areas. It partnered or outsourced much of its operational network activities to companies such as Ericsson and IBM, signaling a shift internally into a new priority area with this "unbundled" design (Osterwalder & Pigneur, 2010).

There Is a Shift in Environment or External Context

Many strategic changes result from shifts in the external context. Three ways this can happen are competitor activities, regulatory requirements, and customer preferences and expectations.

Competitive pressures and moves can cause an organization to rethink its design. For example, faced with competition to its traditional film business from digital cameras, Kodak redesigned in the 1990s to develop a separate digital imaging division (Miles, Coleman, Jr., & Creed, 1995).

Regulatory conditions can require organizations to comply with various legal requirements that impact an organization design. The Sarbanes-Oxley Act of

2002, enacted after corporate accounting scandals including that at Enron, added stricter oversights and controls for financial disclosures. One of the principles of greater internal controls is known as "segregation of duties," where no single person has full ownership of a process so that unethical manipulations might be more easily recognized. With multiple people needing to be assigned to a process, many organizations found themselves under pressure to add more people, rotate jobs, or divide up roles, which has been noted to be a challenge in smaller organizations (Gramling, Hermanson, Hermanson, & Ye, 2010). Similarly, the Affordable Care Act of 2010 contained provisions describing the structure and governance of accountable care organizations (Smith, 2012) that included specific roles and reporting relationships required.

A shift in customer preferences, expectations, and interactions can demand an organization design response. For example, customers today have the ability to engage with a company through any number of social media outlets, and they expect a response to complaints. At Best Buy, thousands of employees across divisions signed up for a program that consolidated Twitter posts from unhappy customers related to experiences at Best Buy. These employees, who included customer service representatives and on-site technicians, could then be deployed to address the customer's problem more quickly (Bernoff & Schadler, 2010).

There Are Internal Changes to Structures, Functions, or Jobs

Organization redesign may be required as a response to other internal shifts in the purpose or mission of another function or to change internal support and partnership requirements. For example, in large organizations many finance and HR functions are organized as mirror structures of the rest of the company, so that internal partners are aligned to research and development, marketing, sales, and other internal divisions. When those divisions change, often the support structure in finance and HR changes in response.

In addition, rapid expansion and growth in the number of employees typically requires introduction of a new or growing management structure, communication and coordination practices, and rethinking of job roles and responsibilities. In a small start-up organization, for example, many employees know one another personally and the scope of the network is relatively contained. Once the organization grows, a more extensive structure and formal policies and practices are required.

Similarly, a reduction in the number of employees or layoffs may require rethinking the scope of divisions or jobs. The introduction of new technologies can decrease the need for manual intervention or administrative processes, resulting in the loss or redefinition of certain roles.

The Organization Has Made One or More Acquisitions

Acquisitions must be integrated, a fact that has clear design implications. Will the joined companies operate as fully independent entities? What will happen with product integration, sales and customer relationships, and clearly duplicated processes such as payroll and accounts receivable? Sometimes these design decisions can be made at the outset, but in other cases design choices are delayed, resulting in confused employees and disgruntled customers. According to a 2008 study, almost half of respondents reported that in the year following an acquisition, they were in need of "merger repair," defined as "several operational, productivity, service, and/or performance issues resulting from poorly conducted M&A integration efforts" (Galpin & Herndon, 2008, p. 7). While there is some evidence that companies that are habitual acquirers have preexisting organization designs that make acquisitions easier to integrate, another study concluded that "undertaking too many acquisitions without major restructuring will likely lead to increasingly suboptimal integration. Restructuring too often, however, will also weaken performance, because of the disruption and costs that it entails" (Barkema & Schijven, 2008, p. 716). Organization design has much to offer the practice of acquisition integration.

The Organization Expands Globally

Consider that in 1960, fewer than 10 percent of companies in the United States faced global competition (Douglas, 1999). As we have seen, that changed with the expansion of multidivisional companies to multinational companies in the 1970s (Galbraith, 2008). Global expansion creates challenges that include product design and supply chain (manufacturing, shipping, customs), customer service (the need for on-site support, perhaps, or local language skills), and branding and advertising (consistency in brand messaging globally). There can also be challenges in finding and training local talent and operating within local labor laws and regulations. These factors create design challenges in the form of structural decisions, questions about centralization versus decentralization, changes to operating models and decision authority, and more.

There Are Cost Pressures

Cost pressures to increase efficiency are often the starting point for an organization, design effort. There may be a move to combine decentralized activities to achieve greater economies of scale, for example, to integrate disparate information technology systems into a single common platform. Unprofitable product lines may be discontinued forcing a reshuffling of existing teams. An organization may shift from using primarily internal talent to contract or freelance labor in an effort to control discretionary costs. Each of these cost decisions has organization design implications.

There Is a Leadership Change

Many new leaders like to "use design to put their personal stamp on an organization" (Nadler & Tushman, 1988, p. 7). A leadership change often occurs in concert with many of the above reasons that would prompt a design change, such as a change in strategic direction or poor results. Thus, new leaders can feel pressure to enact a design change even if it is not necessary, in order to display a visible change to his or her new team (Kesler & Kates, 2011).

Leaders Want to Communicate a Shift in Priorities

Organization design can communicate new or important priorities as a way of encouraging a culture change. A leader of a manufacturing plant may decide to implement self-directed work teams and flatten hierarchical structures to communicate the importance of employee participation, team decision making, and local empowerment.

Unfortunately there are also design efforts that begin with a less coherent rationale. Leaders occasionally desire to redesign solely for political purposes, to increase or reduce an individual's power, to reward members of an inner circle, or to punish those who have been on the losing side of a faction in a debate (Kimberly, 1984). In these cases, organizational members may be confused about what shift in priorities, if any, is being communicated. "At their worst, ill-conceived, poorly managed design efforts generate organizational charades: the illusion of change is created while existing relationships are unchanged" (Kimberly, 1984, p. 122). It is therefore worth the prospective designer's time to investigate the substance behind the motivation to redesign to see what purposes are being served and what priorities are being communicated.

THE DESIGN PROCESS

A formal organization design process consists of a sequence of steps or decisions that provide a logical flow to create a design. Compared to design theory, design processes have received relatively little research attention. As one study put it, "Organization designing is not just the proper assembly of the right blueprint design in a specific situation, but a creative and open-ended process" (Visscher & Fisscher, 2009, p. 121).

The design process is a practical act, often led by internal or external management consultants or organization development consultants who work with design teams to facilitate the process (we will refer to these throughout the book as *design practitioners*). They help leaders and design teams to generate alternative design solutions, to see the implications and consequences of design choices, and to avoid settling on an option too soon. The design process has been described as a process of "divergence" and "convergence" (Visscher & Fisscher, 2009) where an expansive number of design options are generated and discussed, then evaluated according to design criteria before a group converges on a chosen option. Most observers acknowledge that the design process "is an evolving iterative process which sometimes looks and feels messy and complicated" (Stanford, 2005, p. 2).

The design process is often described at the highest level of an organization, but as noted earlier, internal departments such as training, finance, and marketing also have designs and can benefit from following a design process. While any design process may vary depending on the organization's unique needs, a process model can help to focus a design effort and provide a roadmap for a design team. Participants learn a common language and gain a shared understanding about the objectives of each phase of the project. A design process can help to prevent knee-jerk reactions or arriving at a solution too soon, to isolate the underlying needs and correct the root causes of performance problems.

Variations on design process models can be found in a number of research- and consultant-based books (see Galbraith, 2002; Galbraith, Downey, & Kates, 2002; Goold & Campbell, 2002a; Kesler & Kates, 2011; Stanford, 2005; Stanford, 2007). With minor variations among them, most agree that the design process consists of a number of common steps, illustrated in Figure 2.2.

1. **Conduct a design assessment and scope the project.** A design assessment is intended to gather data about the design challenges affecting performance. This stage also involves evaluating the current design, deciding on the scope and approach to the design project, and deciding who will be involved in the discussions and decisions. (Internal and external

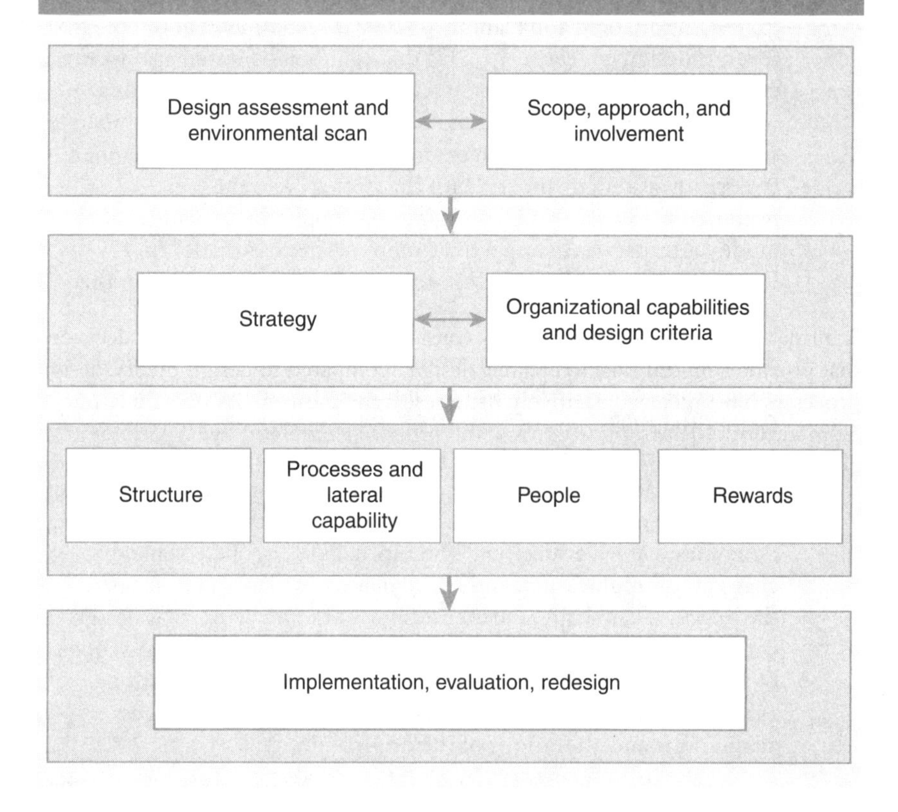

Figure 2.2 The Organization Design Process

consultants will want to engage in contracting at this point; see Anderson, 2017). At this stage, Kesler and Kates (2011) recommend being "clear on the problem to solve" (p. 11), and Stanford (2005) advises articulating "the particular presenting problems or issues" and "your purpose in wanting to re-design" (p. 49). Stanford (2005) notes that problems are not necessarily phrased in the negative. The purpose can also be framed as opportunities such as "How can we accelerate our product development work?" or "How can we delight our customers in our service practices?" At the end of this stage there should be general agreement among the decision makers about the target for the design effort and the project's purpose.

2. **Generate design criteria and determine required organizational capabilities.** This is an iterative process that occurs in concert with evaluating or determining a strategy, which will be covered in detail in the next chapter. Goold and Campbell (2002a) write that most leaders "feel the need to create design criteria at the start of the project, but find this task difficult" (p. 223). In this stage, the design team will agree on a prioritized set of principles and standards by which alternatives will be judged.

3. **Develop a design overview, then test and refine the details.** At this stage, the design team will work on various aspects of the STAR model to change. Structural changes, process changes, and changes to people practices and reward systems should all be considered in an

iterative manner as changes in one point of the star affect the others. Stanford (2005) recommends the development of a "high level design" (p. 133), and Goold and Campbell (2002a) recommend developing several "design concepts" (p. 232) that can then be tested against the criteria with further refinement. Galbraith (2002) recommends a workshop concept where a cross section of organizational members can listen to design alternatives and offer critiques. "In this manner, the organization's members learn the strategy and the logic of the proposed organization. Their opinion is sought, heard, and used to modify alternatives before a final announcement is made" (p. 177). Goold and Campbell's (2002b) "design tests," reviewed later in this chapter, can help to spotlight weaknesses in a design proposal.

4. **Transition and implement, evaluate and adapt**. Even an ideal design can be derailed by a poor implementation process. As Galbraith (2002) puts it, "[B]oth fit and commitment are required for an organization design to be effective" (p. 179). The transition stage "is about placing people in the right jobs, putting new processes into place, [and] making sure you have aligned the systems to deliver the outcomes you have specified" (Stanford, 2007, p. 206). Managing change, communication, and resistance are critical to ensure that the design takes shape. Further design work may happen as design decisions permeate throughout the organization beyond the scope of the original design team. Unanticipated issues and intentional evaluation will both bring concerns to the surface that suggest adaptations and alterations of the original design.

In the next sections we will review stages 1 and 2 of this process.

SCOPE, APPROACH, AND INVOLVEMENT

The designer will need to decide on the scope of the effort. This includes what departments or functions are being designed (e.g., the entire company, the sales divisions, or three of the product divisions) and what levels or layers are included. It can be time consuming to design every new role and job, and such decisions are often best left to later implementation stages. Goold and Campbell (2002a) recommend that "the organization design should go down far enough to make clear the intentions of the designer" (p. 245). In any case, the designer must settle which decisions need to be made early on or by the design team, and which can be delegated to later stages of the process.

There are two ways to approach the design effort: top down and bottom up. Figure 2.3 summarizes these approaches.

Top Down

A top-down design, also called strategic organization design, begins with the organization's strategy and capabilities. By starting with strategy, direction, and required capabilities, this approach ensures that critical activities are included in the design even if no department is currently engaged in those activities today. The introduction of a new strategic capability may result in the creation of a new department that has

Figure 2.3 Benefits and Disadvantages of Design Approaches

	Top-Down Approach	Bottom-Up Approach
Benefits	Can be more forward thinking in terms of design choices. Ensures alignment with strategy.	Best for cleaning up gaps in a current design, reorganizing process flows, and redesigning jobs.
Disadvantages	Organizational details can be missed, resulting in changes that never result in an impact lower down in the organization.	May not be aligned with strategy, so people may end up performing inappropriate tasks.

never existed before to handle that work. This approach has the benefit of not being stuck with today's design choices. But as Nadler and Tushman (1997) point out, the top-down approach can miss many of the details in the organization, designing top-level changes that never result in an impact lower down in the organization.

Bottom Up

The bottom-up approach to organization design is also called "micro" design (Morrison, 2015). It arises out of the sociotechnical systems approach, working "on the alignment of the technology involved in doing the work and the social system that could be created to perform that work" (Galbraith, 2014a, p. 2). A bottom-up organization design begins with an inventory of the activities happening in an organization today. It is especially useful for cleaning up gaps in a current design, reorganizing process flows, and redesigning jobs. Unfortunately, "because they lack strategic perspective, bottom-up designs run the risk of simply making people more effective at performing the wrong work" (Nadler & Tushman, 1997, p. 53). Yet micro design has been called "the real heart of the organization design process. It involves defining all the elements of the design across the organizational system so that the macro vision is implementable" (Morrison, 2015, p. 103).

Nadler and Tushman (1997) recommend that while both are important, the top-down approach should come first:

> Strategic design works from the top down, establishing an architectural frame for the organization as a whole. Operational design works from the bottom up, fleshing out the essential details for each subunit within the organization. Ideally, operational design should flow from, and be consistent with, the overall strategic design. (p. 54)

As we have seen in the design process model described earlier, most consultants and design theorists advise beginning with the top down, strategic approach that begins with a design assessment and follows by generating design criteria.

Deciding Who Is Involved

Another decision to be made early on is who will be involved in the design effort. For design efforts that are small in scope, perhaps designing a small division, a designer can often work one on one with the leader alone. In other cases where the design issues may be contentious or there may be a significant reduction in the size of the senior leadership team, the leader may not want extensive involvement (Kesler & Kates, 2011). Leaders often want to reduce the emotion of a design process, so they decide to keep the effort quiet until they are ready to make an announcement. Unfortunately, this can backfire, as Kesler and Kates (2011) explain:

> The rest of the executive team and broader management corps will have to go through the same thought process as the leader, explore and reject options, and understand the rationale behind the end result. Any time saved by keeping the design process contained is lost in a longer and more complex change management task. (p. 242)

Involving a senior executive team or leadership team can bring more information about the organization into design discussions. The leader can still retain the final decision but benefits from hearing a more diverse set of inputs, and the leadership team's participation can make for a more successful implementation because they understand the design and rationale for design decisions. Unfortunately, because design issues can result in significant changes in jobs or even downsizing of the senior team, design discussions with senior teams can result in pointing blame at others and advocating for conservative choices that reinforce the status quo.

Benefits of a More Participative Approach

Stebbins and Shani (1989) call the above the "Mafia" approaches, with their secrecy and involvement only of the most powerful, often aided by external consultants who leave the "scene of the crime" after their back-room influence. In contrast, many writers advocate that organization design efforts expand participation to more employees throughout an organization. Put simply by Cherns (1977), "[I]f people in the organization are to share in decision making, they must share in the design" (p. 55). On the question of how many people to involve, Goold and Campbell (2002a) agree, "Involve as many as practically possible" (p. 245).

An expanded design team is an option that increases input below the senior team throughout the organization. The team might include high-potential employees that represent multiple levels and functions. Tolchinsky and Wenzl (2014) advocate for this "high engagement organization design" approach that opens up design to a broader audience that engages the whole system in generating and implementing solutions. They argue that today's organizations that need speed, high involvement, and commitment to design changes are best served by being inclusive throughout the design process.

Expanded design teams can take multiple forms, summarized by Lytle (2002), including a steering committee approach that uses subcommittees to conduct further design based on a committee's chosen design principles and a multiple conference approach that uses a sequence of workshops with a large number of participants to develop the organization or plan implementation activities. Heckman (1996) explains the process of a participative design workshop where assessment, design, and implementation planning all happen in the context of a single conference. Kesler and Kates (2011) describe a two-day "design charrette" where a diverse group of participants representing different functions, levels, tenures, and stakeholders collaborate to generate and refine design options.

Table 2.1 Who Is Involved in the Design Effort?

	Leader Alone	Senior Leadership Team	Expanded Design Team
Advantages	• Easier to get "out of the box" thinking • Can freely express opinions about what's working, what's not (reduction in the politics of the process) • Keeps the process from causing anxiety throughout the organization (leaks) • Can be faster for smaller projects	• Those closer to the action provide input • Senior team understands the purpose and rationale for the design • Buy-in may be easier when implementing	• Provides more ideas • Greater commitment to the design throughout the organization • Can provide a role model for more collaborative relationships, empowerment, and participation generally
Disadvantages	• May miss key criteria or facts known by those closer to the action • May be harder to get buy-in from key players • Longer change management process as the organization needs time to understand the design and its rationale	• Typically get more conservative choices • Future structure or design tends to look a lot like current design • Can cause fear or anxiety	• Secrecy is not possible • Leaders must relinquish control or disappointment can result if leaders choose to veto the design team's decisions • Managers are involved in keeping the current organization running and can be distracted by the change effort

When individuals have the opportunity to participate in the design process, they are more likely to support the outcome and commit to implementation (Kilmann & McKelvey, 1975). Similarly, Galbraith, Downey, and Kates (2002) report that a participative process can result in more ideas, a greater commitment to outcomes, a process to role model new relationships, and an opportunity to involve and develop high potential employees.

Choosing the Right Participants

There is not one participation framework that is ideal for all situations and organizations. Lytle (2002) offers an instructive set of criteria to be weighed as leaders and organization designers choose whom to involve in the effort. He advises considering these eight issues:

1. Level of agreement among key stakeholders on the need for rapid change
2. Scope of the design effort

3. Quality of the current relationships in the organization
4. Degree of employee involvement in the design process
5. Amount of direct control that management will exercise over the change effort
6. Resources required and available
7. Organization's past experience with organization design
8. Readiness of the senior leaders to meet the personal requirements of the respective approaches (p. 75)

If the leader has already decided on the design or there are few options to choose from, an extended participative approach may not be the best use of time. If the senior leadership team is frequently derailed by destructive conflict, they may not be prepared to engage in the open discussion required in a design effort. If participants are unclear about the strategic direction or if time is of the essence, a participative approach may not be suitable. Table 2.1 (page 37) summarizes the advantages and disadvantages of the leader-only, leadership team, and expanded team options.

DESIGN ASSESSMENTS AND ENVIRONMENTAL SCANNING

Leaders usually have a sense for why they want to redesign. Typically this is a presenting problem that identifies one or more areas of misalignment or unsatisfactory results, along with the leader's thoughts about what design issues are contributing to that problem. While design assessments are typically internally focused, environmental scans are usually externally focused. Taken together, design assessments and environmental scans can present a more complete picture of the organization and help to ensure that the design effort addresses the right areas.

Design assessments and environmental scans have a number of benefits.

1. They can help to scope the problem and boundaries of the design decisions. A design assessment can help to narrow the scope of the design effort and generate a clear problem statement that the design effort will solve. The design assessment can surface the underlying problems behind why customers are unhappy with the responsiveness of the service department, for example, so that problem is the focus for solutions. Kesler and Kates (2011) advise the development of a concise problem statement that can act as a scope statement such as "There are major disconnects between the customer—represented today exclusively by the sales organizations—and center-led product, product development, and marketing" (p. 44).

It is possible for an organization design effort to become overwhelming, with almost every problem or concern seemingly related to the design. The design assessment can help to reduce the issues to a manageable few. It can also help to refocus a design team on the original issues presented when it gets off track.

2. They can be a force that can spark interest in change. By bringing organizational members together on a common definition of the situation, a design assessment can act as a motivating force for areas they can then agree to change. Nadler (1977) writes that in this respect, "Collection can be used for consciousness raising—getting people thinking about issues concerning them and the organization" (p. 105).

3. They can help to communicate to ensure a common understanding of the purpose of the design effort. When organizational members have a chance to participate in a design effort, they are naturally eager to learn about other people's perspectives on the organization as well. A clear summary of the issues, often gathered and summarized by either an internal or external consultant, can create a common understanding of the goal.

4. They can give insight as to how difficult the change process will be. When the assessment produces a wide variety of issues about which there are strong emotions, the designer can get a sense for how challenging it will be to generate alternative solutions and get agreement on them.

5. They can help to generate alternative solutions early on. When a design assessment involves multiple layers, frontline employees often see with the greatest clarity about what barriers exist for them and can share workable solutions. As Kesler and Kates (2011) write, "Often the interviews bring to light the seeds of big ideas that can later be developed. Sometimes there are seemingly obvious solutions that many people in the organization have tossed around for months" (p. 45).

Design Assessments: Gathering Data

Data gathering for a design assessment generally uses one or more of these common approaches used in most organization development engagements (for more details on these methods, see Anderson, 2017).

1. Interviews
2. Focus groups
3. Surveys
4. Observations and unobtrusive measures

Interviews

Interviews are generally one-on-one meetings during which design practitioners speak directly with individual organizational members. The practitioner is interested in the individual stories and perspectives of organizational members and in a personal setting can explore their history, experiences, beliefs, and attitudes in depth. The primary advantages of interviewing as a method for data gathering include the ability to understand a person's experience and to follow up on areas of interest. Interviews can yield surprises that a practitioner may not know enough in advance to ask about. Even if a practitioner could see the situation personally, interviews can allow the practitioner to better understand how organizational members interpret a situation or what attitudes and beliefs they have about it.

Data gathering through interviews relies heavily on cooperation from organizational members who will only open up to discuss serious issues if they trust the interviewer. Interviews can be threatening, as members may feel defensive if they are personally involved in a problem and they may be motivated to stretch the truth to present themselves in a positive light. Consequently, among the data-gathering methods, interviewing requires the greatest interpersonal skill. To conduct data gathering successfully using interviews, an interviewer should follow these guidelines:

1. Prepare an interview guide. Interviews can be formal and structured, with each interviewee asked the exact same set of questions without straying from the list of questions, or they can be semistructured, with an interview guide containing a general list of open-ended questions addressing the major topics of the interview. Open-ended questions are those that typically require the participant to provide more detailed answers, whereas closed-ended questions can be answered with a word or short phrase. It is usually a better choice to ask a respondent, "How would you describe the goals of this organization?" than "Do you feel that the goals are unclear?" With semistructured interviews, the interviewer adds probes, or follow-up questions, where appropriate, and can explore other areas that were not predicted in the interview guide. In the next section we will discuss how the STAR model can be used as a model for an interview guide.
2. Select participants. When only a small team is involved, interviewing every team member is a reasonable approach. However, because interviewing can be time-intensive and resource-consuming for both the organization and the interviewer, it may not be possible to interview every relevant organizational member. How many interviews to conduct likely will depend on the time available and the scope of the design effort. The selection of interviewees in an organization design project is generally based on the participants' knowledge or involvement in the topic being discussed.
3. Begin the interview and establish rapport. A location for the interview should be selected that allows for the best interaction possible. This means a private location free from distractions such as phone calls and personal interruptions. The interviewer will want to consider how to describe the purpose of the interviews, since organization design projects can be sensitive and cause concern. The interviewer should take the time to explain what he or she will do with the data from the interview and who will see it (if anyone).
4. Conduct the interview by following the interview guide, straying from it when appropriate during semistructured interviews. Interviews are primarily a conversation, albeit one with a specific purpose. Interviewers need to listen carefully to the current response, think about any follow-up questions, remember the other areas that are listed in the interview guide, and be conscious that time is limited.

The best interviewers can maintain the character of the interview as a conversation without being distracted by other tasks.

5. Close the interview. Close the interview by inviting the participant to pose any questions that he or she may have. Conclude by thanking the interviewee and reiterating the timeline for what will happen next and when the participant will hear results, if at all. Most people are naturally curious about what will happen next, and it is important that the conclusion of the interview sets the appropriate expectation. The interviewer can also choose to provide a business card or other contact information in case additional questions arise or the interviewee wishes to clarify something after the interview.

Tips for Successful Interviews

1. Listening is a critical skill in interviewing. It is important to avoid interrupting an interviewee with another question in earnestness to move on to another area. Listening for emotion as well as content can suggest areas for follow-up questions. Noticing hesitancy in the interviewee's voice, the practitioner can ask, "You seem reluctant to talk about the budgeting process. Can you say more about your thoughts?"
2. Avoid indicating agreement or disagreement with the interviewee, or suggesting that the interviewee's responses are similar to or different from other interviews. Even head nodding, nonverbal feedback such as "yes" or "uh huh," used to encourage the interviewee to continue, can be seen instead as a sign of agreement that may change the interview. The best advice is to emphasize interest in the interviewee's experience, not in one particular answer.

While they can be time intensive, they can be well worth the additional effort expended to gain knowledge and background detail into the organization. Because gaining the time to conduct one-on-one interviews can be difficult, many practitioners turn to the group interview, or focus group.

Focus Groups

Focus groups are groups of usually a small number of organizational members facilitated by a moderator who poses questions and then allows for group discussion. Like interviews, focus groups allow the exploration of experiences and situations in depth and to follow up on specific areas of interest. In focus groups, participants can build on one another's ideas. They can brainstorm, discuss, and debate. To conduct a focus group, evaluators should follow a process similar to interviewing. The considerations are somewhat different, however, since the subject matter and structure of a focus group are different from individual interviews:

1. Prepare an interview guide. Interview guides for focus groups are likely to be shorter than those used in one-on-one interviews since the participation level will be much greater for a similar amount of time. Consequently, it is likely that fewer subjects will be covered. In addition to the interview guide, the consultant should prepare some opening and closing remarks that explain the purpose of the interview, what will be done with the data, and how the data will be recorded.

2. Select participants. Groups can be homogeneous, that is, selected based on some criteria they share. Groups can also be heterogeneous, or a mixed group, where the group's composition is more diverse. The advantage of homogeneous groups is that these employees may share a similar background because they have something in common, and they may be able to provide depth and detail into a problem from that perspective. Customer service personnel, for example, may be able to build on one another's contributions to create a more complete picture of quality problems with the company's products. By having different backgrounds or roles in the organization, mixed groups can offer the advantage of seeing patterns common to all organizational members regardless of role or demographic characteristic.

As with interviews, a location should be selected that is free from distractions and interruptions for the length of the discussion. The number of participants per group depends on the subject's complexity but should be somewhere from 5 to 15 people. Successful focus groups can be conducted with more participants, but since time is likely limited, participants may struggle to contribute if the group numbers more than 20.

3. Hold the focus group. The moderator or focus group facilitator should begin by welcoming participants, and reiterating the purpose and explaining the structure of the focus group. Participants should introduce themselves if they do not know one another already, in order to understand one another's organizational roles and backgrounds. The facilitator should explain what and how notes will be taken, as well as what will happen with the results of the focus group(s). The facilitator should next propose several ground rules for participation, including the following:
   - What is said during the course of the meeting should remain known only to the participants and should not be repeated to others.
   - Roughly equal participation is the goal, so the facilitator is likely to intervene from time to time to ensure that all voices are heard.
   - The facilitator may intervene to keep the group on track or focus conversation back to the question under discussion.
   - The purpose is to explore issues; personal comments or attacks are not appropriate.

As the facilitator follows the interview guide, it may be necessary to quiet any monopolizing participants and to encourage those who are shy or have a difficult time jumping into the flow of conversation. The facilitator must also balance the need to get through the interview guide and to explore topics of interest. Since the goal is an in-depth exploration of issues, the facilitator will need to listen carefully to the various contributions and offer additional probing questions.

4. Conclude the meeting. When time has ended or the conversational subjects have been exhausted, the participants should be invited to pose any questions they may have of the facilitator. The moderator should repeat the objective of the project and the focus groups and what will be done next with the data.

Tips for Successful Management of Focus Groups

1. Listening is just as important with focus groups as it is with interviews. Focus groups can be somewhat more complex at times because the facilitator is listening to the speaker, thinking of the next question, and watching group dynamics.
2. Also as with interviewing, it is important to maintain objectivity to the extent possible and to avoid indicating agreement or disagreement with the group's contributions.
3. As in interviews, having two facilitators is an option where one can participate in the conversation and another can take notes.

In summary, focus groups can be an excellent method for gathering data. They can elicit contributions from many people in a shorter time than can be done with one-on-one interviews. Group members can also build on one another's ideas, which can result in better solutions and explorations of a situation. If a facilitator is skilled at managing the conversation and addressing the challenges of a focus group, the data gathered from this approach can be very useful to diagnosis and planning next steps in the design effort.

Surveys and Questionnaires

Surveys are a means by which the design team can solicit input from a large number of organizational members at once. Surveys or questionnaires are typically paper- or Internet-based methods to allow for a large number of participants. Today, a number of free or inexpensive online survey tools (such as SurveyMonkey) make it very easy to survey a large number of organizational members very quickly.

Generally surveys address a broad number of subjects and explore a wide range of issues, as opposed to a deep investigation of one or two issues. Used alone, surveys are best used as exploratory mechanisms, and they are typically inappropriate for sensitive subjects. Some practitioners use surveys following interviews or focus groups to understand how prevalent the issues are that have been brought up in interviews. In combination with other methods, surveys can provide breadth where others provide depth.

The following process can help a practitioner to successfully conduct an organizational survey:

1. Determine the focus of the survey. Surveys can be used to assess one or all elements of the organization design. Each has a different implication for the structure of the survey.
2. Determine who will take the survey. Organization-wide survey topics typically imply that all members will be given the opportunity to participate in the survey. In some situations, a smaller sample of members may be more appropriate, less expensive, and less time consuming.
3. Design the survey. If the survey is too long, participants may become fatigued or busy with other work and may not complete it. If it is too short, it may not provide enough information or detail to act upon. Most surveys use a combination of fixed-response questions (for example, the Likert scale tends to use a 5-point scale with choices of

strongly agree, agree, neutral, disagree, and strongly disagree) and open-ended or short-answer questions. Participants may not take the time to respond to a large number of open-ended questions, and analysis can be complex.

4. Administer the survey. Survey instructions should be clear about how long the survey is likely to take and how participants should return it (for paper-and-pencil surveys) or submit it (for electronic surveys). The deadline should be clearly communicated, and a reminder issued shortly before the survey will close.

Tips for Successful Administration of Surveys

The most common errors in the use of surveys involve the questions or survey items themselves. The following list does not delve into all of the possible errors with question design, but these are a few important issues to consider:

1. Keep in mind the need to translate or localize questions. In a global environment, many organizational surveys need to be accessible in various languages. Survey items will need to be translated as well as localized. That is, translation is a matter of linguistic change, whereas localization is a matter of cultural accuracy for the context. Items should avoid idioms or slang unique to American English as well as U.S. work practices that may not be applicable to employees in other countries.
2. Clarify important terms. Even phrases that might appear to be self-evident such as "senior management" or "your work team" may need to be defined at the beginning of the survey. Employees in a regional office, for example, may wonder whether "senior management" refers to the highest-ranking local management or whether it refers to the executive team at headquarters.
3. Survey items should be tested with a small sample of organizational members who can later be interviewed to determine whether questions were clear and whether the respondent understood the survey items in the manner in which they were intended.

Technological advancements have made issuing and responding to surveys easier than ever before. It is now possible to develop and issue a survey to a targeted population and receive responses within a matter of days. Consequently, surveys remain one of the most popular ways to gather data. The disadvantage of this ease of use is that some organizational members can become oversurveyed, but when used occasionally and conscientiously, surveys can be an excellent addition to a data-gathering approach.

Observations and Unobtrusive Measures

Interviews, focus groups, and surveys all rely on the ability (and willingness) of organizational members to thoughtfully and accurately articulate their thoughts and opinions directly to the organization designer. There are times, however, that designers may want to see for themselves how things really happen. For example, the designer may want to follow a customer service technician to see what challenges are being experienced in a normal day. The designer may follow the recommendation to "staple yourself to an order" (Shapiro, Rangan, & Sviokla, 1992) to observe the order management process first hand, from order generation to order entry to fulfillment, billing, returns, and postsales service.

Observations and unobtrusive measures can provide important data that can corroborate or dispute what organizational members say happens compared to the ideal or intended process. Self-report data can be erroneous because the information relies on the memory of the person being asked. For several reasons, people may report their behavior in error, may not be accurate in their perceptions of the behavior of others, or may represent behavior with a certain slant to give the interviewer a positive impression. Interviewees may not be conscious, for example, of whether telephone interruptions during a task cause them to make more errors or whether they handle customer complaints on a certain product differently from their coworkers. They may report only what they remember (perhaps only the last few days, or an event that was extraordinary and thus stands out) or they may report what they want to make known. Questionnaires may also be unlikely to elicit accurate data on these points. Observations allow the practitioner to get closer to seeing how these issues play out during the course of an ordinary day and to avoid errors in self-reporting.

While observations can give a general sense of how things happen, an observer is not likely to see the entire range of situations. One or two team meetings' worth of observation, or a few hours watching patients in a hospital waiting room, can be very instructive but does not substitute for the knowledge and expertise of those who work there and have seen many more examples. The observer should not overgeneralize from only a small sample of observations and assume knowledge equal to that of organizational members.

Observation would not be a good choice in situations where the phenomenon being observed is rare or infrequent. A practitioner may observe for many hours without witnessing what happens when a machine breaks down if it only happens every 3 months. Observations are less useful for studying unusual problems or infrequent interactions.

Another type of data that can be gathered consists of unobtrusive measures (Webb, Campbell, Schwartz, & Sechrest, 1966; Webb & Weick, 1979). As the name suggests, these data are generally readily available because they are produced during the ordinary course of organizational activity. They can usually be gathered in an inconspicuous manner without changing the data themselves. With unobtrusive measures, the data usually already exist, and gathering the data does not usually change what is being studied. Unobtrusive measures can be a source of data that can give the consultant insight into the organization without making a direct inquiry or conducting observations. Because these data exist separate from the consulting engagement itself, the data are likely to be less influenced by the presence of the observer or practitioner. As a result, unobtrusive measures can be highly valid sources of data. The organization designer may wish to gather strategy documents, job descriptions, training programs, process documentation, employee surveys, business reviews, or other metrics for further investigation.

Each of these methods has different advantages and disadvantages, summarized in Table 2.2.

Table 2.2 Advantages and Disadvantages of Data-Gathering Methods

Method	Advantages	Disadvantages
Interviews	• May prompt interviewees to be more forthright in a personal environment • Interviewer can follow up on important issues and explore situations in depth • More personal than surveys or focus groups • Consultants can capture examples and quotes effectively • Interviews may reveal new issues	• Time and data intensive if many interviews are to be conducted • Potentially expensive • Rapport must be established; interviewees must trust interviewer • Gives only the interviewee's perspective • Interviewers may unwittingly encourage certain response bias • Analysis can be time consuming
Focus Groups	• May save time compared to individual interviews • Access to many people at once, thus can be more efficient at getting information than interviews • Group can build on one another's thoughts, stimulating thinking	• Potential for groupthink or for people to "go along" with one point of view to avoid conflict • Confidential issues may not be discussed with peers • A few members may dominate the group
Surveys/ Questionnaires	• Data from many people can be gathered at once • Can take a short time • Allows a broad range of topics to be addressed • Data can be quantified and compared across groups • Can repeat survey to show differences over time	• Data analysis can be intensive • May require statistical knowledge beyond the capabilities of the consultant • Difficult to follow up in depth on a single issue • Response rates may be low or may bias the results • Respondents may give socially desirable answers
Observations and Unobtrusive Measures	• Observations allow data collection "in the moment" when an event occurs rather than after the event • Already exist or happen "live," more natural • Allow behavior to be seen rather than self-reported • Can substantiate or contradict data gathered elsewhere (triangulation)	• Can be time intensive • Can be expensive • May be difficult to observe multiple instances of a behavior that occurs sporadically • Observer may intimidate or affect the group or individual being observed • Can be more difficult to access

Using the STAR Model as a Diagnostic Framework

The STAR model itself can help to provide a diagnostic framework for interviews, focus groups, and surveys (see box on next page). Categorizing the issues with the STAR model as a guide can help to identify areas where there is the most (or least) concern. In addition, the assessment can help to identify areas of misalignment between points to diagnose where problems may lie, and thus where solutions would be the most impactful.

DIAGNOSTIC QUESTIONS USING THE STAR MODEL

Background

1. Tell me about your role and responsibilities in the organization.
2. How has the organization been performing? What have been some of the most important successes in the past year? What have been some of the most significant problems?
3. What is changing in the external environment? How do you expect each of the following may impact your organization: changes in customer profiles or preferences, regulatory changes, competitive environment (new competitors, competitive moves), changes in technology? What other changes, pressures, or trends do you see coming?

Strategy

1. What is the mission and direction of the organization? Does the organization have a common understanding of the strategy and direction?
2. What do people see as the current capabilities in the organization? How do you use those capabilities to your advantage?
3. Are there new capabilities needed? If so, what are they?

Structure

1. What barriers or problems exist in the structure, and what has been done to address them?
2. What is the level of clarity of roles and responsibilities between people and functions?
3. What overlaps or gaps exist between your group and others? What are the implications of this team's structure on the rest of the organization?

Processes and Lateral Capability

1. What other groups do you work with internally? What coordination processes do you use today? How are joint decisions made? What happens when there are conflicts?
2. What processes are most critical to achieving the strategy or direction?
3. Can you think of additional needs to overcome barriers to collaboration between groups? What infrastructure is needed to enhance and support your core work processes?

People

1. What core competencies (people's skills and abilities) are or will be most important to your success?
2. How do you develop competencies in which you are weak?
3. What is the talent management process? How do you create career paths and succession plans?

Rewards

1. What metrics are required to evaluate and support the strategy or direction?
2. What process is used to develop and cascade goals?
3. What values and behaviors are rewarded, and how?

Environmental Scanning: STEEP and SWOT

In Chapter 1, we made the point that an organization exists as part of a system with its environment, and that its design must change as its environment changes. When customer preferences or buying patterns change, government regulations change, macroeconomic forces change, and so on, organizations must often adapt.

For example, high oil prices, government fuel economy regulations, and consumer environmental awareness all combined to drive higher demand for electronic and hybrid vehicles in the mid-2000s, supported by tax incentives (www.afdc.energy.gov/data/). When gas prices dropped, consumer preferences for electronic vehicles declined according to a 2015 study (Chappell, 2015). Auto manufacturers must carefully monitor all of these environmental trends to remain competitive.

Environmental scanning provides one process by which leaders, designers, and strategists can analyze the organization's future strategy and design requirements. One framework for environmental scanning consists of the acronym STEEP to analyze the social, technological, economic, environmental, and political forces in the organization's environment that may have an impact on the strategy and design. These factors may combine to suggest different scenarios for the organization to consider. For example, future housing construction trends may be impacted by economic, social, and political factors such as rising interest rates, social and cultural preferences for mobility, and reduced tax deductions for mortgage interest. Table 2.3 provides examples of environmental trends using the STEEP model.

A second framework for environmental scanning is called a SWOT analysis. The acronym SWOT refers to a company's strengths, weaknesses, opportunities, and threats. The first two points, strengths and weaknesses, are internal assessments of what the company does well or poorly. A strength might be the company's manufacturing capabilities, while the company might have a weakness in overseas distribution. The latter two points, opportunities and threats, are external assessments of the company's strategic or competitive position in the external environment. An opportunity might be for the company to use its strength in

Table 2.3 Environmental Scanning Using STEEP Analysis

Factor	Examples	Impact on Organization
Social	• Demographic change • Diversity • Work–life balance	• New labor markets • New working practices • Different types of contract
Technological	• Next generation products • Wireless technology • Internet impact	• Keeping systems current • Making best use of investment • Knowledge management
Economic	• Economic cycles • Currency values • Trading relationship	• Outsourcing and subcontracting • Price and tariff changes • Distribution channel changes
Environmental	• Hydrocarbon use • Rain forest destruction • Ocean degradation	• Compliance requirements • Sourcing decisions • Lobby group influence
Political	• Change of government • World trade practices • War	• Regulatory change • Redefinition of competitors • Government support

Source: Adapted from Stanford, N. (2005). *Organization design: The collaborative approach.* Amsterdam, Netherlands: Elsevier, p. 91.

manufacturing to expand into contract manufacturing practices and thereby enter into a new industry practice. A threat might be that a competitor would capitalize on the company's weak distribution channel and expand into that territory.

SWOT analysis and environmental scanning analysis can be used in the process of scenario planning to assess how the strategic direction of the organization may need to change given these trends. Scenario planning encourages organizations to consider several likely possible future states, to consider which of those is most likely, and then to develop plans and actions that could account for a number of possible future situations. In a highly uncertain environment, scenario planning helps to "inform decision making, learn through challenging the currently held mental models, enable organizational learning, and enable organizational agility" (Chermack & Lynham, 2002, p. 373).

Scenario planning "embraces uncertainty by identifying those unknowns that matter most in shaping the future of a focal issue" (Steil & Gibbons-Carr, 2005, p. 17). Scenario planning works best when there are a number of possible options and there is a high level of uncertainty about which options are likely to pan out. City planners may be able to develop contingency plans if this year's rainfall amounts fail to fill the reservoir to capacity (e.g., rationing or price increases). But will the city's infrastructure be robust enough to support the city's needs in 25 years? How will environmental conditions, upstream water usage, tax revenues, transportation, housing prices, interest rates, population increases or decreases, and water rights legislation all affect the future needs of the city? Moreover, which of those factors will be most important to take into consideration? While some data are likely to be available on many of these topics, it may not be possible to predict with certainty how those factors will interact to produce a single likely future state.

A scenario-planning intervention can not only involve creative thinking about uncertain and unknown events but also require the ability to thoughtfully consider ideas and future events that are opposed to one another. Organizational members can have difficulty rationally considering a future in which, for example, the organization's products are obsolete or unnecessary. One purpose of scenario planning is to push these options as topics of discussion.

EVALUATING THE CURRENT DESIGN

Results from the design assessment and environmental scan can be used to evaluate the current design and prioritize opportunities for scoping the design project. For example, a large number of comments from interviews about poor communication between different groups might suggest that the design project begin with processes and lateral capability. If department goals are unclear and people are being compensated for the wrong activities, then structure and rewards might be targets for change. If the organization is investing in a market segment where demographic trends are declining, the strategy may need to change.

There are a number of frameworks and models that can help to identify potential gaps in the current design. Three of these come from Galbraith, Downey, and Kates (2002), Nadler and Tushman (1992), and Goold and Campbell (2002b). Broadly speaking, each framework helps to provide specific suggestions to meet Monge's (1993) recommendation that a design process "focus on misfits and error reduction" (p. 342). Any of these models or tests can be used as instructive suggestions to help scope and focus a design effort.

Figure 2.4 Unaligned Organization Design

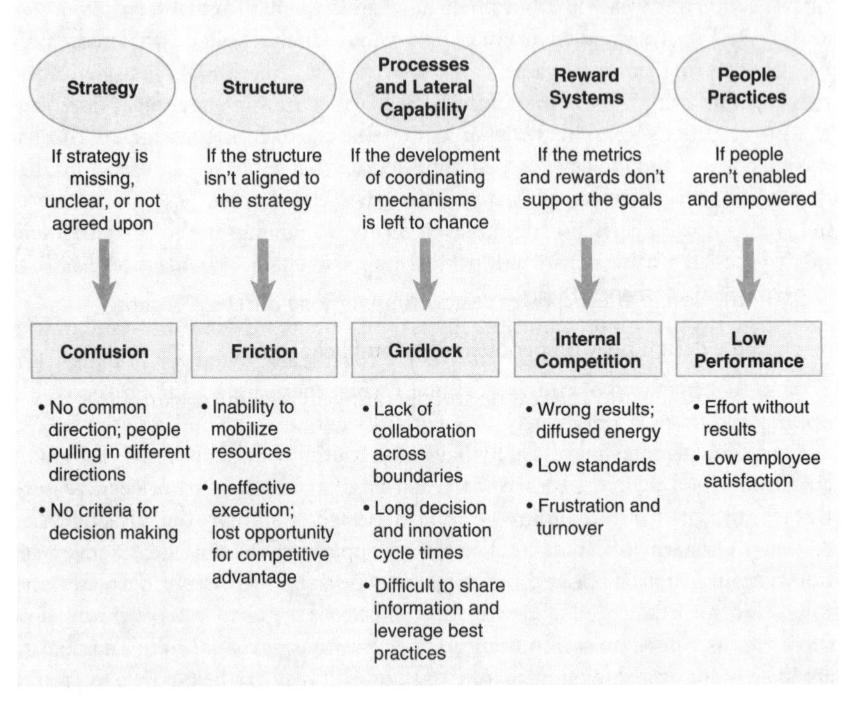
Strategy
Structure
Processes and Lateral Capability
Reward Systems
People Practices
If strategy is missing, unclear, or not agreed upon
If the structure isn't aligned to the strategy
If the development of coordinating mechanisms is left to chance
If the metrics and rewards don't support the goals
If people aren't enabled and empowered
Confusion
Friction
Gridlock
Internal Competition
Low Performance
• No common direction; people pulling in different directions
• No criteria for decision making
• Inability to mobilize resources
• Ineffective execution; lost opportunity for competitive advantage
• Lack of collaboration across boundaries
• Long decision and innovation cycle times
• Difficult to share information and leverage best practices
• Wrong results; diffused energy
• Low standards
• Frustration and turnover
• Effort without results
• Low employee satisfaction

Source: Galbraith, J., Downey, D., & Kates, A. (2002). *Designing dynamic organizations: A hands-on guide for leaders at all levels.* New York, NY: AMACOM, p. 5. Reprinted with permission.

Evaluating Alignment in the Design

Galbraith et al. (2002, p. 5) offer an instructive diagnostic chart to help identify areas of misalignment in the organization's design (see Figure 2.4). Galbraith (2014a) writes that "When the factors are not aligned, frictions develop, people are confused about direction, and time and energy are wasted on unnecessary conflicts" (p. 19). This chart can provide a starting point and focus the scope of a design project. If data from the design assessment echo any of the symptoms in Figure 2.4, that may provide a suggested starting point for the design effort.

Evaluating Strategy/Task Performance and Social/Cultural Factors in the Design

Nadler and Tushman (1992) suggest that change agents evaluate the design's ability to contribute to the strategy and task needs of the organization while appropriately fitting with its social and cultural environment. They write that both perspectives are critical in the design.

> Those who consider only strategies are likely to design organizations that look effective but that somehow do not work, are not implemented, or create as many new problems as they solve. On the other hand, those who consider only the social-cultural perspective may create organizations in which many people feel satisfied but which fail to implement strategies and accomplish the work. (p. 40)

Strategic factors include a design that does the following:

- Supports the implementation of strategy
- Facilitates the flow of work
- Permits effective managerial control
- Creates doable, measurable jobs

Social and cultural factors include examining how

- existing people fit into the design,
- the design affects power relationships among different groups,
- the design fits with people's values and beliefs, and
- the design affects the tone and operating style of the organization.

The design assessment can provide insight into whether strategic factors or social and cultural factors are the sources of misalignment and performance problems in the organization. If the design does not achieve the strategy, then perhaps the design itself is the cause. If the design appears to be accurate but it is not implemented or enabled appropriately, it may be that social or cultural factors are the root cause of performance problems. Nadler and Tushman (1992) put these factors together into a model they call the congruence model of organizations, suggesting that internal factors of people, work tasks, and formal and informal organization must all be in alignment. Any incongruence among these elements suggests a starting point for a design effort.

Goold and Campbell's Nine Design Tests

Goold and Campbell (2002b) list nine tests of whether an organization is well designed—propositions that can also be used to appraise a new design to see whether it is appropriate. They write that the first four of these tests of structure are for "fit" with organizational goals, strategies, skills, and plans. The final five are tests of good design, helping an organization achieve the right level of balance in processes, and may suggest modifications to the design to account for the particular challenges in any organization.

1. **The market advantage test.** Does the structure match how the organization intends to serve its markets? If the organization serves customer segments differently in different geographies, then having geographic divisions makes sense. No customer segment should be missed, and ideally, no segment should be served by multiple divisions in order to provide maximum focus.
2. **The parenting advantage test.** Parent organizations should organize in ways that allow them to provide the most value to the rest of the organization. If innovation is a key value of the parent company, has it organized in ways that maximize innovation throughout the organization?
3. **The people test.** The design should support the skills and energy of the people in the organization. If the design requires that the head of engineering also manage finances, and finding a single replacement for

those dual specialized skills is unlikely if the current leader were to leave, the design may be risky. In addition, the design may be risky if it will frustrate valuable employees who may lose status in the new structure.

4. **The feasibility test.** Will the design require a major cultural shift, such as a matrix design in a culture very comfortable with rules and hierarchy? Will information technology systems require drastic, expensive changes to report performance by customer industry versus geography?
5. **The specialist cultures test.** Some organizational units maintain different subcultures for good reasons. A group focused on the company's core products may think of innovation as a gradual series of incremental improvements to existing products, but a new products division may need rapid innovation for products that have a short life cycle. Combining R&D from both divisions may result in a dangerous culture clash.
6. **The difficult-links test.** How do divisions in the structure develop links between them, and who has authority when conflicts arise? If six divisions each have separate training functions, how do they coordinate the use of instructional resources such as classrooms and trainers?
7. **The redundant hierarchy test.** To what extent are layers of management necessary to provide focus, direction, or coordination for the units in their scope? If the purpose and value of a level of management is the same as the ones below it, it may be unnecessary.
8. **The accountability test.** Does the design streamline control for a single unit, or is authority—and accountability—diffused among different units? Does it encourage units that cannot collaborate to blame one another for poor performance?
9. **The flexibility test.** How does the organization react when there is a change in strategy, goals, or direction? How does the new organization react when a new product is to be designed or introduced? Does the design actually obstruct and confuse rather than streamline and clarify?

Few designs will achieve all of these criteria. Goold and Campbell (2002b) recommend that design planning be an iterative process, and that as a design fails one test, it should be revised and run through the list of tests once more.

DESIGN CRITERIA AND ORGANIZATIONAL CAPABILITIES

Organization design can be a contentious activity that can benefit from the development of objective design criteria. Many teams that attempt to solve problems will engage in an unstructured discussion, sharing problems and concerns, and describing errors and their history and causes. Eventually, a participant will suggest a solution that will be debated until time or enthusiasm for debate runs out, in an approach to decision making that has been called bounded rationality (March, 1994). The heightened emotions and complexity of problems in an organization design project make it even more important that the process begins with a discussion of the design criteria by which the future design alternatives will be judged.

Design criteria and organizational capabilities are generally synonymous (Galbraith, Downey, & Kates, 2002). They consist of the priorities that will guide the design and help leaders design an organization that will achieve the strategy. For example, consider an organization that targets a given market as a low-cost, highly efficient operation. It passes its efficiencies on to customers with lower prices and bare-bones service and it is popular with customers who are cost conscious. It will be designed very differently from an organization that acts as a comprehensive service provider, popular with customers who seek excellent service and a "one-stop shop" for their needs even if it costs a little more. In the first organization, key organizational capabilities might be *continuous improvement in supply chain efficiency* and *ability to deliver products quickly to customers*, whereas in the latter, key capabilities might be *innovation in product development* and *strong customer relationships*. Neither set of capabilities is right or wrong, but each is specific to the organization and its strategic advantage. Many organizations offer similar products (cars, clothing, cell phones) but have different capabilities to distinguish their products from others. This point will become clearer as we delve into strategy in the next chapter.

Leaders must be able to articulate (and agree on) strategic priorities and how those will be prioritized in the design. They should understand what differentiates their product or organization in the marketplace and how their internal design helps them to achieve that differentiation. In addition, they will need to determine how the future needs of the organization and its direction will be enabled by the design to ensure that it remains ahead of competitors. Put differently,

> Organizational capabilities are hard for competitors to match. They may be time-consuming to build, hard to replicate or imitate, or difficult to obtain from others. This is not to say that they last forever. What may be a differentiating organizational capability today could become the baseline in the future as others catch up. (Galbraith, Downey, & Kates, 2002, p. 30)

In summary, design criteria and organizational capabilities are

- unique, integrated combinations of skills, processes, and human abilities;
- created by and housed within an organization; and
- factors that differentiate the organization and provide competitive advantage (Kates & Galbraith, 2007, p. 7).

Benefits of Design Criteria

Design criteria have a number of benefits, because they allow organizational leaders to

- translate the strategy into actionable, tangible statements;
- focus your organization's leadership on what is most important;
- make more objective decisions;

- document and communicate rationale;
- create a framework for making trade-offs;
- provide measures of success; and
- focus on fulfilling the strategy—not just solving today's problems. (Kates & Galbraith, 2007, p. 216)

The development and use of design criteria pushes designers to avoid making changes based on politics and people but instead to make decisions based on a rational evaluation of how the design helps to achieve the strategy. When the design is ready to be implemented and communicated to others, the design criteria can provide a clear explanation for why some options were chosen over others.

How to Develop and Use Design Criteria in the Design Process

It is often helpful to create design criteria by filling in the blanks to the sentence "In order to achieve our business strategy, our organization needs to be able to ______ better than the competition" (Kates & Galbraith, 2007, p. 216). Kates and Galbraith write that good design criteria should be specific, differentiating, actionable, future oriented, and about capabilities (not activities). They recommend a small list of options—no more than five—in order to communicate a clear set of priorities that can inform the design. As Galbraith (2002) put it, "[W]e cannot design simple organizations that provide a variety of products to a variety of customers on short cycle times and also capture economies of scale to provide low cost" (p. 8). The process of generating and prioritizing criteria is intended to focus the process on which of those criteria is most important to the design.

Galbraith, Downey, and Kates (2002, p. 31) provide several examples of effective design criteria:

- Create new products faster than our competitors.
- Offer a diverse product line.
- Encourage innovation.
- Become a low-cost producer.
- Continually increase process efficiency.
- Customize products at a customer's request.
- Deliver high levels of customer satisfaction.

Some authors, however, recommend that design criteria be more detailed in order to provide further direction to the design. Goold and Campbell (2002a) recommend taking the statements above and explaining how those criteria provide implications on design. They advise that "design criteria need to give specific guidance on some aspect of organization design. Criteria such as 'minimize organizational boundaries,' 'maximize the capacity for organizational learning,' or 'cut the time it takes to make decisions' are too general to be useful" (p. 231). For them, successful design criteria include the following (pp. 302–305):

- "Centralize product development and quality control, except for products with clearly different needs."
- "Insure strong leadership is given to the product development and manufacturing functions."
- "Give added attention to new products and Eastern Europe."
- "Avoid creating a 'big team' at the top."

Which of these approaches provides the most appropriate level of detail may depend on the organization. In some cases, the more general design criteria may be enough to guide design, but in other organizations the implications of those criteria may need to be spelled out in greater detail before the next decisions take place. Regardless, having criteria enables designers to compare alternative designs and to explain why one alternative helps to achieve the criteria more effectively than another.

As multiple design options are then developed, design criteria can provide a method for evaluating different designs. Morrison (2015) and Cichocki and Irwin (2011) offer an instructive process whereby each criterion can be weighted on a scale from 1 to 5 (for example, "increase speed to market" can be rated as a 5, "expand into new geographies" can be rated a 3, and "support tax optimization" can be rated a 1 to reflect their differing levels of importance to the organization) (Morrison, 2015, p. 91). Organization design options can then be scored on a scale of 1 to 10 to evaluate how well the design meets (or fails to meet) the criterion, and the weighted calculations can be applied accordingly. For example, assume we were evaluating three design options that a group had considered. For Design Option 1, a score of 8 on the criterion of "increase speed to market" would become 40 points, a score of 7 on "expand into new geographies" adds 21 points, and a score of 6 on the tax optimization criterion would add 6 points, for a total of 67 on these three criteria. We would do the same scoring and weighting for options 2 and 3 and compare the final totals. This method allows a quantitative scoring of multiple design options as an objective measure of each design's match with the criteria. Table 2.4 depicts how the weighted design criteria model works to evaluate different design options.

Table 2.4 Example Application of Design Criteria to Evaluate Design Options

Criteria	Weight	Design Option 1	Design Option 2	Design Option 3
Increase Speed to Market	5	Rating: 8 (x 5 = 40)	Rating: 6 (x 5 = 30)	Rating: 3 (x 5 = 15)
Expand Into New Geographies	3	Rating: 7 (x 3 = 21)	Rating: 8 (x 3 = 24)	Rating: 7 (x 3 = 21)
Support Tax Optimization	1	Rating: 6 (x 1 = 6)	Rating: 4 (x 1 = 4)	Rating: 9 (x 1 = 9)
Total Weighted Evaluation		**67**	**58**	**45**

SUMMARY

The STAR model of organization design provides a framework that has become popular among scholars and practitioners, explaining that important points of a design involve strategy, structure, processes and lateral capability, people, and rewards. Key design concepts include those of alignment and congruence, which explain that the practices of the organization should be internally consistent in order to reinforce one another, and contingency theory, which explains that an organization should be as complicated as its business requires. The principle of complementarity reminds designers that design choices work together in a system, not in isolation from one another. There is no single perfect design, but design is a set of decisions and considerations that involve trade-offs. Today's rapid pace of change challenges organizations to become more agile and redesign regularly.

An organization design process provides a disciplined and logical approach to design. The initial steps of the design include scoping the organization to be designed and deciding who will be involved. The process commonly begins with a design assessment using one or more methods of data gathering such as interviews, focus groups, surveys, observations, or unobtrusive measures. Models and design tests can be used as instructive guides to organize the design assessment and prioritize areas for improvement. An environmental scan looks externally at the organization's environment to analyze the social, technological, economic, environmental, and political trends affecting the organization. A design process proceeds by generating design criteria and understanding the critical organizational capabilities that will form the basis for the new design. Such decisions are difficult if the strategy is unclear, so in the next chapter we will begin with strategy at the top of the STAR model.

QUESTIONS FOR DISCUSSION

1. Consider an organization that you know well. To what extent does it need to be redesigned, based on the principles identified in the chapter?
2. How would you go about gathering data to conduct a design assessment for the organization you identified in the previous question? Which factors in the SWOT or STEEP environmental scanning model affect the organization the most?
3. Locate the website of an organization where you might like to work or where you have been a customer. What do you think are the design criteria for that organization?

FOR FURTHER READING

Galbraith, J., Downey, D., & Kates, A. (2002). *Designing dynamic organizations: A hands-on guide for leaders at all levels*. New York, NY: AMACOM.

Goold, M., & Campbell, A. (2002). Do you have a well-designed organization? *Harvard Business Review, 80*(3), 117–124.

Kesler, G., & Kates, A. (2011). *Leading organization design*. San Francisco, CA: Jossey-Bass.

EXERCISE

ProRunnerGear.com is an online and specialty store retailer of high-end running shoes, apparel, and accessories for the professional runner, competitive runners (e.g., high school, college track) and advanced recreational runners. The company aims to be the first choice for the running athlete by offering a wide variety of innovative products to meet their customers' needs. They may not be the cheapest running store, but they offer exceptional customer service and stock products that cannot be found elsewhere. They have a rapid product delivery timeframe and offer an easy and flexible return policy. Competitors include other online retailers, specialty running stores, and "big box" retailers for some products.

Imagine that you are the executive team of ProRunnerGear.com, and you are beginning an organization design effort. Identify five design criteria that you would use to guide your choices. Make sure to rank your choices in order, 1 to 5, according to your priorities.

CASE STUDY 1: THE SUPPLY CHAIN DIVISION OF SUPERIOR MODULE ELECTRONICS, INC.

Read the Superior Module Electronics case and answer the following questions:

1. Use the STAR model to identify each point of the star in the case. Give specific examples for each point.
2. Work your way around the STAR, and evaluate the design according to each section of the STAR. How would you evaluate how each point of the STAR is consistent or inconsistent with other elements of the STAR?
3. Propose any improvements or changes to any of the points of the STAR that you find to be inconsistent. What STAR model points would you change, and why?

* * *

"Our biggest problem right now is that we are not working together. We are making stupid mistakes, and we know better," admitted Carl Hoffman, senior vice president for supply chain operations at Superior Module Electronics (SME).

"This company looks nothing like the company that my grandfather started more than 50 years ago. We have performance problems that are keeping us from being competitive. Morale in the division is the lowest it has ever been, and we are endangering our reputation for putting out the highest-quality electronics in our industry segment."

Superior Module Electronics creates power supplies, batteries, cables, and switches for large industrial applications. Customers of SME use their electronics components in high-risk industrial applications such as mining (minerals, oil and gas) and hazardous manufacturing (industrial gases, fertilizers, explosives). The company's investment in research and development throughout its history has made it one of the highest-performing companies in its industry. In the past several years, revenues had been steadily rising while competitors reported flat to declining sales. Recently, however, profits at SME have declined and the company is poised to report its first quarterly loss since the recession. Customer complaints about quality have been mounting, and the supply chain division has come under increased scrutiny from the board of directors.

"If one of our power supplies has an electrical surge or it heats up or it causes a fire, it's no exaggeration to say that there would be fatal consequences," Carl stressed. "We distinguish ourselves by developing and manufacturing the highest quality products in our industry. We think it's better to take a little extra time to make it right, because as my grandfather used to say, 'If it's not right, it's wrong.'"

"Government regulations require that our customers adhere to very strict safety practices, and as a result, those same regulations impact us as well. We have to undergo rigorous testing of our products and provide independent data to our customers that certify that our products are safe for use in their environments. But last summer, we had to recall 46,000 power supplies that were shipped out over a 4-month period due to a quality defect in the assembly. There is a possibility that we may face a serious fine for failing to find the defect before the product was sent to customers. If that's true, it will take a long time to regain our reputation and customer trust. Our CEO, my father Avery Hoffman, screamed at me for three hours," Carl remembered. "I still can't get to the bottom of whether the problem was with a supplier or our own internal manufacturing."

"Our problems are self-imposed. I have a bunch of weak managers reporting to me. They bring all of their problems to me rather than sorting them out among themselves. They are supposed to be organized in a flow: advanced manufacturing does the prototype and then trains the other two manufacturing divisions; supplier contracts work with our external suppliers to get the product here for manufacturing to build; planning tells manufacturing how much to build; shipping sends products to customers; project management improves the quality of the whole operation. None of them takes into account the impact of their work on the other divisions. They operate like independent kingdoms instead of an integrated team. It's chaos."

"Many of the problems, I think, stem from the way that we operate as a leadership team. With a few exceptions, we have high-quality people here in the division. The problem is that they are not working together effectively. In addition, there are problems in the attitudes of people. When I go around to meet members of the team, they just don't seem to have any bigger aspirations or commitment. They don't seem amped up or energized. A large number of projects are behind schedule. We are not on the same page with where we are going as a division, where we ought to be putting our resources, or how we determine priorities."

"I have tried to find out more about these issues," Carl continued. "A recent employee survey indicated that two-thirds of the division's staff did not believe that they had the authority to make decisions that allowed them to do a quality job. Almost 80 percent indicated that they had untapped capabilities or that they were unable to use their skills to their full potential on the job. In addition, almost 70 percent of the staff felt that the pay practices did not recognize or reward doing quality work. Finally, 73 percent said that promotion decisions were made for political reasons based on preferential treatment rather than qualifications for the job."

Carl recently called in a consulting team to understand the reasons behind the department's problems. He provided the consulting team with the current organizational chart for the division (Figure 2.5) and recommended that they hold personal conversations with each leader. Excerpts from interviews with members of the leadership team are included below to explain their perspective about the problems that the supply chain division is experiencing.

The Leadership Team's Perspective

Rachel Mills, Supplier Contracts

My division is responsible for negotiating contracts with our suppliers, which includes cost, quality, and delivery expectations. If we order 100,000 feet of copper tubing, we want it at a prenegotiated cost, within a certain quality level, and on our time schedule. If we need a delivery of high purity hydrogen sulfide, then it must contain impurities at a level of less than one-half of 1 percent.

As an incentive to negotiate better rates with our suppliers, my team is compensated with a bonus based on supplier performance, specifically their cost. It is a simple formula: For every percentage decrease in cost, my team gets an equivalent salary bonus. A 10 percent reduction in supplier cost is a 10 percent

Figure 2.5 Superior Module Electronics Organization Chart for Supply Chain Operations Division

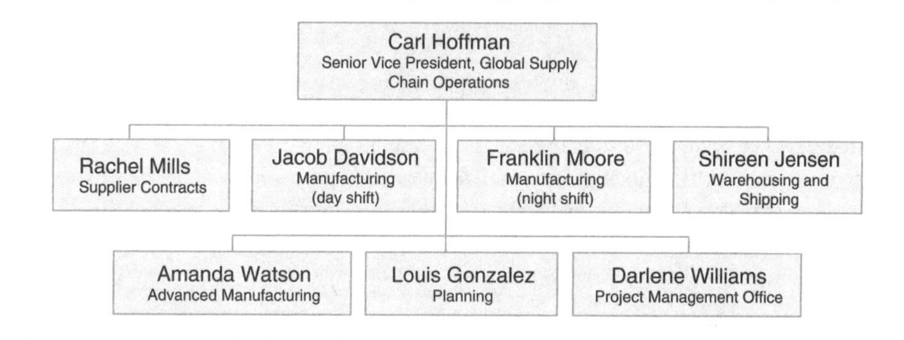

annual bonus. If we can get a part made out of a high-quality composite instead of a pure metal, and the product engineers tell me that it will be the same, then we will change it out with their approval.

Jacob Davidson, Manufacturing (day shift)

"Keep the train moving" is our motto. As the manufacturing engine of the company, the last thing we want is to run out of product and create unhappy customers. It's my neck on the line, so I will do whatever I need to do in order to make sure that we have enough stock, and I don't want Carl and Avery coming in my office. My goals are to ensure 100 percent stocking levels on every product, so I miss my goal any time the warehouse is out of stock.

Frankly, everything else is a distraction that wastes my time. On our management team, we have never worked together very well, and most of my department is a duplication of other functions that can't get their jobs done. I don't know what Darlene's team is supposed to be doing. We have our own project leaders that work to improve manufacturing quality, so I see her team as unnecessary. All of my people are doing their jobs. And Rachel's team lacks the expertise to understand how the products are put together, so when my guys report a quality concern to Rachel's team, they don't understand what we are talking about, so we duplicate their work by calling suppliers ourselves. Same thing with Amanda's team. Her team lacks the basic understanding of what day-to-day manufacturing looks like. They build so few products on her team that they don't know what it's like to have 100 times the workload of what they do, so their manufacturing plans are complicated and we have to rework them before we get started.

Franklin Moore, Manufacturing (night shift)

Typically, the manufacturing plan is published every day at 5 p.m. when Louis's team is leaving for the day. Jacob's team works until 8 p.m., and then my team comes in and works until 6 a.m. A "planning day" is measured at 6 a.m. for the previous 24-hour period, so my team is the one stuck with any plan changes and we have to scramble to meet the goal. We have two opposite problems with this: too much work, and not enough work. Usually, we fail to meet the newly published plan because we are trying to make up the work that Jacob's team did not accomplish during the day and we get impossibly difficult goals to meet. But there are also days that the plan is revised downward, so we have less work to do and I have to send workers home. That causes morale problems.

To make matters worse, my turnover on the night shift approaches 40 to 50 percent. It's rough on the body to have to work the graveyard, so most people stick it out when they first get the job until a position opens up on the day shift. When I have gaps in staffing, I have to turn to our temporary labor until I can get someone hired, which seems to take forever here. Also, no one in our training department is willing to stick around until midnight to run a training program, so we end up doing our own. Most of the training is on the job, led by whoever knows their stuff and has been around the longest.

Shireen Jensen, Warehousing and Shipping

I'm sure you've heard the saying "Keep the train moving," because it's what Carl tells the whole team all the time. My group consists of the warehouse team that ships out the product based on customer orders. I am evaluated based on warehouse stocking levels and our shipping cycle times, or how fast we can ship out orders to a customer. I have no authority to make decisions on warehouse stocking levels other than to tell Jacob's team when we are about ready to run out of stock. If his team does not take action, my team pays the price.

We do not have an effective planning or prioritization process because everything feels like an emergency. If one of Carl's golf buddies complains about an order, he will come down himself to take the materials out of the warehouse and deliver them personally.

Amanda Watson, Advanced Manufacturing

Our job is to take the latest products that are designed by research and development and to actually build them. My team is separate from Jacob's and Franklin's manufacturing teams because we have our own manufacturing line to test out what it's like to build the latest products. Once we create the manufacturing process on any product, we build it for the first 6 months until we feel comfortable that it's ready to go to Jacob's and Franklin's teams.

We're basically our own self-contained supply chain organization, and we need what we need, so we have our own sourcing organization, too. Rachel's team won't help us and is not responsive. For example, when we started our manufacturing plans for the large capacity M4X batteries, Rachel's team insisted that we use an existing supplier for the chemicals that go in the internal chambers. Our team found that the chemical purity was not to the engineering specifications, so we went ahead and ordered our own. Rachel's team is pretty incompetent when it comes to the engineering detail. But I have a team of PhDs who can run circles around them, so we just ask them to step aside while we get the job done.

Contributing to the morale problem in the division is that fact that Carl recently decided to outsource the manufacturing of the M4X batteries after we had spent 6 months on the internal manufacturing plan, meaning that all of the time and effort we invested was worthless. The company ended up paying our external manufacturer to repeat the planning work that we had already done, and no one ever asked us for any of our data or findings about how to manufacture the product. If you want to know why morale is so low, consider that we just took a team of brilliant PhDs and flushed their work down the toilet.

Louis Gonzalez, Planning

My team's responsibility is to create the manufacturing plan, or basically the number of each type of item that our manufacturing teams should be producing. We work with marketing and sales as well as the product managers in the company's product divisions.

Basically, there is no communication or coordination among each of those groups. There is only conflict and disagreement, plus gaming the system. Sales tells us how many of each type of item they expect to sell, but sales generally overestimates how much they are going to sell because they don't want us to be out of stock on any of our products. The product division has their own sales estimates, which are almost always lower. I am caught in the middle but I try to accurately predict how much to tell manufacturing to build based on all of that information. Then I have to use our system to convert all of that into specific orders for our suppliers. I might need to increase our order of sheet metal from a supplier, or reduce our order for coils of 10mm gauge wiring. Sometimes our suppliers need advanced notice of our requirements, as early as a few months in advance. The numbers change all the time, so I put out a new manufacturing order almost every day, which makes our suppliers furious. Rachel's team is supposed to do something about that, but I don't sense that they care that much.

The biggest problems with planning are communication and politics. The lack of coordination is pervasive across this company, and we are rarely if ever informed about important product releases or features. Engineering comes out with a new product that we didn't know about, which means that customers want the newest thing, and we're stuck with a bunch of unsold inventory because we didn't know what was coming. Or the upper management puts the pressure on Carl to make us build more so it doesn't look like we didn't trust their numbers. Carl himself will change the numbers in the system and not tell me until I log in to the system and see the new plan. Then manufacturing has to scramble to get it done. We are always being questioned by upper management and have very little authority to make any decisions.

Darlene Williams, Project Management Office

The mission of my team is supposed to be to orchestrate and manage quality improvement projects across the supply chain division.

I would say that my staff is confused more than anything. Projects are not clearly defined by the leadership team, and there is a great deal of conflict over project priorities. Projects overlap one another and project managers often do not know that they are working on the same thing. Project team members rarely know what their own role is on the team or how they should be working together. Carl himself will come down to the manufacturing floor and shut down a project himself, start another one up, or change the scope or timeline of a project on the spot. The whiplash effect is a demotivator to the whole team. To make it worse, project managers feel that they have no authority over the processes on any of the other teams, so whatever decisions they make can be vetoed by my peers anyway. Decisions about projects and how we allocate resources, including space, time, budgets, and staff, are made arbitrarily by Carl, and there seem to be no priorities to help us decide which projects are the most important. The leadership team does not participate on any project or prioritization process. Sometimes they appear to intentionally undermine the work of my team by starting up teams of their own.

This frustration seems to manifest itself in our relationships with other departments. There is no alignment or engagement with other groups, period. The manufacturing teams feel insulted, defensive, and threatened when my team tries to help them. Manufacturing team members who participate on projects led by my team tend to miss meetings and important deliverables they have committed to. The lack of project stability, unclear roles and responsibilities, and the lack of any kind of rewards for participating on an improvement project outside one's "day job" have meant that any kind of commitment to a project has plummeted.

CHAPTER 3

STRATEGY

Among concepts in the field of management in the past 50 years, perhaps none has been written about or debated more than strategy. Chandler (1962), whose pioneering comparative analysis of four companies we reviewed in Chapter 1, appears to have been the first to apply the strategy concept to the business environment, a concept he likely adapted from his connection with teaching at a military college (Freedman, 2013). Books by Drucker (1964) and Ansoff (1965) created a dramatic rise in the interest in business strategy in the 1960s that has never declined. Since then, consulting companies and publications seem to generate new tools and frameworks every year. As a result, the field of strategy has created a "dizzying sequence of grand ideas, the appearance of gurus . . . [a] proliferation of management fashions and fads . . . with cacophony and inconsistency" (Freedman, 2013, p. 561). It is no wonder that many executives find themselves overwhelmed with strategy concepts and advice. Some observers remark that "it is a dirty little secret that most executives don't actually know what all the elements of a strategy statement are, which makes it impossible for them to develop one" (Collis & Rukstad, 2008, p. 84). If you are hesitant in approaching this topic, you are not alone.

This chapter will introduce foundational ideas and concepts about strategy. This overview is by its nature a selective one specifically for those new to organization design. Strategy can be a difficult concept, full of complex theories and dense writings. Our goal here will not be to convert you into a corporate strategy officer, but to instead, provide enough information so that you can use the organization's strategy decisions as a launching point for the remainder of the organization design. This overview will help you (1) understand why strategy is a compelling concept for design practitioners, (2) recognize when an organization does or does not have a strategy that is agreed upon by a leader or design team, (3) identify what kind of strategy the organization has, and (4) begin to formulate ideas about how the strategy should impact the rest of the design.

Learning Objectives

In this chapter you will learn

- Why strategy is important for organization design.
- Definition of strategy and types of generic strategies.
- Key concepts in strategy.
- New perspectives on strategy that are important for a design practitioner to know.

WHY STRATEGY IS AN IMPORTANT CONCEPT FOR ORGANIZATION DESIGN

Strategy is at the top of the STAR model for a reason. By providing the starting point for the organization's required capabilities (and thus the design criteria as you recall from Chapter 2), strategy has an influence on nearly every other design decision. Specifically, strategy is important for designers for four reasons:

1. **Strategic clarity and agreement are required for effective design.** "If the strategy is not clear, or not agreed upon by the leadership team, there are no criteria on which to base other design decisions" (Galbraith, Downey, & Kates, 2002, p. 3). Without strategic clarity, it will be almost impossible to gain agreement on the prioritized organizational capabilities reviewed in the previous chapter. If a leadership team does not agree on the strategy, it will be difficult to make design decisions affecting organizational structure, key metrics, or required skills of employees to deliver on the strategy. In these cases, it is worth investing additional time up front in strategy development before beginning on the remainder of the design.
2. **Different strategies require different designs.** To reemphasize a point from Chapter 1, "[T]here is no one-size-fits-all organization design that all companies—regardless of their particular strategy needs—should subscribe to" (Galbraith, 2002, p. 14). Just because Nordstrom and Banana Republic are both in the apparel industry and Nike and Adidas are shoe manufacturers does not mean that they should have identical organization designs. Understanding and facilitating organization design thus requires an understanding of how and why strategy has an impact on the design.
3. **Organization design can be a strategic advantage.** If an organization can master a new capability and embed it into its organization design faster or more effectively than a competitor, it can achieve a strategic advantage. Nike's digital capabilities were given strategic focus in 2010 in its digital sports division (Galbraith, 2014b). That capability is visible in its Nike+ sensors embedded in running shoes and in its online NikePlus.com community, which sets Nike apart from competitors that do not offer these features. Unique organization designs can differentiate an organization or help it achieve operating efficiencies that competitors cannot easily replicate.
4. **Organization design can facilitate strategy execution.** Some experts believe that strategies can be copied, but what distinguishes a company's success is its ability to execute on that strategy. As we have seen, many problems with strategy execution can be traced to poor design. Knowledge of strategy can help an organization designer identify creative ways to embed that strategy into each element of the STAR model.

WHAT IS STRATEGY?

Consider these classic and recent definitions of strategy offered by well-respected strategic thinkers:

- "Strategy can be defined as the determination of the basic long-term goals and objectives of an enterprise, and the adoption of courses of action and the allocation of resources necessary for carrying out these goals." (Chandler, 1962, p. 13)
- "Strategy is about positioning an organization for sustainable competitive advantage. It involves making choices about which industries to participate in, what products and services to offer, and how to allocate corporate resources. Its primary goal is to create value for shareholders and other stakeholders by providing customer value." (De Kluyver & Pearce, 2003, p. 1)
- "A company's strategy is management's action plan for running the business and conducting operations." (Thompson, A. A., Jr., Strickland, & Gamble, 2008, p. 3)
- "The dynamics of the firm's relation with its environment for which the necessary actions are taken to achieve its goals and/or to increase performance by means of the rational use of resources" (Ronda-Pupo & Guerras-Martin, 2012, p. 182)

Not surprisingly, in its history, the field of strategy has included many different definitions and schools of thought. Ronda-Pupo and Guerras-Martin (2012) have studied 91 different definitions of strategy in the first 46 years of the field, noting that "the lexicon of strategic management is internally inconsistent and tends to be confusing" (p. 162). Hambrick and Fredrickson (2001) remark that "[s]trategy has become a catchall term used to mean whatever one wants it to mean" (p. 49). Mintzberg (1987; Mintzberg, Ahlstrand, & Lampel, 1988) observes that there are five definitions or perspectives on what strategy means:

Strategy is a plan: We often describe a strategy as a consciously identified path and set of actions. In this definition, strategy is seen as a planning activity that occurs before actions take place. You might have a strategy for getting to work when there is bad weather or a traffic accident that makes your typical route a poor choice.

Strategy is a ploy: Strategy can be a threat of a proposed move in order to draw out the behavior of a competitor or opponent. A poker player might bluff to get a competitor to withdraw. A company may publicly state that it has no interest in acquiring a smaller rival in order to discourage a bidding war.

Strategy is a pattern: Strategy can be something observed in hindsight whether the actions were intended consciously as a plan or not. In this sense, we can distinguish "*deliberate* strategies, where intentions that existed previously were realized, from *emergent* strategies, where patterns developed in the absence of intentions" (Mintzberg, 1987, p. 13). We might infer a company's strategy from the actions it takes.

Strategy is a position: Strategy can be defined in relationship to other competitors within an industry segment or environment. A company might decide to position itself as a provider to the market niche of urban apartment dwellers or environmentally conscious car buyers.

Strategy is a perspective: Finally, strategy can be a worldview, or a company's internal identity and way of perceiving the external world. SOLO eyewear had a mission to help one million people see again in developing countries through a sustainable business model of people, planet, and profit (Schroeder & Denoble, 2014). A compelling vision and laudable goal helped to create a loyal following. Leinwand and Mainardi (2016) write that IKEA's identity "to create a better everyday life for the many people" (p. 22) translates into how they see every aspect of home design.

Scholars make a distinction between corporate strategy and business strategy (Hrebiniak, Joyce, & Snow, 1988; Porter, 1987). A corporate (also called company-wide) strategy is the answer to the overarching question, "What business should we be in?" or as Porter (1987) puts it, "What makes the corporate whole add up to more than the sum of its business unit parts" (p. 43). It might describe the diversification strategy of Berkshire Hathaway, whose subsidiaries include companies in unrelated industries such as Duracell, See's Candies, and Helzberg Diamonds. A business strategy (also called competitive strategy) describes how each of those individual separate businesses compete in their own industries. In this chapter, we will concentrate more on strategy in the latter circumstances.

Sustainable Competitive Advantage

One of the core concepts that has captivated strategists has been that of developing a "sustainable competitive advantage" (for a history and overview, see N. Hoffman, 2000). On this subject, among scholars of strategy in the last several decades, perhaps none is more cited or well known than Michael Porter. It is a fair assumption that virtually every student of strategy since 1996 has been assigned Porter's classic article, "What Is Strategy?" that appeared in the *Harvard Business Review* that year. For Porter, strategy is about "the general principles of creating and sustaining competitive advantage" (Magretta, 2012, p. 93). This means being different—not trying to mimic others or copy a competitor but to find a unique path to stand out in a lasting way. In other words, "A company can outperform rivals only if it can establish a difference that it can preserve" (Porter, 1996, p. 62). How is a company to stand out and perform better than the competition? Porter explains that

> Competitive advantage grows fundamentally out of value a firm is able to create for its buyers that exceeds the firm's cost of creating it. Value is what buyers are willing to pay, and superior value stems from offering lower prices than competitors for equivalent benefits or providing unique benefits that more than offset a higher price. (1985, p. 3)

A company that finds a competitive advantage will be more profitable than competitors because it will operate at lower cost or have the ability to charge a premium price to customers because of the value that is provided.

If you look around your home and ask yourself why you purchased any given item or service, it's likely that the answer will effectively boil down to one of those two reasons. Perhaps you chose the item because it was less expensive, and you judged the competitors to be essentially equal in features. You determined that one brand of stapler or copy paper or orange juice is as good as its alternatives, and you chose the one that cost the least. Or, perhaps you chose the product or service because it was different or unique. You chose premium coffee because you like the taste better, your top-of-the-line flat screen TV because it had unique features, or the more expensive dry cleaner that offers faster service. You were willing to pay more in these instances rather than only evaluating cost. For those companies, your decision criteria formed the basis of their competitive advantage over the alternatives that you did not select.

Activity Systems and Strategic Trade-offs

In Porter's classic 1996 article, he articulated two key principles to define the essence of strategy, including activity systems and strategic trade-offs.

Strategy Rests on Unique Activities

Porter writes that "[t]he essence of strategy is in the activities—choosing to perform activities differently or to perform different activities from rivals" (Porter, 1996, p. 62). In this sense, being different and unique is central to strategy. Most companies that produce a product or service must do similar things such as product development or design, manufacturing and production, service delivery, sales, finance, and marketing. If every company did these activities in exactly the same way, there would be little difference between them. If a company can discover how to manufacture a product at a lower cost, however, that lower cost can be passed on to the customer in terms of lower prices and the company can gain an advantage over a competitor. Or, if a company has a superior product design process that provides an attractive set of new features that no other competitor can match, they also have an advantage. Porter explains:

> Ultimately all differences between companies in cost or price derive from the hundreds of activities required to create, produce, sell, and deliver their products or services, such as calling on customers, assembling final products, and training employees. . . . Activities, then, are the basic units of competitive advantage. Overall advantage or disadvantage results from all of a company's activities, not only a few. (Porter, 1996, p. 62)

Activities are grouped together in activity systems, and when the entire activity system is oriented toward a particular goal, competitive advantage can result. A single activity (lower-cost manufacturing) can provide an advantage, but a sustainable advantage comes from organizing a series of activities into a system that is more difficult for competitors to copy.

Consider the example of Southwest Airlines. Ask most people what Southwest's strategy is, and most will come up with some version of "low cost." But that simple label fails to capture the myriad of activities internally to Southwest that allows them to maintain a cost advantage. Southwest does not just replicate everything that United Airlines does but charge less for the service—to do so would be to settle for lower profitability. Instead, Southwest is able to offer lower prices by also making other choices that decrease costs, such as offering more limited service (no meals, no seat assignments, no baggage transfers to other airlines, no connections). While this has changed somewhat in recent years, Southwest initially chose a smaller lower-cost airport location outside of major hub cities (e.g., Chicago Midway instead of Chicago O'Hare). Using the same fleet of 737 aircraft has meant that Southwest can have standardized training, and pilots and crew members do not have to be limited to only the aircraft they are trained to work. Maintenance costs are lower because spare parts inventory from panels to bolts to coffee pots will all fit every plane, improving the efficiency of maintenance crews. Fast gate turnaround times and efficient boarding practices keep planes flying (when they are making money, versus standing on the ground) and allow more departures per day. In short, everything Southwest does in its major activity system is in the service of providing lower costs to customers. Perhaps another competitor could come along and do the same thing as Southwest by engaging in a few of these activities—charging similarly low prices and offering limited service routes. Other competitors, however, have had difficulty replicating the entire activity system that gives Southwest a unique advantage.

Strategy Requires Trade-offs

Listen to many business executives articulate their strategies, and you may hear some version of "We want to offer the highest-quality product at the lowest cost with the best customer service." This is misguided, in Porter's view. He advises that "a strategic position is not sustainable unless there are trade-offs with other positions" (1996, p. 68). He points to what happened with Continental Airlines (now United Continental Holdings) in the mid-1990s when it decided to compete with Southwest by launching a service called Continental Lite. It offered low prices (one popular incentive invited customers to bring a friend on the flight and be charged only a penny more), no meals, and the same routes. But by maintaining its full-service routes, frequent flier program, and travel agent incentives, it was not able to reduce its costs as Southwest had. Eventually it cut frequent flier benefits and travel agent costs, angering both constituencies. The company's CEO resigned in 1994 and the Continental Lite service was discontinued in 1995 at what is estimated to have cost $140 million (Bryant, 1995).

Porter's view is that "[a] sustainable strategic position requires trade-offs" (1996, p. 68). This means that companies accept the idea that they cannot meet all needs of all customers, and they must make deliberate decisions not to pursue certain types of customer or market. Magretta (2012) describes how the Swedish furniture designer IKEA chose to target price-conscious customers with less expensive furniture designs. IKEA chooses not to design and sell luxury goods or hand-constructed dining tables. Customers agree to the trade-off of assembling the furniture themselves, packing it in their own vehicles, and with almost no individualized sales assistance. Trade-offs are important for three reasons, Porter (1996) writes:

1. "Inconsistencies in image or reputation" (p. 68) arise without trade-offs, because customers will be confused about the mixed messages. If a company is trying to lead the market with a lower-cost product, it will be challenging to convince new customers that a high-end offering is worth the price. If IKEA added an expensive leather sofa to its line with the ability to select among 50 color options, or if Gucci created a $30 sports watch, customers would likely react negatively to the discrepancy with the rest of the company's products.
2. Different strategies require different product configurations, different equipment, and different management systems. Without trade-offs,

these different strategies dramatically increase complexity. IKEA's manufacturing line that is organized to build modular furniture for self-assembly would not be suitable for the leather sofa.

3. Without trade-offs and a clear signal, employees can be confused about priorities. If IKEA introduced a custom-built set of kitchen cabinets that were made to order, employees from designers to procurement to manufacturing would need to stop and rethink how to cope with the offering that goes against the processes used for the rest of the company's product lines. This requires different employee behavior and a different set of skills.

Magretta (2012) concludes that "if there is one important takeaway message, it is that strategy requires choice. . . . Trade-offs play such a critical role that it's no exaggeration to call them strategy's linchpin" (p. 121).

TYPES OF STRATEGY

In this section, we will examine different formulations of types of strategy that scholars have observed. We will cover three strategy frameworks: Porter's generic strategies, Treacy and Wiersema's value disciplines, and Miles and Snow's strategy typology.

As we will see in later chapters, it is important for the organization designer to be able to identify the type of strategy that an organization is adopting in order to be able to disseminate the implications of that choice throughout the rest of the design and ensure alignment.

Porter's Generic Strategies

Porter (1980, 1985) explains that there are three generic strategies from which companies can choose: cost, differentiation, and focus, a typology that Campbell-Hunt (2000) called "unquestionably among the most substantial and influential contributions that have been made to the study of strategic behavior in organizations" (p. 127). As we have seen, Porter has noted that a company must choose one of these strategies to the exclusion of the other two, writing that "sometimes the firm can successfully pursue more than one approach as its primary target, though this is rarely possible" (1980, p. 35), a point that has generated considerable attention (see Figure 3.1).

Cost Leadership

A company enjoys a cost-leadership advantage if it can find ways of operating at a lower cost than competitors. A cost-leadership strategy can work in two ways. First, it can result in higher than average profits even when the company charges generally the same as competitors, because the company's costs are lower and thus its profits will be higher. Second, the company can charge less than competitors and attract more price-sensitive customers, maintaining higher profits by selling more volume. The sources for this advantage can vary depending on the industry, but commonly involve the following:

- Economies of scale (bulk purchasing to reduce costs from suppliers or volume manufacturing, which reduces the cost per unit manufactured)

Figure 3.1 Porter's Generic Strategies

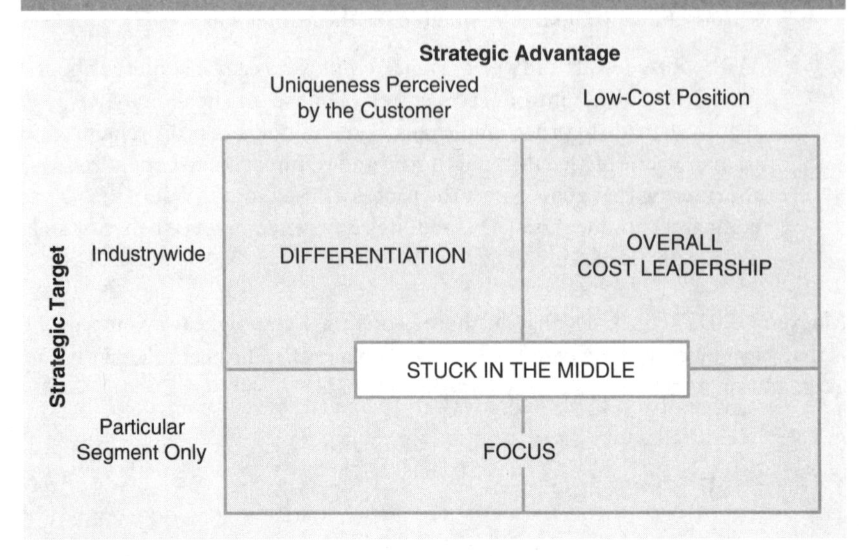

Source: Adapted from Porter, M. E. (1980). *Competitive strategy: Techniques for analyzing industries and competitors*. New York, NY: Free Press, p. 39. Retrieved from https://commons.wikimedia.org/wiki/File:Michael_Porter%27s_Three_Generic_Strategies.svg, licensed under CC BY-SA 3.0 https://creativecommons.org/licenses/by-sa/3.0/deed.en

- More efficient uses of facilities such as manufacturing (perhaps designing products specifically for ease of manufacturing)
- More productive employees (due to more efficient processes) or lower-cost labor (shifting work to lower-cost locations)
- Low overhead costs or cost management in areas such as marketing and information technology
- More efficient uses of raw materials (less waste in the manufacturing process) or using less expensive raw materials
- Outsourcing or vertical integration to take advantage of the capabilities of other companies and thus reduce costs
- Using the Internet or lower-cost distribution channels to sell directly to customers and eliminate a salesforce, distributors, or dealers

Most companies want to be efficient and will look for cost reductions periodically regardless of strategy. A cost-leadership strategy as its primary objective, however, aligns managers and employees to the goal of aggressively examining all internal sources of cost and pursuing cost reductions throughout the organization. A company might invest resources in technology that show real-time inventory levels or automatically package and ship orders from a warehouse. The same can occur with companies that offer services instead of products, making service calls more efficient and thus increasing profitability by performing more services in the same amount of time as a competitor. A low-cost–leadership position can often be sustained by continued reinvestment in efficiencies, new equipment, or new facilities (Porter, 1980).

Differentiation

The second generic strategy is that of differentiation. A differentiation strategy seeks to gain advantage by offering something that no one else offers, and thus can command a premium price. However, creating uniqueness comes at a cost, perhaps in research and development, additional staff, costly raw materials, and more. Differentiation will be profitable only when the premium price that is charged is higher than the cost incurred to create the differentiation (Porter, 1985). Differentiation can take many forms:

- Additional or better features not offered by competitors (a different size, flavor, or color; a new capability such as Internet connectivity; unique, attractive, or specialized design)
- Product quality (premium materials, better reliability, better taste)
- Services that set the company apart (personal assistance or consulting, free installation support or training, free upgrades, overnight delivery, available spare parts, a comprehensive set of services or one-stop shop)
- Removal of something buyers do not want (packaging materials; worry or fear such as in the case of lost computer files; high fructose corn syrup, trans fats, dyes, chemicals, or fragrance)
- Location, delivery, or distribution channel (many locations that offer local convenience, the ability to purchase or maintain an account online, online help or chat)
- Enhancing value to buyers (lowering buyers' costs, saving their time)
- Perceptions of image or reputation (exclusivity, brand recognition and image, technological superiority)

Some features that differentiate a product or service provide an advantage only temporarily, until a competitor can add the same feature (if Tide creates a lemon-scented laundry detergent, then Wisk can do the same relatively quickly). An enhanced feature is not a differentiator if customers do not want it, and it is not profitable if it costs a great deal to invest in the differentiator but customers are not willing to pay extra for it. The differentiation can provide a sustainable competitive advantage as long as competitors cannot duplicate it, customers still desire it, and they perceive that a company has it.

Focus

The third generic strategy is a focus strategy. A focus strategy targets a specific market niche or customer type. Jitterbug, a cell phone provider, targets seniors with simple software on their smartphones, easy to read larger screens, and pre-installed apps that store medical history or dial urgent care with the touch of a button. Law Tigers is a professional association of injury lawyers who specialize in motorcycle accident litigation. Golf Channel shows only programming related to the sport of golf. By focusing on a specific target market, these companies narrow their customer base (to seniors, motorcycle riders, golf enthusiasts) but thereby seek to outperform other companies within that market by specializing. Many companies might target specific market segments, but as Porter notes, for a focus strategy to be effective, "the target segments must either have buyers with unusual needs or else the production and delivery system that best serves the target segment must differ from that of other industry segments" (1985, p. 15). Companies that use a focus strategy hope to demonstrate to customers that they have additional expertise gained by focusing on the target customer segment. They try to show that other companies do not understand the customer and have lost focus with their wider target market.

A focus strategy has two variations—the same two that we have reviewed above—cost and differentiation, and the same principles apply to reduce costs or enhance differentiation. This can be especially desirable as a strategy for smaller businesses that do not have the resources to compete on a large scale against bigger competitors. Thus, focus can be a starting strategy as the business grows. A boutique consulting firm may decide to specialize in consulting on marketing for regional food and beverage companies, leaving McKinsey to consult with globally recognized brands. One requirement for a focus strategy is to identify true differences in the needs of the target customer segments. In addition, there is always the risk that the larger competitors will develop their own segmented brands to compete in the focused market.

Treacy and Wiersema's Value Disciplines

In 1993 (and later expanded in 1995), Treacy and Wiersema articulated their value disciplines approach to strategy, arguing that "no company can succeed today by trying to be all things to all people" (1995, p. xii) and that "to choose a value discipline . . . is to define the very nature of a company" (p. 32). They argued that in earlier decades, customers made choices based on quality or price or some combination, but their observations showed that customers were making more complex buying decisions based on convenience, their customer experience, and postsales service and support. Industry leaders, they wrote, succeeded by focusing on a specific type of customer value. Some customers are more price sensitive than others and seek a no-frills experience, others are willing to pay more for the best product, and still others want their needs met in a customized way with a total solution. They label these three value disciplines as *operational excellence*, *product leadership*, and *customer intimacy*.

Treacy and Wiersema found that top companies were able to "change what customers valued and how it was delivered, then boosted the level of value that customers expected" (1993, p. 84). As they observed market leaders in different industries, they found four rules that seemed to govern the leaders' success:

> Rule 1: Provide the best offering in the marketplace by excelling in a specific dimension of value.
>
> Rule 2: Maintain threshold standards on other dimensions of value.
>
> Rule 3: Dominate your market by improving value year after year.
>
> Rule 4: Build a well-tuned operating model dedicated to delivering unmatched value (1995, pp. 21–25)

They point out that based on Rule 2, "choosing one discipline to master does not mean that a company abandons the other two, only that it picks a dimension of value on which to stake its market reputation" (1995, p. xii). Savvy customers know what they are doing, they point out. Customers who expect an exceptional experience at Nordstrom know that they are likely to pay more for the service, but not irrationally so. Customers who want low prices at Walmart know that personal service is unlikely, but still expect time waiting in line to be reasonable.

Operational Excellence

The operational excellence value discipline means "providing customers with reliable products or services at competitive prices and delivered with minimal difficulty or inconvenience" (Treacy & Wiersema, 1993, p. 84). Companies pursuing an operational excellence approach appeal to customers based on lower prices or convenient, hassle-free service. Costco, for example, has fewer products than most large stores, and does not invest in the ambience of its facilities, which are typically warehouses with huge shelves and industrial lighting. With aggressive supplier negotiations and ruthless product selection, Costco carries and prices items that are popular and where savings can be passed on to the customer. Too many items would contribute too much complexity, which would cost more to organize and operate, so few items and bulk purchasing creates cost effectiveness and simplicity. Operational excellence implies that companies will focus on end-to-end process controls, from sales to supply chain to service, rooting out waste and seeking constant improvement. Companies that are successful in this approach often have standard, simple practices, process checks and monitoring, and management and rewards systems that reinforce process compliance and efficiency.

Product Leadership

Product leadership means "offering customers leading-edge products and services that consistently enhance the customer's use or application of the product, thereby making rivals' goods obsolete" (Treacy & Wiersema, 1993, p. 85). Product leadership companies seek innovation and creative development of new products, new features for existing products, or new ways to use products. Product leaders recognize that success comes from the next innovation, so they concentrate on effective research and development processes and the ability to launch new products into the market and capitalize on product success. They may have any number of new innovations in the portfolio pipeline, and often must balance where to invest resources and where to winnow the portfolio to pursue the breakthrough product. Google, for example, regularly tests and launches new products beyond its initial Search product that have resulted in such innovations as Google Earth, Google Analytics, and Google AdSense (Maxwell, 2009). Further investments in renewable energy or driverless car innovations may or may not pan out, but such projects are the hallmark of a product leadership strategy that rewards experimentation and seeks the next big thing. Product leadership companies are not afraid to create an innovation that may even make the company's own products obsolete, knowing that if they do not, a competitor could.

Customer Intimacy

Customer intimacy refers to "segmenting and targeting markets precisely and then tailoring offerings to match exactly the demands of those niches" (Treacy & Wiersema, 1993, p. 84). Companies pursuing a customer intimacy strategy are not trying to push the latest product or undercut competitors on cost, but instead to build long-term customer loyalty by seeking to understand their customers at such a level of depth that they can design a total solution for them. At Home Depot, for example, clerks do not simply point out that plumbing repair parts are located on aisle 14, but instead they will go to great lengths to inquire about the problem the customer is experiencing and to demonstrate the repair process with the customer in the store. In Hemp's (2002) narrative about his week-long trial as a room service waiter at the Ritz-Carlton, he observes that at the Ritz, customer intimacy is a passion. "If a housekeeper notices that a guest has moved the desk in her room to get a better view out the window, the housekeeper might log that observation on a guest-recognition slip so that the furniture would be arranged accordingly on the guest's next visit" (p. 54). Customer-intimate companies invest heavily in understanding customers and their problems, and in training employees on how to interact with customers to build customer loyalty. A company that chooses this approach "must display the confidence to charge more, because it knows it is worth every dime" (Treacy & Wiersema, 1995, p. 142).

Table 3.1 summarizes the three value disciplines.

Miles and Snow's Strategy Typology

Miles and Snow's (1978) pioneering study concerned the process of organizations' adaptation to their environments. By studying companies in four different industries—college textbook publishing, electronics, food processing, and hospitals—they found that organizations tended to demonstrate one of four different strategic approaches, or types of organizational adaptation.

Defenders

Defenders are companies that presume a narrow and relatively stable market and that seek to improve the efficiency of their operations. They compete primarily on the basis of price, quality, or service, and given that the market is not constantly changing, they can direct their attention to price reductions and quality

Table 3.1 Comparing the Value Disciplines

	Operational Excellence	Product Leadership	Customer Intimacy
Source of Competitive Advantage	Beat competitors on price	Innovation in product with better features, benefits, and functionality	Build relationships and repeat business through superior customer partnerships
How to Maintain the Advantage	Internal cost control; process efficiency; waste reduction	Investment in research and development; product launch processes	Monitor customer preferences and trends; customer feedback that drives improvements
Rewards	Process compliance and efficiency	Experimentation and innovation	Customer satisfaction
Key Internal Processes	Supply chain	Research and development	Sales and customer support

improvements for existing products. The objective of a Defender is not to develop new products or seek new markets but maintain a position within an existing market and seek to provide a full range of services to clients within that market. Growth occurs from extending existing products within the same market, cautiously and incrementally. With an emphasis on stability and efficiency, most Defenders exhibit operations that are formalized, controlled, and prescribed.

Prospectors

Prospectors see their environment with opposite characteristics from Defenders. A Prospector sees a flexible and dynamic environment and defines their market broadly. This requires the Prospector to regularly innovate and extend its product lines, developing new products and seeking new market segments for growth. A Prospector must monitor industry activity, customer preferences, and competitive behavior to ensure that it is positioned for future trends. As an example, Miles and Snow refer to Star Electronics, a company with 20 different divisions, each of which "is relatively free to explore any product, market, or technological development which might lead to an improved version of its present product line or to new markets" (1978, p. 56). Prospectors differentiate themselves through innovation and bringing their products to market before competitors can (Miles & Snow, 1986).

Analyzers

If Defenders and Prospectors are at two ends of a continuum, Miles and Snow (1978) write, then Analyzers try to combine the strengths of both strategies. An Analyzer might have a mix of stable products and ones that are changing or developing, seeking growth in depth of market penetration and through product development. Unlike Prospectors, Analyzers are not likely to be first to market, but instead follow the lead of the Prospectors. There is a balance of emphasis on tight controls and efficiencies and new innovations and continued effectiveness, but the balance must not swing too widely in either direction. Because they operate in both stable markets and changing ones, they aim to develop formal and controlled internal practices for their stable markets and hone their ability to replicate innovations in changing markets. Thus, the Analyzer succeeds through finding the right mix of new products and current ones, new markets and existing customers, efficiency and effectiveness, stability and flexibility.

Reactors

It is a misnomer to call the Reactor profile a strategy compared to the other three types, as it may be better labeled as the lack of a strategy (Parnell & Wright, 1993). Miles and Snow (1978) write that the Reactor "lacks a set of consistent response mechanisms that it can put into effect when faced with a changing environment" (pp. 81–82) likely because it has no strategy, has not been able to link strategy throughout the organization's other structures and processes, or it stubbornly holds to an approach that is no longer viable. Reactors may see the need for change but are somehow unable to execute the necessary actions to adapt successfully.

Table 3.2 summarizes the three strategy frameworks we have reviewed. See the box following Table 3.2 for a discussion of how these strategies have been adapted to global organizations.

Table 3.2 Three Strategy Frameworks

Porter's Generic Strategies	Treacy and Wiersema's Value Disciplines	Miles and Snow's Strategy Typology
• Low cost • Differentiation • Focus	• Operational excellence • Product leadership • Customer intimacy	• Defenders • Prospectors • Analyzers • Reactors

GLOBAL STRATEGIES

You may have noticed that the generic strategy frameworks we have studied do not explicitly address strategy variations for global organizations. Companies that operate in multiple countries often have different approaches to strategy in those countries for different reasons. Beverages and snack foods, for example, display great variation due to food preferences and tastes around the world. For example, Pepsi's Mirinda brand of carbonated beverages is only available outside the United States, and the Walkers brand of potato chips is marketed primarily in the United Kingdom (whose flavors include sweet chili chicken). Many global companies have specific brands only available in certain markets. While Coca-Cola is available around the world, Coca-Cola also markets the Del Valle brand of orange juice available in Latin America and the Ciel brand of bottled water in Mexico. To take into account the complexity of global strategy, there have been many attempts to create a generic strategies approach for global competition (see Rugman & Verbeke, 1993, 2006).

Companies that operate in more than one country generally display one of three broad international strategy types (Bartlett, 1986; Inkpen & Ramaswamy, 2005). Global companies have to consider two requirements: the degree of integration or scale efficiency across countries, and the degree of local responsiveness and flexibility needed.

- Multinational organization: A company that requires a high degree of local responsiveness but has low integration across countries is a multinational organization, operating on an independent country-by-country basis. It might produce different products for different geographies depending on unique local requirements, regulations, or consumer preferences. This strategy is also preferred when shipping or customs costs might be prohibitive.

- Global organization: A global organization displays high integration and scale efficiency but low local responsiveness. The same product may be produced and sold globally with very minor deviations from the standard. There may be centralized activities such as manufacturing to take advantage of cost benefits, with local sales or marketing units physically close to customers.

- Transnational organization: "In contrast to the multinational strategy that seeks to maximize responsiveness to local demands and the global strategy that seeks to maximize scale efficiency at the cost of flexibility, the transnational approach attempts to synthesize the salient benefits of both approaches without many of the disadvantages associated with either" (Inkpen & Ramaswamy, 2005, p. 69).

A company may locate manufacturing in one country to take advantage of costs and a research and development facility in another to take advantage of local expertise. This strategy requires a high degree of coordination across groups, which we will address in more detail in Chapter 5 in the context of global operating models.

For global companies, Porter (1986) modifies his three generic strategies approach to five, to include (1) global cost leadership; (2) global differentiation; and (3) global segmentation, "serving a particular industry segment worldwide" (p. 47). These first three strategies apply to companies whose geographic scope of strategy is a global one. He includes two other strategies for companies whose scope is country centered: (4) protected markets, "seeking out countries where market positions are protected by host governments" (p. 47) and (5) national responsiveness, where there may be a high degree of uniqueness in a particular country even though the industry is global.

Stuck in the Middle

All three sets of authors warn of the dangers of not selecting a defining central and consistent strategy. Porter (1980) writes that "the firm failing to develop its strategy in at least one of the three directions—a firm that is 'stuck in the middle'—is in an extremely poor strategy situation" (p. 41). Similarly, Treacy and Wiersema (1995) write that "not choosing means ending up in a muddle . . . steering a rudderless ship, with no clear way to resolve conflicts or set priorities" (p. 45). Reactors in the Miles and Snow (1978) typology are "inconsistent and unstable" and "will at some point be forced to move . . . to one of the other three types" (p. 154).

Profitability suffers for stuck-in-the-middle companies as a result of their refusal to choose. They are unable to focus on a specific market, losing the battle on cost with other low-cost rivals, and lacking a differentiated product or service. "Achieving cost leadership and differentiation are also usually inconsistent, because differentiation is usually costly" (Porter, 1985, p. 18). Such a strategy can rarely be successful, Porter writes, but only if competitors are also stuck in the middle or if a unique proprietary technology is developed that allows both cost reduction and differentiation at the same time.

The stuck-in-the-middle paradigm has provoked considerable debate. Some agree that too much specialization in one strategy domain can be easy to imitate or that it might leave a company with a myopic view of the competition that limits them from seeking potential innovations (Miller, 1992; Salavou, 2015). But others see examples of successful companies that have bridged multiple strategies. Treacy and Wiersema (1993) acknowledge that "a few maverick companies have gone further by mastering two" of the value disciplines (p. 86), pointing to Toyota's product leadership and operational excellence, and the office supply company Staples's operational excellence and customer intimacy. Salavou (2015) points out that hybrid strategies, as distinct from stuck-in-the-middle strategies, allow shades of gray between the fixed options suggested by earlier models.

Some of the research on hybrid strategies has found that combinations of low cost and differentiation can provide advantages that are more difficult for competitors to copy. The issue may be one of intent and strategy consciousness. In tests of Miles and Snow's (1978) typology, Parnell and Wright (1993) and Parnell (1997) found that companies that had an unsystematic strategy and as "reactors" found themselves stuck in the middle were less successful than companies that intentionally balanced multiple strategic forms. These authors concluded that "low cost and differentiation are not mutually exclusive" (Parnell, 1997, p. 178) and that "businesses can successfully compete with combination strategies" (Parnell & Wright, 1993, p. 32). Faulkner and Bowman (1992) and Parnell (2006) both point out that a more effective lens on strategy may be to examine how companies compete to deliver *perceived customer value* through combinations of the various dimensions. Kim and Mauborgne (2009) argue that in highly competitive industries, a "reconstructionist" strategic approach makes sense whereby a company can redefine an industry in pursuit of both differentiation and low cost.

KEY CONCEPTS

Here we will review several key concepts in the strategy literature that have been widely popular or influential and that are instructive for the organization designer: five forces, core competencies, blue ocean strategy, and the strategy canvas. Each of these concepts will help a designer understand the basis of an organization's strategic priorities and how it intends to execute that strategy.

Porter's Five Forces Model

Porter points out that to effectively analyze competition and strategy, one must understand the underlying economic structure of an industry (Porter, 1979, 1980, 2008). Certainly, the choice of strategy within that industry is critical, but the factors that contribute to the industry's competitive environment strongly influence how profitable the competitors can be. He argues that "the first fundamental determinant of a firm's profitability is industry attractiveness" (1985, p. 4) and that five forces make up the industry's economic structure. Where those competitive forces are intense, profitability is decreased, and where the competitive forces are weaker, profitable returns are more attractive. By analyzing the average industry return on invested capital, Porter (2008) points out that some industries such as soft drinks and pharmaceuticals have a relatively high profitability compared to the average, whereas airlines, hotels, and book publishing have relatively low profitability. The objective of the corporate strategist, then, "is to find a position in the industry where his or her company can best defend itself against these forces or can influence them in its favor" (Porter, 1979, p. 137) to achieve profits that are higher than the industry average. Understanding the five forces can help an organization designer appreciate the underlying rationale for a company's strategic position and why strategic change (and in turn a change to its organization design) might be necessary.

The five forces recast an understanding of a company's competitive environment with a more complete set of factors. We intuitively understand that companies in the same industry compete with one another (Coca-Cola and Pepsi, Southwest and American Airlines, United Parcel Service and FedEx). But this is only one dimension of what shapes the profits and competitive environment of each of those companies. Airline companies compete for profits with alternative forms of transportation as well as with suppliers Airbus and Boeing (airplane manufacturers), who would inevitably desire to be paid more for their planes, and pilot unions that would also like for employees to share in the profits. FedEx's profitability is not only influenced by how much business it gains over UPS, but by how much it pays for its trucks and the drivers who operate them. Direct competition among rivals is, as we will see, only part of the story that determines a company's profitability.

The five forces are not equally impactful in any given industry, and "the most salient force is . . . not always obvious" (Porter, 2008, p. 80). Porter gives the example of Kodak and Fuji, who competed as intense rivals between each other. The biggest threat to their profitability was not the other company but the growth of digital photography and competitors such as Apple. Moreover, underlying industry dynamics can and do change, sometimes rapidly, making any analysis of the five forces temporary. (For a detailed explanation of the five forces beyond this selective overview, consult Porter, 1979, 1980, 2008; see Figure 3.2.)

Threat of New Entrants

A highly profitable industry can attract new businesses that wish to capture some of the profits for themselves. As Porter (2008) notes, this is especially true when competitors can use their size and scale to expand from a related industry. For example, Pepsi expanded into the bottled water market in 1994 with its Aquafina brand, and Coca-Cola responded in 1999 by introducing Dasani. Both companies could leverage their substantial distribution networks, well-known brands, and existing bottling facilities to take market share from competitors such as Evian. Consider what it would take for you to enter the same bottled water industry without those same resources. Several barriers to entry would exist, such as extensive capital requirements to purchase or build a bottling plant, brand recognition of existing competitors that put your unknown label at a disadvantage, and the lack of distribution channels to get your product to consumers. You would lack the same economies of scale that Pepsi has and would need to charge more.

In other industries, the threat of new entrants is kept low because of switching costs. Switching costs refer to the tangible and intangible costs in changing a buyer and supplier relationship. While it does not cost a consumer more to change

Figure 3.2 Porter's Five Forces

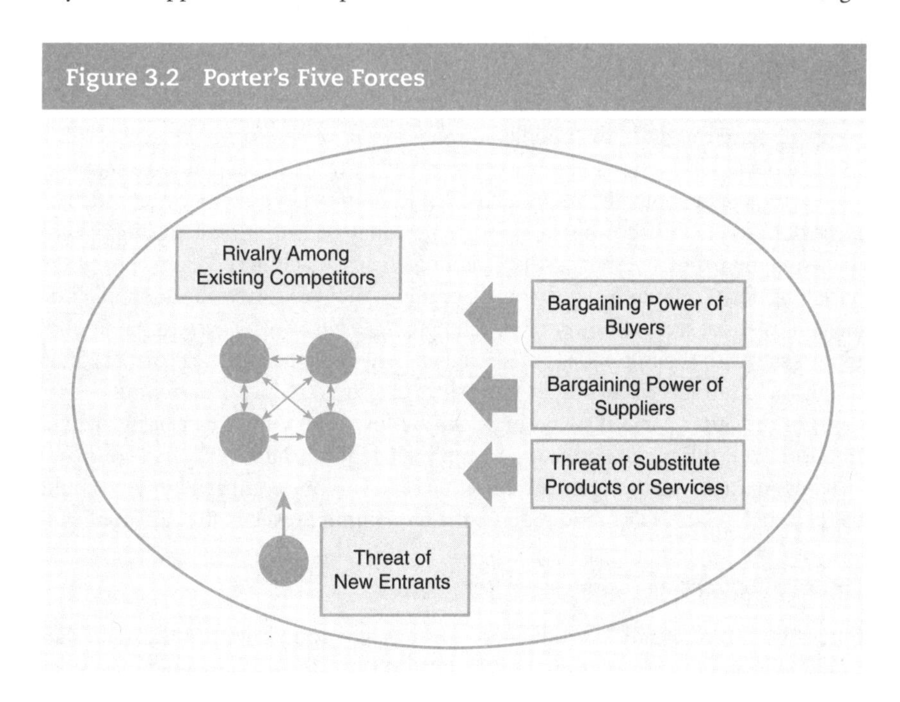

from Dasani to Aquafina, it might cost a consumer to switch from an iPhone to an Android in time setting up the device, moving music files or contacts, and learning how to use the features. All of these entry barriers deter new companies from entering the existing market, leading to higher profitability in the industry. The Internet and mobile phone apps reduce barriers to entry by providing direct access to consumers (instead of traditional distribution channels such as brick-and-mortar stores) and reducing costs (such as a sales force) (Porter, 2001).

Bargaining Power of Buyers

The second force is the negotiating ability of the buyer to extract price concessions or enhanced services from suppliers. If buyers can easily change to another supplier, then suppliers will be forced to keep prices low to retain the business. Consider the shipping and package delivery industry. Amazon.com has been able to negotiate lower shipping costs from UPS not only because the online retailer is a large customer but because Amazon could easily switch to another delivery company. This has made for stagnant profit margins at UPS in recent years and pushed the company to look for internal operating efficiencies (Stevens, 2014). Moreover, the threat of backward integration (such as Amazon.com creating its own shipping division) will frustrate UPS's attempts to raise prices. Buyers also hold power when the products they purchase are not unique or they spend a lot with the supplier and have an incentive to monitor costs, and thus have negotiating leverage.

Bargaining Power of Suppliers

A third force is the negotiating ability of the supplier, the flip side of the previous force. If the supplier has a unique product that is highly differentiated or in short supply, the supplier will retain more profits and charge higher prices to the buyer (who has nowhere else to turn). Microsoft holds negotiating power as a dominant supplier of its operating system, giving personal computer manufacturers few alternatives. With a number of PC companies in the market, consumer buyers have a lot of choices, forcing manufacturers to keep prices low to win customers, but they are also unable to extract price concessions from Microsoft. Thus, PC companies are caught in the middle between two powerful forces.

If a buyer has high switching costs, they will be more dependent on a supplier. For example, if a company has trained all of its employees how to use a particular piece of leased manufacturing equipment, they may be loath to switch suppliers of that equipment and invest in costly retraining on new machinery. When consumers have long-term cell phone contracts that require them to stay with the supplier or pay a substantial fee, the power of switching costs explains why even unhappy customers stay with their provider. It also explains why some cell phone providers offer to buy out contracts to encourage customers to switch (reducing switching costs).

On the other hand, if switching costs are low, then buyers can easily change to another supplier and reduce the supplier's negotiating leverage. A company that has an exclusive arrangement for rental cars with one company but who could easily switch to another brand reduces the bargaining power of the car supplier.

Threat of Substitute Products or Services

The threat of alternative products or services is a fourth force that shapes an industry's competitive environment. "A substitute performs the same or a similar function as an industry's product by different means" (Porter, 2008, p. 84). Some substitutes are easily identifiable because they are almost exact reproductions of a company's product (i.e., they do the same thing). Netflix and Redbox both competed with brick-and-mortar video rental companies; Apple's iPhone became a substitute for film cameras, other digital cameras, and digital video recorders; and Uber became a substitute for hailing a taxi. A movie theater that is a short drive from my house might compete as a direct rival with other theaters that may be slightly farther away on price or customer experience. I might be willing to patronize another theater if the other theater was less expensive, if its seats were more comfortable, or if it offered better popcorn.

However, consider that the competition is broader than just other movie theaters and that substitutes are not always exact. I have a number of entertainment choices on a Saturday evening (including watching live theater, staying at home, or attending a sporting event). The movie theater entertainment experience has a large number of threats of substitute products beyond movies. This is what keeps admission prices stable even where only a single theater exists for hundreds of miles. There may be no other theater to act as competition, but there are plenty of substitute entertainment options to compete with. Because there are virtually no switching costs for substitute entertainment (it does not cost me anything to make the substitute choice), theaters do not just compete with each other, they compete with all other possible ways to spend your leisure time.

In addition, consider what happens when theatergoers do not feel inclined to substitute or when substitutes do not fulfill the same requirements. When the only way to see the popular Broadway play *Hamilton* was to buy a scarce ticket to the New York theater production, there were no other substitutes for theatergoers that wanted the unique experience. The threat of substitution of another Broadway show was lower. Producers were able to raise the base ticket price to $849, a figure they arrived at by studying the resale ticket market (Paulson, 2016).

Porter warns that "strategists should be particularly alert to changes in other industries that may make them attractive substitutes when they were not before" (Porter, 2008, p. 85). When Nomacorc developed a synthetic substitute for real cork in wine bottles, the plastics manufacturer was able to use the innovation to take significant market share from cork makers (Magretta, 2012). New technologies can quickly provide substitutes.

Rivalry Among Existing Competitors

Rivalry is probably the most intuitive of the five forces to understand and is often the most visible in price wars. When Delta drops the price of an airline ticket to earn business, United and Southwest feel pressured to act in kind. As Porter (1979) writes, "[R]ivalry among existing competitors takes the familiar form of jockeying for position—using tactics like price competition, product introduction, and advertising slugfests" (p. 142). In a city where there are a fixed number of hotel rooms, hotel chains have a perishable product (because last night's unsold hotel room has no value) and will be pressured to keep prices low to lure customers. They may need to offer enhanced features such as a free breakfast, airport shuttle services, or late check-out to distinguish themselves from other chains. When competitors are roughly equal in size and growth is slow, the rivalry is likely to be intense and price competition can be destructive to profitability.

Analysis of Porter's Five Forces can help an organization designer understand why a company might be responding to its competitive environment with a strategic shift. Porter (1985) explains that

> from a strategic standpoint, the crucial strengths and weaknesses are the firm's posture vis-à-vis the underlying causes of each competitive force. Where does the firm stand against substitutes? Against the sources of entry barriers? In coping with rivalry from established competitors? (p. 29)

The five forces might explain why a company adds a new division to diversify and enter a profitable new market or why it wants to set up a new manufacturing unit to reduce the reliance on a supplier. With knowledge of this rationale, the organization designer will be in a better position to identify how the organizational structure, processes, rewards, and people practices can enhance this competitive positioning.

Core Competencies

In contrast to the positioning-based view of strategy described in the five forces model that sees strategy as a company's relationship with its environment, there is an alternative perspective that looks inside the company. That is, it sees the company's internal capabilities as being the most important resource for a company's success and development of capability as critical for strategy. (This perspective, called the resource-based view of the firm, is generally traced to the pioneering work of economist Edith Penrose, 1959). This point of view has given rise to the concept of "capabilities-based competition" (Stalk, Evans, & Shulman, 1992, p. 57) or "core competencies" (Hamel & Prahalad, 1994; Prahalad & Hamel, 1990). Prahalad and Hamel (1990) write that "the real sources of advantage are to be found in management's ability to consolidate corporatewide technologies and production skills into competencies that empower individual businesses to adapt quickly to changing opportunities" (p. 81). A successful strategy long term, they write, is more about developing and using core competencies over time than any short-term winning product strategy.

Consider that an innovative new product may help a company to differentiate itself from competitors, but what gave rise to the innovation in the first place? The organization likely made use of its unique skills and abilities in some aspect of product development. Apple's ability to design products with elegant and functional simplicity is at the root of many of its successful products, and is taught at its internal university (Chen, 2014). Color photocopiers and single-lens reflex cameras exist in two different industries, and Canon seeks to demonstrate how its products differ from Xerox or Nikon. To do that, Canon has been able to exploit its core competencies in precision mechanics and fine optics. Individual product lines may come and go, customer preferences change, and markets shift, but what remain consistent over time are a company's underlying skills and abilities.

Competencies transcend individual products and are "a bundle of skills and technologies rather than a single discrete skill or technology" (Hamel & Prahalad, 1994, p. 202). This means that core competencies are less about a single area such as product design, and more about how that product design exists in a web of functions that bring that design to the market, including manufacturing and marketing.

Companies should distinguish between core competencies and other activities that they may do well but which are not core. A core competence should pass three tests (Prahalad & Hamel, 1990, pp. 83–84):

1. A core competence provides potential access to a wide variety of markets. The competence should be extendable to other markets or

applications beyond the current or even obvious ones. If it is unlikely that the competence could be applied elsewhere, it is not likely to be core to the company.

2. A core competence should make a significant contribution to the perceived customer benefits of the end product. Even if customers cannot articulate the exact competence, they know that it forms one of the reasons behind why they chose the product or service. Customers may not know how Apple designs its products, but they know that product design and usability is a key benefit.

3. A core competence should be difficult for competitors to imitate. That is, if other competitors already have the competence as well, those skills are likely "table stakes" required as a minimum ability rather than differentiating the company. Over time, in fact, many core competencies are likely to become copied and routine for most competitors.

Many organizations can identify 20 to 30 activities that seem critical, but in reality, only five or six are likely to contribute to the company's leadership position (Prahalad & Hamel, 1990). Hamel and Prahalad (1994) write that "other traps include mistaking assets and infrastructure for core competencies and an inability to escape an orthodox product-centered view of a firm's capabilities" (p. 225). Once they are recognized, opportunities can be identified to extend existing competencies into current and new markets and to identify new competencies that will provide significant prospects in the future.

Galbraith and Lawler (1998) conclude that the core competencies concept reminds us that a company cannot succeed through imitation. "It must also develop new competencies so that it can create the next innovation. . . . What results is a constantly shifting strategy requiring multiple and combinable competencies," they write, "very different from conventional thinking about sustainable advantage" (p. 2).

Organization designers can benefit from the concept of core competence in several ways. Companies that operate independent and isolated business units may be missing an opportunity to take advantage of core competencies that exist in other units, indicating opportunities to align structures and processes. Prahalad and Hamel (1990) point out that reward systems that encourage business unit independence may create competition rather than cooperation in the use of core competences. Some organizations trace the company's core competencies down to the individual employee level to ensure that the competencies are nurtured and retained, highlighting the people point of the star.

Blue Ocean Strategies and the Strategy Canvas

The Ringling Bros. and Barnum & Bailey Circus held its first performance in New York in 1919 as a joint entity. With its trademark moniker, "The Greatest Show on Earth," the circus has long been a feature of American culture, showcasing clowns and trained elephants and tigers. In the mid-1980s, however, the circus was performing poorly, and revenues were mediocre. Using Porter's Five Forces language to explain the industry's decline, there were plenty of substitutes for children more interested in video games, talented performers had supplier power, and audiences (buyers) felt increasingly wary about the use of animals.

What would possess a new entrant from wanting to enter this declining market? Enter Cirque du Soleil, founded by Guy Laliberté, to "reinvent the circus" (Kim & Mauborgne, 2015). Now with more than 40 original shows, Cirque du Soleil has entertained an astonishing 155 million audience members in dozens of countries with acrobats, unique stories, and exclusive music.

Kim and Mauborgne (2015) coined the term *blue ocean strategy* to describe what made Cirque du Soleil successful. They did not set out to duplicate existing competitors in an established market space. Instead, they redefined the market, creating a new type of circus experience more akin to a theater production. They redesigned the classic circus tent to create an upscale venue, eliminated costly and controversial animal acts, created intellectually stimulating storylines and characters threaded throughout the production, and designed lighting and music to enhance the visual production. They redefined the boundaries of the traditional circus market by creating something entirely new that was not exactly a circus, a concert, or a Broadway production, but all of those at once, appealing to adults as well as children.

Blue ocean strategies like this seek to reinvent the market. They make competitive analysis somewhat unnecessary, because no competitor precisely duplicates what the organization is doing. They "create and capture new demand, break the value-cost trade-off, and align the whole system of a firm's activities in pursuit of differentiation *and* low cost" (Kim & Mauborgne, 2015, p. 18). A good blue ocean strategy has three characteristics: focus, to not compete on every dimension but selective ones; divergence, to create a new market space with differentiators that are not seen among competitors; and a compelling tagline, an authentic message that resonates with customers.

By contrast, red ocean strategies presume the boundaries around a given industry or market space and assume that competition occurs only within that market space. Red ocean strategies aim to "beat the competition, exploit existing

Red Ocean Strategy	Blue Ocean Strategy
Compete in existing market space	Create uncontested market space
Beat the competition	Make the competition irrelevant
Focus on existing customers	Focus on non-customers
Exploit existing demand	Create and capture new demand
Make the value-cost trade-off (Create greater value to customers at a higher cost or create reasonable value at a lower cost)	Break the value-cost trade-off (seek greater value to customers and low cost simultaneously)
Align the whole system of a firm's activities with its strategic choice of differentiation **or** low cost	Align the whole system of a firm's activities in pursuit of differentiation **and** low cost

Source: http://www.comindwork.com/weekly/2016-06-13/productivity/red-ocean-strategy-vs-blue-ocean-strategy

demand, make the value-cost trade-off, and align the whole system of a firm's activities with its strategic choice of differentiation *or* low cost" (Kim & Mauborgne, 2015, p. 18).

To assess the competitive environment and develop a blue ocean strategy, Kim and Mauborgne advise use of a concept they call the strategy canvas. The canvas "captures the current state of play in the known market space . . . [and] the offering level that buyers received across all these key competing factors" (Kim & Mauborgne, 2015, pp. 27, 29). Table 3.3 gives an example of the strategy canvas for Cirque du Soleil and the Ringling Bros. circus. By comparing the two companies on the dimensions important to buyers, we can see the *value curve*, or each company's comparative position on the points most critical for competition in that industry.

The Ringling Bros. and Barnum & Bailey value curve displays high value on areas where other circuses traditionally competed, such as animal shows. Notice the shaded dimensions at the end of the table, however. Cirque du Soleil competes in dimensions where traditional circuses have almost no competitive position. By adding entirely new dimensions to the competitive environment, Cirque du Soleil redefined market boundaries. When public appetite for animal shows decreased due to pressure from animal rights activists, ticket sales for Ringling Bros. shows waned. In May 2017, the Ringling Bros. circus closed permanently.

Table 3.3 Cirque du Soleil Strategy Canvas

Value Dimension	Cirque du Soleil	Ringling Bros. and Barnum & Bailey
Price	–	+
Star Performers	–	+
Animal Shows	–	+
Aisle Concessions	–	+
Multiple Show Arenas	–	+
Fun and Humor	0	0
Thrills and Danger	0	0
Unique Venue	++	–
Theme	++	–
Refined Watching Environment	++	–
Multiple Productions	++	–
Artistic Music and Dance	++	–

+ = advantage, 0 = neutral/equal, – = disadvantage

Source: Adapted from Kim, W. C., & Mauborgne, R. (2015). *Blue ocean strategy*. Boston, MA: Harvard Business Review Press, p. 43.

Every strategy canvas differs depending on the industry segment, but such a framework can help to guide a company's evaluation of its competitive position and potential strategic moves. Actions to create blue ocean strategies follow four categories (Kim & Mauborgne, 2015, p. 31):

1. **Reduce:** Which factors should be reduced well below the industry's standard?
2. **Eliminate:** Which of the factors that the industry takes for granted should be eliminated?
3. **Create:** Which factors should be created that the industry has never offered?
4. **Raise:** Which factors should be raised well above the industry's standard?

NEW TRENDS IN THINKING ABOUT STRATEGY

In the past several years, thinking about strategy has changed. Noting that more industries are operating in a hypercompetitive state (D'Aveni, 1994) where constant change is the norm, the idea of a sustainable competitive advantage is becoming a rarity (McGrath, 2013a, 2013b). S. L. Brown and Eisenhardt (1998) called

TESTS OF STRATEGY FORMULATION

Synthesizing many of the recommendations in this chapter from strategy research, the following questions and principles can stimulate an evaluation of whether an organization has a robust enough strategy to create design criteria and guide a design effort.

Principles of Strategy (Markides, 2004)	**Elements of a Strategy** (Hambrick & Fredrickson, 2001)	**Questions to Ask to Test Strategy** (Hambrick & Fredrickson, 2001, p. 59)
• Strategy must decide on a few parameters. • Strategy must put all our choices together to create a reinforcing mosaic. • Strategy must achieve fit without losing flexibility. • Strategy needs to be supported by the appropriate organizational context. • No strategy remains unique forever.	• Arenas: Where will we be active? • Vehicles: How will we get there? • Differentiators: How will we win in the marketplace? • Staging: What will be our speed and sequence of moves? • Economic logic: How will we obtain our returns?	• Does your strategy fit with what's going on in the environment? • Does your strategy exploit your key resources? • Will your envisioned differentiators be sustainable? • Are the elements of your strategy internally consistent? • Do you have enough resources to pursue this strategy? • Is your strategy implementable?

this "competing on the edge," noting that competition is becoming more uncontrolled, unpredictable, and often inefficient as companies regularly must fail before they find success. Thus, Reeves and Deimler (2011) concluded, adaptability is the new competitive advantage.

Many of these authors question the assumptions of the classic strategy frameworks and concepts that we have reviewed in this chapter and advocate for a view of strategy grounded in change. They point out that past ideas assumed relatively stable industries and markets which do not exist today, and that 5-year strategic planning horizons become obsolete almost as soon as the plans are created. As Reeves, Love, and Tillmanns (2012) put it, "[G]lobal competition, technological innovation, social feedback loops, and economic uncertainty combine to make the environment radically and persistently unpredictable. In such an environment, a carefully crafted classical strategy may become obsolete within months or even weeks" (p. 79). This perspective questions the need to engage in exhaustive strategic planning practices and highlights the need for a new approach to strategy.

Kotter (2012) concludes that previous definitions of strategy need to evolve. He writes that "strategy should be viewed as a dynamic force that constantly seeks opportunities" (p. 47), and McGrath (2013a) sees "the end of competitive advantage," arguing for a series of short-term advantages that, taken together, keep a company in a leadership position. Product cycles of ramp up, sustainability, and decline occur with much more speed. Many companies find themselves in a difficult position having invested so much in a product that is rapidly declining; their only solution is to conduct a painful reactive restructuring. McGrath (2013b) advises that companies develop the ability to exit declining businesses as much as they need to recognize new areas of opportunity.

Reeves and Deimler (2011) describe four organizational capabilities that foster rapid adaptation:

1. The ability to read and act on signals of change. "In this environment, competitive advantage comes from reading and responding to signals faster than your rivals do, adapting quickly to change, or capitalizing on technological leadership to influence how demand and competition evolve" (Reeves, Love, & Tillmanns, 2012, p. 76).

2. The ability to experiment rapidly and frequently—not only with products and services but also with business models, processes, and strategies. McGrath (2013a) argues that this can be achieved by encouraging "intelligent failures" and an "experimental orientation" (p. 102).

3. The ability to manage complex and interconnected systems of multiple stakeholders. Whether they are suppliers, distributors, outsourced providers, or joint ventures, the ability to rapidly adapt requires a coordination and communication capability.

4. The ability to mobilize. For organization designers, this means creating flexible structures, teams, and decision rights practices that allow for flexibility in strategy execution. Leading adaptive businesses use their organization designs to their advantage and learn how to become "shape shifters" (McGrath, 2013a, p. 27), reconfiguring and morphing themselves as the opportunities require.

We will return to this perspective in Chapter 9 to examine how this focus on agile, flexible organizational strategies translates into changes in every point of the star.

SUMMARY

An understanding of strategy can help a leader or organization designer identify ways to embed that strategy in the design and develop creative and innovative structures, processes, rewards systems, and people practices that differentiate the organization. Strategy has traditionally been seen as a sustainable competitive advantage, and we have reviewed three different strategy frameworks: Porter's generic strategies of low cost, differentiation, and focus; Treacy and Wiersema's value disciplines of operational effectiveness, product leadership, and customer intimacy; and Miles and Snow's strategy typology of Defenders, Prospectors, Analyzers, and Reactors. While originally most of these authors argued that companies must choose a single strategy or face limited success by being "stuck in the middle," some now argue that such an approach is possible (or even preferable). We have also reviewed several critical concepts in strategy that are important for organization design. Porter's Five Forces explain how industries are economically structured and shape strategies in those industries. The concept of core competencies helps designers understand how nurturing an organization's competencies can create long-term future success. Blue ocean strategies explain how success can be found by redefining a market boundary beyond its traditional margins. Current themes in thinking about strategy concern speed and adaptability, as the timeframes for competitive advantages continue to shrink and erode. As we have seen, even a perfect strategy can fail without proper execution, and the organization's design is a major part of the ability to execute.

QUESTIONS FOR DISCUSSION

1. Imagine that you're working with a group of executives at the start of an organization design project using the STAR model, and the conversation turns to strategy. Some say that strategy is a 5-year business plan, others argue that strategy is a set of high-level goals, another says that strategy is the method for getting to the vision of what we're trying to achieve. Everyone sitting around the table looks at you, and it's your big moment. One asks you, "In three sentences or less, how do you define strategy?"
2. In this chapter, we have focused on strategy as an umbrella concept that applies to an entire company. Yet, we know that organization design applies throughout an organization. How might you apply these concepts with other divisions inside a company, such as marketing, supply chain operations, customer service, or human resources? How might the ideas need to be adapted to that purpose?
3. It is evident that much has changed in the business world since many of the concepts in this chapter were originally developed, and scholars continue to debate these ideas. To what extent do the concepts such as generic strategies, value disciplines, five forces, and core competencies still apply today?

FOR FURTHER READING

Kim, W. C., & Mauborgne, R. (2015). *Blue ocean strategy.* Boston, MA: Harvard Business Review Press.

Miles, R. E., & Snow, C. C. (1978). *Organizational strategy, structure, and process.* New York, NY: McGraw-Hill.

Porter, M. E. (1979). How competitive forces shape strategy. *Harvard Business Review, 57*(2), 137–145.

Porter, M. E. (1996). What is strategy? *Harvard Business Review, 74*(6), 61–78.

Porter, M. E. (2008). The five competitive forces that shape strategy. *Harvard Business Review, 86*(1), 78–93.

Prahalad, C. K., & Hamel, G. (1990). The core competence of the corporation. *Harvard Business Review, 68*(3), 79–90.

Treacy, M., & Wiersema, F. (1995). *The discipline of market leaders.* New York, NY: Basic Books

EXERCISES

1. Find two similar organizations that do the same thing (e.g., two companies that offer cell phones or services, two department stores, two car companies) and identify their different strategies.
2. Choose a well-known company and look at its website. Use some of the concepts in the chapter to identify that organization's strategy (what is its competitive advantage?). If you can find it out, try to locate its design, too. You might check the "About us" or "About the executive team" pages on the website.
3. The Appendix to this book contains an organization design simulation game involving a dice roll. Begin Part I of that activity now. Before you turn to the Appendix, roll a single six-sided die six times (the type of dice roll you would use in a board game) and keep track of your numbers in order. You will end up with a sequence like this: 4, 2, 3, 2, 5, 1. Duplicate numbers in your sequence are fine. Refer to the Appendix (Part I) to learn what your dice rolls mean for the type of organization you will create for this simulation exercise.

CHAPTER 4

STRUCTURE

Learning Objectives

In this chapter you will learn

- Different options for structuring organizations into departments or groupings.
- The advantages and disadvantages of each of those structure types.
- How structure includes other decisions such as span of control and centralization.
- How different strategy choices affect structure options.

When a strategy is in place and is agreed upon by the leadership team, and the design team has created a set of prioritized design criteria, then it is appropriate to consider options for the organizational structure. The design criteria may naturally and easily lead to an obvious structure option, but more often than not, complex organizations make this choice more challenging. Multiple criteria can suggest multiple structure options which may even appear contradictory on the surface.

The task is to be conscious of the structure options available, their advantages and disadvantages, and to design the structure point of the star with a full realization that not all criteria can be addressed through organizational structure alone. Will creating a set of geographic divisions provide important focus on the unique needs of customers in different global regions, or will this choice frustrate customers who want a single global solution? If we create different product units, will that mean enhanced innovation or will we lack consistency between products? The leadership or design team must be able to follow the structure's implications on people's behavior, since "the structure of an organization importantly influences the flow of information and the context and nature of human interactions" (Miller, 1987, p. 7). Where structure provides clarity, it can also obscure or create barriers. Thus, the design team must make structure choices that do not impede organizational members' ability to get their work done and that have the greatest benefits with the fewest obstacles.

In this chapter, we will look at multiple pure or classic structure types (though many organizations have blends and adaptations of these). We will examine the advantages and disadvantages of each so that the designer can understand the trade-offs involved in selecting one type and address the drawbacks with other design decisions later. Because the structure point of the star involves more than the organizational chart, we will look at other structure considerations, such as span of control, centralization, roles and responsibilities, and job design. We will conclude by returning to the link between strategy and structure to provide a starting point to examine which structure options might correspond most appropriately with different strategies.

CONNECTING STRATEGY AND STRUCTURE

How Strategy Influences Structure

Recall that in Chapter 1, we reviewed the pioneering work of Chandler (1962) and Burns and Stalker (1961), whose studies of organizational evolution first proposed the idea that strategy influences choice of organizational structure. In Chandler's study, it was the growth of the organization into new product lines or new geographic field offices that prompted the organization to add new divisions to focus on the expanded areas of strategic emphasis. In the Burns and Stalker study, it was clear that structuring for unpredictable conditions (organic structures) was very different from structuring for routine ones (mechanistic structures).

Hrebiniak, Joyce, and Snow (1989) summarized management research over the decades and concluded that "there is widespread belief . . . that in high-performing organizations structure needs to be properly fitted to strategy" (p. 13). Nadler and Tushman (1997) agree, writing that "certain forms of organizational grouping are better suited to achieving particular strategies" (p. 73). Strategy focuses the organization on a limited set of choices as to what markets to pursue and what approach to take; similarly, structure focuses organizational members' attention on a limited range of tasks and activities for a given department. Structure is considered to be one of the methods for executing and implementing strategy, by acting as a lens to help members make day-to-day operating decisions.

How Structure Influences Strategy

It might seem counterintuitive that structure could influence an organization's strategy, but several research programs have demonstrated the validity of this observation. Simons (2005) argues,

> On the one hand, structure follows strategy. But on the other hand, organization design—through its defining effect on information flows—influences future strategies. The structure of an organization determines how information from the market is processed and acted upon. The design of an organization determines who receives information, to whom it is forwarded, and what actions are ultimately taken. In other words, not only does strategy determine structure, but structure also determines strategy. This two-way flow must be incorporated into any successful design. (p. 9)

The configuration of strategy and structure form a powerful combination as a lens on information and the environment. Organizational members become accustomed to interpreting and acting on customer needs and competitors' moves in a regular routine. They may become blind to or ignore information that does not fit their preexisting categories. As a result, the organization "may have difficulty pursuing activities outside its normal scope of operations" (Miles & Snow, 1978, p. 7).

Following our discussion of common organizational structures, their advantages and disadvantages, and related structure concepts, we will return to the connection between strategy and structure.

DIMENSIONS OF ORGANIZATION STRUCTURE

The structure point of the star contains four dimensions (Galbraith, 2014a):

- Departmentalization or Groupings
- Shape/Configuration
- Centralization/Decentralization, or Power Distribution
- Division of Labor and Specialization

As organization designers work out the structural design, they need to make decisions in each of these four categories. We will discuss each of these points in detail throughout this chapter.

DEPARTMENTALIZATION OR GROUPINGS

The concept of departmentalization or groupings reflects what we typically think of as the organizational structure, that is, the organization chart that displays reporting relationships and the different departments or teams that make up the organization. Mintzberg (1979) argues that "it is through the process of grouping into units that the system of formal authority is established and the hierarchy of the organization is built" (p. 104). When we refer to common organization structures below, we will be referring to the different options for departmentalization. Because this is arguably the most consequential decision that a designer will make with respect to structure, we will cover this subject in depth.

The Purpose of Department Groupings

Mintzberg (1979) writes that "grouping is a fundamental means to coordinate work in the organization" (p. 106) with four purposes:

1. **"Grouping establishes a system of common supervision among positions and units. . . .** Thus, unit grouping is the design parameter by which the coordinating mechanism of direct supervision is built into the structure." Most commonly, each department is led by a manager who oversees the activities of that unit.
2. **"Grouping typically requires positions and units to share common resources"** such as budgets, office facilities, and equipment. They may all use the same information technology systems, filing systems (virtual or physical), or even people (shared services such as administrators or finance support).
3. **"Grouping typically creates common measures of performance"** in that organizational members in a single unit are often responsible for a common set of work activities or results. Groups are often created based on their contributions to key strategic objectives such as a product grouping responsible for designing the next generation of a company's successful product. Nadler and Tushman (1997) write that "grouping decisions determine what the organization will be able to do well and

deemphasize other work" (p. 73), providing limits on the activities to be performed in a given department.

4. **"Grouping encourages mutual adjustment."** When people work together in common groups they tend to coordinate more frequently with those in their same department. This is especially true when members share the same space, for example, when members of a department all work on the same floor of the same building. A widely replicated finding of social psychology is that when people are put into groups and are given a group identity, an "ingroup–outgroup" effect takes place. As we will see later, this advantage of structure is its central disadvantage, as "the same reason that grouping encourages strong coordination *within* a unit . . . creates problems of coordination *between* units" (Mintzberg, 1979, p. 107).

Structure Options

Designers can organize work by knowledge or skills, by activity, by output, by client, by place, or by process step (Mintzberg, 1979; Nadler & Tushman, 1997). In combination and variation, there are an infinite number of structural grouping possibilities. Based on the size of the organization and strategic lens, most organizations choose one of the following. The most common structure options that we will discuss are:

1. Functional structure
2. Product structure
3. Geographic structure
4. Customer/Market structure
5. Process structure
6. Network structure
7. Front–Back structure
8. Matrix structure

Each of these is described below in its purest form, with its advantages and disadvantages.

Functional Structure

The functional structure is arguably the most common and well-known hierarchical structure. In this design, divisions are organized by the type of work they do, so that divisions of marketing, finance, sales, manufacturing, product development, and so on are led by a single executive who reports to a chief executive officer, for example. Those who work in marketing work with other like-minded marketing professionals on marketing-related concerns, so its chief advantages lie in its ability to help divide labor and focus on narrow areas of specialty. When they are all in the same department, marketers can share problems and solutions with other marketers, coordinating and sharing best practices. The organization can develop its capabilities, knowledge, and skills in the functional area, and employees can see a clear career growth path. It can also be a highly efficient structure. The marketing budget, when centralized in this manner, can be used for leverage to develop a contract with a single vendor for all printed materials, advertising, and events. Standard processes can be developed for the department to reduce duplication of work and streamline functional decision making (Galbraith, 1995). Figure 4.1 shows an example of a functional structure.

Disadvantages of the functional structure include interdepartmental coordination and complexity. "The functional structure lacks a built-in mechanism for coordinating the work flow" (Mintzberg, 1979, p. 125). Coordination between functions generally is expected to happen at higher management levels, which can slow down interdepartmental information sharing unless other lateral or horizontal capabilities are developed. Marketing may see the need to add a new capability to an existing product, but Research and Development may see as its priority to invent new products. Thus, the organization can be slow to respond to changing environmental demands as internal coordination challenges bog down decision making.

When the organization becomes more complex, with multiple products, services, and markets, the demands placed on the functional structure can exceed the capacity of the system to cope with the decisions and information needed. The same efficient marketing practices and decisions that worked well in the past for a single product now could be weighed down by the challenge of adapting to marketing in Spain, marketing a new product sold only in Asia, or developing marketing plans that work for both large businesses and individual consumers. Customers can become frustrated by the finger pointing between groups that claim that a problem is another department's responsibility. Galbraith (1995) explains that Apple used a functional structure until the addition of laptops, mobile devices, and different distribution channels added too much complexity to manage with that structure. "This kind of variety overwhelms the decision-making capacity of the general manager and the functional leadership team" (Galbraith, 1995, p. 24). Leaders in a functional structure may have little time or energy to focus on long-term strategic challenges when they spend most of their time solving day-to-day coordination problems between departments. Thus, the functional structure is best for smaller companies with fewer product lines that have a long life cycle. Because of this, many observers believe that the once-dominant functional structure has been outgrown, since in many (perhaps most) organizations, speed and fast product turnover have become the norm.

Figure 4.1 Functional Structure

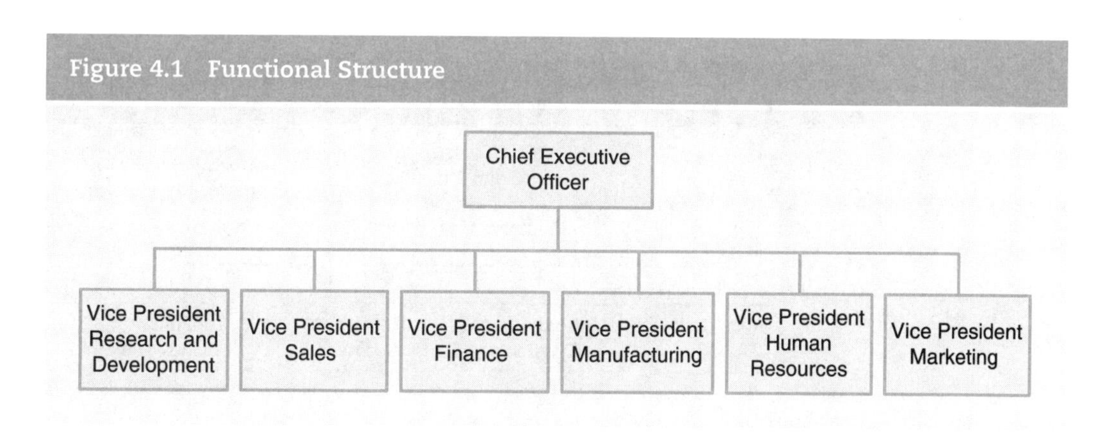

Product Structure

A product structure is an alternative to a functional structure, and it divides responsibilities by the product that the department creates. For example, Campbell Soup Company is an $8 billion global food company organized by its three product divisions: Americas Simple Meals and Beverages (producing the classic well-known soups), Global Biscuits and Snacks, and Campbell Fresh. In 1968, Walker and Lorsch called the choice between a functional structure and product structure "one of the thorniest" (p. 129) issues that a manager had to address. Should the organization choose a functional structure as above, but subdivide by products underneath that top layer, or should it choose a product structure at the highest level and include functional specialization underneath it? Where there are multiple products to be managed,

> developing highly specialized functional units makes it difficult to achieve coordination or integration among these units. On the other hand, having product units as the basis for organization promotes collaboration between specialists, but the functional specialists feel less identification with functional goals. (Walker & Lorsch, 1968, p. 131)

A financial services company might choose to organize by a product structure, with divisions for auto loans, mortgage loans, retirement accounts, and banking, which are essentially the different products that the bank offers to customers (shown in Figure 4.2). Instead of a single division to handle all customer accounts, there might be separate loan officers, financial advisers, and processing and billing departments in each of those divisions. When implemented at its fullest, each self-contained product unit may also have its own human resources, information technology, finance, sales, and marketing departments. As a variation, a blend of a functional and product structure is also possible where these functions are centralized and shared among product divisions.

With a product structure, coordination and focus within a single unit is clear, since in the auto loan department, there are specialists who work solely on auto loans, and attention is not diverted to the special and distinct challenges of mortgage loans. Decisions can sometimes be made more rapidly because each department controls the resources needed for rapid implementation. Employees in product divisions often develop camaraderie with colleagues, pride, and motivation in seeing their product line succeed.

Figure 4.2 Product Structure

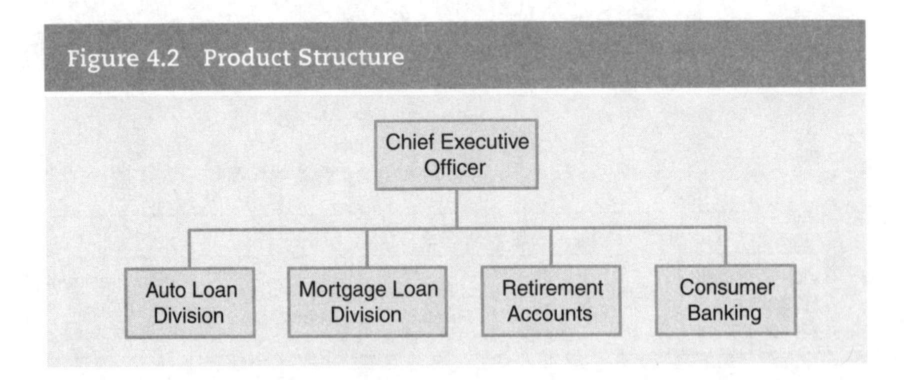

However, the product structure can also lead to duplication of work and inefficiencies, since multiple departments may not be sharing skills and resources most effectively. (They may unnecessarily duplicate purchases of information technology, for example, and the functional IT specialists in each division may not be sharing needs, common goals, or processes). Because different divisions may operate independently, they may not share information or knowledge effectively. Customers who buy products from more than one division can have the feeling that they are purchasing from multiple companies, as different practices can exist in each division. Products might not look or feel the same to the customer or even work together. Customers can be frustrated when they experience different policies and processes, such as billing and invoicing, or experience the lack of information sharing between divisions (global customers may need coordinated points of contact in each geographic division). In the financial services example, customers who have an auto loan may receive different communications from the mortgage loan division, and the two divisions may not share customer information between them, leading to a fragmented customer experience. In addition, when the wider organization might benefit from discontinuing a product line that is not succeeding, the same dedication that employees feel to that product might also discourage them from making a decision to stop producing it.

Customer/Market Structure

Galbraith (2005) observed that product-centric companies, in organizing themselves around their product lines, develop a mindset that pushes the company's existing products on customers. Their goal is to find customers for their products rather than to create products for customers. However, some customers desire long-term relationships; complete packages of solutions that include products, services, consulting, and support; customization; and a consistent global experience. This is only possible to deliver if organizations adopt a customer-centric mindset versus a product mindset.

A customer or market structure is intended to provide a focus on the unique needs of customers in a given market segment or industry group. Individual consumers who purchase a house have different real estate transaction needs from large global companies who may own hundreds of properties. Consumers and government customers both want security for their information technology systems, but the practices of sales, invoicing, and postsales support are likely to be very different for these customer types. Structuring by customer or market type means that the different customer divisions have the responsibility to understand the customer segment and to design products and processes with that segment in mind.

Translating this mindset to the organization design can mean anything from a relatively simple, "light" use of customer teams to account managers for the largest global customers to complete structuring by customer type. (A front–back organizational structure, described later, is yet another example of a customer-centric structure.) A global account director for a bank who works with the bank's largest clients might have the responsibility for understanding the client's requirements in depth, coordinating all salespeople who work with the client around the world, and customizing products and services to meet the client's needs.

Figure 4.3 shows an example of a customer/market structure, a marketing organization for a book publisher where the customer segments include K–12 students, college students, and professional and technical readers. The marketing

Figure 4.3 Customer/Market Structure

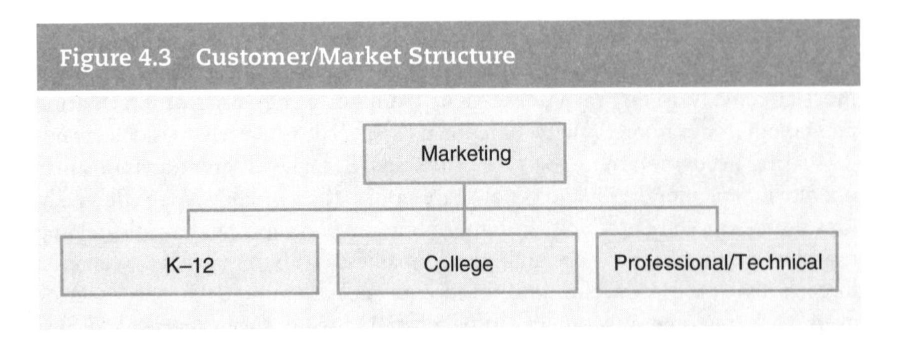

department treats different customer segments differently (e.g., different marketing strategies, advertising messages, social media campaigns). This structure has the advantage of focus, where divisions can dedicate their energies to the given market. Notice again in this structure type how a disadvantage is that resources can be duplicated in each division, losing potential economies of scale.

Geographic Structure

A geographic structure is organized by location or place. Some organizations provide products or services where there is a requirement (or competitive advantage) to having a physical presence where customers are located, such as restaurants, dentists, hotels, and housecleaning services. Figure 4.4 displays a sales organization structured by continent where the sales resources are located. In a geographic structure, resources can be placed physically closest to where the work happens, and the structure offers the advantage of local customization and knowledge of regional needs. Buyers for a retail clothing chain know what the trends and customer preferences are for swimwear in Miami versus warm coats in Minneapolis.

While digital technologies can reduce the perceived distance from the company to its customers (e.g., call centers that can serve customers from anywhere in the world), there remain some compelling reasons to maintain a physical presence in a location. Human resources and legal specialists know that local employment laws differ significantly between the United States and Europe, for example, and a geographic structure may be the most appropriate option to facilitate regional specialization and offer the most accurate policy advice. Government regulations may require a local professional to sign financial statements. The organization, even if global in scope, may wish to portray itself as being a local company. There can also be cultural and language challenges that require local knowledge in order to adapt organizational practices to operate in a certain country. In some locations, using a third-party distributor or agent is preferred or more cost effective, requiring a geographic approach to manage. If shipping costs are prohibitive, local manufacturing may be necessary. Consider the drawback, however, in duplicating these resources in different physical locations. If the team in Europe is experiencing a slow period while demand is high in Asia, it can be expensive to shift people from one geography to another.

Process Structure

Process designs became popularized in the 1980s and 1990s as a way to structure an organization to achieve flexibility as a principal objective (Anand & Daft, 2007; Bahrami, 1992). These designs are also sometimes called "boundaryless" or

Figure 4.4 Geographic Structure

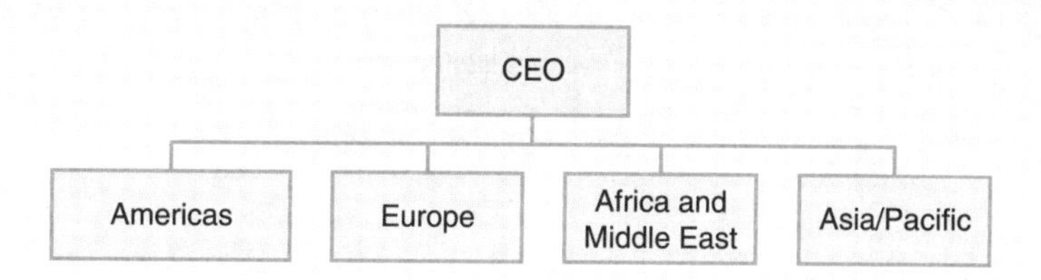

"horizontal" organizations. The boundaryless design emerged primarily in high-technology companies where creativity and innovation, along with rapid product development cycles and quick time to market, were necessary to remain competitive. The boundaryless design breaks down the traditional hierarchy and replaces it with cross-functional, often self-managed teams that form and restructure as the business changes. Roles, titles, jobs, and teams are no longer rigidly built into the structure of the organization, but negotiated and flexible depending on the needs of the organization. The ability to rapidly form teams, set objectives, adapt to change, and build relationships are all key skills in boundaryless organization.

One more structured version is to design by process steps that cut across the old hierarchy. "The vertical structure is based on units that are organized around core processes" with "process owners at the top management level" (Nesheim, 2011, p. 110). In this design, the core processes of the organization that create customer value are the dominant organizing principle. There may be a division focused on the process of gathering customer requirements and developing new products. Another division may be focused on creating customer demand and processing orders. A third may focus on manufacturing orders and delivering products to customers. A process leader may be in charge of each process step.

Boundary-breaking designs like this one are good when rapid cycle time is necessary, since there are fewer boundaries to interrupt process flow and decisions to revise the process can be made at the local level. The workflow and each department's connections to the customer are much clearer to all organizational members. The process-based organization can "enhance the coordination among people and activities and increase the company's flexibility allowing it to respond to market changes and customer needs efficiently and effectively" (Angelo et al., 2010, p. 51).

Galbraith (2002) notes that the process structure was once a popular organizational structure, but that the structure is less useful in organizations that have automated or outsourced many processes and thus do not have jobs assigned to them as the structure intends. The design is challenging "because of the need for horizontal and vertical management structures to co-exist and indeed be coordinated with one another" (Angelo et al., 2010, p. 51). Figure 4.5 shows an example of a boundaryless or process structure.

In a case study of developing a process-based organization, Angelo et al., (2010) note that deciding on process boundaries and articulating the relationship between the process owners and functional units can be especially complex. The task of leadership and management is particularly challenging in the process organization, as old ways of managing in the traditional hierarchy no longer apply. In an organization accustomed to traditional vertical decision-making authority,

Figure 4.5 Process Structure

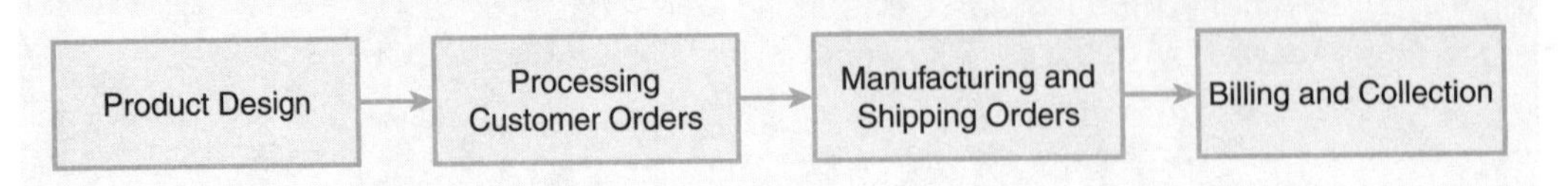

a process structure can be a foreign way of managing. Leadership now performs an integrative function (Shamir, 1999), managing tensions among authority, tasks, politics, and identities (Hirschhorn & Gilmore, 1992). Leaders in the process organization must help to form teams, negotiate between teams, sort through role conflicts, balance competing interests between groups, and encourage employees to maintain an organizational connection even while teams are being disbanded and re-formed.

Network Structure

A network structure also dissolves the traditional hierarchical functional structure. Indeed, the network structure reduces the organization's functions down to its central competencies, and a network of suppliers and partners provides services that the organization does not consider central (or that are not cost effective to perform internally). For example, in the 1980s, Harley-Davidson began to work with a network of suppliers instead of producing all components itself, reducing cycle times and costs (Miles & Snow, 1992).

In one type of network, organizations may design their own products internally, but may contract with an outside manufacturer and shipping company to build and deliver products to customers. They may work with local distributors or third-party providers who may sell directly to customers on behalf of the company, but these distributors are independent entities, not in-house sales agents. "The network model suggests that these companies can be more innovative by setting up special units focused on innovation in which brokers bring resources together and later transfer results to the larger operating system" (Miles & Snow, 1986, p. 72). In some networked organizations, the "external" suppliers may be so tightly integrated with the organization's people, processes, and technology that the line between being internal and external to the organization is blurred. The organization may even ask outside suppliers, manufacturers, and distributors to integrate their own processes and technology on behalf of the company. The organization therefore becomes a "broker" of services among the various players (Miles & Snow, 1986).

This network organization has four characteristics, according to Miles and Snow (1986):

- Vertical disaggregation: The separation of product development, manufacturing, shipping, and logistics into unique activities performed by different organizations.
- Brokers: A hub-and-spoke model where one or more parties brings the network together.

- Market mechanisms: Market needs and contracts for services hold the network together.
- Full-disclosure information systems: "Broad-access computerized information systems are used as substitutes for lengthy trust-building processes based on experience" (p. 65).

"A properly constructed network can display the technical specialization of the functional structure, the market responsiveness of the divisional structure, and the balanced orientation of the matrix" (Miles & Snow, 1986, p. 65). Because each organization specializes in a core competency, the dynamic network organization brings together the strengths of each organization in a way that maximizes scale and flexibility. An example of this type of network is presented in Figure 4.6. Other types of networks exist as well (Miles & Snow, 1992).

Network organizations can be cost effective and flexible, and they can focus the organization on its central purpose. They can also cause problems when the organization must rely on the performance (and organizational health) of an external company over which it may have little control. Unless the multiple organizations comprising the network are monitoring the external environment, they can become blind to trends and the need to change. The transition from internal ownership to external control can also be challenging if organizational knowledge or processes are not robust enough to share effectively.

Front–Back Structure

The next two structures that we will discuss are hybrids of the first six. By hybrid, we mean a structure that incorporates two or more of the previous structure types. The front–back structure is a hybrid of the customer structure on the front end, and a product structure on the back end. Figure 4.7 displays an example of a front–back structure. In the late 1990s, Citibank structured using a front–back structure comprising global product units and global customer units, each with its own authority, accountability, and profit goals (Galbraith, 2000).

Figure 4.6 Network Structure

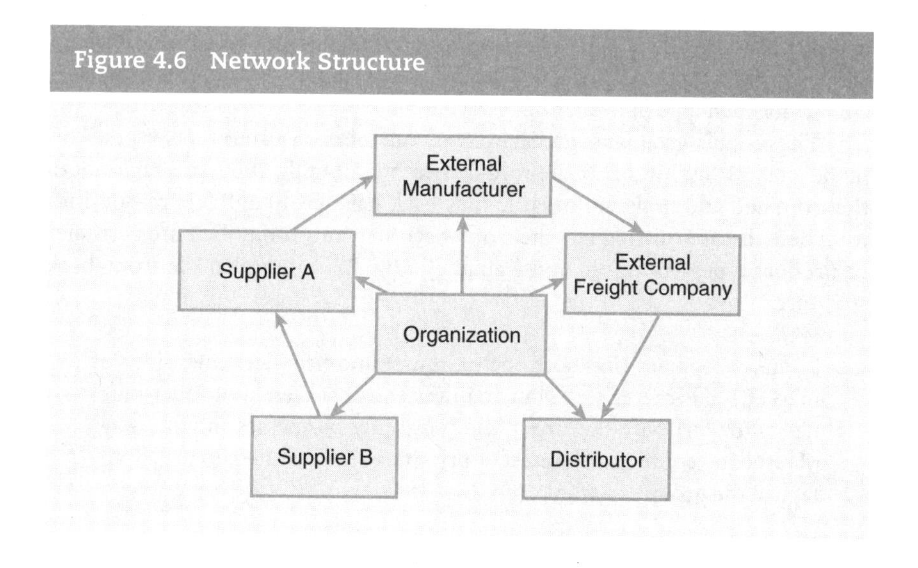

Figure 4.7 Front–Back Structure

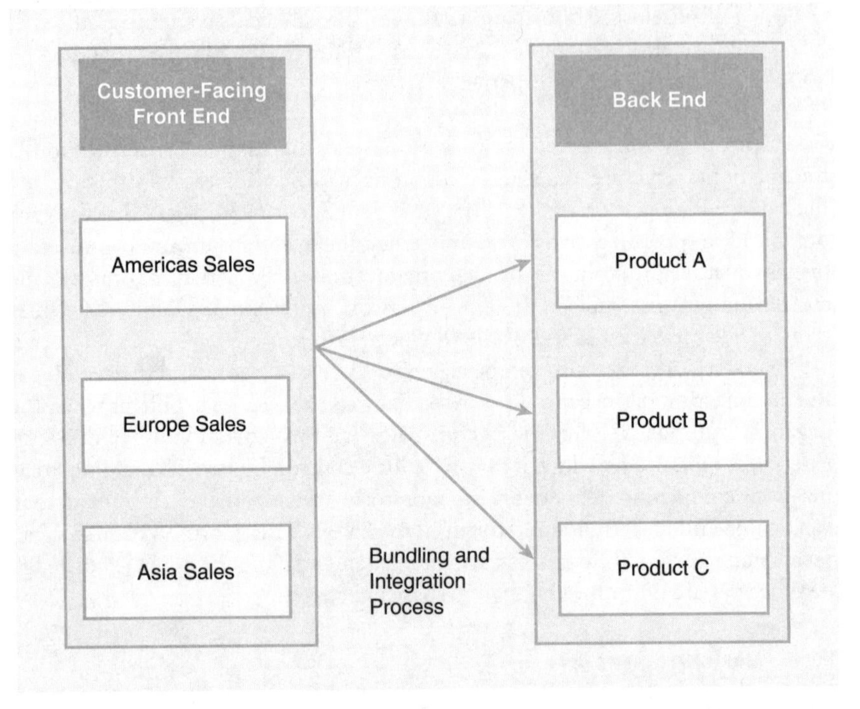

The front end is intended to be a customer-focused operation, for example, as a single point of contact for a global customer who wants one point of entry to the organization. It can be a geographic structure or a customer/market structure as defined earlier. On the back end are the product groups that develop the products sold by the front end (put differently, the front end purchases products from the back end). For example, the Americas Sales division might bundle a product A and product B together for a customer who is interested in buying both. The insurance company Allstate offers policy discounts for customers who purchase auto, home, and life insurance in a single policy, making it unnecessary to have a separate sales contact for each type of insurance.

The product groups are global in scope and focus on all customer types. This model creates "multifunctional profit centers" (Galbraith, 2000, p. 240) for both the front end and back end because they each have profit and loss responsibility. These features distinguish the front–back structure from the pure customer or product types. As Goold and Campbell (2002a) state about the front–back structure,

> [T]his recognizes that both the customer and product dimensions of market focus are critical, but requires the "back-end" product businesses to work with the "front-end" customer businesses and find ways of resolving conflicts of interest or priorities between them to the advantage of the group as a whole. (pp. 183–184)

This model helps to alleviate the disadvantages of a product structure, where a single customer purchasing multiple products would have to interface with multiple contacts. Global customers who want a single contract for all product types do not want a different salesperson for every product (as would be the case in a product structure). These customers are driving organizations toward the front–back hybrid model. This model also helps to alleviate the disadvantages of a customer structure, where different products might be designed for different customer needs with little integration between them.

There are several forces that might prompt an organization to adopt a front–back structure (Galbraith, 2000, p. 251):

- Customers can buy all products.
- Customers want a single point of contact.
- Customers want a sourcing partnership.
- Customers want solutions and systems, not components and products.
- Opportunities exist for cross-selling and bundling.
- Value-added is becoming increasingly customer specific.
- Advantage can be gained through superior knowledge about customers and customer segments.

Implementing a front–back hybrid structure can be difficult, because the front end and back end have different priorities and goals. Power struggles can result from front-end customer account managers who demand customization from a back end that does not want to invest precious resources. Back-end product managers may be frustrated at the inaction of the front end in promoting their product lines. The front end will want speed and responsiveness in addressing customer needs, while the back end will want to focus on economies of scale and innovation, making conflicting priorities a point of contention. The back end can lose sight of customer needs without communication from the front end, and the front end can lose sight of the organization-wide efficiency benefits of the back end.

Matrix Structure

Matrix organizational forms were first developed in the 1960s and 1970s as an attempt to address some of the disadvantages of other structure forms and to maximize their advantages. Large global companies want to develop superiority in multiple areas. A company may need first-to-market innovations with strong product expertise, but at the same time it may also want the ability to have an efficient supply chain manufacturing function or consistent global marketing. Neither the functional structure (with its cross-functional communication challenges) nor the product structure (with its duplication of functional resources) would meet the need to focus on both goals, and the organization refuses to choose between them.

In a matrix form, the specialist functions and product or geography structures both exist, in some respects. Imagine a technology company that manufactures personal computers, printers, software, and handheld devices. If it operates in a matrix structure as depicted in Figure 4.8, it might have teams in each division

Figure 4.8 Matrix Structure

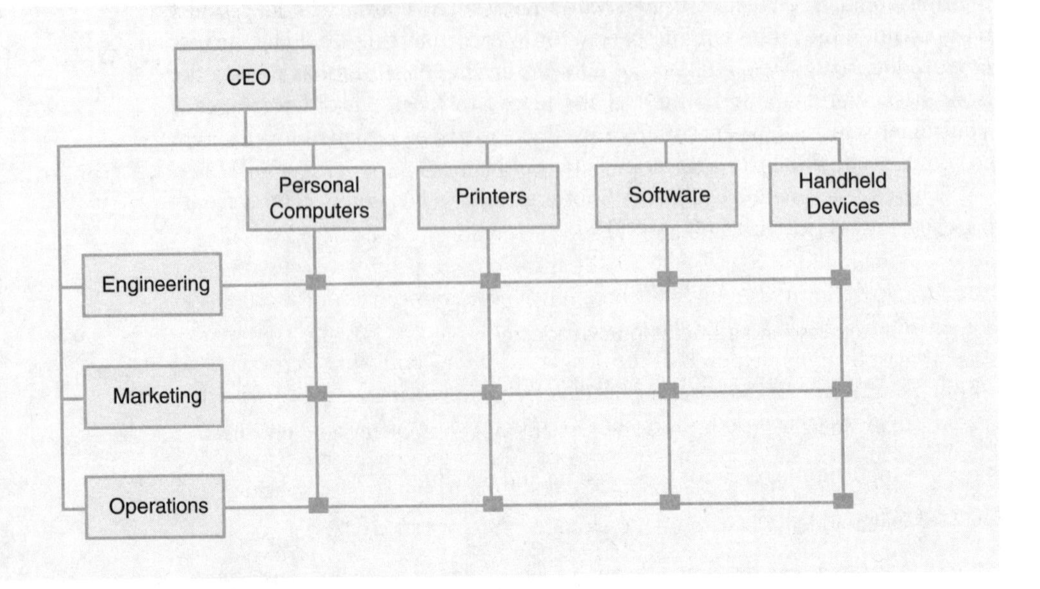

with responsibility for engineering, marketing, and operations. Each of those latter functional groups would have a leader to oversee the company's overall strategy for that function. For example, the leader of marketing would be responsible for ensuring a consistent marketing strategy across all divisions, while the leader of the printer division would be responsible for the success of the company's printing products. The matrix structure has the advantage of excellence in the product line while increasing communication and coordination among functions.

Note that a requirement for the matrix is that the organization maintains dual perspectives (e.g., function and geography, or product and customer segment), with an equal balance of power between both perspectives. Employees (the squares at the intersections in Figure 4.8) report directly to the two bosses that manage these dual areas. Often a subproject manager will be identified to coordinate the work of the product team and functional team. Galbraith (2009) writes,

> When the matrix is working well, the two bosses communicate with each other to detect issues early and prevent unnecessary conflicts. Usually they jointly select the person to be the subproject manager. They then agree on a set of goals against which the manager will be evaluated. This agreement minimizes giving conflicting goals to the manager with two bosses. The subproject manager is then jointly evaluated, and both bosses sign off on the performance review. (p. 5)

Some organizations create "dotted line" reporting relationships where one reporting line is the employee's direct boss while the dotted line manager is a coordinator but does not have direct line authority. Purists argue that dotted line relationships are not matrix structures, strictly speaking.

Matrix organizations work especially well under three conditions (Davis & Lawrence, 1977). First, they work well when there exist pressures for *multiple areas of focus*, such as when a group needs to focus on both technical expertise in a certain field (functional or product expertise) and unique customer requirements of a given market (customer focus). A focus on costs and efficiency is maintained by the functional line, and the focus on innovation and product excellence is maintained by the product line. Second, matrix organizations work well when *the work is especially complex or interdependent* and additional coordination is required. When people are interdependent in multiple ways, a matrix may help to improve communication patterns. In the example above, information can be shared at both the product line and functional level. Finally, a matrix is appropriate when *resources need to be shared* for maximum efficiency. When skills are scarce and resources are at a premium, a matrix facilitates reassignment of the scarcest resources to the necessary areas. Imagine that each of the dots at the intersecting lines represents an employee or team. In these cases, resources can be shifted among the engineering team from personal computers to printers if the workload demands it, making the matrix responsive and adaptable to the work. A marketing manager could move from personal computers to handheld devices. Employees can also develop their skills across multiple product lines.

Matrix structures can be challenging to implement and can cause role conflict for the individual who can be caught between the demands of two managers. The clarity of decision rights and control in the pure functional or product structures is lost, and the competing priorities of the two lines of the matrix can create conflict. For example, an engineering manager who wants to design a product for efficient manufacturing can come into conflict with the leader of the printer segment who wants a specialized feature for the product that is more expensive to produce. Decision processes can be complicated by seemingly needing the approval of managers at many levels in order to proceed. The matrix structure can thus lead to power struggles among managers. However, notice that the existence of conflict is not a fault of the matrix structure, but an intentional choice to have multiple areas of focus. When the conflict becomes destructive and power struggles and politicking outweigh the flexibility of the structure, the benefits of the matrix are lost.

While Figure 4.8 depicts the most basic of matrix structures, organizations have evolved ever more complex versions in the decades since the matrix was originally popularized, particularly in organizations that do business globally and need a strong geographic dimension to their structure. Consider how Figure 4.8 might look if we added three geographic regions reporting to the CEO. Each of those geographic divisions might also have connections to the other lines of the business, to create a department responsible for marketing printers in Europe, or engineering software in Japan. Galbraith (2009) explores what more complex matrix structures look like, including a discussion of the challenges of planning, leadership, and human resources policies that these structures present. We will discuss some of these more complex matrix structures in the next chapter.

Advantages and Disadvantages of Structure Types

As you can see from the discussion above, no structure is perfect. Table 4.1 summarizes the advantages and disadvantages of each of these structures.

Table 4.1 Advantages and Disadvantages of Structure Types

Structure Type	Advantages	Disadvantages
Functional	• Efficient for small or single-product or service businesses • Allows for economies of scale • Ease of collaboration among like-minded professional groupings who have similar specialization and worldview • Can develop common processes and approaches within divisions • Clear career paths	• Collaboration across functional departments is challenging. • Challenging to address multiple product or service lines • Single-minded devotion to professional activity can mean less visibility into bigger picture or wider needs. • Can be slow to respond to changes in the environment
Geographic	• Can enhance local customer relationships • Allows adaptation for regional customs, language, or regulations • Local focus when required for regulatory purposes • Customers perceive organization as local	• Physical distance can make it difficult to share resources across divisions. • Difficulty in sharing information and best practices • Lost economies of scale when regions operate as unique entities, duplication of resources
Product	• Encourages innovation by product line • Ability to change more quickly to environmental demands • Employees develop pride of ownership around product line. • Ability to measure profitability of a product line	• Too much dedication to product can make the division overlook alternatives. • Less likely to advocate dissolving or discontinuing a product line • Lost economies of scale across product lines, duplication of resources
Customer	• Creates long-term relationships with customers • Allows getting to know customer requirements in depth • Knowledge of customers allows more opportunity for bundling or creation of packaged solutions beyond products or services alone. • Creation of additional value helps avoid price wars.	• Lost economies of scale or duplication across divisions, possibly reinventing the wheel • Challenging to share information across divisions
Process	• Rapid communication and reduction in cycle time of work done	• Separation of business activities into process and non-process functions may be problematic.

	• Individuals working together on teams develop broader perspective, more flexible and empowered roles. • Rapid organizational learning is facilitated. • Improved customer responsiveness (Anand & Daft, 2007, p. 332)	• Teamwork could get in the way of functional specialization. • Traditional departments may instigate turf battles (Anand & Daft, 2007, p. 332).
Network	• Allows organization to focus on its core competencies • Allows organization to take advantage of best of breed partnerships to gain best technologies or skills • Can be more cost effective • Can be more flexible	• Reduced control due to reliance on external partnerships • Requires investment in the partnership, metrics and monitoring • Reduction of in-house skills
Front–Back	• Attempts to provide advantages of customer and product types, with both customer focus and product excellence and innovation • Single point of contact for customers • Effective and efficient selling • Ability to cross-sell and bundle products for customers	• Can be tricky to get alignment between front and back and resolve resulting conflict • Back end can lose touch with the business or customer requirements • Front end can advocate for divergent directions, compromising functional or product standards • Power struggles between front and back
Matrix	• Allows multiple areas of focus • Facilitates movement of resources across divisional lines • Allows for specialization • Encourages coordination	• Creates substantial conflict, requiring interpersonally skilled leaders to resolve • Organizational members can be confused by dual lines of authority, slowing decision making. • Can be costly to implement

It should be clear based on this chart that there is no one structure that is right or wrong, or a single choice that is best for the occasion with no drawbacks. Kesler and Kates (2011) point out that the organization designer may find that more than one structure option would be appropriate. The designer should weigh several considerations to choose among them, namely, "the degree of change and disruption, primacy (what needs to change first), the management team's capacity to manage complexity, what changes will have the biggest positive impact, what will be most visible to customers or employees, and the fit with the existing culture" (p. 15). Indeed, because there will always be disadvantages with any structure choice, the most that a designer can do is to make the best choice with the information available and to be conscious of the flaws of that choice.

Choosing a Structure and Evaluating the Options

Some observers have noticed that as organizations grow, they tend to structure themselves following predictable patterns of evolution. A single-product business works well for a functional structure, but as new products are added, the complexity overwhelms the functional organization. The organization then pursues a product or business-unit structure with functional units underneath. As the organization continues to grow into a global operation, it requires a geographic or customer structure to manage customer relationships in different countries. The complex, multidimensional priorities of the operation then require a matrix for flexibility and efficient resource allocation. A crisis of red tape occurs (Greiner, 1998), frustrating managers who spend too much time resolving conflicts and dealing with bureaucracy. The organization simplifies and refocuses with a network structure (Galbraith, 2014a; Snow, 2015).

Kesler and Kates (2011) write that leaders often want to simplify the organization structure and choose one of these pure forms to avoid too much complexity. They may feel that a front–back structure or matrix structure would be too difficult to implement or execute, so they choose a functional or product structure instead. "There is no value in purity," Kesler and Kates (p. 89) argue, pointing out that more complex structures may give some organizations a competitive advantage and be worth the investment.

In addition, most organizations have multiple structure types at multiple levels. For example, at the highest level, a small hotel chain might choose a functional structure, with leaders for hotel operations, new real estate development, finance, marketing, and human resources. Underneath the hotel operations leader, the organizational structure might be a customer structure because the hotel chain offers lodging for families on a budget, extended stay properties for business executives, and timeshare properties sold to investors. Under the family lodging segment, the structure might be geographic to manage four regions across the United States. In each case, the structure option best meets the strategic need, priorities, capabilities needed, and results required at that specific level.

For this reason, Kesler and Kates (2011) state that "generating and evaluating strategic grouping options is an iterative process. Organizations are multilayered, and it is very difficult to understand the pros and cons of a given option without imagining at least two layers deep" (p. 88). Some levels will naturally lead to one of the pure structure choices covered earlier, but subsequent layers of the organization could prove more challenging to design. "The key is to find ways to blend and balance the strengths and weaknesses of the varied options," walking through the implications of various choices (p. 89).

To choose a grouping option, Galbraith, Downey, and Kates (2002) advise returning to the design criteria (as discussed in Chapter 2) to ensure that the new model addresses the organizational capabilities specified by the criteria. In addition, Nadler and Tushman (1997, pp. 77–79) offer six questions to consider:

1. To what extent does the option maximize the utilization of resources?

With its emphasis on grouping people who share the same activities, the functional structure allows economies of scale and sharing of resources. By duplicating resources in different product groups or geographic units, those structures lose the maximization of resources, but this may be an investment that the organization explicitly wishes to make in order to gain the benefits of those structure choices.

Complexity of the design should also be evaluated. An organization design that is unnecessarily complex will require a significant amount of management attention to introduce and manage, wasting resources.

2. How does grouping affect specialization and economies of scale?

Mintzberg (1979) writes that "groups may have to be formed to reach sizes large enough to function efficiently" (p. 123). Every department in a university needs a human resources contact to help with hiring paperwork and answering payroll questions, but that does not mean that every department needs a full-time specialist. There is unlikely to be a need for a specialized human resources representative because of the unique needs of the business department compared to the sociology department, so a centralized function makes sense. However, a university that has a business school may want to invest in its own library separate from the central university library, making the trade-off of enhanced specialization for lost economies of scale. Network organizations may choose fewer internal specializations to gain the benefit of external knowledge and economies of scale.

3. How does the grouping form affect measurement and control issues?

Functional and product structures make measurement relatively easy, as the activities of the manufacturing or sales departments and the profitability of product A can all be tracked. Measurement is made more complicated in a front–back hybrid structure, where both the front end and back end may have responsibility for revenue, profit, and market share. The front end may wish to gain market share by reducing prices whereas the back end may wish to maximize profits (Galbraith, 2000), creating conflicts over control.

4. How does the grouping form affect the development of individuals and the organization's capacity to use its human resources?

Functional organizations allow clear professional identifications and communities to develop. Matrix organizations encourage functional identification as well as maximize cross-product knowledge and resource sharing. Structuring by product, customer group, or geography might isolate functional experts from like-minded professionals and make it more challenging to develop employees. If there is only one finance director in a certain country, the employee will develop a wide-ranging perspective on the business but will often have less frequent interactions with other finance professionals.

5. How does the grouping form affect the final output of the organization?

Mintzberg (1979) draws a distinction between "natural" and "unnatural" workflows where "members of a single unit have a sense of territorial integrity; they control a well-defined organizational process; [and] most of the problems that arise in the course of their work can be solved simply, through their mutual adjustment" (p. 118). Each structure type creates barriers between groups. If those barriers are "unnatural" divisions, organizational members will need to work harder to overcome them. "If people are grouped together in ways that give them control over an end-to-end process, bottlenecks and weak points in the process can be easily discerned and changed" (Galbraith, Downey, & Kates, 2002, p. 96), allowing the organization to be more adaptable.

6. How responsive is each organization form to important competitive demands?

Functional structures develop disciplinary excellence but, as we have noted, are not especially attuned to rapid responsiveness in competitive environments. Product, customer, and front–back structures are more driven to innovate for customer needs. Network organizations may be able to more quickly mobilize a new network to rapidly take advantage of a competitive need.

PRINCIPLES OF STRUCTURE

As leaders choose a grouping option, it is also useful to keep in mind other additional choices that need to be made with respect to organizational structure.

Shape/Configuration: Span of Control and Layers

What should be the ideal size of the departments that have been created? How many managers will be needed to accomplish the work, and how many management layers are ideal? The shape of the organization concerns how tall or flat the hierarchy will be. The determining factor for the number of managers is the number of employees that each manager will supervise—called the span of control.

Consider this example: In 2014, McDonald's made headlines by announcing that it was changing its structure to give local franchisees more authority to make decisions about their menus. Reports indicated that the company

> is eliminating layers of management and creating a new organizational structure in the U.S. as it seeks to better respond to consumer tastes amid falling sales and profits. . . . As part of the change, the company is creating four zones—Northeast, South, Central and West—that it says will be organized around local consumer tastes and preferences. The new zone structure replaces one consisting of three divisions—West, East and Central. . . . "You've told us that there are too many layers, redundancies in planning and communication, competing priorities, barriers to efficient decisions making, and too much talking to ourselves instead of to and about our customers," [McDonald's U.S. President Mike] Andres wrote. "If we want to grow beyond our current results, we need to evolve beyond our current model." (Jargon, 2014)

For McDonald's, the fewer divisions, the more franchises that existed in each division. Thus, the taller the hierarchy, and by implication, the more layers necessary to reach the executive in charge of that division. By adding a new division, the number of layers can decrease, streamlining communication throughout the hierarchy.

The choice can be described on two ends of a continuum. One option is to add more people per manager or unit, which means a flatter hierarchy with fewer managers and layers. This is referred to as a wide span of control. Another is to assign fewer people per manager, increasing the number of managers and thus layers in the hierarchy. This is referred to as a narrow span of control (see Figure 4.9 for an example).

Figure 4.9 Span of Control

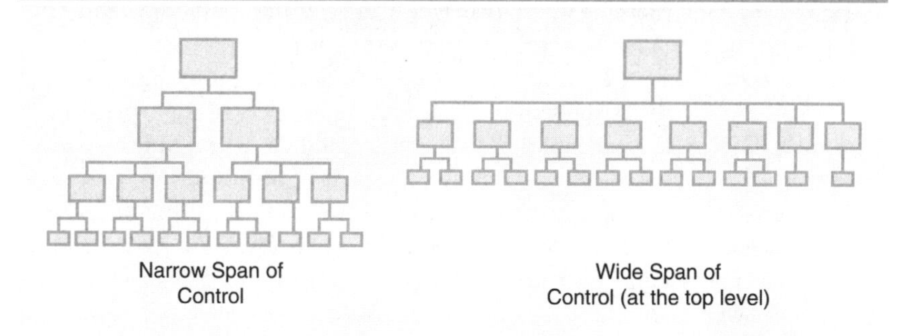

Flatter hierarchies and wider spans of control have a number of benefits. Fewer managers are needed, reducing costs. Employees can have a greater degree of autonomy and authority in their jobs. This can lead to more rapid decision making from which customers can benefit. Conversely, a narrower span of control can also have advantages. More management roles give employees a chance to grow into supervisor responsibilities (Galbraith, Downey, & Kates, 2002). Managers with a narrow span can become more closely attuned to the work, can pay attention to needed coordination across a team or across departments, and can handle day-to-day responsibilities while upper-level managers attend to long-term strategic challenges.

As Hamel (2011) provocatively described, a 1:10 ratio of managers to employees seems reasonable for a small organization, but comes at a steep price for a large organization of 100,000 employees. The same ratio would require more than 10,000 managers, but would also require more than 1,000 additional managers just to manage the work of the other managers. Thus, management can be expensive, with pressures to reduce layers when costs need to be addressed. For the most part, "leaders have no good method for assessing which parts of the management structure are needed and which are superfluous" (Topp & Desjardins, 2011, p. 213). A thoughtful evaluation of span of control needs to consider several factors about the employees, managers, the work, and the organization (Galbraith, 2002; Galbraith, Downey, & Kates, 2002; Topp & Desjardins, 2011).

Questions about the ideal span of control for a manager go back to the beginnings of the field of organization design. Urwick (1956) claimed that the average business executive could handle a span of control around six subordinates, explaining that with the various combinations of relationships and interactions among six people, a manager would need to keep 200 different permutations and cross-group relationships in mind (person A's relationship with B and C, person B's relationship with C and D, subgroup D-E-F, and so on). Others argued that at lower levels in a hierarchy, greater spans of control were possible, leading to quantitative studies that attempted to create complex mathematical formulas to construct the ideal span per level in the organization for best performance (Keren & Levhari, 1979). Recommendations and realities vary considerably, from an advised span of 7 or 8 (Davison, 2003) to 5 to 10 for an executive team (Galbraith, Downey, & Kates, 2002). Davison (2003) found that in health care organizations the span averaged 16, but it was fewer than 5 in information services organizations.

Galbraith (2002) pointed out that spans of control of 17 or even 75 are possible depending on the circumstances of the work and management style. A span of control of 17 is achievable with a manager who delegates most of the authority and spends time coaching. In a factory where three self-managed teams of 25 individuals organize their own work and schedules, run their own team meetings, and work according to policies and standard practices, a single leader can manage all 75 employees. There is less need for direct supervision of the work of every employee. The point is that there is not one right answer for span of control for any given industry, company, or layer within a company. See box for span of control considerations.

Moreover, the most appropriate span of control for a given department or organization may change over time. During the start-up of a new product division, a narrower span might be appropriate as employees work out roles and

FACTORS INFLUENCING SPAN OF CONTROL

Employee Factors

- Employee experience: If employees have a great deal of knowledge and experience in dealing with the work, they can be more autonomous and a manager can supervise more people.
- Employee independence: If employees are able to manage their own work schedules and priorities and are disciplined and self-motivated, a wider span is possible.

Manager Factors

- Competence in delegation and coaching: Managers who are skilled at delegating work to team members and who can coach and guide (versus control and direct) can manage more employees.
- Diversity of responsibilities: A manager who is responsible for multiple functions may need a narrower span of control to be able to focus on the varied nature of the work.

Work Factors

- Interdependence of work: If the work is independent and employees can work on their own, a wider span is possible. If, however, the work requires a great deal of coordination among members of a team, a smaller team may be required unless team members are capable of coordinating as a self-managed team.
- Work complexity: If the work is especially complex and requires management supervision, a narrower span may be needed. If the work relies on standardized policies and procedures, managers can create rules to direct the work and may be able to supervise more employees.
- Predictability of work cycles: When the work is regular, predictable, and routine, a manager may be able to supervise more employees, but a narrow span may be required when the team is overloaded with work one minute and has excess capacity in the next.

Organizational Factors

- Geographic dispersal of team: With a team that is virtual or not co-located, a manager may need to invest more time in connecting with team members across multiple locations and require a smaller team.
- Amount of turnover: A high turnover rate means that managers may need to spend time with new employees to train, coach, monitor, and mentor, and thus require a narrower span.
- Amount of change: Organizations undergoing a transition or in an unstable environment may need managers who take an active role in helping employees manage change and thus have a narrower span of control.

responsibilities and managers coach the team to coordinate work on the new product. Over time, as the product matures and the team gains more experience in self-managing, fewer managers may be required.

For the last several years, the trend has been to reduce the number of managers, flatten hierarchies, and give employees more ownership and control over their work. Hamel (2011) describes how tomato processor Morning Star relies on self-management, commitment to colleagues, and clarity of mission to direct employee work instead of supervisory control by a boss. Employees have a great deal of authority to make decisions but also the responsibility to do so in the best interests of the company, so they will almost always quickly consult with team members rather than make unilateral decisions. Such practices can increase employee loyalty and engagement. Flatter hierarchies can change the traditional role of management and require delegation and empowerment, so this practice may be countercultural for some organizations.

Distribution of Power: Centralization/Decentralization

Another design decision relates to what decisions or activities will be centralized in a single function and which will be delegated or decentralized to different groups to manage on their own. At its heart, it is an issue of authority and power in decision making, with standard practices and policies that apply to everyone, or with each group having the authority to decide. These are issues about which citizens have heated arguments; for example, should school district superintendents decide on the curriculum and teaching practices for all schools in the region, or should school principals and faculty have the authority to make those decisions alone.

This was the impetus for Ouchi's (2006) study of three school districts. He noted that a traditional school district structure consists of a centralized administrative office that made decisions about school curriculum, budgets, special education curriculum, and faculty development programs. In Edmonton, Seattle, and Houston, some decisions were decentralized to principals at the local school level. Some functions such as computing services and bus transportation remained centralized at the main office where other decisions such as staffing (the number and mix of full-time or part-time teachers, number of administrative staff) and scheduling were made at the individual school level, giving principals greater control. Ouchi (2006) concluded that the principals were able to innovate, customize, and adapt to the needs of students more easily by having local control.

Figure 4.10 displays the "hub and spoke" model of centralization and the dispersed decision making in a decentralized model.

An example of a centralized function is a shared services center. Shared services groups are centralized functions that are pulled out "to provide services to meet the needs of other units cost effectively and responsively" (Goold & Campbell, 2002a, p. 171). They may be responsible for transactional activities such as accounts payable and payroll, or they may require substantial expertise such as software development. In performing the same function for everyone, shared services units should see themselves as an internal provider or supplier with internal units as their customers. Efforts to reduce costs and streamline operations by growing centralized functions often result in unhappy internal customers. According to a 2014 report, "fewer than 10% of the companies reported that they were highly satisfied with the effectiveness of headquarters" functions (Kunisch, Müller-Stewens, & Campbell, 2014).

Figure 4.10 Centralization and Decentralization

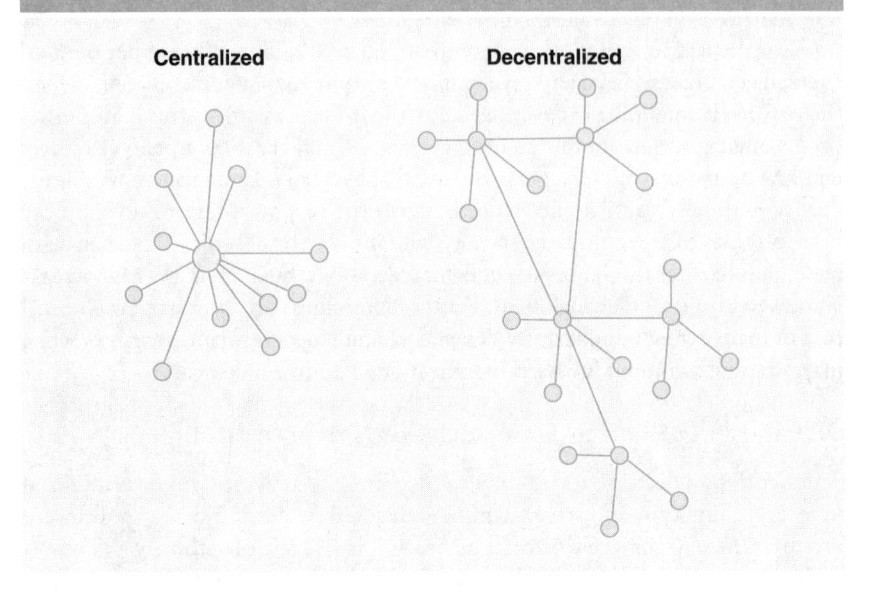

For example, on the one hand, creating a centralized contracts group as a "shared service" that serves all product groups to manage all customer agreements can result in economies of scale and standard processes. This practice makes sense until the company's new product X requires specialized contracts knowledge and a unique process, or when the geographic expansion into Japan means necessary language support that the centralized group is ill-equipped to handle. Suddenly subgroups are created for product X contracts and geographic support for Japan, eventually leading to the creation of subgroups for any number of apparently unique needs, losing the benefits of centralization in the first place. It is no wonder that the centralization-decentralization decision has been called "one of the most vexing questions in organization design" (Kates & Galbraith, 2007, p. 141).

Centralization of decision making can have a number of benefits. A centralized group can create one standard process that can be applied with consistency, as in the case of a group that creates common reports for every department, or in the design of policies or resource allocations that apply to the whole organization. It can have the advantage of economies of scale, such as when a centralized manufacturing operation can create products for every department rather than undertaking the expense of setting up separate facilities for each product line. Similar to the advantages of a functional structure, these units can develop deeper expertise and share knowledge and talent. The company can negotiate with vendors for global needs that apply to everyone such as training or information technology, gaining the benefits of common procurement practices. An organization experiencing a crisis where fast decision making needs to be conducted quickly, a centralized function can do so more effectively than spending time coordinating decentralized functions. In addition, separating out an activity in a centralized group allows the remaining units to focus on the core competencies that matter most (whether product development or customer focus) rather than investing resources and management attention in operational activities.

Taken too far, however, too much centralization can be damaging. Centralized groups may ignore the special requirements of different units, leading to reduced effectiveness. If training needs really are different in a given geography, it is unnecessary to force employees to participate in corporate global programs. Centralized groups may miss what is happening on the ground and lack responsiveness to customer needs or important trends. They may become slow to innovate or adapt to change. It may also be the case that the organization confuses centralized decision-making authority with the need to coordinate, communicate, and share information across divisions.

Decentralization also has advantages. By giving the authority for decision making to the local unit, they can remain responsive to customer needs. A related advantage is speed; rather than waiting for the central group at headquarters to develop a plan, a local unit can do so more quickly. Decentralization can help when there are real distinctions between units. If a competitor only operates in Europe, there is no need to develop a global marketing strategy in response; instead, the local marketing group can develop and manage the action plan. Another advantage is that local units can pilot alternatives to common problems at a lower cost, experimenting on a small scale to see if a practice will work. A regional pricing strategy can be adopted to see if it brings in more customers before the effort and expense of a global implementation is considered.

Yet too much decentralization, at the extreme, can be equally damaging. Decentralization comes at a cost, where duplication of an activity in different units is intended because the organization seeks to achieve the advantages described above. Managers who want to build an empire and retain control will explain that every aspect of their unit is unique and requires them to own the decentralized activity. Without intentional communication efforts, local innovations may never be seen by other units that could benefit from the learning. Table 4.2 compares these advantages and consequences of centralization and decentralization.

Table 4.2 Comparing Centralization and Decentralization

Centralization	Decentralization
Benefits	**Benefits**
• Common processes and consistency • Economies of scale and lower costs • Negotiating power • Ability to develop deep expertise • Allow other groups to focus on their core competencies	• Activities remain closer to where the work is needed • Ability to adapt different practices to unique requirements of a geography or department • Speed • Can pilot innovative solutions for potential application elsewhere in the organization
Problems When Taken Too Far	**Problems When Taken Too Far**
• Common processes do not meet the needs of different groups • Slow to change and innovate • Failure to listen to customers	• Duplication and higher costs • Failure to share innovative solutions with other groups that could benefit • Every group claims uniqueness

Kates and Galbraith (2007) recommend starting with the principle that activities should be decentralized, but then carefully examining which activities are managed by multiple units and thus could be good candidates for centralization. For those activities, ask yourself the following questions:

- What capabilities are essential to our success and need to be guided rather than left to chance?
- Where can we benefit from commonality?
- What are the few critical business and management processes that should be designed and maintained by the center?
- What information and knowledge needs to be shared?
- Where are we confusing the need for coordination with the response of centralization? (p. 164)

Division of Labor and Specialization

A third decision that leaders and design teams need to make with respect to the structure point of the star concerns the division of labor and degree of specialization of the various people and departments. Recall that in Chapter 1 we reviewed the work of F. W. Taylor (1911) who proposed the idea that an assembly process with five steps could be broken down so that each worker performed the same step before handing the next step off to a colleague. Each worker specialized in one step of the process and could build expertise and familiarity with what it took to do the task most effectively, with a performance and productivity gain resulting from that knowledge. With less specialization, a single worker might handle the entire end-to-end process alone. The benefits of less specialization and more variety are greater rewards and satisfaction with the job, less burnout due to repetition, and the ability to learn other job tasks (Staats & Gino, 2012).

A greater degree of specialization may result in more departments with a narrower scope of work. A lower degree of specialization (greater scope of job tasks or more generalists) will mean a broader scope of responsibility for the person and department, which may result in fewer departments. Consider the role of the human resources professional. In a small business, the same HR person may perform the activities of benefits contact, training specialist, organization development consultant, and employee relations adviser. Larger organizations permit the ability to add more specialists who focus their skills and time in each of these areas. Expertise and depth of knowledge can be developed.

When work-related uncertainty is high, "organizations must specialize enough to match task and/or environmental complexity" (Nadler & Tushman, 1988, p. 79). For example, in pharmaceutical research or high tech, where competitors are developing new scientific and technical capabilities, an organization may not be able to develop expertise in the new specialties with enough depth quickly enough using existing staff. Galbraith (2002) writes that in low to moderate skilled tasks, less specialization tends to occur as automation removes some of those tasks. For highly skilled task areas, on the other hand, greater specialization occurs because of the fast pace and complexity in today's research and development fields.

Signs to watch out for occur at both extremes. Underspecialization may simplify the organization, yet it can result in an inability to develop skill depth and respond appropriately to environmental or strategic threats. Overspecialization creates more roles and departments, and while it allows depth of knowledge and increased capabilities, it can also increase costs and create conflict between specialists that may have trouble finding common ground (Nadler & Tushman, 1997).

CONNECTING STRATEGY AND STRUCTURE: REVISITED

Let's return to our discussion of strategy to follow the link between strategy and structure. Several of the authors whose work we reviewed in Chapter 3 on generic strategies also have offered observations about the most appropriate organizational structure for those strategies. While these recommendations do not address all of the eight types of structure we have studied, the thought process to draw logical implications for structure is instructive. These are suggestions and hints at a starting point for a structure choice based on strategy archetypes.

The operational excellence strategy and the Defender strategy both emphasize the importance of maintaining a competitive advantage through cost efficiency. For the Defender, technological efficiency, a stable market, incremental growth plans, and deep expertise in a narrow domain all suggest that it benefits most from a functional structure (Miles & Snow, 1978). For operational excellence companies, Treacy and Wiersema (1995) suggest that process discipline and low-cost transactions can result from a structure with centralized functions.

Prospectors and product leadership companies excel at and succeed in their competitive environment when they are innovative, developing prototypes that they hope to bring to market. They demonstrate a "tendency toward [a] product structure with low division of labor and low degree of formalization" (Miles & Snow, 1978, p. 66). Product leaders also prefer "loose-knit structures" (Treacy & Wiersema, 1995, p. 90) that "allow resources to move toward the most promising opportunities" (p. 95). A greater degree of decentralization permits local resource utilization where experiments can be tried out. "The logical extension of this approach to structure is the product organization, in which all of the resources required to research, develop, produce, and market a related group of products are placed in a single, self-contained organizational subunit" (Miles & Snow, 1978, p. 62).

The Analyzer's choice to pursue both the stability of existing markets and to pursue flexible growth plans suggests both the efficiency and routine of a functional structure and the new product focus of a product structure. In other words, the appropriate structure type for the Analyzer is a matrix. Miles and Snow (1978) share an example of an Analyzer company whose functional and product groups operated independently for existing products but in a highly matrixed collaborative structure for new products.

For Treacy and Wiersema's (1995) customer intimacy strategy, structural components suggested include "entrepreneurial client teams" and "high skills in the field" implying decentralized customer/market or front–back hybrid structures. They suggest that some highly customer-intimate companies can offer a broad range of services through network structures, since "the strength of these companies lies not in what they own, but in what they know and how they coordinate expertise to deliver solutions" (Treacy & Wiersema, 1995, p. 137).

SUMMARY

The choice of organizational structure may be the most visible aspect of the design. By making a structure choice, the design team and leadership are signaling to the organization what it considers to be one of the most dominant strategic priorities, and the lens through which decisions should be made, resources should be allocated, and power should be distributed. We have reviewed eight of the most common types of organizational structure (functional, product, geography, customer/market, process, network, front–back, and matrix), though in practice there are many combinations and variations of these options. All structures offer advantages and all come with consequences so the designer must be aware of the implications of the choice. Three additional structure considerations include span of control, centralization, and specialization of job roles, which have consequences for the number of managers and expected management style, where power is located, and the division of responsibility in each department.

Choice of structure should be driven by the strategy and the required organizational capabilities (design criteria) needed to be successful. Creating departments to focus on strategic outcomes also creates barriers between those same departments. What is required to solve the disadvantages of organizational structure and cross-organizational barriers is the design of lateral capability, the design issue we will turn to in the next chapter.

QUESTIONS FOR DISCUSSION

1. Reflect on an organization structure that you have experienced. Do the advantages and disadvantages of that structure presented in this chapter resonate with your experience? What additional advantages or disadvantages would you add to Table 4.1?
2. We have discussed at length the idea that the organization's strategy needs to be reflected in or translated to its structure. What happens when the structure is inconsistent with the strategy? Can you imagine an example of how that might happen? What symptoms might you see as an employee or leader in that organization of an inconsistent link between strategy and structure?
3. Many of the structure decisions presented in this chapter follow trends, where the pendulum might swing from one extreme to the other, such as from narrow to wide span of control or from centralization to decentralization. Why do you think this is the case? Have you seen this pendulum swing happen in your own experience?

FOR FURTHER READING

Anand, N., & Daft, R. L. (2007). What is the right organization design? *Organizational Dynamics, 36*, 329–344.

Davis, S. M., & Lawrence, P. R. (1977). *Matrix*. Reading, MA: Addison-Wesley.

Galbraith, J. R., Downey, D., & Kates, A. (2002). *Designing dynamic organizations*. New York, NY: AMACOM.

Kates, A., & Galbraith, J. R. (2007). *Designing your organization: Using the star model to solve 5 critical design challenges*. San Francisco, CA: Jossey-Bass.

Miles, R. E., & Snow, C. C. (1986). Organizations: New concepts for new forms. *California Management Review, 28*, 62–73.

Miles, R. E., Snow, C. C., Fjeldstad, Ø. D., Miles, G., & Lettl, C. (2010). Designing organizations to meet 21st-century opportunities and challenges. *Organizational Dynamics, 39*, 93–103.

Mintzberg, H. (1979). *The structuring of organizations*. Englewood Cliffs, NJ: Prentice-Hall.

EXERCISES

1. From Strategy to Structure

Read the profiles of the organizations below. Explain what you think is (or should be) the company's strategy. What might be on the top of their list for design criteria? How might you structure this organization using one of the designs covered in this chapter? Why?

Organization A

We are a national network of grand piano tuners, specializing in the tuning, maintenance, and repair of high-end performance instruments (at universities, concert halls, churches, etc.). There aren't that many of us around these days, of course, and we've struggled in the last few years, since this tends to be a limited market.

Organization B

We provide online computer training courses to the "older generation" who are still learning how to use their laptops. We offer courses in basic word processing, e-mail, and Internet browsing, but also more advanced courses in PowerPoint, Excel, and Photoshop. We also have a small set of courses delivered here in the state at different recreation centers and senior centers.

Organization C

We are one of the fastest growing small businesses in the country—we provide fitness programs for kids. Now that school districts are cutting their physical education programs and camps are too expensive, parents turn to us for after-school programs to keep their kids up and moving. We have a franchise model, so we develop and design the programs and then work with the franchisee to get the program running.

Organization D

We are a third-party producer of video games for various platforms. We have developers that work on the Nintendo Wii, Nintendo DS, the Xbox, the Sony PlayStation, and more. Each of these is a unique skill area (developers for the Wii and DS don't know how to develop for the Xbox, for example). We're now expanding into the online gaming area as well. To be successful, we need to differentiate ourselves from the rest of the market and continually be first to market in providing innovative video games.

2. Structure Pros and Cons

Imagine that you are attending a friend's holiday party and you meet a fellow party guest who describes the organizational structure of his or her department. For each party guest that you meet, try to

a. identify the organizational structure (or structures) being described. Try to sketch it out on an imaginary cocktail napkin.

b. explain to your fellow guest what you think are the likely problems that the organization suffers from based on what you now know about the advantages and disadvantages of organizational structure choices. Begin your response with "It sounds like you are organized in a ______ structure. You are probably very successful in doing ______. I would imagine that you have challenges with ______."

Party Guest 1

"I am the vice president of an internal IT support group. We support the rest of the company with its IT development needs. So, if someone needs a customized application, a new website, or some IT work done, they call us. We have a group of business analysts assigned to support each function in the company (sales, services, product development, HR, and so on). These internal customers are very demanding and have unique needs. Our analysts work to understand their business, and they scope the projects based on their understanding of the outcomes. Then they hand off the projects with the scope document to the project management group to lead. The PM has the scope document from the customer, and works to form a team from the applications, website, and quality and test groups to deliver the customer's request. The business analyst still maintains the primary relationship with the customer, so if the scope changes, the timeline can't be delivered, or the customer isn't happy, the business analyst plays the primary liaison role."

Party Guest 2

"I lead a financial services consulting business in the midwestern United States. We currently have 22 on-site consulting operations centers that we lease inside chain discount stores, but we also have a national for-fee telephone service where we can help customers over the phone. The way it works is that we help consumers on a walk-in basis for a fee with setting up and managing investment accounts, financial planning, and doing tax returns. We also have a subscription service where consumers can buy hourly access to consulting services via a 1–800 number to get basic questions answered, such as 'What's the difference between different kinds of retirement accounts?' and 'Do I qualify for a certain tax deduction?'"

Party Guest 3

"We are the sales organization for a national manufacturer and installer of solar energy products. I have five sales leads reporting to me representing our four different sales geographies, plus a separate group for federal accounts, since those take government clearance and government customers tend to have special needs. Each region is usually broken down into subregions (for the East, for example, they have a territory representing the upper East consisting of Maine, New Hampshire, Vermont, a mid-Atlantic region of Virginia and Maryland, and so on). Each region has its own local human resources, administration, and finance support, though all regions use the same order management system to place customer orders."

Party Guest 4

"I'm the head of our quality division. Reporting to me are several groups. First, there are five leaders who run our test engineering programs, making sure that what comes out of manufacturing meets the specs that we have for our products. There is also a training group that conducts all of our safety and quality training for our manufacturing division. I also have a policy group that determines all of our quality policies and creates documentation and standards for our processes. They also lead our compliance activities when we have to create reports for ISO 14001 certification or EWRA (Electronic Waste and Recycling Act). Last, I have a machinery division that creates the tools that the test engineers use to test our products in the final test stages."

CHAPTER 5

PROCESSES AND LATERAL CAPABILITY

Learning Objectives

In this chapter you will learn

- Why lateral capability is important (and difficult).
- The forms of lateral capability and their advantages and disadvantages.
- How to decide which form of lateral capability to implement in a design.
- How governance models and decision processes enhance collaboration.

In 1943, new Disney employees were provided with an employee handbook titled *The Ropes at Disney's*. In addition to a discussion of holidays, vacation time, sick leave, and absences, the handbook contained a unique organizational chart to explain how the organization worked.

Instead of visually depicting the formal hierarchy with its common pyramid shape as in a traditional organizational chart, it graphically displayed how departments worked together in the production of a Disney film (see Figure 5.1). This chart, and others of the era, helped employees understand in graphical form and written narrative not only the roles and responsibilities of the various departments, but how they interacted (Watts, 2001). A note at the bottom of the chart reads, "This chart designates operations and not authorities." In other words, the chart depicted a flow of how work activities, information, and communication passed between different departments, which was seen as distinct from the hierarchical authority and management structure within those departments. The Disney chart highlights, in brief, what is meant by the processes and lateral capability point of the STAR model.

To underscore the importance of this point of the STAR, consider these examples:

- In 2009, during the financial crisis, many homeowners took advantage of a government program designed to help them with their mortgage payments if they qualified. Banks created internal departments to work directly with borrowers to reduce their mortgage premiums and allow homeowners to stay in their homes. However, those departments failed to coordinate with the foreclosure divisions inside the same bank. Witnessing the subsequent reduced payments from borrowers, the foreclosure divisions began seizing the same homes whose owners were participating in the bank's loan revision program (Tett, 2015).

Figure 5.1 Organizational Chart From *The Ropes at Disney's* (1943)

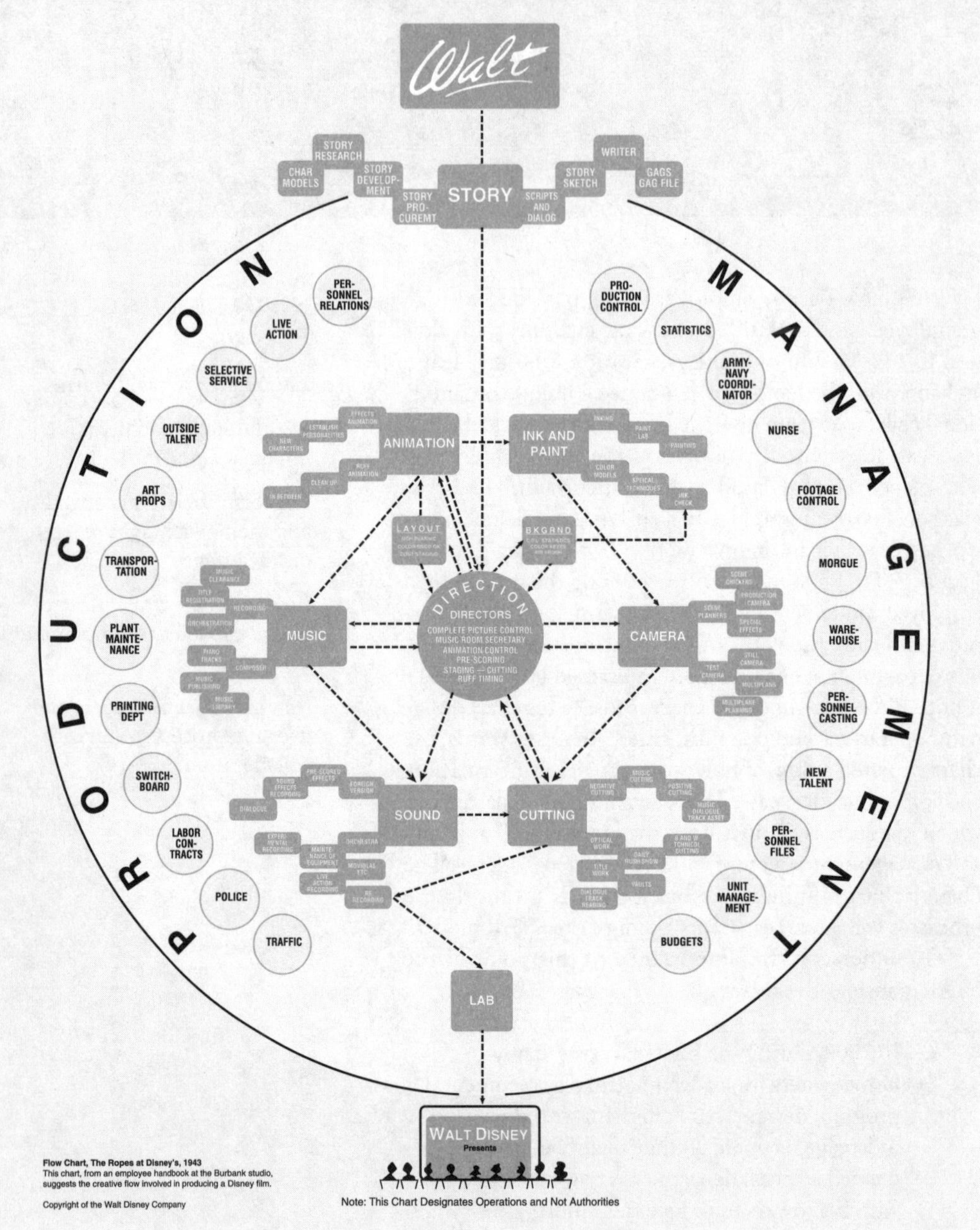

Source: © Disney. Used by permission.

- At Ford, intercompany conflict between finance and engineering functions resulted in delays in upgrading the profitable Lincoln Town Car since finance would not permit engineering to design upgrades that had an increase in cost. The Ford Focus redesign in 2003 highlighted poor coordination between the North America division (where only minor updates were made to the Focus) and Europe (where a new design was developed), resulting in the inability to gain economies of scale (A. Taylor, 2006).

- Having reorganized nine times in 15 years (from 1994 to 2009), Sony has divested itself of unsuccessful lines of business, laid off thousands of employees, and closed a majority of its stores. In part, this was the result of internal divisions not collaborating with one another, including the Walkman division and the Vaio computing division, which worked on separate solutions to allow consumers to download music. The Sony Music Entertainment division refused to help with the projects, afraid for the impact on revenues from compact discs (Dhillon & Gupta, 2015; Tett, 2015).
- In January 2018, Walmart proudly announced that it would raise its minimum wage and give employees a bonus of up to $1,000 due to benefits from a lower corporate tax rate. Distracting from the positive news were scathing reports on social media that Walmart-owned Sam's Club quietly intended to close 63 stores, potentially putting more than 9,000 employees out of work. "Walmart representative Greg Hitt told CNNMoney that the company did not intend to make both announcements on the same day. 'The tax issue has been a floating target for some time, in terms of when we would actually discuss it,' he said. 'Both of those actions or announcements originated in different parts of the business.'" (Wiener-Bronner & Sanicola, 2018).

In each of these examples, the organization's performance suffers as a result of insufficient lateral capability, or poor cross-department collaboration. The barriers created in the structure become insurmountable to coordination even where it is needed most, to the detriment of both the organization and its customers.

As we saw in Chapter 4, designers choose structural groupings to encourage collaboration among a group of colleagues who have the same mission or set of strategic goals. However, even though "organizations group positions to minimize coordination costs" (J. D. Thompson, 1967, p. 57) by creating structural departments to accomplish strategic objectives, the barriers to collaboration between those same groups can be significant. At worst, the organization falls into the trap of allowing the groupings to become "silos" and "stovepipes." In short, we have taken the pieces apart, and now it is time to put them back together.

In this chapter, we will examine the benefits and costs of developing lateral capability, and we will learn what forms of lateral capability help to address the disadvantages of the structure point covered in Chapter 4. We will look at symptoms of underdeveloped and overdeveloped lateral capability and understand how the designer should balance which forms to choose. Finally, we will look at how governance mechanisms and clear decision practices can result in more effective processes and greater lateral capability.

LATERAL CAPABILITY: THE HORIZONTAL ORGANIZATION

It is widely recognized that the vertical structure is unable to deal with a high amount of complexity and speed of change. Emphasis on the vertical hierarchy alone creates numerous problems in managing the organization (Ostroff, 1999, p. 6):

- Its internal focus on functional goals rather than an outward-looking concentration on delivering value and winning customers
- The loss of important information as knowledge travels up and down the multiple levels and across the functional departments
- The fragmentation of performance objectives brought about by a multitude of distinct and fragmented functional goals
- The added expense involved in coordinating the overly fragmented work and departments
- The stifling of creativity and initiative of workers at lower levels

Duplication of effort, fragmentation, and lack of information sharing are problems that are unlikely to be worked out naturally unless designers make efforts to enhance lateral capability and support it through other mechanisms (such as the rewards and people points of the star). While many organizations might prefer to leave lateral capability to chance, assuming that people will naturally figure out what coordination is needed, there are good reasons to intentionally design lateral capability into the organization.

Lateral capability is defined as "information and decision processes that coordinate activities spread out across different organizational units, providing mechanisms for decentralizing general management decisions" (Galbraith, 2002, p. 38). Another way of describing lateral capability is to think of it as the horizontal organization, whereas the formal structure is the vertical organization (see Figure 5.2). The structure "provides the clarity and sense of stability that people need in order to function in large organizations" (Galbraith, Downey, & Kates, 2002, p. 136) through the process of grouping around a common mission and lens. Lateral capability consists of the coordinating mechanisms for those people and groups to work collaboratively across departmental boundaries.

Rather than having all decisions work their way up through the vertical structure to be addressed by the senior management team, lateral capability practices encourage coordination throughout the structure.

> In lateral organizations, personal relationships and informal contacts become much more powerful than formal structures and reward systems for achieving the organization's goals. . . . People closest to the decision who have to live with the consequences of their decision are empowered to make the decision. . . . Interdisciplinary collaboration on projects mandates that traditional departmental lines become blurred. Loosening horizontal boundaries places greater emphasis on processes, and requires improved communication, leadership, and resolution of turf issues. (Joyce, McGee, & Slocum, 1997, pp. 22–23)

Figure 5.2 Structure and Lateral Capability

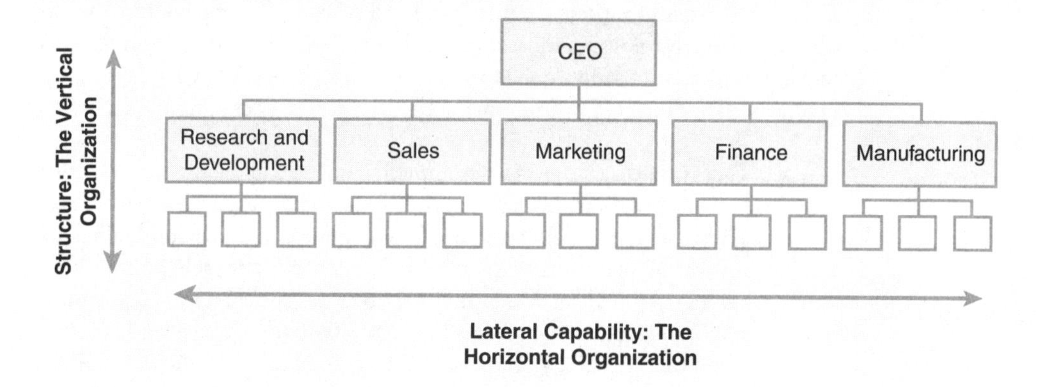

Recall the classic Lawrence and Lorsch (1967) study discussed in Chapter 1, where the authors found that organizations had to balance differentiation, or the separation of the organization's tasks into different departments, with integration, or the connection and coordination between those units. They argued that different organizations have different integration needs. In some organizations, lateral capability is unnecessary. For example, the Carlisle companies, a global conglomerate with diversified divisions in food service and construction materials products, may have little need to integrate common processes in each unique division.

In many organizations, however, close coordination is required to introduce new products and effectively and consistently market a global brand message. More than 50 years ago, J. D. Thompson (1967) observed that "positions or components of complex organizations are not unidimensional" and that "their components serve different purposes for the larger organization, they employ several processes, they frequently serve more than one clientele, and for the most part they are geographically extended" (p. 57). Consider also that

- customers buy products from multiple divisions in multiple geographies;
- customers speak to employees in different divisions;
- geographic units experience similar problems that need to be resolved the same way around the world;
- common or core processes cut across several functions.

Galbraith (2002) noted that lateral capability is increasingly required when organizations face a diversity and variety of tasks, a rapidly changing environment, a high degree of interdependence among functional units, common technology platforms, and requirements for faster cycle time and speed across the organization. All of these factors point to the importance of developing lateral capability in an organization's design.

Why Developing Lateral Capability Is So Difficult

Despite the obvious need for lateral capability, developing it can be difficult. Enhancing an organization's lateral capability can be challenging because the effort can run up against power, politics, and turf wars that have become commonplace in many organizations. The collaborative behavior advocated by lateral capability practices is counteracted by internal competitive forces, including the following:

- **Turf wars** that develop when limited resources and a pressure on costs encourage departments to carefully guard what resources they have. They may be suspicious of change and engage in destructive games such as withholding information from other departments, self-promoting, sabotage, or scapegoating other departments (Buchanan & Badham, 2008). Indeed, Buchanan and Badham (2008) report on a study that found that 89 percent of managers agreed that those "who use political tactics should expect to have similar tactics used against them . . . implying an attitude of 'you stab my back, I'll stab yours'" (p. 25).
- **Stronger identification** with one's own internal group, also called the "enemy within syndrome" (Ashkenas, Ulrich, Jick, & Kerr, 2002), where internal departments see other units as the enemy instead of the external competition.
- **Rewards** for department goal achievement versus corporate goal achievement. These can encourage leaders to seek gains for their local function at the expense of other departments and thus the overall company.
- **Mistrust** of other groups that creates barriers to collective action. The sales organization predicts how many of a given product it will sell next quarter, but when the planning organization finalizes the plan to tell manufacturing what to build, it changes the numbers. Manufacturing then changes the numbers again, preferring to rely on its own estimates.

Benefits and Costs of Lateral Capability

When done well, however, organizations can experience a number of areas of improved performance as a result. There are several benefits of enhancing lateral capability, summarized in Figure 5.3:

1. **More decisions.** "The lateral organization increases the capacity of the entire organization to make more decisions more often" (Galbraith, 1994, p. 6). Teams can be given the authority to manage some activities themselves within boundaries without approval from senior management, allowing them to alter activities as necessary when they are empowered to do so.
2. **Increase in senior management time.** No longer are the number of decisions to be made conditional on the available time of senior management to make them. The time of senior management is freed up to address different concerns.
3. **Faster and better decisions.** Decisions can be faster when they are made at the local level by knowledgeable employees who can address problems immediately with the most up-to-date information and data.

Figure 5.3 Benefits and Costs of Lateral Capability

Benefits
Costs
More decisions
Increase in senior management time
Faster and better decisions
Flexibility and adaptability
Successfully deal with complexity
Individual employee benefits
Innovation
Employee time
Increased conflict
Personal costs

They can use their skills to solve problems instead of dedicating time to summarizing the issue for higher-level management.

4. **Flexibility and adaptability**. Not only are the decisions often better as a result, but so is "the organization's ability to adapt to a dynamic environment" (Joyce, et al., 1997, p. 3). The lateral organization can often be changed and adapted more quickly to needs than a large-scale restructuring. A project team can be quickly created and deployed to solve a customer's problem and then disbanded or re-formed at a different time on a different problem.

5. **Successfully deal with complexity**. Organizations often have a complex mix of different products and services, geographies, and customer types with a complex array of activities required to manage them. By implementing lateral capability, designers can "increase the capability of their organization to handle the high information-processing requirements of such diverse activities" (Joyce et al., 1997, p. 3). Thus, "the lateral organization allows the resources of the entire organization to be marshaled to focus on these various dimensions" (Galbraith, 1994, p. 7).

6. **Individual employee benefits**. Individual motivation and learning can increase from lateral connections. When employees are empowered to decide and implement the decision on their own, they are often more engaged in their work and motivated for success. When employees collaborate with others who have a different perspective because they work in a different division, they see a problem or decision through another lens and take on a broader general-management perspective which increases personal learning.

7. **Innovation**. Organizational innovation can be another benefit of lateral capability. As managers in functional units interact with managers of customer-facing units, "problems will be discussed, best practices shared, and new ideas generated" (Simons, 2005, p. 118). They may come up with a better solution to problems than either could have come up with alone.

Nevertheless, such benefits also come with added costs:

1. **Employee time**. Employees will spend additional time in meetings and conversations with colleagues in different divisions. They will need to develop a common language and terminology, decision-making

practices, and negotiate norms and working agreements. This time "is time not spent with customers or suppliers or developing new members" (Galbraith, 1994, p. 8).

2. **Increased conflict.** As Walker and Lorsch (1968) observed, "The more two functional specialists or their units differ in their patterns of behavior, the more difficult it is to bring about integration between them. Nevertheless . . . achievement of both differentiation and integration is essential if organizations are to perform effectively" (p. 131). Employees representing different functions will have different perspectives that can result in conflict. If they are unable to resolve the conflict, the benefits of increased innovation and speed are unlikely to be achieved.

3. **Personal costs.** Joyce, McGee, and Slocum (1997) found that participation in challenging lateral relationships increased an employee's stress, caused feelings of role overload, and resulted in loss of commitment. Personal and politically motivated conflict, the challenges of dual reporting relationships, ineffective meetings, the challenges in sharing resources, and barriers to performing one's job were all personal costs identified in their study.

FORMS OF LATERAL CAPABILITY

Forms of lateral capability vary widely. "Some are simple, obvious, and inexpensive. Others are more sophisticated and costly and also require more design attention" (Galbraith, 1977, p. 112). They also differ significantly in the investment required and value gained. Some can be encouraged easily because they tend to come naturally to employees whereas others require implementation work. Here we will review the five types of lateral capability illustrated in Figure 5.4.

Networks

Much of the communication and interaction in organizations does not always follow the formal vertical structure or chain of command. Instead, informal communication provides an important channel for getting work done. Indeed, management scholar Chester Barnard wrote in 1938 that "informal organization gives rise to formal organizations" (p. 123), and Mintzberg (1979) concluded that "centers of power exist that are not officially recognized; rich networks of informal communication supplement and sometimes circumvent the regulated channels; and decisions processes flow through the organization independent of the regulated system" (p. 46). When new employees are "learning the ropes," they are often learning about the informal organization network. Building the new employee's network contributes to understanding how to get work done in ways that supplement the formal structure, learning who to contact, how to get information, and how to participate in the social fabric of the organization. This point is graphically displayed in Figure 5.5.

Networks are informal and voluntary communication patterns that can facilitate information sharing across department boundaries by exposing members of one group to those in another. Imagine making an acquaintance in another division at a training program or office party, then later needing a contact in that division to help solve a problem you are experiencing. This is such a natural occurrence in so many organizations that organization designers Goold and Campbell

Figure 5.4 Continuum of Lateral Capability

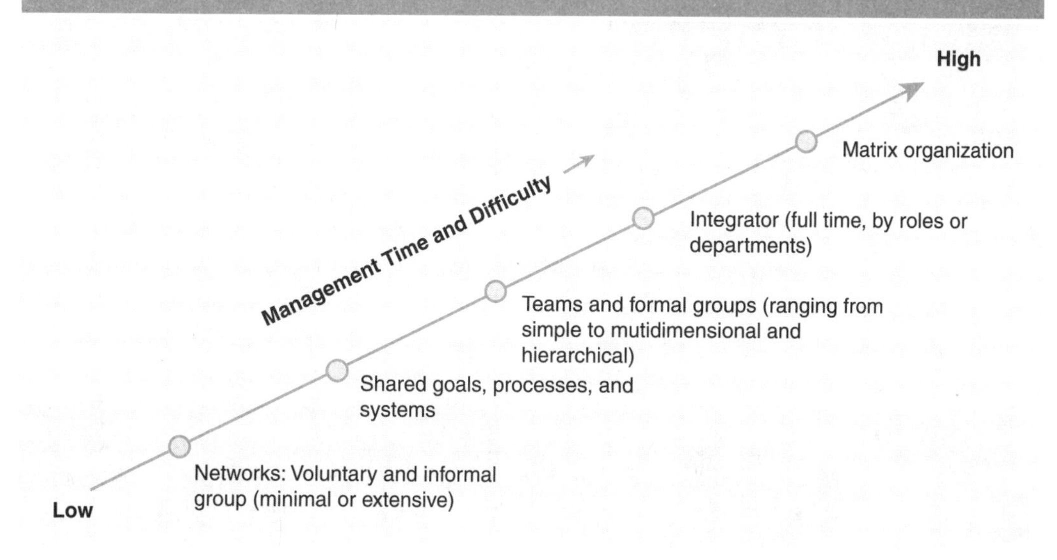

Source: Adapted from Galbraith, J. R. (2008). Organization design. In T. G. Cummings (Ed.), *Handbook of organization development* (pp. 325–352). Thousand Oaks, CA: SAGE, p. 331.

(2002) write that they prefer to design organizations with fewer rules and less hierarchy and more opportunities for self-managed networking. Galbraith (1977) refers to this mechanism of coordination simply as "direct contact."

Charan (1991) writes that networks can create a "small company inside the large company" (p. 105). In some of the cases Charan observed during his research, the network was a formally identified grouping of managers representing functions across the company and hierarchy responsible for key strategic outcomes. In other cases, networks were informal. In both cases, successful networks rely on social architecture, trust, and influence as forms of power instead of formal hierarchy and authority. Networks may help Barbara in San Francisco to contact Amanda in London to learn how another geography has solved a problem. However, the voluntary nature of the relationship does not necessarily mean that Barbara must implement the same solution.

Cultivating Networks

Networks are so critical to organizational functioning that some are turning to social network analysis (also called organizational network analysis) to understand and actively manage the networks in their organizations. Network analysis in organizations has had a longer history in the academic literature (Tichy & Fombrun, 1979) but more recently has become of interest to practitioners such as executives and human resources professionals (Cross, Kase, Kilduff, & King, 2013). Cross, Dowling, Gerbasi, Gulas, and Thomas (2010), reporting on a study of network analysis in an information technology organization, stated that the data from the analysis were used to identify highly connected and overloaded contributors (with whom many people consulted) along with different subgroups across different geographies. Since the goal was to increase cross-geography collaboration, they were also able to identify underutilized cross-functional coordination channels.

Figure 5.5 Hierarchical Perspective versus Network Perspective

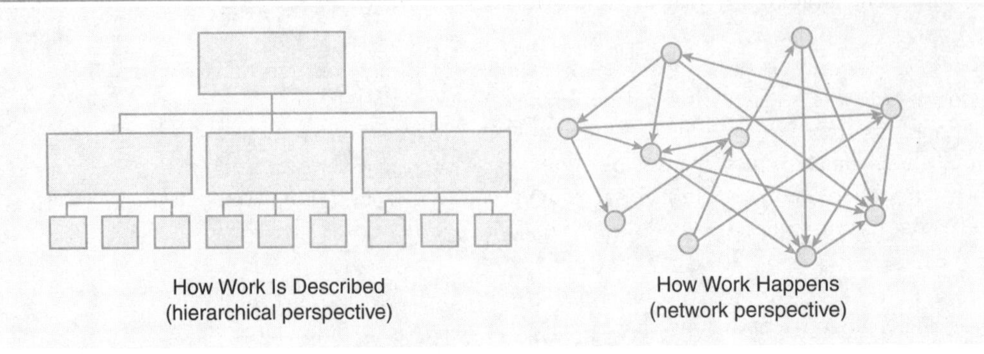

Some people naturally gravitate to informal roles where they have the opportunity to build and manage their networks. Burström and Jacobsson (2011) have coined the term *glue people* to describe those with no formal authority or position but who have a personal commitment to facilitate communication across the organization. As we will see later with formally defined integrative roles, such liaison positions are important to cross-functional collaboration. However, they do not need to be formal positions and often can be an important resource to an organization's success. Glue people willingly adopt these tasks based solely on their personal commitment to connecting people. When they are formal positions, such liaison roles are often called "boundary spanning roles," or a defined point of contact in one division for the purpose of communication with another.

Networks are often easier when employees are located in the same building or floor. More organizations are taking this into consideration by redesigning physical spaces to encourage collaboration. They are designing fewer fixed, high wall offices or cubicles and creating more spaces that can be reconfigured as a spontaneous meeting takes shape. Software developers at 3M respond positively to the "collaborative spirit and energy in an open area," remarking that it is "wonderful in encouraging impromptu collaboration" (Cohn, 2010, p. 413). Some organizations create separate work zones for collaboration and quieter areas for individual work and social activities. Several factors are critical to the success of these designs, researchers have found, including the ability to also have private conversations and support from senior leaders that such impromptu meetings are not wasted social time but important for the accomplishment of work (Fayard & Weeks, 2011).

Finding opportunities for face-to-face collaboration can be a challenge in today's virtual global organization and where more people are making the choice to work part-time, work flexible hours, or telecommute. Instead of relying on networks to naturally form, Galbraith, Downey, and Kates (2002) highlight a number of ways that organizations can purposefully cultivate networks, including job rotations, training programs, communities of practice, and electronic social networks.

Job Rotation Programs. Even short rotation periods of weeks or months can "be an effective technique to build awareness of the issues faced by employees in different units" (Simons, 2005, p. 119). Indeed, studies have found that managers who have worked in different divisions have a larger network and tend to communicate to a larger number of colleagues outside their division than those who have not experienced such rotation opportunities (Galbraith, 1977). Galbraith (2002) has called rotations "the most powerful tool of the organization designer" (p. 48) in encouraging the growth of networks.

Training. Training programs that include members from different functions and geographies can foster networks and encourage people to meet who may never have had the opportunity. Leadership development programs where managers engage in simulations can allow participants to see how other leaders in other situations solve problems differently. They can share views of the company from their different vantage points, contributing to each leader's broader knowledge of the organization.

Communities of Practice. Communities of practice are "groups of people informally bound together by shared expertise and passion for a joint enterprise" (Wenger & Snyder, 2000, p. 139). Members are generally self-selected and participation is voluntary. A community of practice might consist of a group of marketing representatives who work in different groups but get together over lunch for a brown-bag talk by a member or to share what they are working on. They are not teams because there is no specific task to be achieved and there is no formal nomination or assignment process to participate. Instead, they are a forum for exchanging information among colleagues, helping one another solve problems, providing opportunities for informal peer review and feedback, and keeping up-to-date on professional trends. In some organizations where communities are encouraged, they can contribute to the strategy of the business when members can pool information across different lines.

Wenger and Snyder (2000) write that communities of practice can have a number of benefits, including rapid problem solving, sharing best practices, development of professional skills, and recruitment and retention of talent. Communities of practice are likely to form voluntarily and spontaneously in most organizations, but their development can also be encouraged and cultivated (Wenger, McDermott, & Snyder, 2002). Communities frequently have a coordinator who communicates with members and brings them together. They work best when they are organic and change as needed according to the energy of members.

Electronic Social Networks. Some organizations provide collaborative technology platforms (CTP) where people can share ideas in an asynchronous discussion board and related files. They can be simple shared file systems where employees can post presentations they have given or financial models that may be of use to others. Others are more complex, allowing employees to have the ability to interact and hold online conversations as they would on Facebook or Twitter.

> Rather than having the content curated by a website editor or database manager, excellent CTPs allow users to add or modify content themselves. They can comment on or respond to others' posts, rate or recommend existing content (e.g., by clicking the "like" button), download and distribute materials, and interact in real time. (Gardner, 2016, p. 176)

Employees can use these systems to find other experts and reach a knowledgeable person more quickly. Salespeople can locate others who have information about a current or potential client. Service engineers can learn which customer problems have already been solved.

These are different from other kinds of technology systems that connect people (discussed below) because they are voluntary. One danger is that employees may not use it or see the value in participating. Some companies have found great success, however, in designing systems that have high value for users and in encouraging usage through advocates and sponsors. Consulting firm PwC implemented such a system called "Spark," and now finds that more than 95 percent of employees have used the system within the last 90 days (Gardner, 2016).

Advantages and Disadvantages. Networks can encourage innovation, knowledge sharing, and a broader organizational perspective. Because they are ubiquitous but also voluntary, employees can build and maintain networks as they prefer. They are generally not costly to implement or support (although electronic social networks may have a cost), and networks can be personally and professionally rewarding for employees. As a device for achieving the strategy, however, networks may not be robust enough mechanisms for coordination. An auspicious chance meeting of a knowledgeable colleague in the hallway might save an employee time in figuring out an internal process, but chance meetings are too random to rely upon when determining which new features should be added to the next generation of a product line or how to respond to a competitor's recent move.

Shared Goals, Processes, and Systems

A second set of mechanisms to connect departments consists of shared goals, common processes that cut across divisions, and common information technology systems to which the groups contribute.

Shared or Superordinate Goals. If manufacturing, order delivery, and installation support all have the same goal to contribute to 98 percent on-time delivery of a customer order, they will be more likely to coordinate in the service of that goal. The goal should be an overarching one to which each group can contribute. Each group may have unique actions that help to achieve the goal, such as a manufacturing goal to develop "on-demand" manufacturing capabilities that speed cycle time, or an order delivery goal that raises delivery quality to prevent time-consuming rework.

Even more effective to bring groups together are superordinate goals. A superordinate goal is one that is "*urgent*, *compelling*, and highly appealing for *all* groups involved" (Sherif, 1979, p. 261) and is "beyond the resources and efforts of one group alone" to accomplish (Johnson & Lewicki, 1969, p. 10). That is, it is often not enough for the goal to simply be shared—it must be one that each group could not reach if it were to try to do so alone. Conflict is reduced when teams come together in a cooperative context to reach a goal that is important to them, and when team members witness members of the other team working hard on an interdependent task.

Lateral Processes. A lateral process is a key organizational process that crosses major divisions. Management practices are included here, including those such as planning and budgeting, where resources are allocated to different groups. Many designers recommend concentrating on the three to five core processes that serve customers and create the most value for the company. Consider a process such as new product design, which might involve employees from service, sales, marketing, operations, and research and development. In Chapter 4, we reviewed the structural version of a process-based organization, where organizational units were formally structured under core processes. Many organizations choose not to take process focus to this extreme, preferring instead to develop "a process-based model simply by imposing process management as an additional dimension on top of the existing functional or product dimension" (Angelo, Alessandro, Massimo, & Davide, 2010, p. 51). In this alternative, processes become a form of lateral capability added onto other structure types in order to connect the structural units.

One of the most challenging aspects of identifying lateral processes is deciding on their boundaries, because the starting and ending points of processes are not always clear. Some organizations use standard process models designed by an industry consortium, such as the Supply Chain Operations Reference (SCOR) model, which organizes supply chain activity by the steps of plan, source, make, deliver, and return (Bolstorff & Rosenbaum, 2012). Examining these standard models can have the benefit of ensuring that process descriptions are complete and no step is overlooked. In addition, industry standard models often allow an organization to benchmark its performance against comparative organizations.

Typically, once the organization's key processes are identified, each is led by a process owner who "is responsible for planning and controlling functions regarding the governing" of the process, including "setting goals and expectations, identifying, formalizing, and documenting work processes, providing resources, and implementing processes" (Nesheim, 2011, p. 110). Process owners may be responsible for measuring the quality of the process and making necessary process changes to ensure the quality, quantity, or timeliness of the output. Galbraith et al. (2002) advocate mapping out lateral processes as a way of clarifying handoffs and key interfaces between departments. Process maps contain descriptions of who is involved, decisions to be made, and key performance indicators (KPI) that focus process owners on the important metrics.

Information Technology as a Coordinating Mechanism. Technology can also connect departments. Enterprise Resource Planning (ERP) systems integrate different functions such as finance, human resources, and manufacturing. Where formerly data about a manufacturing plan, new orders, inventory levels, back orders, and purchasing contracts existed in separate department systems, an ERP system integrates that data into a single planning system accessible to multiple departments. Customer Relationship Management (CRM) software can integrate sales and customer support by providing information about customer contacts and addresses, which products or services they have ordered, billing information, and the customer's most recent service calls. Human resources systems can contain knowledge about performance reviews, salary data, past positions and promotions as well as information accessible to others in the organization such as areas of expertise, languages spoken, and certifications.

Advantages and Disadvantages. Processes, goals, and technology add another level of formality that can help managers and employees see how they are connected. Employees can see a tie between the process step they engage in and the value that is delivered to the customer. With shared goals, no group can profit at the expense of another, encouraging groups to see the shared impact of their work. Process mapping and technology implementations can be time consuming and costly, however, and thus are best for the organization's few core processes. Finally, there can be a tendency for the process or the technology to direct the work rather than the other way around, and people may find themselves at the mercy of a required process or technology step that adds no value to customers.

Teams

Teams are arguably the most common form of lateral capability in use today. Indeed, some have observed that "the effective functioning of groups and teams is central to the effective functioning of organizations" (Woodman & Pasmore, 2002, p. 164). Carl Larson and Frank LaFasto (1989) explain that "a team has two or more people; it has a specific performance objective or recognizable goal to be attained; and coordination of activity among the members of the team is required for the attainment of the team goal or objective" (p. 19). A product sales team, with representatives from each geography, can meet regularly to share best practices and solve problems they have in common related to selling a particular product.

For example, a set of geographic sales divisions may decide to structure themselves in a mirror image (Galbraith, 2002) for consistency and to simplify the lateral connections between groups. Each division may have a person focusing on sales contracts, sales training, and sales compensation (see Figure 5.6). To facilitate information sharing and consistent practices and procedures, they form a team made up of the members of the other divisions. The global sales contracts team may have no manager, but one of the members may take responsibility for scheduling meetings, facilitating problem resolution, or escalating problems that the team cannot solve on its own (e.g., a team lead). Notice that the geographic structure is chosen as the main structure type, with different work functions beneath that. The functions become the basis for the teams, but not all functions will need a team. Instead, their connection might be addressed with a different form of lateral capability.

Cross-Functional Teams

Cross-functional teams are a response to the increasing complexity of operations in many organizations and the demand for rapid pace, focus, and problem solving (Parker, 1994). A cross-functional team is "a small collection of individuals from diverse functional specializations within the organization" (Webber, 2002, p. 201). Members are not usually part of the same department but represent varied departments, units, or geographies, and they are often brought together for a defined period to work on a specified project or problem. Team members usually report to a project team leader but also report to a functional unit "home" manager who directs their day-to-day work.

The same benefits of implementing cross-functional teams are also its major challenges. First, "functional diversity" of membership brings multiple perspectives together to enhance a team's knowledge and problem-solving ability (Webber, 2002), yet it also means that teams can have trouble communicating and finding common ground as team meetings become organizationally "multicultural" experiences (Proehl, 1996). Members may use different points of reference or vocabularies and exhibit different values. Second, cross-functional teams can have the benefit of including members who can be brought together for a short time to work on a project and then disband. A task force (or ad hoc team) is a specific kind of team, perhaps called together for a single purpose and a short period, maybe even self-directed without a manager to guide the work of the team. Yet dedication

Figure 5.6 Teams Formed From Mirror Image Departments

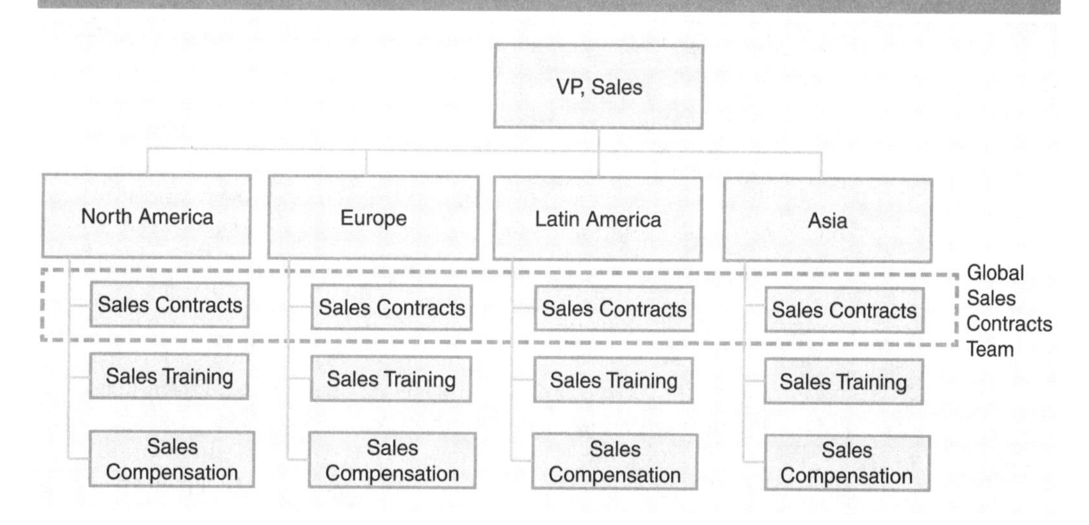

of time can vary among organizational members, causing team conflicts and mismatched understandings of commitment to the team. This is "largely because the projects are not directly related to the members' immediate work, and members have many competing responsibilities and varying degrees of immediate management support for participating in organizational initiatives" (Proehl, 1996, p. 7).

Studies of cross-functional team success point to the need to address some of these common challenges early on in the formation of a cross-functional team. Leaders can develop a common team mission and identity in the early stages so that team members who represent multiple functional areas can feel a common sense of belonging, commitment, and accountability to the success of the cross-functional team. Parker (1994) specifically recommends clear, overarching team goals to reduce ambiguity and confusion about the team's authority and responsibility. Webber (2002) recommends both training for team leaders and team leaders establishing working relationships early with functional managers to explicitly negotiate time expectations for those members working on the team, and to agree on a performance appraisal and rewards process.

Much work has been done by researchers to identify the characteristics that distinguish high-performing, effective teams. In an extensive survey of different types of teams in different types of organizational environments and circumstances, Carl Larson and Frank LaFasto (1989) conducted detailed interviews of members of high-performing executive teams, project teams, sports teams, government, and military teams. They concluded that eight characteristics set the successful teams apart:

1. *A clear, elevating goal.* That is, the goal is understood and seen as challenging to team members.
2. *A results-driven structure.* Team members must have clear roles, effective communication processes, and an ability to use available data to evaluate progress and take corrective action when necessary. Members must also understand how their roles interrelate.

3. *Competent members.* The team must comprise members with the right technical knowledge and interpersonal skills to contribute to the team's goal.

4. *Unified commitment.* Team members must be willing to dedicate effort and energy to the team.

5. *A collaborative climate.* Team members must develop a climate of trust in one another in order to collaborate.

6. *Standards of excellence.* High-performing teams have high standards for individual performance and members feel pressure to achieve.

7. *External support and recognition.* Teams need external rewards but also support in the form of resources necessary for the team to accomplish its work.

8. *Principled leadership.* Leaders provide the necessary motivation and alignment to complete the team's work.

Advantages and Disadvantages. Teams can empower individuals throughout the hierarchy to make local decisions quickly. They are commonplace and can be easily formed quickly and flexibly when needed to address a problem or opportunity. However, team members require team skills to be productive. The team needs a clear charter and purpose with defined decision authority. Members need time to sort out roles and responsibilities among members of the team, or conflict can result. Unproductive conflict can inhibit the team and stall the work.

Integrator Roles

Integrator roles are formal positions with the responsibility to share information and coordinate across the structure. These are appropriate in situations where successful execution of the organization's strategy hinges on integrating different people and groups together. The integrator also adds capacity to the general manager's role when it is too complex for one person to handle. As Lawrence and Lorsch (1967a) put it,

> The integrator's role involves handling the nonroutine, unprogrammed problems that arise among the traditional functions as each strives to do its own job. It involves resolving interdepartmental conflicts and facilitating decisions, including not only such major decisions as large capital investment but also the thousands of smaller ones regarding product features, quality standards, output, cost targets, and so on, . . . much like the customary job description of any company general manager. (pp. 142–143)

Common roles such as product manager, project manager, and brand leader have as their primary objective the responsibility to coordinate diverse functions with a common objective. As Nadler and Tushman (1997) put it, "[T]heir purpose is to identify someone who will share a general management perspective with other, specialized managers who bring to the table essential expertise but relatively narrow concerns" (p. 97). Walker and Lorsch (1968) wrote that the integrator could help manage the dilemma of whether to organize by product or function, so that product managers could help to integrate specialists in various functions on common product goals while still allowing the specialists to retain their functional alignment.

Integrators are often designed as neutral positions who can gain trust by being objective and making decisions without being seen has having a personal stake in any outcome except for the common good of the organization. They often do not have the formal authority of having members of the team report to them (as they would in a management role) but must influence others to act without relying on position power.

Galbraith (1994) argues that the selection of the integrator is critical, and the skills are difficult to find. Lawrence and Lorsch (1967a) also make the following observations about successful integrators, who

- prefer to take significantly more initiative and leadership; they are aggressive, confident, persuasive and verbally fluent;
- seek status to a greater extent; they are ambitious, active, forceful, effective in communication, and have personal scope and breadth of interests;
- have significantly more social poise; they are more clever, enthusiastic, imaginative, spontaneous, and talkative;
- prefer more flexible ways of acting; they are adventurous, humorous, and assertive. (p. 150)

Integrators often succeed because of their personal influence and competence rather than formal authority. They are skilled at conflict resolution, negotiation, and persuasion to bring about agreement in times of contentious conflict. They will be comfortable proactively connecting with others in different departments and divisions to gain agreement. For global organizations, the integrator must be skilled at cross-cultural negotiation and communication. They must be able to see the bigger picture in addition to being able to see a situation from the perspective of any single function or unit (where they may have developed their own expertise). They will be comfortable in ambiguous situations where the role is not clearly defined.

As a result, Galbraith (1994) recommends developing integrators internally versus hiring externally, because the best integrators will not only be technically skilled and interpersonally competent, but also aware of the organization's internal dynamics in order to navigate the political waters effectively. To make an integrator successful, Galbraith also recommends granting the role status through title or reporting relationships, such as having the integrator report to a high-status individual. In some organizations the location of the integrator's office or past career experience can also grant status.

Advantages and Disadvantages. Where the work is strategic enough, integrator roles have the advantage of formalizing responsibility for coordination and communication across multiple groups. It adds general management capacity that can save upper management time by negotiating resolutions between parties. The primary disadvantage is the cost associated with the role and the investment in hiring an additional manager solely for cross-functional coordination. Additionally, it can be difficult to find skilled employees to fill integrator roles.

Matrix Organizations

We discussed the use of the matrix as a type of structure in Chapter 4. Notice how it also falls under the category of a lateral capability. Imagine an integrator becoming a solid-line boss instead of a dotted-line one, or the team lead in Figure 5.6 becoming a line manager of the team. These would be examples of moving these forms of lateral capability to a matrix structure. In each of the former examples, the organization's distribution of power and authority is clearly placed on one dimension, whether product or geography. The organization's structure communicates the importance of those dimensions as primary and the functional team as secondary. The matrix organization, in adopting two or more forms of structure in a single design, formalizes the lateral capability as well along the second dimension. Whereas the other forms of lateral capability described above add some level of coordination to the structure in order to cross the department boundaries, the matrix establishes this coordination within the structure itself. Power is equalized, and no dimension is primary.

While it might be tempting to jump quickly to the matrix as an option that resolves both the structure and the processes and lateral capability points of the star, remember that the challenges of a matrix are significant, with a greater level of coordination investment required, skills needed to manage it, and greater potential for conflict that can result from employees having two bosses.

In Chapter 4, we reviewed the basic two-sided (two-dimensional) matrix, where the matrix exists on two dimensions such as product and geography or function. Here we will review two more complex matrix structures, including the two-hat matrix and the three-dimensional matrix.

Two-Hat Matrix. For many organizations, one disadvantage of a matrix structure is that it adds management resources, which may not be an acceptable option for smaller organizations or divisions. One alternative is the two-hat matrix (Galbraith, 2009), which gives each manager responsibility over two dimensions of the matrix. Figure 5.7 graphically illustrates what this might look like in a human resources organization. Each leader has responsibility for a geography as well as a function. The North America leader supervises human resources business partners focused on that region. In addition, instead of adding a new leadership role for the head of global training and development, the organization adds

Figure 5.7 A Two-Hat Matrix

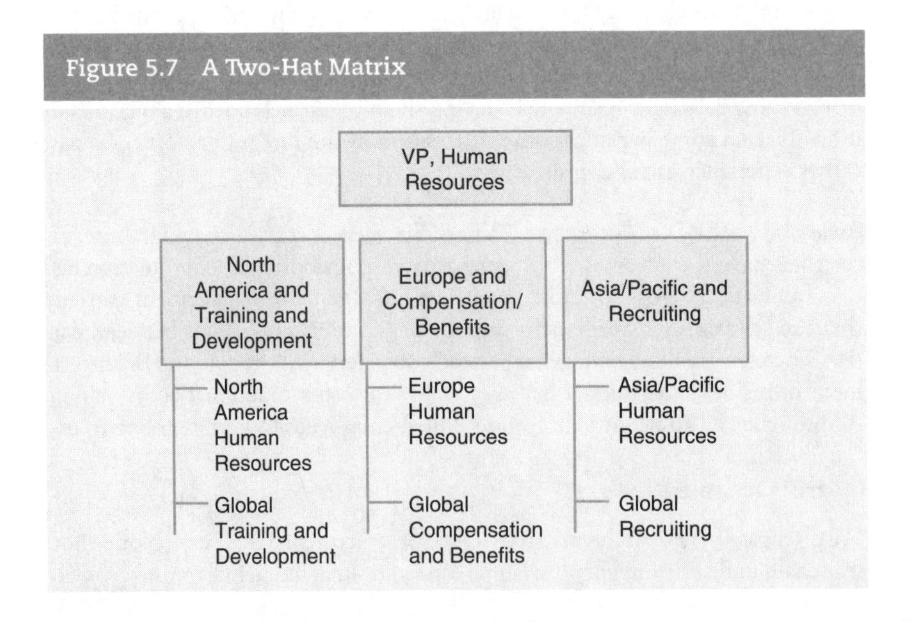

a second hat to the North America leader as the owner of global training and development, a role that affects the other two regions.

This approach has several benefits. It can reduce headcount and cost, since the model does not require three additional management resources. It encourages the leaders to maintain a broader focus on the issues and challenges of other divisions, promoting cross-organization information sharing and collaboration. Galbraith (2009) writes that sales organizations can benefit from this structure when sales leaders own both their own regional accounts and a set of national accounts. For these groups, the two-hat matrix has the potential to reduce turf and territory issues, since the leaders are all mutually responsible for shared success in one another's divisions. The model can also be an appropriate interim step as the organization graduates to a full matrix model.

There can also be challenges of the two-hat model. It can be hard to implement, the most evident difficulty being the increased workload placed on the leadership team. In addition, without a collaborative leadership team, the global responsibilities that affect other divisions may not end up being truly global, and a leader could choose to manage in a self-serving capacity, prioritizing North America needs in training and development, for example.

Three-Dimensional Matrix. Three-dimensional matrix organizations most frequently include a geographic dimension added to product and functional dimensions (Galbraith, 2009). Some call this kind of organization an international matrix or transnational organization (Burton, Obel, & Håkonsson, 2015). The three-dimensional matrix "is appropriate when both global integration and local responsiveness are needed" (Galbraith, 2008, p. 337). This structure allows for global product divisions as well as regional divisions focused on sales and customer relationships in a given geographic market. Figure 5.8 shows an example of a three-dimensional matrix.

In the three-dimensional matrix, the company maintains business/product units and geographic regions. Within geographic regions there are often country leaders who focus on specific product lines, reporting directly to the business unit and the geographic leader. There might be a global product line leader for the division of mobile devices (under the group of "hardware products") and a leader for Asia. Reporting to both leaders would be the head of mobile devices in China, supervising the sales, marketing, and finance functions, for example.

The international matrix can place more emphasis (power) on the geography dimension or the business dimension, or the two dimensions can be relatively equal. Three factors determine how to balance the dimensions: the amount of cross-border coordination needed (giving more power to the business dimension), the amount of interaction with local government (giving more power to local geographies), and the diversity of the international product portfolio (with more diversity of products giving more power to the business dimension) (Galbraith, 2009).

Making the Matrix Work

Galbraith (2009) lists actions required of leaders to make a matrix successful:

Seeing That Conflicts Are Resolved. Leaders must create an environment where those who manage lines of the matrix can resolve conflicts themselves without escalating every disagreement. They must ensure that the

Figure 5.8 A Three-Dimensional Matrix

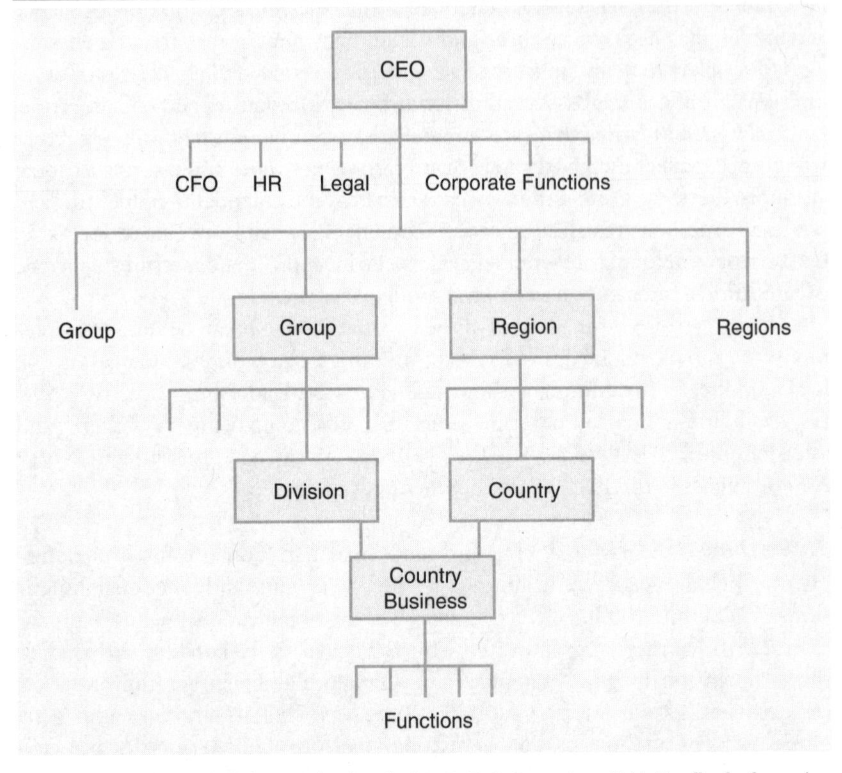

Source: Galbraith, J. R. (2008). Organization design. In T. G. Cummings (Ed.), *Handbook of organization development* (pp. 325–352). Thousand Oaks, CA: SAGE, p. 337.

organization understands that such disagreements are a natural part of the organizational model and not the fault of individuals and that conflict does not degenerate into interpersonal disputes or have lasting consequences. As Galbraith (2009) reminds us, "[W]hen conflict arises, it indicates that the structure is working" (p. 202).

Managing the Top Team. Leaders must address escalations that both (or multiple) matrix leaders bring for resolution only after they cannot resolve the issue themselves. Ideally the leader will work collectively with the top team to bring issues to a resolution rather than contribute to misunderstanding through one-on-one discussions. The latter can result in two people hearing different messages if they are not in the room: "She told me to spend the money when needed," one manager reports, while another responds, "She told me to avoid the unnecessary expense."

Balancing Power. In two-hat and three-dimensional matrices, the leader must address a sensitive equilibrium of power and authority issues. Galbraith advocates collective team decision making that can allow the leader to witness team decision making in the moment, observing the capabilities of the top team to manage at the same time as the leader can make responsive adjustments to those decisions as needed.

In addition to this list of leadership actions, Galbraith (2009) provides a list of capabilities that an organization needs to make a matrix successful (see box on next page).

Advantages and Disadvantages. These were reviewed in Chapter 4, and to that list, we can add advantages and disadvantages of the more complex forms of matrix. For the two-hat or three-dimensional matrix models, these can provide additional focus on different markets or geographies while maintaining focus on both product excellence and functional expertise. Managers learn how to think through problems from multiple perspectives. One disadvantage of these other models is complexity; the model must often be explained to employees. As a result, leaders often shy away from implementing them.

GETTING THE LEVEL OF LATERAL CAPABILITY RIGHT

With several different forms of lateral capability to choose from, the organization designer must weigh which to choose. The organization assessment can provide data about whether more or less lateral capability is needed, or whether a more or less sophisticated form is required. Table 5.1 presents common symptoms from the organization assessment that indicate a mismatch between the organization's needs and current state.

There is some evidence that managers may underestimate how much collaboration is required between organizational units, suggesting that there

Table 5.1 Symptoms of Mismatched Lateral Capability in an Organization Design

Symptoms of Not Enough Lateral Capability	Symptoms of Too Much Lateral Capability
• Top management experiences communication overloads.	• Significant time is spent in unproductive meetings.
• Top executives are drawn into day-to-day decisions to the detriment of strategy development.	• Too many people (or the wrong people) are involved in a group's decisions or too much consultation in decision making.
• It takes too long to get decisions from top executives and execution is inhibited.	• Long cycle time or missed deadlines as a result of confusion over decision authority
• "The left hand does not know what the right hand is doing."	• Stress, overload, and burnout
• Reinventing the wheel or dedicating resources to solving problems that have been solved already in other groups	• Job dissatisfaction due to increased conflicting demands on time or unresolved matrix conflict
• Work falling through the cracks, missed handoffs, or quality errors between groups who fail to understand upstream or downstream impacts	• Excessive cost investment compared to the need (e.g., integrative roles where informal liaisons would suffice)
• Turf disputes, blaming, and finger pointing between groups that should be coordinating	

SUMMARY OF ORGANIZATIONAL CAPABILITIES TO MAKE A MATRIX WORK

- The company possesses high social capital or no silos.
- People work effectively in teams across organizational boundaries.
- The teams are interconnected.
- People are trained in the skills of team problem solving and conflict management.
- Managers in key roles are naturally collaborative, and they live the values.
- Managers in key roles can influence without authority.
- Performance management is based on full and fair assessments of performance.
- There are multidimensional accounting systems to track multidimensional performance.
- The planning process is also the conflict resolution process.
- There is a spreadsheet planning process that aligns the goals of the different dimensions of the matrix.
- The leadership builds networks and values networkers.
- The leadership ensures that roles, responsibilities, and interfaces are clearly defined.
- Joint escalation processes are known and used intelligently.
- Problems are jointly addressed.
- The health of the organization is monitored.
- A strong leadership team sets the example.

Source: Galbraith, J. R. (2009). *Designing matrix organizations that actually work*. San Francisco, CA: Jossey-Bass, pp. 231–234.

is a need for greater lateral capability (Sherman & Keller, 2011; Worren, 2011). Sherman and Keller (2011) found that this underestimate occurred in more than 30 percent of the cases where integration was needed. This was most commonly due to a manager choosing a lower form of lateral capability than required because of a misunderstanding of task interdependence or information needs of another group.

Yet, researchers have found that the opposite situation is also true, where too much lateral capability can be just as bad as too little. Recent research indicates that employees are experiencing "collaboration overload," with time spent in collaboration increasing by more than 50 percent in recent decades (Cross, Rebele, & Grant, 2016). The amount of time collaborating through e-mail, meetings, and phone calls now approaches more than 70 percent of an employee's time (Cross & Gray, 2013). Mankins and Garton (2017) find that 25 percent of a manager's time is wasted in unnecessary meetings or responding to unnecessary e-mails. Research organization CEB has found that 60 percent of employees must actively interact with more than 10 colleagues every day, and half of that number had to collaborate with more than 20 others each day (Mankins & Garton, 2017). Using organizational network analysis, Cross and Gray (2013) report that one overwhelmed individual in their study ("Scott") was listed as a key contact by more than 150 people, with 77 mentioning that they wish they had even more of Scott's time. Clearly there are also times when too much coordination and communication are an overinvestment and a waste of resources.

How to Decide Which Form to Use

These situations both result from a mismatch between the integration needs and the kind of lateral capability in use. It might be tempting to look at all five forms of lateral capability and decide that if one is beneficial, implementing all of them might be even better. However, most organization design researchers advise differently, preferring to base the form of lateral capability on the required integration of the groups based on the strategy. "The organization designer must match a company's cross-functional coordination requirements with the appropriate types and amounts of lateral processes" (Galbraith, 2002, p. 47). Lawrence and Lorsch (1967a) refer to "requisite integration," where certain groups in their study had greater integration needs than others. Worren (2011) notes that the role of the organization designer is to find the "sweet spot" "to ensure that there is a match between work processes and the formal structure of the organization" (p. 26).

If more lateral capability is needed, the designer should examine whether it is worth moving up one form at a time rather than attempting too much all at once. As Galbraith (1971) puts it, "Probably a sequence of moves until the bottlenecks disappear is the best strategy; this will allow for the proper attitudinal and behavioral changes to keep pace" (p. 39). Casual networks can grow into informal communities of practice. Groups with shared goals can establish formal teams; teams can be connected by an integrator; integrators can become leaders of matrix organizations.

To evaluate the forms of lateral capability required, the organization designer should consider the following:

Degree of Interdependence. The primary way to evaluate the method or amount of lateral capability to select is to understand the degree of interdependence of divisions. Even though departments might be interdependent, the relationship between those departments can differ in complexity. J. D. Thompson (1967) observes that organizational units can be interdependent in several ways, displayed in Figure 5.9. Each escalating form of interdependence requires greater lateral capability. Reciprocal and team interdependence will require more sophisticated forms of lateral capability than pooled or sequential interdependence.

Business Strategy. Conglomerates and holding companies with a diverse portfolio may have little need for cross-business coordination. Global companies with global strategies and activities that need to be connected around the world will require much greater lateral coordination. Galbraith (1994) advises that "these latter multinationals will require country teams with business representation, business teams with country representation, and business and country managers. They must commit to a substantial amount of lateral organization" (p. 44).

Task Uncertainty and Complexity. As Nadler and Tushman (1988) put it, "More complex linking mechanisms can handle more information and deal more effectively with uncertainty than can simpler linking mechanisms" (p. 100). Teams, integrator roles, and matrix structures empower employees to see and address problems or opportunities themselves, coordinating resources as required. The formality of their practices can handle more complex problems than a community of practice or informal network. Completing a business case for a potential acquisition is a complex task that requires a commitment from a dedicated team instead of a casual effort from voluntary participants.

Figure 5.9 Forms of Interdependence

Pooled interdependence: Each unit operates relatively independently but contributes to the whole. For example, three different regional sales units may be coordinated with the corporation's standard rules or sales processes. Their sales activity is independent from each of the others, and their relationship with one another generally is because of their contributions to the overall organization's success.

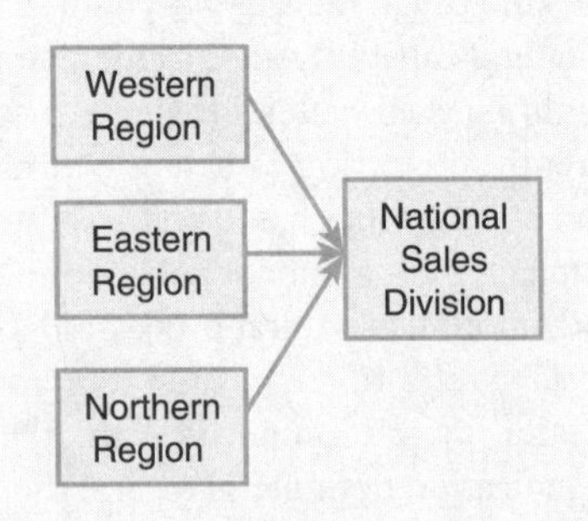

Sequential interdependence: Departments are sequentially interdependent when one produces an output that becomes an input for another group and a handoff process occurs. Here the relationship is asymmetrical, with one group dependent on the tasks of another. Sequential interdependence generally occurs as a one-way flow of information or tasks, as is the case when order entry sends new orders to the fulfillment department, for example. Their activities can be coordinated with schedules, plans, and service-level agreements that specify the quantity, quality, and timing of the handoff.

Order Entry → Order Fulfillment

Reciprocal interdependence: Reciprocal interdependence between departments occurs when "the outputs of each become inputs for the others" (J. D. Thompson, 1967, p. 55). Production and maintenance divisions in manufacturing each rely on one another to provide equipment needing to be fixed and newly fixed equipment ready to be used. Each department's decisions affects the others, and coordination is achieved less through rules or agreements than through feedback, negotiation, and adjustment.

Maintenance ↔ Production

To J. D. Thompson's (1967) list, some researchers have noted a fourth:
Team interdependence: A fourth form of interdependence occurs when multiple departments have multiple forms of interdependence with others (McCann & Galbraith, 1981; Van de Ven, Delbecq, & Koenig, Jr., 1976). Legal, contracts, and sales divisions are all interdependent to resolve contract negotiations with customers. New product development involves the departments of engineering, marketing, manufacturing, and finance, which must all coordinate their activities, determine decision authority, allocate resources accordingly, agree on a shared timeline and activities, and so on.

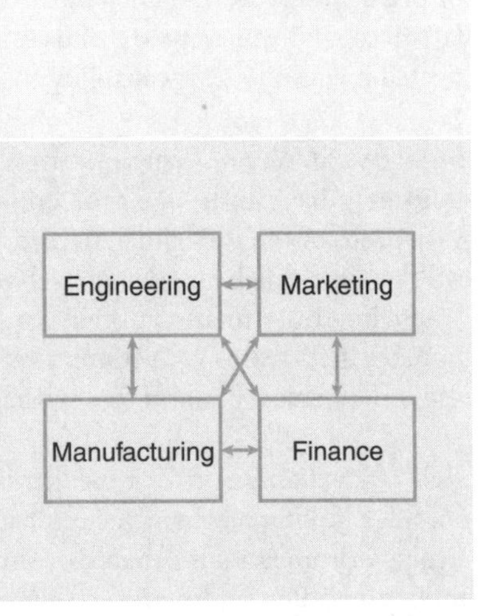

Cost. The more advanced the form of lateral capability, generally the greater the cost in people, time, and management attention. Matrix organizations require attention to teams and meetings to integrate activity on both dimensions of the matrix whereas informal networks have little to no cost.

Interpersonal Skills. Some forms of lateral capability require more skills than others. Matrix organizations challenge the conflict resolution ability of managers; integrator roles require the ability to influence without authority.

Trust and Existing Relationships. If two divisions trust that the other will make effective decisions for the benefit of both, they may be successful with less formal lateral mechanisms. If two divisions have engaged in destructive turf battles for some time, it may be more difficult to implement lateral mechanisms that rely on healthy negotiation and conflict resolution.

Changes Over Time. As the work changes, so will the interdependence of the work and the above factors. Designers should not assume that lateral capability will remain static over time but that it is a dynamic capability that must change as the organization changes. One of the major advantages of lateral capability is that it can be adjusted without the painful need for large-scale restructuring.

GOVERNANCE MODELS AND DECISION AUTHORITY

A critical factor for success in globally matrixed organizations is a platform to hold the right conversations (Kesler & Kates, 2016) that provide a mechanism for collaboration. Two formal routines are helpful to cross-organization collaboration: (1) a governance model and planning process that results in a set of shared agreements (Kesler & Kates, 2016, call this a "business handshake"), and (2) a clear set of decision practices that allow everyone involved to understand the decision to be made and the authority to make it.

Governance and Planning Processes

Earlier we reviewed the benefits of a superordinate goal or shared goals to connect departments and ensure alignment on activities. When these are developed during an annual or regular goal-setting process, there is shared agreement and clarity with a minimum of misunderstandings throughout the year.

Consider a technology firm where one division does software development for new products and another creates training programs for the products. A successful product launch requires both groups to integrate their activities so that the product is ready for customers and the training is ready to accompany it. If the divisions do not clearly agree on the product portfolio, including which products are priority, features, launch timelines, and other details, a breakdown is likely as each group is likely to make its own priority and resourcing decisions independently. Or consider a matrix organization where sales divisions in different geographies must collaborate with global product leaders on how to allocate resources to maximize product sales—because based on the competitive environment in different regions, different products will sell better than others. Both sales and product leadership must agree on resource investments (e.g., advertising and marketing funds, where to invest in sales representatives).

A shared planning process and handshake allows for mutual agreements to be established. As Kesler and Kates (2016) put it, "[T]hese joint conversations produce better plans, but they also produce alignment and ownership" (p. 91).

After the initial agreement is made about the priorities and plans, a regular review process (monthly or quarterly) can ensure that the plans are still appropriate. If circumstances have changed, the review meeting can provide a forum to renegotiate the previous agreement to ensure alignment.

Kesler, Kates, and Oberg (2016) outline four collaborative governance forums that can create an opportunity for effective planning and allow "the right people to focus on the right topics with shared data" (p. 37). These are standing committees with a clear mission and objective to focus on four areas of the organization:

- Direction: A forum for cross-organization discussions of corporate strategy
- Oversight: A forum for discussions and review of important metrics, goals, and appropriate resource allocation across the organization
- Innovation: A forum for decisions on the product portfolio and organizational growth
- Strategic Intentions: A forum for "unique aspects of the strategy" including customer experience, brand, talent, and acquisitions

Decision-Making Practices

"If you can't make the right decisions quickly and effectively, and execute those decisions consistently, your business will lose ground," write Rogers and Blenko (2006, p. 53). One danger of the increased collaboration in many organizations today is that by having so many people participating in and consulted on decisions, the decision process is slow and cumbersome. Rogers and Blenko (2006) explain that decisions are commonly stuck between at least four competing groups: global versus local decision makers, center versus business unit, function versus function, and inside versus outside partners. For example, should the annual plan for a product advertising strategy be made by corporate marketing, the local product manager, or the company's contract advertising agency?

The responsibility charting technique (Beckhard & Harris, 1977), often called RACI charts, can help an organization with its decision-making processes so that members understand who is responsible and involved with what actions and decisions. It can reduce conflict by specifying up front, before the situation occurs, what involvement is necessary in what ways by which people. It consists of the development of a chart or grid on which are written the major activities and which members are given the responsibility of completing (see Table 5.2 for an

Table 5.2 A RACI Chart Example

Activity	Product Manager	Marketing Lead	Event Planning Coordinator
Finalize event budget	R	C	I
Confirm event location	A	R	C
Decide on key product messages	R	C	
Schedule and coordinate vendors	I	A	R

example RACI chart for a marketing product launch event). The simplicity of the design belies its power, since completing the chart can be a focal point to pull a group out of a conflict or confusion and surface unexamined difficulties.

Team member names are listed at the top of the grid, and down the left-hand column are listed the team's major activities. One of the following letters is placed under each team member's name, in the row for each activity, representing that team member's responsibility for the activity (or it may be left blank if the member is not involved, as shown in Table 5.2):

- *R: Responsible.* This person is responsible for ensuring that this action is carried out.
- *A/V: Approval or veto.* This person has authority to approve or veto actions and decisions for this item.
- *S: Support.* This person supports the activity with time or other resources.
- *C: Consulted.* This person should be consulted or included in the action.
- *I: Informed.* This person should be communicated to or informed about the status of the activity.

Variations exist among practitioners in which letters should be included. Some, for example, call a role analysis chart a RACI chart and leave out the *S.* Golembiewski (2000) advocates adding a *D* (for decision; for example, *R–D* and *A–D*) to signify responsibility or authority for a decision and *Imp* to signify responsibility for implementation. Rogers and Blenko (2006) use the acronym RAPID: Recommend, Agree, Perform, Input, and Decide.

Beckhard and Harris (1977) advocate a number of useful constraints or "rules" regarding the use of responsibility charts. First, they recommend that every activity line must have one and only one person responsible—only one *R.* If more than one person must be responsible, the activity should be segmented so that the boundary of each member's responsibility is documented clearly. Second, a large number of approvals—*A*s—might be an indication that there are too many approvals, and team activity might be streamlined by reducing the number of necessary approvers. Similarly, having too many people consulted on an action may be unnecessarily involving others and inviting input, which can lead to those consulted becoming surrogate or informal approvers, again slowing down implementation.

Kesler, Kates, and Oberg (2016) write that RACI charts (and the like) can help to clarify roles for relatively straightforward sets of activities. They point out that in their experience these tools do not help with strategic, complex decision practices such as which products should get the most marketing investment next year or which products engineering should begin to phase out. People also waste time and make the RACI process bureaucratic by trying to decide what the differences are between being responsible and accountable and what that might mean in practice.

Instead, the authors argue for developing decision practices that can relieve tension in complex decisions. "Insist that the partners engage in conflict and debate on the important items in the handshake" (Kesler & Kates, 2016, p. 129). Decision principles and shared values such as "winning faster in the market with customers is the starting point for our decisions" (Kesler & Kates, 2016, p. 131) will focus the debate. In addition, a "golden vote" process that switches a RACI into a single binary choice will streamline decision making. In this practice, one party is given the final decision authority. The point is not to remove consultation or debate, but to clarify who will determine the outcome when consensus cannot be reached and a decision must be made to move forward.

ENABLERS FOR SUCCESSFUL LATERAL CAPABILITY

We discussed earlier why the development of lateral capability is so difficult. As Ashkenas, Ulrich, Jick, and Kerr (2002) argue, structures provide a sense of stability, and thus provide a psychological security that is often shattered with an emphasis on cross-functional processes, meddling integrators, and multidimensional matrix organizations. Lateral capability is enabled through several means:

Leadership and Management Skills. We have alluded to a number of interpersonal skills required to make lateral organizations successful, including negotiation, communication, and conflict resolution. In addition, Kesler and Kates (2016) provide a helpful set of competencies to develop matrix-ready leaders, including inquisitiveness, cognitive complexity, building trust, influencing stakeholders, global mindset, building organization, and building community. What is clear is that success of the lateral organization from a leadership point of view requires personal traits to bring about results.

Shared Values. The organization must develop a culture of collaboration where information sharing is a core value. Fjeldstad, Snow, Miles, and Lettl (2012) give the example of how Accenture, a global management consulting firm, needed to develop increased collaborative capacity among its more than 200,000 employees. Rapid knowledge sharing around the globe was critical to support client projects. There is an electronic infrastructure system to help connect employees, but what makes the system function effectively is a set of core values to which employees adhere, such as "one global network" and "respect for the individual" (p. 740). Ashkenas et al. (2002) advocate the development of new "mental models" (p. 129) for collaboration that can replace old mindsets. Galbraith (2008) writes that lateral capability depends on a foundation of social capital including trusting relationships.

Authentic Empowerment. As we have seen, one of the benefits of lateral capability is the additional capacity in the time of senior leadership. If senior leaders intervene in decision processes or second guess the priorities of a team, the purpose of the lateral mechanism is undermined. When team members represent their department, "participants must have the authority to commit their department," Galbraith (1977, p. 121) writes.

People Practices. We will discuss these in depth in the next chapter, but Joyce et al. (1997) write that lateral structures depend on the enabling processes of the people point of the star. These include talent programs such as rotations to build networks and expanded thinking. In addition, lateral capability is enhanced when employees hold a broader definition of career development that encourages career growth outside one's own department or function.

Reward Systems. Clear metrics that measure the result of shared resources and collaboration will support lateral capability (Ashkenas et al., 2002). The development of reward systems (discussed in greater detail in Chapter 7) can reinforce the achievement of team goals or superordinate goals, the attainment of lateral process metrics, and the resolution of matrix conflicts. Employees can be rewarded for contributions to a lateral team or sharing knowledge in a community of practice. If employees perceive that an assignment to cross-functional teams is a punishment, or if such contributions are not valued (or do not count toward an annual performance appraisal), they will be less likely to dedicate their full energies to the task.

SUMMARY

Lateral capability supports the structure by connecting the different divisions that have been established. It can help to reduce problems of duplication and fragmentation and provide a mechanism to share information across the hierarchy. We have reviewed five categories of lateral capability. Networks are easily formed, low cost, and generally informal ways of supplementing formal communication channels. Shared goals and processes help to ensure that different divisions have aligned priorities and are connected. Teams can cut across the hierarchy and provide a mechanism for action and decision making when empowered by leadership. Integrator roles use influence to organize and connect the activities of multiple departments. Finally, matrix organizations create formal solid line structures across multiple dimensions. More sophisticated forms of lateral capability provide more formal mechanisms to ensure collaboration, but they also come at a cost, including time dedicated to collaboration. Too much lateral capability is an overinvestment of time and excess cost, which can be frustrating, but too little leaves the organization susceptible to continued solos. The task of the organization designer is to find the right level to support the strategy. Supporting practices such as governance models and clear decision authority can also enhance an organization's lateral capability. Achieving successful lateral capability also requires enabling mechanisms, including a culture where core values support collaboration, leadership and management skills, and elements of the people and rewards points of the star.

QUESTIONS FOR DISCUSSION

1. Consider common points of contention in organizations such as headquarters and field or subsidiary offices, day shift and night shift, sales and support, kitchen and wait staff, back office, and front office. Why do you think many organizations struggle with lateral capability? What are some of the barriers to cross-department coordination in your experience?

2. Think about any of the forms of lateral capability you may have experienced. For example, how would you assess your own professional network? What would be some of the benefits to you or your organization to growing your network?

3. Consider a problem you have experienced with cross-department coordination. How

was the problem addressed? Should a "greater" or "lesser" type of lateral capability have been chosen? What would have been the consequences of using a different type? What benefits or drawbacks did you witness?

FOR FURTHER READING

Ashkenas, R., Ulrich, D., Jick, T., & Kerr, S. (2002). *The boundaryless organization.* San Francisco, CA: Jossey-Bass.

Galbraith, J. R. (1994). *Competing with flexible lateral organizations* (2nd ed.). Reading, MA: Addison-Wesley.

Galbraith, J. R. (2009). *Designing matrix organizations that actually work.* San Francisco, CA: Jossey-Bass.

Kesler, G., & Kates, A. (2016). *Bridging organization design and performance: 5 ways to activate a global operating model.* Hoboken, NJ: Wiley.

Ostroff, F. (2009). *The horizontal organization.* New York, NY: Oxford University Press.

EXERCISE

1. Continue with Part II of the organization design simulation activity. Turn to the Appendix to follow the instructions and complete the (1) structure and (2) processes and lateral capability points of your organization design.

CASE STUDY 2: COLLABORATION AT ONDEMAND BUSINESS COURSES, INC.

Discussion Questions

1. How would you describe the strategy of ODBC and the structure of the online product development division?
2. Summarize the issues brought up by the managers. What are the problems that the division is experiencing? How do those problems reflect the organization design (consider strategy, structure, processes, rewards, and people)?
3. Several managers suggested centralizing some functions such as project management or quality assurance and testing. What are the advantages and disadvantages of that option? What is your opinion about that suggestion?
4. Explain what lateral capability mechanisms discussed in Chapter 5 you might suggest to Robyn Trevino to increase collaboration across the teams.

* * *

OnDemand Business Courses, Inc. (ODBC) is a provider of corporate education and training for business professionals. ODBC originally began as an onsite training company offering one- to two-day courses on such topics as "Customer Service Essentials," "New Manager 101," and "Leading Your Best Team." Seminars were presented at a customer's location for a flat fee for up to 25 employees. Organizations that hired ODBC liked the flexibility of bringing in a trainer whenever they liked for a fixed rate (plus expenses) without the overhead costs of maintaining an entire in-house training department. Customers tended to be small or medium-size businesses or city government agencies with fewer than 1,000 employees, so they could not generally afford to hire their own trainers. ODBC used freelance trainers and acted as a broker between customers and the training staff. In addition, ODBC offered "public" courses in hotel ballrooms where anyone could enroll and register for a course for a fee ranging from $59 to $259, depending on the seminar. This option was especially popular with health care and financial services professionals who were required to earn a minimum number of continuing education hours per year to maintain their professional certifications or licenses. Following this model, ODBC was among the market leaders.

Five years ago, following significant revenue shortfalls at the hands of e-learning companies that offered training entirely online, ODBC experimentally converted just a few of their popular courses to an online platform. With no experience in designing online learning, ODBC staff was unsure how to make the courses engaging, so the online courses were simply long, digitized video lectures of an ODBC onsite course. Each year the video department would add a course or two, but ODBC did not invest heavily in e-learning.

ODBC's CEO at the time, Belinda Patton, was known to say that online learning would only ever amount to a small trend in the corporate education industry, since "no company will ever want all of their training done completely online," as she put it. ODBC remained stubbornly committed to the on-site course model for the next several years even as on-site course revenue declined substantially—by more than 44 percent—and the online course revenues increased by more than four times. Still, the online course revenues only made up less than one-third of ODBC's overall business. Patton remained unconvinced about the future of online learning for ODBC.

Two years ago, as it became clear to the board of directors that ODBC was losing market share in the e-learning market and that demand was continuing to shrink in the onsite training market, Robyn Trevino was brought in as CEO to replace Patton. Trevino had been the mastermind behind the success of one of the fastest growing e-learning companies and immediately created a new business model. She announced that ODBC would be in the business of designing and delivering online training courses that would run on ODBC's own website.

"Our strategy is to take our leadership role in onsite courses to an online experience," Trevino said at an all-employee meeting in her first few months on the job. She continued,

> Our customers are loyal and dedicated to us. They appreciate the flexibility that we have always offered them, to be their training organization on demand. I am announcing today that our plan is to create an online platform where our customers will have access to a single "all you can learn" product. Our customers will pay an annual subscription based on how many employees they want to give access to our learning. We will become the premier e-learning company in our industry. If we all pull together under this new strategic approach, we will be unstoppable. Our rallying cry must be "One ODBC," Trevino said.

Knowing that the company was lagging well behind other leading companies in the market, but also knowing that ODBC had the strength of brand recognition and instructional quality, Trevino recognized the need to move quickly. She directed almost all of the company's resources to new online course development and hoped that the onsite training revenue would hold steady for long enough to provide the profitable income needed to fund development of the online products. It was a race against the clock and she quickly restructured the company's online product development division into seven new departments focused on content specialty, depicted in the following organizational chart and department descriptions:

1. Management skills (courses include "Leading Your Team" and "Managing Poor Performers")
2. Communication skills (courses include "Ace That Presentation!" and "Telephone Etiquette")
3. Interpersonal skills (courses include "Conflict Management" and "Listening Skills")
4. Customer Service skills (courses include "Calm an Angry Customer" and "Emotional Intelligence")

5. Computer software and technology skills (courses include "Word Processing" and "Mastering Spreadsheets")
6. Sales skills (courses include "Negotiation" and "Sales Presentations")
7. ODBC Learning Platform (the technical backbone of the operation, responsible for the website and user interface)

Within each of the six content departments, there are three identical roles:

- Project Managers, who work with marketing to prioritize courses to develop, create project plans, assign resources, and coordinate the various players (including content development, technical development, legal, finance, sales, and marketing)
- Content Developers, who are instructional design experts who conduct topic research and write the courses, including video scripts and postcourse quizzes
- Technical Developers, who maintain the team's website, organize digital files, conduct technical quality assurance and testing, organize video production, and provide customer service when customers have problems.

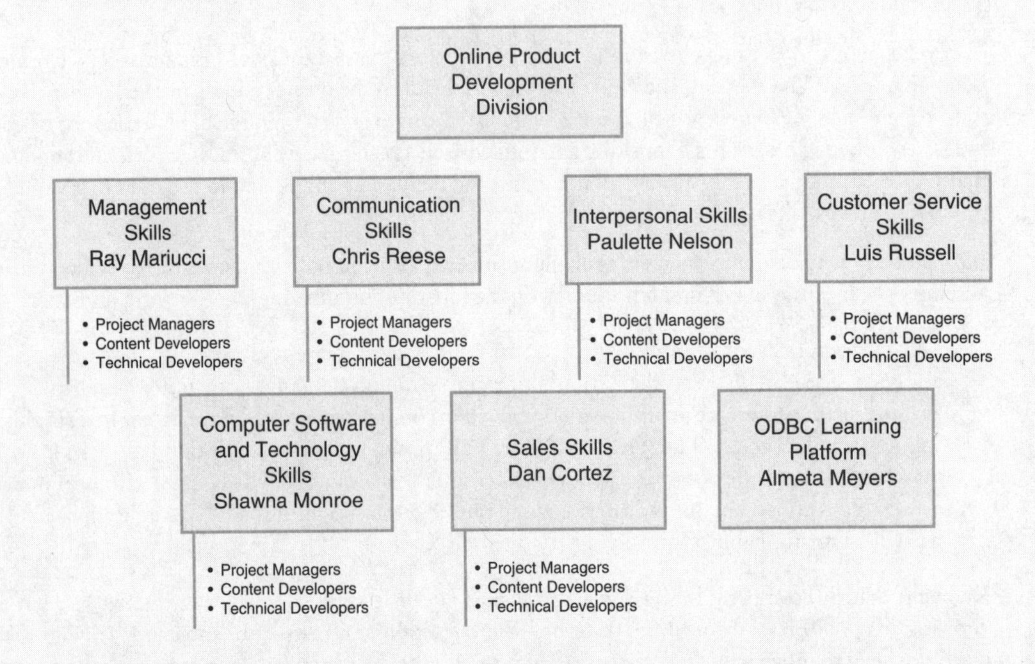

Trevino pushed the teams hard and within a year, revenue for the online courses had almost doubled. Recently, and unfortunately, customer complaints and costs have now increased substantially as well.

To get to the root cause of the problems in the product development division, Trevino hired a consultant to speak to members of the management team and to issue a report with findings and recommendations. Following are notes from the consultant's interviews.

Ray Mariucci, Management Skills

We've done a tremendous amount of work in this division to get all of our courses ready to be presented online. What's remarkable is that the courses weren't just the old curriculum that we put online; we have revised each program from scratch. They now look and feel like online courses rather than an afterthought. We have short videos, interactive exercises, quizzes, and simulations. It's really amazing what we have accomplished.

Our end goal is to create the ability for customers to subscribe to a service and get access to take as many of the online courses as they would like, purchasing login accounts and paying a fee for each employee. We have never really made it to that point. We still allow our customers to purchase individual courses from us as they used to in the onsite model. Every sales agreement with a customer is different since we allow customers to buy only the management skills and sales skills curriculum, or just the communication courses.

This team is really a conglomerate of seven isolated groups. We have been so focused on Robyn's mission of expanding our online products as quickly as possible, we have retreated into our own silos and have never had time for any collaboration. That has become a problem. We have never had a staff meeting where we share our course roadmaps or plans. I have no idea what courses are coming up in the sales skills department or communication skills. Robyn says, "One ODBC," but right now it's more like "Seven ODBCs."

Chris Reese, Communication Skills

What's going well is that my team is highly skilled and we are executing very quickly on the goals that we have for development of communication skills courses. My biggest problem with this division is that we are fragmented into different pieces. It's like we each work for a different company. We each develop our own content and have our own goals for the year. Are we aligned on the same path? I have no idea. It's nice to say that we should all be part of one ODBC vision of a single all-you-can-learn product, but what does that mean for me and my goals? We might share updates with each other at a very general level but information sharing is kept to a minimum. People are tight lipped, like they don't want you to know what they are working on. Dan's team designed a course on "Sales Presentations" earlier this year and was working literally next door to my team who was working on a course on "Executive Presentations." Neither of us had any idea about the duplication and both of us ended up calling the same external trainer as a subject matter expert. For some reason, Dan also thinks that his group should own the course on telephone communication skills in sales but we are going to design it anyway.

Paulette Nelson, Interpersonal Skills

I'm sure people will complain about the isolation of each of our groups. Do you know why? I get my bonus based on how many customers I have who take interpersonal skills courses. If I have less revenue attributed to interpersonal skills courses compared to Luis's department, Robyn wants to know why. We have monthly operations reviews where I have to show exactly how much I am contributing to our online product revenue.

I push my team to develop our courses as fast as we can and to get our sales teams to sell the interpersonal skills curriculum. I can't afford to waste time collaborating with another team. So yes, there is a lot of duplication as my team designs parts of courses that should be standard. We design our own unique websites, so we all have our own registration and login pages and instructions on how to use the website. We each have our own customer service teams in case there are technical bugs or complaints. We each have our own quality assurance and testing groups. We each have our own video production resources. All of those could be standardized but no one seems to feel the burning need to change because we all want to control our own destiny.

Almeta's team should be helping us but they do not understand what we need and frankly they are too slow to keep us on schedule. She is always trying to standardize on one approach, but since we all have unique requirements, most of her suggestions do not make sense. Our technical developers understand our course content and work very closely with our course developers. They come up with innovative ideas that might not work for other groups.

Luis Russell, Customer Service Skills

Our customers want one solution but we are selling them six different products that all look different and work differently. Ray's office is right next door to mine, but I can't tell you what he or his team is working on. On Monday, I saw that Ray had hired an external contractor to conduct a video shoot, and I just shook my head because it is the same contractor that my team will be using tomorrow. We are going to pay thousands of dollars in duplicate setup fees just because we didn't coordinate our schedules.

Here is another example of our failure to coordinate: We are designing one of our new customer service skills courses, and my team felt that there are concepts from communication skills courses that would be beneficial for us to use. We heard that Chris's team is working on a "six-step method" for communicating clearly in a presentation. I could use that same concept for customer service agents, and we could actually have consistency in the methodology we teach to our customers. However, the communication course does not exist, and it might be several months away or even a year if it is not on schedule. So, I had to decide whether to invest my own team's time in creating content that really should come from another team, and keep us on schedule, or whether we should delay so that we could use content that fits our standards. Delaying would have made Robyn furious, so we did what we had to do as quickly as possible to get the course out, even though that was the wrong answer for our customers.

The irony is that my team develops all of these customer service courses, but we are terrible at customer service as a collective function. When a customer calls my team to complain that the website isn't working, and I find out that the customer is not complaining about my website but Ray's or Paulette's, we just pass the customer on. We have no control over what those other teams are doing. We refer the customer to another group since we have our own problems to deal with. It's just another way that we look like seven different companies to our customers.

Shawna Monroe, Computer Software and Technology Skills

My group is a little different from everyone else. Since we design computer software courses that use industry standard, common software applications, we need special licenses and interactive technology to create our courses. For example, if we are designing an enhancement to our Intermediate Spreadsheets course, we spend a lot of time creating an interactive experience so that students actually try to do what we are demonstrating as we select this row or shift-click this column. In our experience, that is the only way to show the student how to perform complex technical programming calculations. It also takes a special learning platform to accomplish.

As a result, there is really no need for me to collaborate with anyone else. No, our division is not a very cohesive team but we are each doing our own thing and I think that's fine.

Dan Cortez, Sales Skills

If we are going to succeed and turn things around in this company, we absolutely need to coordinate and collaborate more than we do today. Customers do not want to buy six different categories of skills courses. They want to buy one set of courses that covers all skill areas. For example, when I talk to customers about sales skills, they want to teach telephone communication skills, dealing with challenging customers, and listening, in addition to making sales presentations. That means our customers have to buy four different packages to cover those areas unless I direct my team to develop those topics in our own group. Yet if I want my customers to buy from me, and enhance my team's revenue, I have to offer what they want even if it's also offered in another group. Robyn has been coming down to our building every few months for the past year, yelling at us constantly that we need to work together to provide a seamless customer experience, but we still operate in isolation. One opportunity for improvement that I have considered is that we should have a single group that focuses on quality assurance and testing before our courses are published, to find any errors. If I could design courses and turn them over to another group to test and publish, that would save my time.

Almeta Meyers, ODBC Learning Platform

My team is the technology group that manages the software foundation of the entire operation to make sure that our platform can support the course designs. We design the standards and help the other teams create live or recorded video, online polling, or other interactive features. The problem is that we can design all of the standards we want, but if none of the technical developers in each of the departments listens to us, it doesn't matter what my group decides. There is a lot of duplication between what we do and what the technical developers do in each department.

For example, last year we purchased a company license for an instructional learning platform that allows all course developers to more easily create and publish their content. Then I just learned a few weeks ago that Shawna's team went out and bought their own learning platform for their own use without consulting anyone else. If I had known about their needs, I could have found a solution for the whole company instead of duplicating our technology purchases.

I don't understand why all of the technical developers on each team do not report directly to me, since my group is given the responsibility to make all technical decisions. If I don't control them and have the authority over them, how am I supposed to ensure consistency in our technology platform?

CHAPTER 6

PEOPLE

Learning Objectives

In this chapter you will learn

- Why the people point of the star must be customized to the business strategy.
- How to create differentiated workforce plans and unique people strategies by understanding "A" positions and pivot roles.
- How to design strategic talent practices such as career development, learning and development, and performance management to support the organization design.

We begin this chapter with three brief case studies that illustrate the importance of the people strategy in organization design.

Case 1: Coca-Cola

In 2004, Neville Isdell came out of retirement to lead the Coca-Cola Company during a difficult time. Investors and analysts pointed to poor stock performance, while internally, employees suffered through layoffs and reorganizations that resulted in low morale. To turn around the company, Isdell engaged 150 senior leaders in setting a new strategy, a "manifesto for growth," through a global and collaborative process that lasted 8 months. The leadership team identified critical organizational capabilities for the growth strategy: brand marketing, franchise leadership, innovation, and people development.

A year into the strategy-setting process, Isdell changed the organizational structure by integrating the marketing, strategy, and innovation functions under a single leader to encourage collaboration among those groups. Yet, Isdell reflects that "we changed the structure, but it's not about central versus de-central. We want leaders making decisions and we want those decisions to fit inside our manifesto for growth" (Kesler, 2008, p. 20). The growth strategy also meant "building or acquiring many new skills," Isdell says, to achieve success in the core business while adding to the product portfolio (Kesler, 2008, p. 20). To support employee growth and learning, Isdell notes that "we've invested a lot more management time in people development over the past three years—again, tied to the realization we are fundamentally a creative-service business." Managing a global business requires global leadership so Isdell "made it a point to ask managers to take more lateral assignments, and we want them to move across markets, and sometimes functions" (p. 20). Extensive talent reviews of the senior team gave them personal feedback to improve their performance and provided input to succession plans. "The manifesto for growth was the basis of that work," Isdell remarks, but "the job isn't done by any means" (Kesler, 2008, p. 21).

Case 2: AT&T

AT&T's business today bears little to no resemblance to its first instantiation, the 19-century American Telephone and Telegraph Company. Today it looks much more like a technology giant than the company that originally focused on making Alexander Graham Bell's invention a household presence. Due to rapid changes in communications technology and consumer preferences, and because the telecommunications industry is "moving from cables and hardware to the internet and the cloud, AT&T is in a sprint to reinvent itself" (Donovan & Benko, 2016, p. 69). Many of AT&T's long-tenured employees began their careers with a company that has changed dramatically to wireless technology and entertainment. However, replacing those 280,000 employees with new employees who have the required skills in "cloud-based computing, coding, data science, and other technical capabilities" (Donovan & Benko, 2016, p. 70) is not an option. The supply of such talent is scarce, and the competition for them is fierce.

Instead, AT&T has embarked on an ambitious reskilling program. New job roles and profiles have been created along with an updated set of skills and capabilities required for each role. The objective is to develop flexible and transferable skills that allow more internal career movement. Employees are provided not only with career planning and self-assessment tools but also with significant learning opportunities. Options for employee learning include individual courses, short tutorials, packaged course bundles for popular technical certifications, and accredited online degrees in partnership with a university. The company expects that employees will change roles and skills every 4 years to keep up with the demands of rapidly changing technology.

AT&T has spent more than $250 million on the education programs so far. "AT&T wants to invest in, rather than leave behind, those who helped build its position in the marketplace. But to remain profitable in the future, it has to move beyond the skills that once made it great" (Donovan & Benko, 2016, p. 73).

Case 3: Lafarge

French construction material company Lafarge began its global expansion in the 1990s with acquisitions in China, Eastern Europe, Indonesia, the Philippines, India, and South Korea. Global expansion prompted a global organization redesign to integrate the new divisions but also allow local responsiveness. The cement division, for example, now had operational staff in Western Europe but also Turkey, Latin America, Africa, Asia, and the Middle East. To address the gaps between the new divisions, cross-functional teams were created, but the management decision-making style remained focused on authority at the top of the hierarchy. One manager observed, "[T]he organizational challenge is to be a group and not to work in silos as divisions. Our strength was to gain synergy from Lafarge resources but now there are too many internal borders" (Som, 2008, p. 84).

The company decided to invest in global talent and take advantage of the skilled employees that had joined Lafarge from the different acquisitions. Instead of the career path remaining solely within a country or geography, the new high-potential talent program would promote the best employees to roles throughout the world. The new talent program was designed "to promote future growth and build up a pool of international managers trained to be business heads of Lafarge" (Som, 2008, p. 91). "Expatriation or a transfer was meant to be a career-oriented move and taken as a means to gather international experience for further career growth" (Som, 2008, p. 93). The company also recruited talent from respected global business schools and developed learning and development programs that included not only formal classroom training but apprenticeships and learning on the job.

* * *

What these cases have in common is a concentrated attention on people practices that change and evolve as the organization's design changes. Coca-Cola's growth strategy required innovation in product development, and while a new structural division was formed to address that need, new leadership behaviors were also required. Executive talent reviews, lateral and geographic job moves, and succession plans supported the needed growth in the capabilities of leaders. As a company enters new areas in which to compete like AT&T has in wireless and entertainment, new skills are needed and the company's approach to learning and development adjusts to support that need. Lafarge required senior leaders to have an understanding of the global market, so they developed international mobility programs to grow talent from within.

This chapter is about how the people strategy supports the organization design. Like other aspects of an organization's design, the people strategy can accelerate and reinforce the business strategy and other points of the star, or it can inhibit the design and provide barriers to success. The people point of the star emphasizes the importance of having the right people with the right skills contributing to the strategy but also continuing to grow and develop as the strategy changes. Regardless of whether the structure or processes are perfectly designed, having talent practices that are incompatible with the rest of the design will result in failure.

When we refer to the choices in the people point of the star, we consider this point to encompass all of an organization's human resources and talent management practices. These include the identification of strategic talent and learning and development practices to enhance employee skills. We will look at performance management and evaluation processes, career development practices, and learning and development. Most leaders may say that "people are our most important asset," but struggle to understand why and to decide how to design a unique and customized people point of the star that achieves the strategy. We will examine how these practices work together to differentiate an organization's people design.

We will refer to these issues as being a matter of human resources, both the concept and the function, though the human resources (HR) department itself should not be responsible for all design decisions that concern people. Just as all employees have a responsibility to managing an organization's finances appropriately, not only the finance department, so too do all managers have the responsibility of effective management of people.

TRADITIONAL APPROACHES TO PEOPLE PRACTICES

In recent years, a number of observers have remarked that though the workforce and workplace have changed significantly since the 1950s, many organizations have retained the same practices to managing HR that have existed for more than 50 years. Here we will review the evolution of people and talent practices before turning our attention to an approach driven by the business strategy.

In the 1950s, writes Cappelli (2008b), the rapid growth of organizations and the continuing need for skilled managers demanded that organizations hone their ability to identify skilled talent and develop employees quickly. Cappelli notes that "careers advanced inside organizations because companies no longer brought in talent from the outside," citing a study showing that when executives retired, "40 percent had been with their firms more than forty years" (p. 53). Predictable advancement was the rule, with many employees remaining in their jobs for less than 2 years before moving to another role, typically moving upward along a defined career path.

As time passed, both the demand and supply of managers became less predictable, and organizations reduced their investments in internal development and training. With changes in deregulation in the 1970s and greater global competition in the 1980s, it became increasingly difficult for businesses to predict both the life cycle and demand for products, and as a result, the skills that would be needed in the future. By the 1990s, outside hiring increased as organizations looked externally for skilled candidates, and the average job tenure (the number of years employees remained with one company) declined substantially. Few companies wanted to invest heavily in training employees who would be leaving for a competitor, and for their part, employees saw fewer career advancement opportunities. By the 2000s, many companies surrendered to the volatility of their talent needs and stopped both talent planning and internal training programs, and employees found the situation just as unpredictable. Leaders in many organizations decided that "years-long programs for developing talent create a false sense of accuracy and no longer make sense" (Cappelli, 2008b, p. 9).

As a result, most organizations have not invested in developing an approach to talent from a strategic standpoint. "They continue to treat employees as raw materials to be acquired and then made useful through training and development" versus "building human capital as a core source of competitive advantage" (Bartlett & Ghoshal, 2002, p. 37). At its extreme, Lawler (2008) refers to the former as a structure-centric approach to people. In this approach, a hierarchical bureaucracy determines the design of "McJobs" that are rigidly defined with narrow job duties and specified procedures. Career paths are absent or minimal. Indeed, Cappelli (2008b) notes that 30 percent of recent business school graduates could not identify their next logical career move at their current employer (p. 95).

The result is that, as Boudreau and Ramstead (2007) write, today's HR practices in most organizations are generic and interchangeable.

> How concerned would you be if your competitor had a copy of your HR strategy? Too often, the answer we get to that question is "Not very concerned, because ours probably looks a lot like theirs anyway." Indeed, if you compare the HR strategies of two competitors, without indicating the names of the companies, it is often hard to tell which strategy goes with which company. (Boudreau & Ramstead, 2007, p. 71)

Many organizations follow common programmatic approaches to talent management, learning and development, and performance reviews. Indeed, typical talent decisions in organizations, according to Boudreau and Ramstead (2007), take one of three poor approaches:

1. **The organization's practices focus on compliance**. Decisions about policies, rules, compensation, hiring, or learning programs are made based on threats of legal action or regulatory requirements. Such

policies might be legally necessary, but they do not specifically address how these programs can go beyond mandated procedures to contribute to the organization's need for innovation or customer focus.

2. **The organization's practices follow fads and fashions**. Decisions are made and practices implemented based on popular approaches from the latest book by a well-known (usually successful) business leader or article from a respected academic author. HR leaders end up adopting Google's approach to people selection or GE's approach to conducting performance evaluations without regard to whether it makes sense for their organization. We also learned in Chapter 2 how isolated and disjointed design decisions have little effect on an organization's performance, and this is true for HR practices as well.

3. **The organization's approach focuses on equality and programs apply to all employees equally**. There is little difference between practices for high performers and lower performers, resulting in the occasional tolerance of poor performance. All employees are provided with the same access to learning and development opportunities regardless of role. Career moves are not intentionally planned to accelerate the development of top employees but may be haphazard or ad hoc.

Surveys of HR practitioners that design people strategies support the notion that HR practices are generic and driven by programs and rules. "All too often, HR is largely an administrative function headed by individuals whose roles are focused on cost control and administrative activities" (Lawler & Boudreau, 2015, p. 4). A longitudinal survey of how HR practitioners spend their time shows little difference in strategic activity from 1998 to 2012, and that the HR role in most organizations is not seen as a strategic partner. While HR is rated highly at providing HR services, business leaders generally rate HR's effectiveness as low in strategic involvement.

A STRATEGIC APPROACH TO PEOPLE PRACTICES

Despite the generic HR practices used in many organizations, there are good reasons to consider a strategic and targeted approach. In today's knowledge-intensive work where innovation is prized and high engagement and employee commitment lead to increased participation, organizations that focus on their talent have a competitive advantage. When the organization's strategy is frequently adapting to a rapidly changing environment, the organization requires talent that can adapt as well, as the examples from Lafarge, Coca-Cola, and AT&T demonstrated earlier. Starting with the strategy ensures alignment between practices and prevents disjointed and isolated talent decisions. A strategic approach to people practices answers questions such as these (Boudreau & Ramstead, 2007):

- "Where does our strategy require that our talent and organization be better than our competitors' to work?" (p. 3)
- "Where do our talent and organization systems need to be different from competitors' and why?" (p. 3)

- "Where would an improvement in the quality of talent and organization make the biggest difference in our strategic success?" (p. 50)
- "If we shifted our strategic goals, which of our employees or organizational structures would have to change the most?" (p. 3)
- "When the strategy changes, how should you change your talent and organization?" (p. 75)

While talent management must start with the strategy, notice that the STAR model also suggests that the people strategy affects the business strategy. A human capital-centric organization takes seriously a reflexive relationship between people and business strategy. That is, "business strategy is determined by talent considerations, and it in turn drives human capital management practices" (Lawler, 2008, p. 9). As the business strategy is developed, considerations about the availability of talent should help to shape the organization's approach. Scarce talent needs may mean that the organization will have difficulty finding the right skills. If the organization is unable or unwilling to invest in the hiring or internal development of talent to help drive the strategy, then the strategy is unlikely to be successful.

Research findings suggest that organizations that adopt a strategic approach to talent perform better than those that do not. Huselid and Becker (2011) argue that "business and strategic initiatives drive the design and implementation of HR management systems, which in turn affect workforce levels of skill and motivation, as well as the design of work, which then affects productivity, creativity, and discretionary effort, which subsequently drive profitability, growth, and ultimately, shareholder value" (Huselid & Becker, 2011, p. 422). (See Figure 6.1 for a display of this relationship.)

A strategic talent approach has four characteristics:

1. It is driven by and fully integrated with business and talent strategies. The strategic approach translates to all aspects of HR such as recruitment and employee development.
2. It is managed as a core business process. It is an integral part of senior executive activity, not a process delegated to the HR department.
3. The planning cycle matches the business strategy and operational timelines. "Leading organizations . . . place as much emphasis on the strategic talent reviews as they do on the strategic planning process and the annual operating reviews" (Silzer & Dowell, 2010, p. 39).
4. It is ingrained with a talent mindset throughout the organization. A focus on talent is a shared value through the organization, role modeled by top leadership (Silzer & Dowell, 2010, p. 38).

There is no single and agreed-upon definition of *talent management* because the term has been used as both an umbrella description for all HR practices and as a narrow term for talent planning and pipelines. One instructive (albeit lengthy) definition of *strategic talent management* is the following:

> We define strategic talent management as activities and processes that involve the systematic identification of key positions which differentially contribute to the organization's sustainable competitive advantage,

Figure 6.1 Organizational Performance Impact of Strategic HR

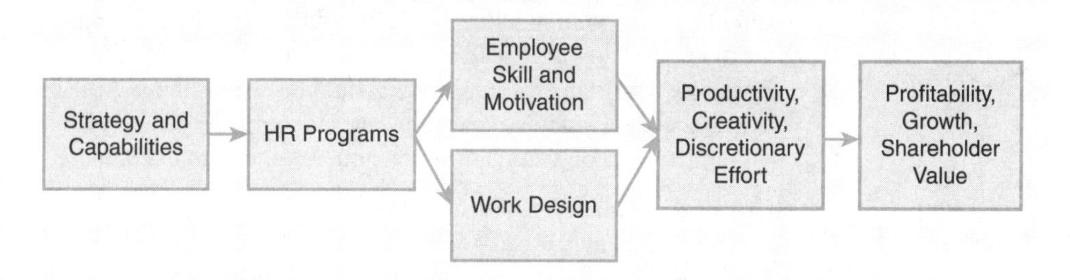

Source: Adapted from Becker, B. E., & Huselid, M. A. (1998). High performance work systems and firm performance. *Research in Personnel and Human Resource Management, 16*, pp. 53–101.

> the development of a talent pool of high potential and high performing incumbents to fill these roles, and the development of a differentiated human resource architecture to facilitate filling these positions with competent incumbents and to ensure their continued commitment to the organization. (Collings and Mellahi, 2009, p. 304)

To summarize, this definition implies three actions to be taken to follow a strategic approach to talent. Each of these actions will be explored in the following sections.

1. Understanding key positions for differentiation
2. Identifying a talent pool of high-potential employees
3. Creating an aligned architecture of HR programs such as career development, performance management, and learning and development to support the strategy

KEY POSITIONS AND THE DIFFERENTIATED WORKFORCE

An initial approach to strategic HR was to create generic workforce strategies, often based on the typologies we saw in Chapter 3. For example, using the Treacy and Wiersema (1995) strategy framework, Beatty and Schneier (1997, p. 32) propose different performance measures, selection criteria, development, and rewards based on the strategy, as follows:

- **Operational excellence**: In these organizations, work is centralized and controlled with strict procedures, so performance should measure total cost, errors, waste, and lost customers. Employees should be selected for process competence, and development should be based on teaching employees procedures and rules. There should be high skill depth in different operational functions. There should be a predictable career ladder with pay based on skills and team productivity.
- **Product leadership**: Work is often coordinated across teams to seek innovation, so performance measures should be on patents and

copyrights, industry recognition, sales on new products, and sales and customer growth. Employees should be selected for technical competencies, willingness to experiment, ability to deal with ambiguity, and innovative thinking. Employees should demonstrate "humility, creativity, and versatility" (Treacy & Wiersema, 1995, p. 97). In employee development, employees should be responsible for their own learning with mandatory growth in certain competency areas. Rewards should be based on team innovation and development of competencies.

- **Customer intimacy**: Knowing customer needs is especially critical, so this strategy should measure customer retention rates and referrals. Employees should be selected for being active learners and being able to network, "adaptable, flexible, and multitalented" (Treacy & Wiersema, 1995, p. 136). Development should be based on building skills in partnerships and consultation with customers to develop a long-term relationship. Rewards should be for broad-based creative thinking that drives customer success.

Similarly, Miles and Snow (1984) posit that an organization pursuing a Defender strategy with a functional structure and stable product line is most likely to build its own internal human resources, with an emphasis on hiring at lower levels and providing substantial training and development to provide predictable staff growth and depth. The innovation required in the Prospector strategy would suggest the opposite approach, bringing in ("buying") skilled staff through sophisticated recruiting practices and providing limited opportunities for training. The mix of stability and change in the Analyzer strategy suggests a focus on both acquiring skills and development internally.

Considering the generic strategy is one option for organizations at an early stage of differentiating the workforce. However, such an approach presumes that there exist only a few HR strategies to match the generic business strategies. Following this logic, all organizations pursing "low-cost" or "product-leadership" strategies would follow the same HR practices.

Becker, Huselid, and Beatty (2009) offer an alternative to the generic strategy approach that proposes a stronger fit between the organization's unique strategy and its workforce. To take a differentiated approach means that human resources practices will move beyond the "peanut butter" approach that spreads investments equally in all employees. As they put it, "Differentiating the workforce strategy ultimately means investing disproportionately in certain employees and groups of employees, based on their strategic roles" (p. 24). An analysis of strategic roles requires an understanding of the processes by which the competitive advantage is realized and which roles contribute to a greater degree to that advantage.

In this regard, the leader can return to the organizational capabilities and design criteria (what Becker, Huselid, and Beatty [2009] call the "strategic capabilities") for guidance on how to prioritize workforce investments. They point out that the analysis of strategy for the workforce has two implications: "First, the workforce strategy should be aligned directly to the human capital requirements of the strategic capabilities. Second, just as those capabilities are unique or differentiated relative to competitors, the workforce strategy should be differentiated accordingly" (p. 32).

For example, two different organizations may have similar priorities to grow through expansion into new markets. In one organization, the growth strategy may play out through partnerships with other organizations in many geographies where the two companies' products can be bundled together. In another organization, the growth strategy may be to establish a physical presence in new countries. In the former organization, the key to success will be the ability to partner effectively and negotiate with locally established companies; in the latter, the key to success will be identifying and placing leaders who can grow a business with a start-up mentality. Notice how similar business strategies take different approaches and thus imply very different human capital requirements and people strategies such as career paths and skill development needs. As Sparrow, Scullion, and Tarique (2014) put it, "[T]he success (or failure) of the business model may become crucially dependent on the job design of a small number of mission-critical jobs" (p. 55).

In a differentiated workforce, different choices are made with respect to employee selection, rewards, performance management, and employee development for those in strategic roles. The jobs may have a more extensive analysis of the work design of the role and the competencies required. There may be an in-depth investment in an intensive interview and recruiting process to ensure the right employees are selected for strategic roles. Employees in those roles might be provided with more coaching, greater development opportunities such as training courses or job rotations, and more frequent feedback on performance. HR practices might invest in developing successors specifically for those strategic roles to build a strong bench of candidates who are prepared when vacancies arise. There might be special investments in strategic talent to ensure that they understand the direction of the organization and how they contribute to its future. See box for signs an organization is failing to provide enough differentiation.

Before leaders can decide on programs to differentiate strategic jobs, those jobs must be identified.

"A" Positions and Pivot Roles

Some argue that leaders should always seek the best talent for every position, known as "topgrading" (Smart, 1999). Topgrading is the practice of hiring and retaining only *A* players—the people in the top 10 percent of talent available,

SIGNS AN ORGANIZATION IS NOT DIFFERENTIATING ENOUGH

Among the signs that an organization is not differentiating enough, Becker, Huselid, and Beatty (2009) mention these:

- There is no explicit workforce strategy.
- No one can really explain how the company's workforce strategy contributes to the organization's strategic success.
- There is no clear line of sight between value of workforce practice and strategic success.
- The financial conversation with HR largely focuses on controlling its overall budget.
- The value of workforce practices is based on how they compare with external best-practice standards.
- Concerns about some employees feeling "left out" makes it difficult to disproportionately invest in high-value employees. (p. 8)

while clearing out the low-performing *C* players. This focus on high-performing talent makes intuitive sense. Nathan Myhrvold, the former chief technology officer of Microsoft, once remarked that "the top software developers are more productive than average software developers not by a factor of 10 or 100, or even 1,000, but 10,000" (Trost, 2014, p. 19). Top-performing managers can increase productivity of a division by 40 percent, and top salespeople contribute 67 percent greater revenue (Silzer & Dowell, 2010). The worst-performing customer service agents can destroy value and anger customers. It is no wonder that most managers would seek to hire and develop the best performance for every position.

As others argue, however, "it is neither desirable nor appropriate to fill all positions within the organization with top performers" (Collings & Mellahi, 2009, p. 305). Significant resources and expenses are required to recruit, compensate, and develop the top performers in every position, so most organizations must make choices about where to invest. As a result, Huselid, Beatty, and Becker (2005) argue that "businesses need to adopt a portfolio approach to workforce management, placing the very best employees in strategic positions, good performers in support positions, and eliminating nonperforming employees and jobs that don't add value" (p. 1).

A focus on positions, versus people or players, recognizes the contribution that the role (not person) makes in the achievement of strategy. "Jobs located in strategic business processes have more value than jobs located in other areas of the business, even if they have the same title" (Becker & Huselid, 2010, pp. 356–357). A pharmaceutical company that stakes its strategy on innovation in cholesterol-lowering medications will differentiate among the biochemical engineers working on those products compared to those engineers with similar job titles working on important (but less strategic) high blood pressure medications.

Huselid et al. (2005, p. 111) list two defining characteristics of an "A" position:

- It holds a "disproportionate importance to a company's ability to execute some part of its strategy."
- There is "wide variability in the quality of the work displayed among the employees in the position."

The concept of disproportionate impact on strategy may be intuitive, but the second characteristic may be less so. To make a differentiated investment worthwhile, there must be variations in performance so that the extra investment ultimately has a performance impact on the strategy. If everyone in a strategic role is already performing with a great degree of skill, or at a level equivalent to other competitors, there is "little opportunity for competitive advantage since everyone's performance is already at a high level" (Huselid, Beatty, & Becker, 2005, p. 113).

The authors define three types of roles that make a differential impact in an organization:

"A" Positions: Strategic

- These roles have high strategic impact and there is an observable difference between high and low performance.

"B" Positions: Support

- These roles may assist or aid those in strategic roles but do not make a direct strategic contribution.

"C" Positions: Surplus

- These roles are necessary for the organization to exist but do not have strategic importance.

Strategic "A" positions have the following characteristics:

- Strategic positions feature a high degree of variability in performance.
- Strategic positions often require a high level of expertise.
- Strategic positions aren't determined by hierarchy.
- Strategic positions aren't defined by how hard they are to fill; workforce scarcity doesn't equate to workforce value.
- Not all positions in a job category have to be considered strategic for some of the positions in a job category to be considered strategic.
- Strategic positions typically represent less than 15 percent of the workforce. (Becker, Huselid, & Beatty, 2009, p. 73)

There may be several strategic jobs, and such roles are likely to be found throughout the organization. Notice that neither hierarchy, decision authority, or title appear as defining characteristics of "A" positions. An engineering think tank that develops innovations and then sells the patents or establishes partnerships with other organizations who take the innovations to market might have two "A" positions: the engineer and the business development agent who negotiates partnership agreements.

Boudreau and Ramstead (2007) define "A" positions as "pivot roles," noting that many jobs are important but only a few are pivotal. At Starbucks, the pivot role is the barista who has the immediate impact on the customer experience, differentiating Starbucks through not just high product quality but through a personal touch that keeps customers loyal. They can offer a high degree of customization, adapting drink orders as the customer desires. Baristas will often know the orders of their regular customers and start the drink order even before the customer reaches the counter. The cashier experience is important to many organization's customer service strategies, but at Starbucks it is a pivotal aspect of the experience.

At Costco, where the strategy relies on low prices and product availability, the role of the purchasing manager is pivotal. This is likely to be an important role in many other organizations, too, but at Costco, the strategy hinges on the strategic aspect of the purchasing manager's ability to identify, source, and negotiate prices on the right products.

Boudreau and Ramstead (2007) also point out that even within pivot roles there are pivot points (interactions or activities) within a role that are strategically important. At Boeing, the aircraft engineer is a pivot role, but within the role there is more strategic importance to engineering coordination versus design activities. This is because the rapid design time required of new aircraft means more partnerships and collaboration with other organizations.

As an exercise, think for a moment about the pivot role that Disney considers critical at its theme parks. When you think you have the answer, read the explanation in the box on page 168.

PIVOT ROLES AT DISNEY

If you are like most people who consider pivot roles at Disneyland, you might have thought that the pivot roles were the characters such as Mickey Mouse, Snow White, Donald Duck, or the princesses that are popular with young visitors. You might have guessed the Disney Imagineers who design the rides and unique experiences that Disney is known for. You might have pointed to Disney's marketing department to recognize the importance of generating demand for vacations and park visitation.

While Disney characters are a differentiator, and the others all might be important roles, our definition of pivot talent includes both strategic importance and variation in performance. There is little difference between those who play the role of Mickey Mouse, so an investment in training would not make much impact.

Instead, Disney considers the pivot role to be the sweepers that clean the park. Sweepers who know the park and can provide surprising and exceptional service are likely to noticeably improve the guest experience. They are often nearby and can point out directions to rides, services, food, and gift shops. They can help families solve problems and satisfy customer needs in a way that Mickey Mouse does not (e.g., no one asks Mickey where the nearest restrooms are located!). By recognizing the customer service role of sweepers in addition to their cleaning role, Disney can differentiate itself from competitors through additional customer service training for sweepers. They select employees who have both the interest and capability for engaging with guests and desire to create an exceptional experience.

> In employee development, sweepers receive different training in customer interaction than Mickey Mouse. Sweepers get opportunities to learn from experience that will increase their familiarity with the park and those areas of the park that are most asked about by guests. In fact, while all Disney cast members go through the famous Traditions orientation and training program, there is also a formalized on-the-job training program for Disney sweepers [that] includes specific guest service elements.
>
> Notice how the portfolio of practices is directly connected to the pivotal interactions and actions. . . . Just as with well-executed marketing or financial decisions, Disney's talent investments are targeted to where they will have the largest effect. (Boudreau & Ramstead, 2007, p. 62)

Creating workforce differentiation can be challenging. Some leaders and employees may react negatively to a judgment that their role is "nonstrategic." It can be difficult to separate the evaluation of a person in a role from the strategic contribution of the position. Others may find it unfair to provide certain career opportunities, development, or rewards to some employees and not others. If appropriately implemented, however, the analysis of "A" positions and pivot roles can help leaders to make talent decisions in a way that is more focused, nuanced, and targeted.

TALENT IDENTIFICATION AND PLANNING

A second concept important to strategic talent management is the ability to identify key talent and to plan for future talent needs.

Talent Identification: Focus on Potential

Competitive environments, scarce skills, uncertainty, and strategic change combine to form a "war for talent," a term coined by McKinsey in the late 1990s (Michaels, Handfield-Jones, & Axelrod, 2001). "As organizations spend more time and resources on talent, interest in identifying and developing the needed talent inside the organization has been growing" (Silzer & Church, 2010, p. 213). The challenge is to identify participants in the talent pipeline who can become part of the organization's pool of future leaders and candidates for "A" positions.

In the past, such identification took the form of assessments of IQ, personality inventories, or job competencies that a given individual needed to possess. In an increasingly changing world, however, many organizations are moving to an assessment of potential "to contribute to the organization in the future, usually in a different capacity, doing different and broader kinds of work" (Silzer & Church, 2010, p. 220). There is growing agreement that leaders must "learn how to spot potential, effectively retain people who have it, and create development programs to help the best get better" (Fernández-Aráoz, 2014, p. 51). This means not only searching for who has a certain set of skills today, but who has the potential to learn new skills in the future as the organization's requirements continue to change.

One common approach to talent identification is a nine-box grid that visually maps an assessment of an employee's past performance and future potential. Evaluating employees on their past achievements and potential for future contributions (on a high, medium, low scale) results in placement in one of the nine boxes in Figure 6.2.

Figure 6.2 Nine Box Talent Grid

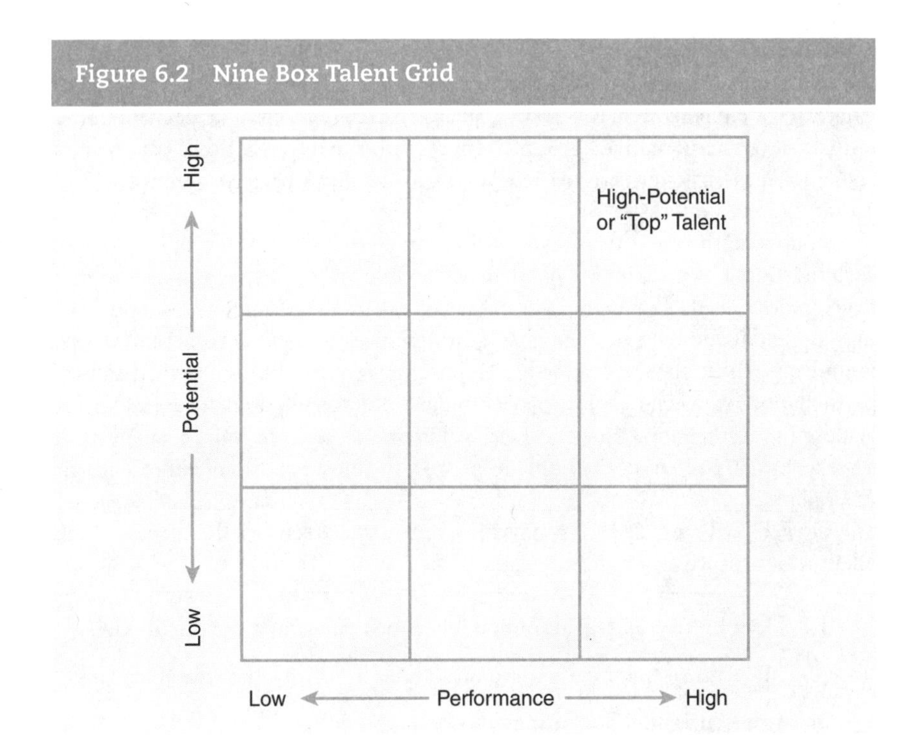

There is significant variation in the definition of high potential (Silzer & Church, 2010), but three definitions are most common:

1. **Role**: the potential to move into top or senior management roles
2. **Level**: the ability to move and perform two positions or levels above current role
3. **Breadth**: the capability to take on broader scope and a leadership role and develop long-term potential (p. 222)

By contrast, Fernández-Aráoz (2014) points to five personal characteristics of those with high potential:

1. **Motivation**: "a fierce commitment to excel in the pursuit of unselfish goals" (p. 51), ambition, and aspiration
2. **Curiosity**: a penchant for seeking out new experiences, knowledge, and candid feedback, and an openness to learning and change
3. **Insight**: the ability to gather and make sense of information that suggests new possibilities
4. **Engagement**: a knack for using emotion and logic to communicate a persuasive vision and connect with people
5. **Determination**: the wherewithal to fight for difficult goals despite challenges and to bounce back from adversity (p. 52)

Some talent review processes include every member of the organization in the review, whereas others include only the top two levels of management, strategically important positions, or certain functions or geographies (Dowell, 2010). A talent review meeting among the leadership team is common when the team will review each person on the talent grid and discuss demographic data about the individual (educational background, tenure with the organization), past results (accomplishments over the past few years), leadership strengths and needs, and career goals and interests.

Following the identification of performance and potential for all employees, each individual receives an action plan for career growth, next possible roles, and development needs. For high potential or top talent (in the upper right corner of high potential and high performance), the action plan might consist of development experiences such as leadership training programs, rotation opportunities, participation on special projects, coaching and mentoring, or exposure to senior leaders. In most organizations the distribution of high potential talent ranges from 5 percent to 20 percent of the population, with the most common being 9 percent to 10 percent.

Dowell (2010, pp. 431–434) advises seven lessons to ensure the success of the talent review process.

1. Hold line leadership accountable for the management of talent pools.
2. Make talent judgments based on standards drawn from strategic plans.
3. Value current contributions and future potential.

4. Focus as much on development as on assessment.
5. Include the individual in the planning process.
6. Emphasize the dialogue over the review format and technology.
7. Focus on the follow-up rather than the review.

Talent Planning, Pipelines, and Talent Pools

The identification of talent is often a closely guarded secret. Household products company Proctor & Gamble considered its top talent to be a competitive advantage. "One of its biggest trade secrets wasn't a clothes-cleaning technology or diaper formulation, but its Talent Portfolio, a blue binder that listed pertinent data on every candidate for the top 120 jobs—as well as their potential replacements several levels down" (Reingold, 2016, p. 176). Many organizations use talent identification practices to develop talent pools and plan succession management. The goal can be either simply to identify replacement candidates for existing roles or to provide intentional development opportunities for successors to ensure that they are prepared when the role opens up.

Yet, planning for future talent needs is no small matter. A high-potential pool of future leaders with a 10 percent turnover rate will see half its candidates gone in a 5-year timeframe (Cappelli, 2008b). It is no surprise that almost two-thirds of executives remain concerned about finding key skills, and less than one in four were confident in their talent pipelines (Fernández-Aráoz, 2014). Keller and Cappelli (2014) call the talent pipeline process a "guessing game for most organizations" (p. 117). Will we have the right number of engineers with specialized skills in 4 years, assuming our current strategy is a success? Do such candidates even exist? How many leaders will we need with experience starting up a new manufacturing site overseas? Should we begin to aggressively hire candidates from competitors (and can we afford to) or should we begin our own internal programs to develop candidates from within (and can we afford to)?

Cappelli (2008a; 2008b; 2009; Keller & Cappelli, 2014) advocates a supply chain model of talent in order to forecast demand, borrowing from a profession that has had a longer history in ensuring that the right product is available at the right time for customers. A supply chain model addresses the question "How do organizations ensure a sufficient supply of human capital when both demand and supply are uncertain?" (Keller & Cappelli, 2014, p. 118). Just as manufacturing organizations have moved to a just-in-time approach to production to minimize excess inventory, leaders can forecast talent in a "talent on demand" approach (Cappelli, 2008a). Forecasting concerns both supply and demand of talent, so leaders need practices to reduce uncertainty in forecasting accurate talent demands as well as the supply or availability of talent when it is needed. Cappelli (2008b, p. 78) offers four recommendations to address the uncertainty of the talent pipeline. The first two recommendations address uncertainty in talent demands, the second two address uncertainty in available supply.

1. **Make *and* buy to manage risk**. Having a deep bench of available talent is an advantage to mitigate the risk of uncertain needs. However, those who are identified as successors are often frustrated by waiting until an opportunity arises. Leaders can plan to have some high-potential employees for some positions but plan to recruit externally for others.

2. **Adapt to the uncertainty in talent demand.** Forecast talent needs for shorter periods, and create cross-division talent pools to develop employees "with broad and general competencies that could be applied to a range of jobs" (Cappelli, 2008b, p. 80).
3. **Improve the return on investment in developing employees.** Some companies have policies for employee development that ask employees to share in the cost of development, or agree to stay with the organization for a certain length of time.
4. **Preserve the investment by balancing employee–employer interests.** When employees desire a new career opportunity internally, the employee's desires and the employer's needs are balanced to ensure the right moves make sense for both.

As more organizations adopt a supply chain model of talent planning, more sophisticated models and tools are becoming available. Uncertainty is unavoidable, but such methods allow leaders to make better decisions about future talent needs.

CAREER DEVELOPMENT

Many organizations have developed career development systems internally to retain and motivate employees, to develop employees internally and promote from within the organization, and to provide opportunities for upward mobility (Gutteridge, Leibowitz, & Shore, 1993). Some even hire career counselors (Niles, 2005). The concept of an organizational career development system originated from organizations' interests in balancing what employees want for career growth and personal development and what the organization needs given its strategic objectives. Yet, most organizations still believe that the primary responsibility for career growth and development remains with the individual. Given the frequent downsizing and restructuring in the contemporary organizational environment, changes to the notion of careers, and changes in the employment "contract," it makes more sense than ever for individuals to be conscious of their own career plans and development. Career development programs and one-on-one career interventions can help employees through a forced transition such as a merger, restructuring, or downsizing. They can also help employees proactively choose to take action in anticipation of a transition in the future (seeking out new skills to plan for a new job).

The Classic View: Stages of the Career

Early research and writing on career development emphasized a linear progression of career shifts throughout an employee's life, though recent research indicates that this concept has now been outgrown.

Consider Schein's (1978) book *Career Dynamics*, in which he outlined nine stages of a career life cycle:

1. *Growth, fantasy, exploration.* During this stage, individuals explore career options and make educational choices based on careers they find desirable.

2. *Entry into world of work.* Individuals search out, interview for, and experience the first job. They experience the transition to becoming an employee, working for an employer, and navigating the challenges of completing initial job tasks.
3. *Basic training.* The individual begins to develop job skills, becoming an effective contributor. The individual is in a learning mode as a novice organizational member, learning not only job skills but also interpersonal skills in relating to and working with colleagues. He or she may be highly concerned with developing competence and meeting performance expectations of a supervisor or colleagues.
4. *Full membership in early career.* Individuals experience first major job assignments not in a training or apprentice role. They learn how to accept work assignments and the complexities of working with coworkers for extended periods. They evaluate whether this work represents what they would like to be doing in the future or whether a different job or organization would better suit them.
5. *Full membership, midcareer.* Individuals develop self-assurance and trust in decisions and job skills. They may have increasing responsibility and a professional reputation. They consider how to remain current in their areas of expertise and how to continue to grow and develop.
6. *Midcareer crisis.* Individuals begin to reassess their career choices and options. They may evaluate their strengths and weaknesses and think through their goals for their lives and how their careers fit or do not fit with that vision.
7. *Late career.* Individuals will customize a path based on the previous stage to determine the next steps. Those who take a leadership role will learn how to manage the work and performance of subordinates and make broad-ranging decisions, while those who do not choose a leadership path may develop breadth or depth in their areas of expertise.
8. *Decline and disengagement.* Individuals begin to change job roles and perhaps take less responsibility. They may develop increasing interests outside of work.
9. *Retirement.* Individuals transition from a day dominated by full-time work to nonwork concerns. They may reevaluate their personal identities in noncareer terms and may decide how to use work skills in a different capacity.

Schein (1978) writes, "People in different occupations move at different rates through the stages, and personal factors strongly influence the rate of movement as well" (p. 48). Some individuals may remain in one stage for an extended time, and some may find themselves rapidly progressing through stages.

The Contemporary View: Boundaryless Careers

While this once may have been a relevant description of most employees' career development experiences, many observers now suggest that these stage theories no longer fit for the majority of employees. As organizations have evolved, so has the concept of the career.

In the changing work environment in which individuals may change careers or jobs or choose to be away from the workforce for any period (e.g., to raise children, take a sabbatical, travel, obtain an advanced degree), some research suggests that people no longer progress through their career stages in the sequence presented earlier. Instead, they cycle through them quickly and return to previous stages (Sullivan, 1999). Rather than presuming that individuals follow a single, well-defined career path through stages, some have proposed the concept of the "boundaryless career" (Arthur & Rousseau, 1996), which transcends any individual job, occupational function, profession, and organization. Career progression in a boundaryless career is defined more by learning milestones and skill capabilities rather than age and job titles. With the rise of flexible contract work, part-time, and temporary project work, employees may choose to work independently, taking advantage of their multiple and diverse skills to work for several employers. Thus, in a boundaryless career, employment may be with many firms rather than a single company, and job security exists not because of tenure and long-term loyalty to the organization but because of the individual's ability to successfully perform the work and contribute to organizational goals (Sullivan, 1999).

Career Lattice Versus Career Ladder

Within a company, the concept of the boundaryless career implies that upward mobility may not be the only option for growth and development, but employees can develop their careers by gaining a diversity of experiences in a variety of areas. The term for this is the *career lattice* (Benko & Anderson, 2010) as distinct from the career ladder. Employees may want vertical career growth into management and senior leadership positions, or they may desire to increase technical depth and expertise in a given professional area. They may even desire both. Junior accountants in product division A may not need to wait for a senior accounting position to open up, but may gain useful experience in product division B before moving to a senior role in product division C when there is a vacancy. Thus there is no single development path for all employees, but a customized evolution that makes sense for each individual depending on their needs or interests. Automobile manufacturer BMW has implemented a career development practice called a knight's move. Similar to the pattern that a knight follows on a chess board, employees move up vertically but then subsequently move over or across to another division as a way of enhancing cross-functional skills (Galbraith, 2014a). See Figure 6.3 for a graphic illustration of the career lattice versus ladder.

Lattice career pathways have several features (Benko & Anderson, 2010, p. 68):

- Create multidirectional development options, expanding choices for individualized career moves
- Provide transparency about the range of possible roles, along with the benefits and trade-offs
- Focus the culture less on upward moves and more on development and contribution
- Build cross-silo relationship and knowledge, thereby improving collaboration, coordination, and execution.

There is also evidence that different generations experience career paths differently and hold different expectations for their careers. According to a study by

Lancaster and Stillman (2010), the most recent generation entering the workforce (the Millennial generation) has a higher expectation for career development, with 82 percent of Millennial respondents noting that "career paths advance too slowly where they work" (p. 181). The authors recommend that employers offer rotation programs that can enhance skill development and provide a breadth of knowledge gained from a variety of positions.

Table 6.1 compares traditional and boundaryless careers.

Figure 6.3 Career Ladder Versus Career Lattice

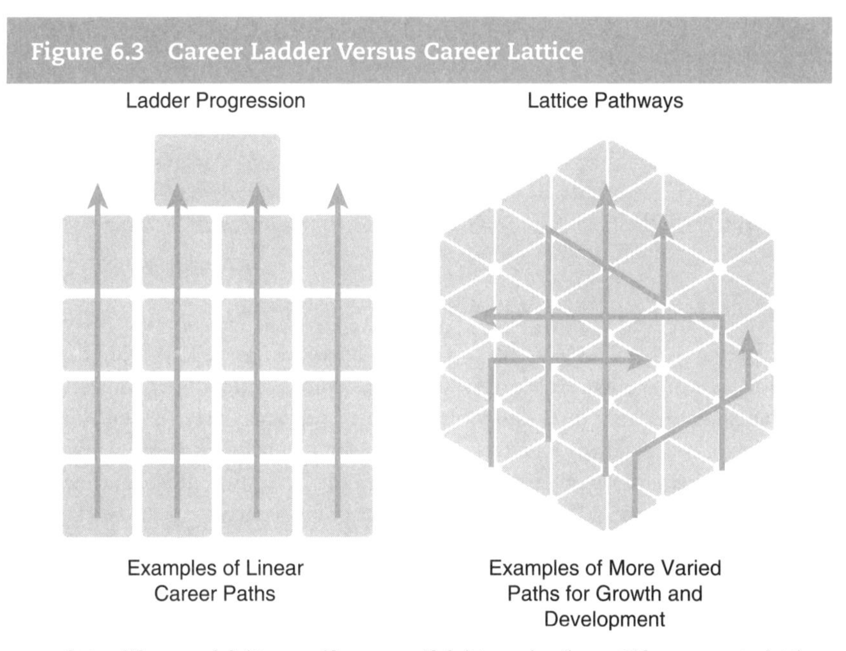

Source: https://dupress.deloitte.com/dup-us-en/deloitte-review/issue-8/the-corporate-lattice-rethinking-careers-in-the-changing-world-of-work.html

Table 6.1 Traditional Versus Boundaryless Careers

	Traditional Careers	Boundaryless Careers
Employment Relationship	Job security for loyalty	Employability for performance and flexibility
Boundaries	One or two firms	Multiple firms
Skills	Firm specific	Transferable
Success Measured By	Pay, promotion, status	Psychologically meaningful work
Responsibility for Career Management	Organization	Individual
Training	Formal programs	On the job
Milestones	Age related	Learning related

Source: Sullivan, 1999, p. 458.

"Lattice organizations understand how to achieve high performance in this changing world of work. To engage a diverse workforce, they make it possible for their employees to tailor aspects of career and life" (Benko & Anderson, 2010, p. 50). Recognizing the multiple and diverse ways that careers develop can help leaders design talent programs that find talent throughout the organization, not just in the same division or function. Such an approach can build engagement and loyalty and increase employees' connections within the organization.

TALENT DEVELOPMENT AND LEARNING PROGRAMS

Traditional approaches to developing talent took the form of formal training programs, typically classroom events led by an in-person trainer. While such programs still exist, today's emphasis is much more likely to be on new forms of learning in addition to formal training, and recognizing that growth and development come from a wide variety of experiences beyond a formal classroom.

New Forms of Learning Versus Formal Training

In their review of learning trends, Noe, Clarke, and Klein (2014) write that the global nature of the workforce, cost pressures, and workload demands all have constrained the use of formal classroom learning programs. Instead, they point out that learning can occur through technology-driven mechanisms, through informal means, and through social channels. "Learning is becoming more learner controlled, socially affected, and recognized as naturally occurring in the workplace" (p. 248). Learning is now considered to occur during the work process itself and often is initiated based on the learner's interests and motivations. Today, workplace learning includes a diverse blend of multiple types, delivery mechanisms, channels, lengths, content producers, and forms. It is no longer episodic, confined to a classroom, but continuous and integrated into the job role and processes (see box).

WORKPLACE LEARNING TODAY

- Is directed by the learner rather than an instructor
- Can be short and informal versus lengthy and formal
- Occurs in multiple modalities versus in a face-to-face classroom
- Learners choose when and where to learn versus controlled delivery
- Content comes from everyone versus content coming only from external experts
- Learning just in time versus training just in case
- On demand versus scheduled and controlled
- Integrated into the job process versus disconnected from the real world application
- Can occur as part of a social network or team versus learning in isolation

E-learning. E-learning generally refers to learning programs that use technology as a delivery mechanism for content, reducing the need for instructors to teach courses. Employees can often access content on a smartphone or tablet, learning beyond their office walls while traveling on a business trip or commuting on a train. E-learning can include video lectures, games or simulations, and they can be synchronous (all learners participate at the same time) or asynchronous (learners access the content when they want). Some organizations provide access to MOOCs (massive open online courses) which often provide a course structure containing videos, readings, quizzes, and discussion boards for student interaction. Access to on-demand content can often provide just-in-time learning when employees require knowledge, immediately before they begin a task or activity. This can provide faster knowledge acquisition (immediate access instead of waiting for the next available training course) and greater retention (employees are able to use the knowledge immediately instead of forgetting what they learned in a course months ago).

Informal Learning. There is greater recognition of the pervasiveness of informal learning that occurs through self-directed learning, self-reflection, and conversations with or observations of managers or peers. It can occur through networking or interaction with internally recognized experts inside a company. Informal learning appears to be greater in organizations where managers establish a culture of learning, provide tools and resources for access to learning, and support connections with colleagues who share knowledge with one another and are invested in a team's development. Mentoring programs are growing in popularity in organizations to facilitate learning. A mentor is a counselor, adviser, and teacher who usually works in a one-on-one relationship with a protégé. In some apprentice-like models of mentoring, the mentor may demonstrate how a task is accomplished or provide an example, watch the performer complete the task (or assess completed work), and then provide feedback or an assessment on how it was done.

Social Learning. Social learning includes the electronic coordination tools and communities of practice that we reviewed in Chapter 5. In addition, many organizations are going beyond these to invest in social technologies where employees can generate their own content to share with one another. An employee can record a video for other employees demonstrating a unique solution to a problem, or post a tip on an internal bulletin board or wiki site. Such content is usually current and highly relevant to employees, making use of expertise that already resides within the organization. However, it can often be of low quality, difficult to locate, and lack integration with other content.

Development Through Experiences

Stretch assignments provide the opportunity for employees to learn new skills while contributing in a given job role. One study found that the assignments that offered the most development opportunities were "a position with larger scope; turning around a business; starting a new business; a large, high-profile special project; and working outside their home country" (Michaels et al., 2001, p. 104). Intentional job rotation programs provide "logically ordered job assignments where high-potential leaders are systematically given increasing challenges in different strategic or operational areas of the business to develop the expertise, capabilities, and perspective needed to perform effectively in future leadership roles" (Yost & Plunkett, 2010, pp. 315–316). Many organizations have arrived at the conclusion that "you can't have an agile company if you give employees lifetime contracts" (R. Hoffman, Casnocha, & Yeh, 2013, p. 50), leading some authors to advocate a "tour of duty" model. R. Hoffman, Casnocha, and Yeh (2013) argue that a new employment contract of short-term, 2- to 4-year roles that take advantage of an employee's entrepreneurial spirit also helps to increase employee retention.

Development through experience can push leaders outside their comfort zone but through an experience that allows them to try new skills and learn from both success and failure. For example, an organization might design rotation experiences to allow high-potential leaders to develop a diverse background in multiple functions or geographies. Sales leaders might rotate through different geographic regions, and product leaders might be asked to take on roles in marketing.

One key to ensuring that the job experience is a learning opportunity is to be intentional about the specific skills, competencies, relationships, and learning outcomes expected. Yost and Plunkett (2010) recommend the completion of a taxonomy required of leaders as they rotate into new roles:

- Experiences needed: a turnaround scenario, international experience, start-up experience, sales roles
- Competencies: strategic thinking, technical expertise
- Key relationships: partners, key customers, senior executives
- Learning outcomes or growth: comfort with ambiguity, openness to feedback (p. 316)

Once a potential experience need is identified, Yost and Plunkett (2010) recommend an analysis of it to include the following:

- The types of job assignments in the organization that map to this experience
- A list of smaller development-in-place assignments that also might be available or created
- Strategies to navigate through the experience
- A description of the key elements that must be present to make the experience strongly developmental (e.g., supervisory support, risk, profit and loss responsibility) (p. 321)

These considerations can help to ensure that the new experience will provide the right development opportunity for the given individual. In addition, the stretch assignment should provide the right amount of challenge. Too little challenge and the individual will not learn from the experience because he or she will fall back on familiar skills; too much challenge and the individual could become demoralized from the struggle and fail to learn from the experience.

PERFORMANCE MANAGEMENT

The consulting company Deloitte made headlines in 2015 when it announced that it would follow several other large companies in no longer conducting traditional annual performance reviews. The Deloitte practice followed what many other organizations do: set annual performance goals for every employee and then conduct a lengthy evaluation process in which managers write evaluations of employee performance and assign a rating. Not only were ratings of skills inaccurate and highly variable among raters, the feedback from an annual process came too late to be valuable to employees being rated. More strikingly, members of the organization spent close to two million hours collectively on the process of completing forms and holding meetings.

Lawler (2008) writes that any performance management system must accomplish four goals:

1. It needs to define and produce agreement on what type of performance is needed. Shields and Kaine (2016) write that performance has three components: Inputs, such as the employees' skills, knowledge, and competencies; Processes, including behaviors, work effort, and activities; and Outputs, such as results achieved.
2. It needs to guide the development of individuals so that they have the skills and knowledge needed to perform effectively. Employees should receive feedback on their skills to know where to develop for growth.
3. It needs to motivate individuals to perform effectively. It should feed a rewards system that is commensurate with performance.
4. It needs to provide data to the organization's human capital information system. (pp. 99–100)

Done well, performance appraisal systems can have a number of positive benefits, but done poorly, they can have unfortunate negative consequences, as displayed in Figure 6.4.

It is no wonder that performance management is one of the most unpopular talent programs that most organizations use (Lawler, 2017). Managers are unhappy because they must take significant time to prepare the reviews and occasionally hold difficult conversations. Employees are unhappy when the manager's ratings tend to be lower than self-ratings (a common practice because employees tend to rate themselves more highly, with 80 percent of employees believing that they are above-average performers; Mohrman, Resnick-West, & Lawler, 1989).

Lawler (2017) observes that major alterations are needed to performance management practices in most organizations, and he advises that there are several critical features that should be part of an effective performance management process.

1. **The process should be led by executives**. "Unless there is a top-down commitment to doing it well and senior managers acting as role models of effective performance management behavior, there is little to no chance it will be a key driver of business strategy" (Lawler, 2017, p. 92).

Figure 6.4 Benefits and Consequences of Performance Appraisal Systems

Benefits of Performance Appraisal Systems	Negative Consequences of Performance Appraisal Systems
• There may be increased motivation to perform. • Self-esteem of person being appraised may increase. • Person doing the appraisal gains new insight into the person being appraised. • Job of the person being appraised may be clarified and better defined. • Valuable communication can take place among the individuals taking part. • Participants may gain a better understanding of themselves and of the development activities that are of value. • Rewards such as pay and promotion can be distributed on a fair and credible basis. • Organizational goals can be made clearer, and they can be more readily accepted. • Valuable appraisal information can allow the organization to do a better job planning and developing training programs.	• Individuals may quit as a result of the way they are treated. • False and misleading data may be created. • The self-esteem of the person being appraised and the person doing the appraisal may be damaged. • Large amounts of time may be wasted. • The relationship among the individuals involved may be permanently worsened. • Performance may be lowered for many reasons including the feeling that poor performance measurement means no rewards for performance. • Money may be wasted on forms, training, technology, and a host of support activities. • Expensive lawsuits may be filed by individuals who feel unfairly appraised.

Source: Republished with permission of John Wiley & Sons, Adapted from *Designing performance appraisal systems*, A. M. Mohrman Jr., S. M. Resnick-West, and E. E. Lawler III, pp. 3–4, © 1989; permission conveyed through Copyright Clearance Center, Inc.

2. **The process should not be an annual one.** Annual ratings and feedback do not match the flow of work for most employees. Technicians who fix broken Internet service at customers' homes could get performance feedback daily. Other employees manage work processes such as sales or service engagements with customers that may last for weeks or months. Goal setting and feedback practices should occur immediately after those projects end. The process thus becomes adapted, customized for employees' needs, and a regular ongoing part of the work. The frequency of the process (including goal setting) should match the pace of organizational change.
3. **Use technology**. Technology can help to provide a repository of feedback throughout a performance cycle and allow the observation of trends over time.
4. **Measure effectiveness**. Surveys of employees and managers can provide data about how well the system is meeting its goals.
5. **There should be no ratings**. Ratings can take a number of forms from a simple "Does not meet," "Meets," "Exceeds" 3-point scale, to a forced distribution or stack ranking of employees from best to worst. These are bias-prone measures prompting some organizations to eliminate ratings but still insist on performance feedback discussions.

6. **The process should be based on data.** Technology can increasingly provide detailed and objective data that can provide input on employee performance.

At Deloitte, major changes have been made to the performance management process. Since the primary work at Deloitte consists of consulting teams collaborating together on projects, the goal of performance management is to reward high performance, create stronger teams, and drive individual performance through feedback. To rate team members, after each project or no less than quarterly, team leaders are now asked, "Would you always want this person on your team?" "Would you award this person the highest possible compensation increase and bonus?" "Is this person at risk for low performance?" and "Is this person ready for a promotion today?" (Buckingham & Goodall, 2015, p. 46). Over time, and experience with different employees and team leaders, a reliable set of trends can be observed about an employee's performance. Weekly check-in conversations and quarterly or project-based reviews provide the opportunity for dialogue and feedback.

Redesigning a performance management system to support strategic needs and the rest of the organization design should be done thoughtfully and with appropriate input from employees and managers. Effective design of a performance management process, according to A. M. Mohrman, Jr., Resnick-West, and Lawler (1989, pp. 28–30), entails five principles:

1. Get the right people involved. Employees should be included in the appraisal system design team to build commitment.
2. View performance appraisal as part of a complex system. Changes to the process may have impacts on other practices such as rewards or may imply needed management training.
3. Learn from implementation. Evaluate the results of pilot programs and make modifications.
4. Remain flexible. The process should be adaptable as business needs change.
5. Be patient. Implementing a new system may take training, increased communication, or manager support.

Different strategies will require different behaviors to be performed to accomplish it. A matrix organization may place a premium on collaboration across different dimensions of the matrix, so the performance management system can reflect input from multiple managers. An organization with a strong global operating model may desire to include feedback from peers on shared strategy development and clear decision practices. Ultimately each organization has the opportunity to design a performance management process that is aligned to their unique business needs.

STRATEGIC ANALYSIS AND DESIGNING THE PEOPLE POINT

Clearly there are a number of different approaches to identify and develop talent, from job rotations and career lattice programs, to e-learning, employee-created learning content, and updated performance management programs. We have also emphasized the importance of designing a unique portfolio of practices created

BUILDING A GAME-CHANGING TALENT STRATEGY

Based on their experience with financial services company BlackRock, authors Ready, Hill, and Thomas (2014) conclude that the best talent strategies "are relentlessly focused on supporting, and in some cases driving, the companies' business strategies. . . . Their talent policies are built to last but are constantly under review, to ensure that they can respond to changing conditions on the ground and to cultural differences across the globe" (p. 64).

BlackRock's commitment to its customers provides an enduring value and purpose that drives all of its human resources practices, as are its values of "collectivism, collaboration, trust, and respect" (p. 67). We will discuss the role of organizational culture and design in more depth in Chapter 8, but the authors point out that a successful culture of talent management is "purpose-driven, performance-oriented, and principles-led," (p. 68) with the following characteristics:

1. My company places "purpose" at the heart of its business model.
2. My company has a high-performance culture.
3. Leaders in my company follow well-understood guiding principles.
4. Our people policies help drive our business strategy.
5. Our talent management practices are highly effective.
6. Our leaders are completely committed to excellence in talent management.
7. Our leaders are deeply engaged in and accountable for spotting, tracking, coaching, and developing the next generation of leaders.
8. Our talent practices are strategically oriented, but they also put a premium on operational efficiency.
9. Our talent practices engender a strong sense of collective purpose and pride yet work very well for my career as an individual.
10. Our talent practices strike the right balance between global scale and local responsiveness.
11. My company has a long-standing commitment to people development, but we are very open to changing our policies when circumstances dictate. (p. 67)

together to achieve the organization's strategy (see box for an example). Unfortunately, as Hunt (2014) observes, "one of the reasons for poorly integrated development programs is a tendency for companies to treat [these approaches] as separate programs managed by separate groups" (pp. 257–258). As leaders and organization designers, we know that misaligned programs send inconsistent messages and lead to a decrease in performance.

To organize a people strategy based on the business strategy, a tool such as the one in Figure 6.5 can help to organize the designer's priorities. It follows a logical thought process from the design criteria through the important competencies required and talent needs in "A" positions. An action plan helps to specify important and unique elements to the human resources strategy and to ensure that they are connected with one another for the same purpose of achieving the business strategy.

Figure 6.5 Example of a People Strategy Analysis

Design Criteria or Strategic Priority	Competencies Required	"A" Positions and Pivot Roles	Talent Needs	Actions (talent management, learning and development)
Provide custom bundles of products and services	• Ability to assess customer needs • Business acumen • Broad product knowledge	Customer account managers	• 25% growth in account managers forecast in 2 years • Gap in coverage of retail accounts	• Identify successors for critical account roles • Create on-demand product training • Develop talent pool for retail accounts • Customer feedback incorporated into performance management

GLOBAL CONSIDERATIONS

Organizations must manage a talent pool that is globally diverse as the workforce becomes increasingly global, mobile, and virtual. Many organizations see their talent pool as global and focus on identifying and developing talent anywhere, believing that an employee's location is not critical (Tarique & Schuler, 2014). Indeed, most employees in global companies are expected to work and collaborate with others around the world no matter their home location. Yet, there is also evidence that demographic trends and talent needs vary across countries and regions. For example, growing investment by multinational companies in India and China has created a need for deeper technical skills. At the same time, the working population in China is aging while India's growing population will create a younger workforce (Doh, Smith, Stumpf, & Tymon, 2014). The growth of domestic companies in both countries adds to the competition for talent. Doh, Smith, Stumpf, and Tymon (2014) observe that talent management practices in India and China are beginning to look like those in the West. Similar studies of talent management practices in various countries and geographies have been done in Brazil, Japan, Thailand, China, Poland, and Finland (see Al Ariss, 2014, for a review), to name just a few.

The central issue has been framed as one of balancing local needs with global consistency, or divergence versus convergence of talent practices. To what extent is there necessary uniqueness in approach in a given geography or should all regions be following similar talent practices across an organization? Not surprisingly, we can look to the rest of the organization design for answers. "An organization's approach to [global talent management] is largely defined by its corporate strategy and corporate structure, and whether operations are more centralized (globally integrated) or decentralized (locally responsive)" (Sparrow, Farndale, & Scullion, 2014, p. 266). Where the strategy requires close coordination between regions, and information and knowledge must move freely between them, an approach to talent that moves talent between geographies horizontally might be preferred. Where depth of expertise or relationships within a region is more important, a local approach to talent management might be best suited to the organization.

More likely, such decisions are not wholly either-or, but a matter of a series of decisions about how best to manage global talent.

There are practical problems, however, in that research has demonstrated that different cultures approach talent practices differently. The meaning of high performance and high potential differs across cultures, complicating a global approach to talent identification. Certain behaviors that are preferred and rewarded in one culture (for example, directness, or a strong sales orientation) may be seen as shortcomings in another (Ruddy & Anand, 2010). Chinese companies have been observed to emphasize team spirit and attitudes toward work in performance appraisals and use more general criteria allowing more manager leeway in interpretation of performance (Boudreau & Lawler, 2014). Employees in China may be culturally discouraged from positive self-presentation and high self-ratings on performance evaluations (Ruddy & Anand, 2010). Thus, the measures of performance may not be consistent and require alignment conversations to ensure calibration. Most organizations, however, appear to discount cultural differences in talent identification.

In the past, an expatriate assignment was a preferred method for the development of global leaders who could become familiar with business conditions experienced around the world. In recent years, the trend has been toward increasing development of local leaders who are prepared to take broader leadership roles rather than bringing in leaders from outside the country (Ruddy & Anand; 2010; Sparrow, Farndale, & Scullion, 2014). Not only are such expatriate assignments expensive, many expatriates struggle to learn the local language, culture, and business customs.

Stahl et al. (2012) recommend that global talent management practices balance local and global needs. Where global standards are important (such as leadership competencies that support the organization's strategy), global consistency may be required. Where local or cultural considerations are critical (e.g., preferences in training modalities or compensation practices to reflect inflation rates), regions should be given discretion. As Sparrow, Farndale, and Scullion (2014) conclude, "We think the label optimization (or hybridization) might better describe what has to be done to GTM [global talent management] practices as they are used across different geographies" (p. 272).

SUMMARY

In this chapter, we have covered ways to approach the people point of the star to support the strategy and the rest of the organization design. The objective is to design a people point that looks unlike any other organization's or competitor's so that it is as unique as the organization's strategy. Creating a differentiated workforce approach means conducting an analysis of "A" positions or pivot roles that have a disproportionate impact on the achievement of strategy. These roles also display variations in performance so that investments in the roles will elevate results and improve strategic impact. Talent management, including the identification of high-potential employees and the planning process for future talent, allows leaders to thoughtfully assess talent gaps to strategic needs and design appropriate development actions. Career development today looks more like a lattice of diverse moves than a single upward ladder of advancement. Leaders should consider learning activities that take advantage of continuous, social, and informal learning options as well as development moves for high-potential talent that provide varied experiences to stretch and challenge employees. Finally, we reviewed performance management approaches that give employees feedback on their work. A well-designed people point of the star should consist of aligned and coherent talent approaches in each of these areas.

QUESTIONS FOR DISCUSSION

1. What is your reaction to the idea of a differentiated workforce? What do you see as the practical advantages or challenges in implementing this concept?
2. In this chapter, we reviewed the distinction between a career ladder and a career lattice. How do you expect your career to evolve? What will be the important considerations to you in changing jobs or career paths?
3. Which of the trends in workplace learning have you seen in practice? How do you imagine learning will occur throughout your career? What forms of learning will help you stay current in your career?

FOR FURTHER READING

Becker, B. E., Huselid, M. A., & Beatty, R. W. (2009). *The differentiated workforce.* Boston, MA: Harvard Business.

Cappelli, P. (2008). *Talent on demand.* Boston, MA: Harvard Business.

Lawler, E. E., III. (2008). *Talent: Making people your competitive advantage.* San Francisco, CA: Jossey-Bass.

Lawler, E. E., III. (2017). *Reinventing talent management.* Oakland, CA: Berrett-Koehler.

Silzer, R., & Dowell, B. E. (Eds.). (2010). *Strategy-driven talent management.* San Francisco, CA: Jossey-Bass.

EXERCISE

In this exercise, we will practice developing a strategic approach to the People point of the star based on the strategy, structure, and process points. Note that you will need to make some assumptions about the organization. You may also research a real organization where you think this organizational capability would be a top design criterion.

Key Organizational Capability From Strategy or Important Structure or Process Feature	Key Pivot Positions (those few targeted roles and skill sets in the new organization that will have a disproportionate impact on results)	How You Would Design Other Key "People" Features (Talent management, learning and development, performance feedback)
Develop new product ideas		

(*Continued*)

(Continued)

Key Organizational Capability From Strategy or Important Structure or Process Feature	Key Pivot Positions (those few targeted roles and skill sets in the new organization that will have a disproportionate impact on results)	How You Would Design Other Key "People" Features (Talent management, learning and development, performance feedback)
Ensure an exceptional customer experience in our retail stores		
Ensure that we produce products at the lowest cost		
Expand our products into new geographic markets		
Coordinate best practices across global lines		
Deliver project management support throughout the organization to support team projects		
Sell packaged solutions of bundled products to meet unique customer needs		
Push decision making down to cross-functional teams		
Ensure that customer services professionals are familiar with solutions to common customer problems (troubleshooting)		

CHAPTER 7

REWARDS

Learning Objectives

In this chapter you will learn

- How the rewards point of the star influences motivation for individuals to achieve personal and organizational goals which support the strategy and the rest of the organization design.
- Why rewards are often misaligned and how rewards can have unintended consequences.
- How to design metrics through the balanced scorecard to focus attention on what is important.
- How organizations can approach elements of a rewards system, such as pay for performance, skill-based pay, and team compensation.

In Chapter 6, we considered how leaders design talent practices that support the important skills and competencies that are required for the organization to be successful. Closely connected with the talent strategy is the rewards strategy, the final point of the star. When done well, an effective rewards strategy can propel the business strategy and attract and retain key talent.

A rewards system also helps to connect individual performance behaviors to the accomplishment of organizational goals, acting as an incentive for individuals to enact the right personal actions that will help the organization achieve its strategy. Rewards support other star points as well, by focusing attention on the structural lens (rewarding division performance, whether product, customer, matrix, and so on), lateral capability (supporting participation in cross-functional teams and communities of practice, or balancing the multiple dimensions of the matrix), and people (supporting skill development, or rewarding top talent). The primary purpose of a rewards system is to motivate employees, as it helps to draw a connection between their personal goals and those of the organization (Galbraith, 2014a).

An important component of the rewards system is the set of metrics that indicate success, because "before you reward people, you have to be able to measure their contribution" (Galbraith, Downey, & Kates, 2002, p. 191). The design of goals and metrics, preceding implementation of rewards, communicates what results are desired and will be rewarded. Leaders must consider what outcomes are wanted and how those outcome and process variables will be measured. Tools such as the balanced scorecard, reviewed in this chapter, help to communicate goals to achieve the strategy.

By now, it will come as no surprise that we will emphasize the importance of alignment of the rewards point of the star with the strategy and the rest of the design. Unfortunately, as we will review in this chapter, misaligned rewards and metrics are common. The consequences of this misalignment may be significant in providing barriers to the achievement of the strategy. As we will see, it makes sense for designers to pay careful attention to rewards, because a poor rewards system can encourage employees to act in ways that may counteract the rest of the design objectives that the designer has worked so hard to reach through the other four star points.

When we use the term *rewards*, we are referring to both financial and nonfinancial incentive practices. Financial incentives include monetary compensation such as base pay, bonuses (based on individual, team, or organization-wide performance), pay for performance (commission or piecework), and stock, profit sharing, or equity programs. Other financial incentives include benefits, vacation time, and gift certificates. Nonfinancial incentives and recognition are also an important component of rewards programs. These include praise and thank-you recognition from managers and peers, employee-of-the-month programs, commendation in employee events and newsletters, a certificate, personal trophy or plaque, or name inscribed on a sign or panel hanging in a public place in the organization. Additional nonfinancial incentives include "status indicators such as an enhanced job title, a more flexible work schedule, greater job autonomy, paid sabbaticals, more interesting work, . . . training and development, tuition reimbursement, coveted parking spaces, a gym membership, a new piece of furniture" (Aguinis, Joo, & Gottfredson, 2013, p. 247). While the concept of rewards most often conjures images of monetary payments to employees, it is also important to include this broader range of nonfinancial recognition opportunities.

APPROACHES TO REWARDS

Researchers distinguish between two prevailing rewards practices:

- **A traditional, hierarchical, or bureaucratic approach** (J. Kerr & Slocum, 1987; Lawler, 1990, 2017). The primary determinants of rewards in this approach are tenure (defined as time in the job or organization) and performance, based on a supervisor's subjective evaluation (J. Kerr & Slocum, 1987). In this approach, rewards increase as hierarchical level in the organization increases.
- **A performance-based strategic design approach**, which generally began in about the mid-1980s (J. Kerr & Slocum, 1987; Ledford, 2014). The performance-based approach "objectively defined and measured performance and explicitly linked rewards to performance" (J. Kerr & Slocum, 1987, p. 102). Salary increases in this model are generally based on the overall market rate, but bonuses are given based on a manager's individual or division results. In this approach, achievement of results that contribute to the strategy is the greatest criterion for a reward.

Despite evidence for the effectiveness of the performance-based approach, Lawler (2017) reports that the traditional approach still dominates. "The reward systems in most organizations do not focus on skills and competencies, business strategy, team and organizational performance. . . . Instead they still follow a traditional bureaucratic model and are based on job evaluation systems, merit pay, and fixed set of fringe benefits" (p. 75). As a result of the challenges in aligning rewards to strategy, many organizations' practices look the same as they did decades ago. Ledford (2014) reports that the strategic approach has even waned in recent years "to a less strategic, more mechanical, and less important position" (p. 170), yet Lawler (2017) exhorts that the "traditional reward system practices do not fit well in organizations built for the new world of work" (p. 88).

Aligning strategy and rewards is a complex endeavor, one that has been called "daunting given the number of different work units and occupations that make up a major corporation" (Scott, McMullen, Shields, & Bowbin, 2009, p. 46). Finding the right metrics that will drive the right behavior for different jobs and divisions is a difficult process. Research suggests that it is worth the effort, however, and that careful alignment between business strategy and rewards increases organizational performance. "An organization's pay system should take into consideration its strategy, structure, and the broader environment (that is, there should be both internal and external fit), as well as employees' needs and expectations. If this is done effectively, it increases the likelihood of improved employee and organizational performance" (Samnani & Singh, 2014, p. 9). Yet this alignment between rewards and business strategy may only be substantial for about a third of organizations, according to studies of compensation professionals (Ledford, 2014).

MISALIGNED REWARDS: WHEN REWARDS FAIL

Creating an effective rewards system that supports the organization design is much easier said than done. The primary reason a rewards system does not support the design is that it is misaligned. There are many opportunities for the rewards system to fail to support desired behaviors, or worse, provide an incentive for the wrong behavior. When rewards are inappropriately designed to support organizational goals, unintended consequences can occur. An employee "behaves as encouraged, obtains a good 'score,' and receives expected rewards, but the organization is worse off" (Hambrick & Snow, 1988, p. 348). Here are some outcomes of a poorly designed rewards system.

Unethical Behavior

In 2013, a *Los Angeles Times* investigation alleged that Wells Fargo bank employees, under pressure to retain customers and encourage them to maintain more ties to the company, opened credit card accounts and bank accounts without customers' knowledge or consent. Former employees describe a sales environment with high quotas for selling additional products and services to customers. Employees who failed to reach the quotas reported being forced to work overtime without compensation or risk public humiliation in front of coworkers (Reckard, 2013). Wells Fargo executives would later announce a change that "refocused the retail bank's incentive plan to reward employees for higher customer satisfaction, not product sales" (Colvin, 2017, p. 144).

Aguinis, Joo, and Gottfredson (2013) tell the story of the vegetable producer Green Giant, who once rewarded employees for finding insects in food processing. They discontinued the practice once employees started planting insects in the food in order to later report discovering them and receive a reward.

Counterproductive Behavior

Workplace accidents are a serious threat to employees. When worker's compensation claims increased in the 1980s, insurance premiums became a large expense for many organizations. Some managers began to adopt incentive programs to encourage employee safety, giving bonuses to employees whose work sites had no accidents. What some observers found as a result is that the accident rate may not have changed, but what decreased was the reporting of accidents by employees in order to receive the bonus (Hunt, 2014; Mattson, Torbiörn, & Hellgren, 2014; Miozza & Wyld, 2002).

The city of Albuquerque, New Mexico, struggled with mounting overtime compensation expenses in its trash collection division. To reduce overtime and encourage speed by trash collectors, the city implemented a pay plan where drivers would be paid for 8 hours of work, regardless of how long it took to complete their route. Drivers drove faster, causing accidents and insurance claims, they missed or skipped pickups, causing complaints, and they omitted mid-route trips to the dump drop-off site to save time, causing the city to incur fines for driving overloaded trucks. The end result was an increase in expenses, not a decrease (Pfeffer, 2007).

Counterproductive behavior may also be seen in a focus on short-term results at the expense of the organization's long-term success. Managers may delay equipment maintenance or employee training to save costs in the short run and meet budget goals, only to see more serious equipment malfunctions or employee skill gaps in the long run.

Conflict and Competition

Rewards practices can increase employee conflict and accelerate internal competition. Research on workplace bullying suggests that the incidents of bullying increase when the organization has a competitive environment, as is the case when employees must compete for scarce rewards. Employees who are bullied may leave the organization or lower their productivity so they are not seen as a threat to the bully. The researchers conclude that "workplace bullying may represent a particularly important unintended consequence of zero-sum performance-enhancing compensation practices" (Samnani & Singh, 2014, p. 14).

Roth (2014) argues that the bell-shaped performance curve is one culprit of increased competition and conflict. He points out increased internal competition comes from practices that rank employee performance and demand that 10 percent to 20 percent of lowest-ranked employees be terminated. Even when leaders advocate cooperation among employees, a bell-curve rating system rewards competition.

Internal conflicts and poor cooperation can also result when "decisions are made to optimize performance in one unit contrary to the needs of the larger organization" (Schuster & Kesler, 2011, p. 40). To speed cycle time and reduce rework costs, a unit decides to reduce the number of quality checks on outgoing products, only to see greater customer complaints that must be addressed by the service department. Rewards can unintentionally drive one division to maximize its goals to the detriment of another, causing negative downstream impacts and exacerbating interdepartmental competition.

Slower Change and Resistance

When the strategy or other element of the organization design changes, but rewards remain the same for behaviors that were important in the old system, it should come as no surprise that the old behaviors remain. Leaders may be reluctant to change rewards practices, conscious that these practices are sensitive, complex, and sometimes emotional. They may have seen how effective the practices were in the old organization and be afraid of instituting too much change at once. The result is confusion due to mixed messages about what is important, resistance to change, and a slower adoption of the new organization design.

WHY DESIGNING REWARDS IS SO CHALLENGING

Each of these cases demonstrates a situation where a reward prompts an unintended consequence—an undesirable byproduct of the reward system. This fact was pointed out in a classic article by S. Kerr (1975) titled, "On the Folly of Rewarding 'A,' While Hoping for 'B.'" In it, Kerr argues that reward systems can frequently reinforce the exact opposite of desired behaviors, citing examples from medicine, politics, and education. He argues that faculty members find greater promotion opportunities at a university (and external recognition) for prominent research even while most universities hope for good teaching but fail to reward it. "Managers who complain that their workers are not motivated might do well to consider the possibility that they have installed reward systems which are paying off for behaviors other than those they are seeking," Kerr (1975, p. 781) observes. As Hunt (2014) aptly concluded, "[Y]ou get what you pay for, but what you pay for may not be what you want" (p. 23).

Misaligned rewards may be due, in part, to the lack of comparative attention that organization designers pay to rewards. While the fields of psychology and management have studied employee motivation and compensation for years, the discipline of organization design has generally focused more on the first four points of the star that we have covered than on the rewards point. Schuster and Kesler (2011) go so far as to state that "design practice is not well-defined, and the literature is nearly silent on how to align rewards systems to an integrated organization design initiative. Rewards systems are the *orphan star point*" (p. 39). They point out that many organization design professionals are not well educated in designing rewards or compensation strategies. Designers may consider rewards system design to be outside the scope of an organization design effort or they may fail to consider its importance.

In addition, organization designers and compensation professionals often lack a common language and frame of reference, operating at cross-purposes. "Organization designers seek to differentiate the organization by creating unique, hard-to-replicate capabilities that can produce lasting and sustainable competitive advantage" (Schuster & Kesler, 2011, p. 40). Yet, compensation professionals are driven by the need to ensure that an organization's practices are not out of step with the majority of competitors. As Lawler explains,

> [M]ost organizations seem obsessed with finding out what other organizations are doing in the pay area.... Instead of trying to gain competitive

advantage by doing different things, most companies seem happy to copy what other companies do and thereby to avoid being at a competitive disadvantage. (Lawler, 1990, p. 3)

Salary surveys, compensation consultants, and prevailing wage data and market pricing all combine to provide a set of ranges that most organizations strive to fall within. As Ledford (2014) puts it, there is "safety in copying" (p. 169). Even within the same organization, business units may be unable to gain approval to implement unique compensation practices that are considered to be out of step with the rest of the organization.

MOTIVATION

One purpose of the rewards point of the star is to direct employee motivation. Theories in the fields of psychology and management have long attempted to explain employee motivation and how rewards impact behavior and performance. Many of these theories date back to the mid-1960s, what some writers called "the golden age" of motivation theory (Steers, Mowday, & Shapiro, 2004). In order to understand if, how, and why rewards will motivate employee behavior, we will review some of the key concepts in motivation research, including expectancy theory, goal setting, and equity; intrinsic and extrinsic motivation; Herzberg's motivation-hygiene theory; a debate on the relationship between financial rewards and motivation; and how jobs can be designed to increase intrinsic motivation.

Expectancy Theory, Goal Setting, and Equity

The implicit model that drives the development of most rewards systems in organization design is as follows, displayed in Figure 7.1.

Hambrick and Snow (1988) refer to this as the "long-linked framework" of rewards, pointing out that there are a number of causal connections that must work effectively for the framework to successfully connect incentives with performance. The important point is that there should be a clear line of sight between the metrics and expected results or the performance to be measured, and the reward. That clear line of sight should increase motivation.

For the purposes of organization design, expectancy theory has been a popular explanation to underlie the above design of rewards systems (Lawler, 2000;

Figure 7.1 A Model for Rewards Systems

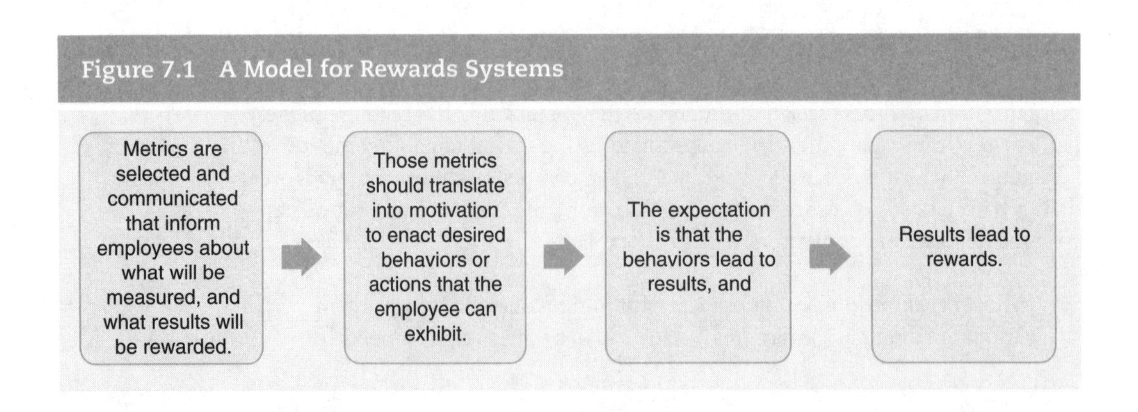
Metrics are selected and communicated that inform employees about what will be measured, and what results will be rewarded.
Those metrics should translate into motivation to enact desired behaviors or actions that the employee can exhibit.
The expectation is that the behaviors lead to results, and
Results lead to rewards.

Samnani & Singh, 2014). Expectancy theory posits that behavior is a result of a person's ability and his or her motivation to complete a task (Gerhart, 2010). Expectancy theory contains three major tenets or concepts: valence, instrumentality, and expectancy (Vroom, 1964).

1. **Valence**: Defined as the perceived outcome of performance, positive or negative. A reward must be an attractive one that is desired by the individual. It "must be clearly perceived as large enough in amount to justify the additional effort required" (D. Katz & Kahn, 1966, p. 353). An employee may not be motivated by a monetary incentive that is perceived to be too small to be worth the additional work. An additional vacation day may be highly motivating for some, and less motivating for others. Some employees are gratified by public acknowledgment of their performance, but others are embarrassed. Thus, valence can be a very personal matter. As Lawler (2000) has described, "The first key to a motivating reward system is to use only rewards that are valued" (p. 76). "Offer the wrong carrot, and employees will feel insulted, misunderstood, or just apathetic" (Lawler, 1990, p. 104). Importantly, expectancy theory does not presume that all rewards must be monetary. Valence consists of any outcome, including a sense of accomplishment, personal satisfaction, and self-esteem.
2. **Instrumentality**: The individual must have confidence that if performance is achieved, the reward will be granted. The reward "must be perceived as directly related to the required performance and follow directly on its accomplishment" (D. Katz & Kahn, 1966, p. 353). If employees perform according to the expectation that their performance will result in the reward, and the reward is not given, they will be less likely on subsequent occasions to perform.
3. **Expectancy**: The individual must believe that the outcome required to receive the reward is achievable through personal effort or behavior. As Vroom (2013, p. 272) has explained, "Motivating people is not just a matter of increasing the importance to them of doing well but also of enhancing their belief in their own capability of doing so."

Expectancy theory suggests that all three elements must be in place for the reward system to work. Individuals must see the reward as something they want to earn, that reaching the expected performance level is possible through their own actions, and that the results will be rewarded if achieved (that the promised reward will be administered). Expectancy theory research confirms that employees are "proactive, future-oriented and motivated to behave in ways that they believe will lead to valued rewards" (Lawler & Worley, 2006b, p. 2). It explains work motivation by suggesting that people will pursue activities that will maximize their benefit (and by consequence, minimize punishments or pain). It also emphasizes the importance of trust, because "the belief that performance will lead to rewards is essentially a prediction about the future. For individuals to make this kind of prediction, they have to trust the system that is promising them the rewards" (Lawler & Jenkins, 1990, p. 1015).

Goal setting is an important variable of motivation, connected to expectancy. Goals that are perceived as too difficult, or outcomes that are perceived as random and impossible to affect, will not be motivating for some people (e.g., they produce low expectancy). For others, "stretch" goals that are perceived as extremely difficult will be highly motivating. These individuals may seek the heightened sense of accomplishment that comes from attaining a very difficult goal. Goal-setting theory (Locke & Latham, 2002) identifies the conditions under which a goal will be motivating:

1. A specific high goal leads to higher performance than no goal setting or even an abstract goal such as "to do your best."
2. Given goal commitment, the higher the goal, the higher an employee's performance.
3. Variables such as participation in decision making, performance feedback, incentives, and competition increase performance to the extent that they lead to the setting of and commitment to a specific high goal (Latham & Locke, 2008, p. 322).

Lawler (1990) concludes that "goals that are perceived to be achievable but challenging should be the objective because they are the most motivating and produce the highest levels of performance" (p. 105).

Feelings of justice and equity in rewards also affect an employee's motivation to achieve goals and seek rewards. A sense of fairness impacts whether rewards will motivate performance. Rewards "must be perceived as equitable by the majority of system members, many of whom will not receive them" (D. Katz & Kahn, 1966, p. 353), because employees will compare their own rewards to those of others. Two types of justice are important in the rewards system:

Distributive justice: the perception that the outcome is a fair one. An employee will perceive an outcome as fair by comparing his or her reward to the rewards that others receive. It will be perceived as fair if others who made similar contributions received similar bonuses (i.e., everyone who sold 20 units earns $500). In addition, "People compare their ratio of inputs to outcomes with that of other people" (Weibel & Rota, 2002, p. 176), so the outcome is perceived as fair not necessarily if the bonus is identical, but as long as the bonus or reward is connected to the input or work. Employees compare levels of education, years of experience, workload, number of projects, and a host of other variables with the rewards received such as titles, pay, and promotions. High-performing employees will be dissatisfied if all employees receive the same pay regardless of performance input. If employees think that the outcome is unfair, they are likely to reduce their work, demand an increase in rewards, find a different comparison point, or leave the organization.

Procedural justice: "the procedures and rules followed when making decisions and that culminate in certain results" (Weibel & Rota, 2002, p. 177). Employees want to know that the process for determining rewards is a fair one. For example, if a reward is based on a manager's performance evaluation of the employee, employees want to be evaluated consistently without prejudice or bias in the process. If some employees' pay is reduced due to tardiness, but not all employees', then the process will be perceived as unfair. Procedural justice is increased when employees have a voice in the process, when decisions are explained, and the procedures and criteria are clearly defined.

Comparison points complicate the judgments of distributive and procedural justice. Organizations can design rewards systems with internal equity or internal comparisons, that is, a similar process and fair outcome across the company. All new hires, or engineers with 8-years' experience, are paid within the same relative scale or band within the company. Organizations can also compare their rewards systems externally with other companies, as can employees. However, there can be innumerable comparison points (including education, tenure, industry type, performance levels), which can be highly subjective. While it may be difficult to eliminate all possible perceptions of unfairness, considerations of distributive and procedural justice should be made in designing a rewards system that motivates employees.

Intrinsic and Extrinsic Motivation

Motivation to perform can be of two types: *intrinsic and extrinsic.*

People are intrinsically motivated if the work activity itself is a source of motivation. Employees in a nonprofit social services organization derive a sense of personal satisfaction and self-gratification by helping citizens with necessary services. The process of doing research and solving challenging problems might fascinate a research biochemist. A musician might find enjoyment in learning a challenging piece of music. A teacher finds personal satisfaction in helping a child struggle through a difficult concept and eventually master it. A weekend sports enthusiast enjoys camaraderie and meets a desire for social connection by participating in a softball team, even when the team loses every game. In addition, the achievement of a personal goal can be intrinsically motivating, as in the case of running a marathon when the process of training might be arduous but eventually satisfying.

Extrinsic motivation comes from external sources, such as pay and external recognition. The job or work activity itself is not the primary reason for the motivation, but it is the instrument by which the extrinsic rewards are achieved. An employee works at a job that is highly disliked because it provides the money to pay for expenses such as housing, food, transportation, and so on. Money is not the only extrinsic motivator; people can also be motivated by approval of or praise from others, fame or publicity, good grades, a trophy, or a positive performance rating.

Intrinsic and extrinsic motivation do not have to be independent of one another. The biochemist may find the work rewarding but also enjoy the publicity that comes from published research and granted patents. The marathon runner may also derive extrinsic motivation in the form of praise from family members.

The relationship between intrinsic and extrinsic motivation on job satisfaction and performance has been called "one of the most heated debates in the applied psychology literature" (Cerasoli, Nicklin, & Ford, 2014, p. 981). In the next sections, we will explore this relationship.

Motivation-Hygiene Theory

In a research program beginning in the late 1950s, Frederick Herzberg began to explore the attitudes that people had about their jobs in order to better understand what motivates people at work. A number of studies had sought to answer the question "What do workers want from their jobs?" throughout the previous decades, with contradictory results. In interpreting the studies, Herzberg suspected that job satisfaction was not the opposite of job dissatisfaction. In other words, he believed that different factors might be at play when workers were satisfied with their jobs than when they reported being dissatisfied with their jobs.

Through a series of in-depth interviews, Herzberg and a team of researchers set out to investigate. They asked people to reflect on important incidents that had occurred to them in their jobs—both positive and negative—and asked participants to explain what it was about that event that made them feel especially good or bad about the job.

> The results showed that people are made *dis*satisfied by bad environment, the extrinsics of the job. But they are seldom made satisfied by good environment, what I called the *hygienes*. They are made satisfied by the intrinsics of what they *do*, what I call the *motivators*. (Herzberg, 1993, pp. xiii–xiv)

In the initial 1959 publication and through subsequent studies, Herzberg explained the key motivators that contributed to job enrichment, in what has been called his motivation-hygiene theory:

- Achievement and quality performance
- Recognition for achievement and feedback on performance
- Work itself and the client relationship
- Responsibility
- Advancement, growth, and learning

At the same time, Herzberg, Mausner, and Snyderman (1959) point out that hygiene factors will not necessarily contribute to job satisfaction, but can cause job dissatisfaction. "When feelings of unhappiness were reported, they were not associated with the job itself but with conditions that *surround* the doing of the job" (p. 113), such as these:

- Supervision
- Interpersonal relationships
- Physical working conditions
- Salary
- Company policies and administrative practices
- Benefits
- Job security

Herzberg et al. explain that their research on motivation illustrates why contemporary managers had such a difficult time motivating employees. Then-popular management programs for supervisors and wage incentive programs addressed hygiene factors of supervision and monetary compensation, but did little to address the factors such as achievement and work itself that truly motivated employees. Herzberg's motivation-hygiene theory provides an important reminder that money is not the only reward that employees value.

Intrinsic Motivation and Extrinsic Rewards

Consider this scenario: A graphic artist has been struggling for years but loves creating art. His work is shown in galleries and earns critical acclaim but generally does not sell. One day after reviewing his work, an advertising agency offers him a lucrative job. He accepts the offer, motivated by the process of design and gratified that his work will be showcased in public. The job pays very well and for a while he is given substantial bonuses based on customer satisfaction surveys and speed of project completion. After a difficult few years, the agency discontinues the bonus system. Eventually the enjoyment of producing art is gone, and he quits the job, the love of art muted by the experience.

This scenario has been called the "crowding out effect" or the "undermining effect." "The undermining effect refers to the idea that the presentation of incentives on an initially enjoyable task reduces subsequent intrinsic motivation for the task" (Cerasoli et al., 2014, p. 981). The motivational effect provided by the monetary incentive displaces the intrinsic motivation of job enjoyment for its own sake. Vroom (2013) explains:

> It is not the receipt of the money that does the damage. The cause lies in its contingent nature; in other words, the fact that it is linked to the level of performance. Monetary compensation changes the meaning of the task from something which is done for personal gratification to something which is done for financial gain. (p. 273)

Eventually the person being rewarded appears to see the task as something that must be done or is done in order to receive a reward rather than a task that was appealing or satisfying personally. In other words, task performance and satisfaction have become contingent on receiving the reward. Deci, Koestner, and Ryan (1999), in an analysis of more than 100 studies, offer the conclusion that "tangible rewards tend to have a substantially negative effect on intrinsic motivation" (pp. 658–659).

Popular business authors Kohn (1993a, 1993b) and Pink (2010) have made these findings public, arguing against instituting financial rewards to motivate performance. Kohn (1993b) explains that "rewards succeed at securing one thing only: temporary compliance. When it comes to producing lasting change in attitudes and behavior, however, rewards, like punishment are strikingly ineffective. Once the rewards run out, people revert to their old behaviors" (p. 55). Kohn (1993a) argues that rewards actually punish (by controlling employees and withdrawing a perceived benefit), they break relationships, they are often separated from the reasons for the reward, and they discourage risk taking. Pink (2010) concludes that rewards can undermine creativity, encourage game playing and cheating, and encourage short-term behavior.

Yet many authors argue that they have conclusively determined the opposite effect, that "financial incentives relate positively to performance, do not reduce intrinsic motivation, and, in general, are *more* effective than we previously thought" (Shaw & Gupta, 2015, p. 281). This line of research suggests that the graphic designer example provided above is an unrealistic (or at least uncommon) scenario. These research programs contend that conflicting findings about the relationship between rewards and motivation can be explained by the design of the rewards system, not the use of rewards in and of themselves (Shaw & Gupta, 2015). Pfeffer (2007) points out that incentives may work too well, resulting in the counterproductive behaviors described earlier. Rewards systems tend to increase surveillance, evaluation, and control over employees, which appears to be a significant influence on the reduction of intrinsic motivation, as can the induced stress, pressure, and competition of the organizational context. When these are removed, and the reward is not contingent and held out as a prize but is an unexpected bonus, intrinsic motivation does not decrease (Deci, Koestner, & Ryan, 1999; Pink, 2010). Cerasoli, Nicklin, and Ford (2014) point out that the connection between types of motivation is more nuanced, and that the effectiveness of a rewards system may depend on the kind of task or job being rewarded. They find that

> tasks that are straightforward, highly repetitive, and perhaps even less inherently enjoyable, should be more closely linked to extrinsic incentives. . . . On the other hand, tasks that require a great deal of absorption, personal investment, complexity, and overall quality should be less linked to incentives and much more closely linked to intrinsic motivation. (pp. 998–999)

This finding is likely due to the fact that intrinsic motivation is already relatively low for tasks that are not very interesting or personally compelling. Ledford, Gerhart, and Fang (2013) conclude:

> If the reward is appropriately implemented, it should enhance, rather than undermine, intrinsic motivation—making the incentive effect that much more powerful than if it relies on extrinsic motivation alone. This requires appropriate communication about the importance of the task and the nature of the incentive; specific, meaningful performance goals; appropriate feedback and support from supervisors; selection systems that help sort out those who do not fit the desired culture (and reward strategy) of the organization; and an organizational culture in which incentives are supported by managers and employees. (p. 28)

Importantly, researchers have concluded that intrinsic and extrinsic motivation may work in combination (Cerasoli et al., 2014; Shaw & Gupta, 2015). If rewards are designed and implemented properly, then intrinsic motivation may actually be increased and performance positively affected.

Researchers continue to work out the situations in which these combinations are counterproductive and when they support one another in tandem. Employees may be effectively rewarded and compensated for work they find meaningful and gratifying. The bottom line is that "there is no reason to make a trade-off between designing interesting work and motivating through extrinsic rewards" (Lawler, 2000, p. 79). The job itself can be designed in motivating ways, a point to which we now turn.

Motivational Impact of Job Design

As we saw above with Herzberg's motivation-hygiene theory, employees point out that the reason they are satisfied with their jobs has generally to do with motivators such as achievement, challenge, and learning. Hackman and Oldham (1976, 1980) have explained that there are dimensions of jobs that can be designed in such a way that will increase an employee's satisfaction, work quality, motivation, and performance. Hackman and Oldham (1980) describe job design as the answer to the question "How can work be structured so that it is performed effectively and, at the same time, jobholders find the work personally rewarding and satisfying?" (p. 71). When jobs are designed well, people find them more motivating and contribute more effectively to the outcomes that the organization seeks.

Hackman and Oldham (1976) identify three psychological states that are associated with increased motivation.

- Experienced meaningfulness of the work: the degree to which the individual experiences the job as one which is generally meaningful, valuable, and worthwhile
- Experienced responsibility for work outcomes: the degree to which the individual feels personally accountable and responsible for the result of the work he or she does
- Knowledge of results: the degree to which the individual knows and understands, on a continuous basis, how effectively he or she is performing the job (pp. 256–257)

These three outcomes can be reached if jobs are designed to increase or maximize five different dimensions:

1. **Skill variety**. The degree to which a job requires a variety of different activities in carrying out the work, which involve the use of a number of different skills and talents of the person
2. **Task identity**. The degree to which the job requires completion of a "whole" and identifiable piece of work; that is, doing a job from beginning to end with a visible outcome
3. **Task significance**. The degree to which the job has a substantial impact on the lives or work of other people, whether in the immediate organization or in the external environment
4. **Autonomy**. The degree to which the job provides substantial freedom, independence, and discretion to the individual in scheduling the work and in determining the procedures to be used in carrying it out
5. **Feedback**. The degree to which carrying out the work activities required by the job results in the individual obtaining direct and clear information about the effectiveness of his or her performance. (Hackman & Oldham, 1976, pp. 257–258)

They point out that contextual and individual factors are also at work, such as an individual's personal value for growth and development, the knowledge and skill applied to the job, and satisfactory organizational conditions. When these conditions are met, designing jobs with these characteristics in mind can increase the internal motivation of employees and make the jobs themselves more rewarding.

Since the original job design theory and research was done, jobs themselves have changed (Oldham & Hackman, 2010). Job redesign today may not require a large-scale organizational intervention driven by senior executives. Today, employees are more likely to have greater freedom in participating in the design of their own jobs, even customizing them based on their own interests and skills. Considering the factors above as jobs are designed and giving employees the autonomy to adapt them may increase the intrinsic motivation of a job.

METRICS AND THE BALANCED SCORECARD

Designing the right metrics is important in creating goals that are just challenging enough and that clarify what results will be rewarded. Metrics help translate the strategy into performance goals to be achieved. For example, a company may have a goal to capture 50 percent market share with a new product being introduced this year, or to sign up 25 new customers to increase revenues by 15 percent. These goals at the corporate level can then be the starting point for identification of goals at the unit or division level, and eventually the team and individual level. A corporate goal to increase gross profits by 10 percent next year can be translated down to multiple units. Manufacturing can contribute to the goal by decreasing the cost per unit sold by 5 percent. Sales can target an increase in sales of profitable product bundles by 15 percent. Marketing can target business development efforts and increase the number of profitable new customers by 20 percent.

M. W. Meyer (2002) writes that performance measures have seven purposes, displayed in Figure 7.2:

1. They allow the organization to **look backward** to evaluate prior performance.
2. They permit **compensation** based on achieved performance.
3. They allow the organization to **look ahead** to focus everyone on future performance objectives.
4. They **motivate** attention to future performance.
5. They allow goals to **cascade down** throughout the organization, from top to bottom.
6. They allow goals to **roll up** to check whether unit goals will achieve overall objectives.
7. They permit **comparisons** between individuals, teams, and units.

Implicit in these purposes of performance measures is that they communicate consistently throughout the organization what goals are important. They focus everyone's attention on how the strategy will be operationalized.

One popular method for designing strategic performance measures was first developed in the 1990s, called the Balanced Scorecard (Kaplan & Norton, 1992, 1993, 1996, 2001). Many observers at the time had criticized prevailing organizational metrics for being overly focused on financial results, causing leaders to assume a myopic, short-term focus. Others argued that more important were metrics such as product quality, cycle time, and customer satisfaction, pointing out that financial successes came to those that focused on these metrics.

Figure 7.2 The Seven Purposes of Performance Measures

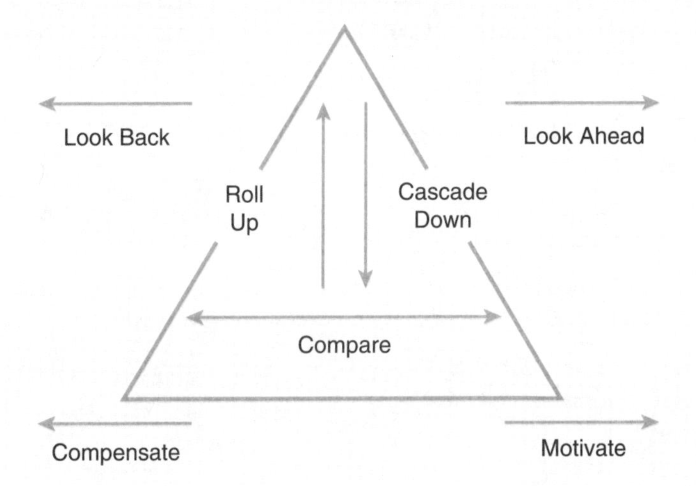

Source: Meyer, M. W. (2002). *Rethinking performance measurement*. Cambridge, England: Cambridge University Press, p. 31.

Kaplan and Norton (1992) responded that financial metrics and operational metrics were both critical, and that there was no need to choose between them. They integrated the most important metrics into a balanced scorecard that would provide a dashboard of past financial performance and operational indications that could give insight into future performance. They point out that the scorecard combines important data into a single place and that it provides a balance of metrics to avoid the scenario where "improvement in one area may have been achieved at the expense of another" (Kaplan & Norton, 1992, p. 73). The balance occurs between external and internal metrics, quantitative and qualitative metrics, and past performance and future orientation. The scorecard has four purposes (Kaplan & Norton, 1996, p. 10):

1. *Clarify and translate vision and strategy.* The senior leadership team decides on key metrics together after a discussion of the strategy and important objectives. They must decide on the relative importance of revenue growth, profitability, entering new markets, or investing further in existing ones.
2. *Communicate and link strategic objectives and measures.* The scorecard provides a mechanism for communicating the important goals throughout the organization at all levels.
3. *Plan, set targets, and align strategic initiatives.* The scorecard development process can act as a future-oriented planning process. Goals are set for each of the strategic objectives, sometimes 3 to 5 years in the future, with annual milestones to indicate progress. Initiatives can be identified and action plans created to address each goal.
4. *Enhance strategic feedback and learning.* The scorecard provides feedback on whether the strategy is working or whether different actions should be taken. If the planned actions are being taken but are

not realizing the expected results, leaders can investigate the cause and plan appropriately.

The scorecard identifies goals and performance metrics in four categories (Kaplan & Norton, 1996, p. 9):

1. **Financial Perspective**: To succeed financially, how should we appear to our shareholders?
2. **Customer Perspective**: To achieve our vision, how should we appear to our customers?
3. **Internal Business Process Perspective**: To satisfy our shareholders and customers, at what business processes must we excel?
4. **Learning and Growth**: To achieve our vision, how will we sustain our ability to change and improve?

Examples of the goals and metrics in each of these categories appear in Figure 7.3.

Identifying the right performance measures is critical; indeed, Niven (2014, pp. 239–241) lists dozens of possible metrics in each category of the balanced scorecard. Kaplan and Norton (1996) note that "the essential objective in selecting specific measures for a scorecard is to identify the measure that best communicates the meaning of a strategy" (p. 306), calling this process an "art." Clarity and consensus among the executive team are critical in creating a scorecard.

Effective performance measures have several characteristics, according to Niven (2014):

Figure 7.3 Example Metrics for the Balanced Scorecard

Financial Perspective	Customer Perspective	Internal Business Process Perspective	Learning and Growth Perspective
• Revenue growth • Revenue from new products • Profit growth • Gross margins • Working capital • Days inventory • Inventory turns • Accounts receivable • Return on assets • Return on equity • Earnings per share • Debt	• Customer satisfaction index • New customer acquisition • Customer retention • Market share • Customer profitability • Customer likelihood to recommend • Brand recognition • Products returned by customers • Customer complaints	• Manufacturing cycle time • Product quality • Rework rate • On time delivery to customers • Innovation cycle time; new product introductions • Service delivery responsiveness • Order to delivery cycle time • Process cost • Number of patents	• Employee engagement survey results • Employee retention • Top talent turnover • Employee productivity • Training and development • Competency levels • Completed performance evaluations • Recruiting for pivot roles

1. They are linked to the strategy and are narrow or focused. Hundreds or thousands of metrics might be available, but only a few may provide real insight into strategy execution. Most organizations have too many performance measures, creating as many as 50 to 60 goals. This overwhelms employees and creates a tremendous workload in order to monitor (see Meyer, M. W., 2002). Too many metrics dilutes strategic focus.
2. They are accessible. Many leaders desire to measure something that is difficult to measure, or for which data are not yet available. Lawler (1990) agrees, writing that "sometimes the issues are not so much as what to measure as how to measure it" (p. 15). A hotel chain that wanted employees to reduce costs and increase customer satisfaction had cost data readily available, but gathering customer satisfaction data required further investigation and planning.
3. They are timely and actionable. Metrics should be updated frequently, so employees can take action as needed. Metrics should also be the foundation for action to correct gaps. A weighted index that combines a number of metrics into one may obscure important issues. For example, a customer satisfaction index comprising five different satisfaction areas might hide one critical negative satisfaction score if four are very high. An employee engagement survey can provide a comprehensive score of overall engagement, but there may be specific issues that need to be addressed when examined in detail.
4. They are focused on more than just financials and include counterbalanced metrics to avoid unintended consequences. A metric to reduce cycle time may result in shortcuts to quality, so a second quality-related goal can ensure that both remain important.
5. They are relevant and outcome based. Good performance measures identify standards to be achieved, not strategic initiatives. Good metrics are often quantitative to allow consistent evaluations and comparisons over time, but the discussion about the metrics and actions to be taken is often more critical.
6. They track past performance and future trends. In other words, good performance measures contain a mix of lagging and leading indicators. Past financial performance is a lagging indicator. Mentions on social media can be a leading indicator of future sales of a soon-to-be-released product.

Kaplan and Norton (2001) have enhanced the balanced scorecard with a concept they call a strategy map. In a strategy map, the metrics in the balanced scorecard are graphically depicted in relationship to one another to show how different performance measures influence others. "Each measure of a Balanced Scorecard becomes embedded in a chain of cause-and-effect logic that connects the desired outcomes from the strategy with the drivers that will lead to strategic outcomes" (p. 69). For example, training on how to spot and respond to quality errors in manufacturing (learning and growth perspective) will increase product yields and reduce rework in manufacturing (internal business process perspective). With greater product quality, customer perceptions of the product will increase as will the customer's satisfaction (customer perspective). Increased customer satisfaction should translate to increased profitability and revenue (financial perspective).

Noting that the balanced scorecard has been difficult for HR professionals to adapt to HR, Huselid, Becker, and Beatty (2005) have created the workforce scorecard. As we learned in Chapter 6, the organization's talent strategy should identify the *A* players that have a greater proportional impact on the organization's strategy. The workforce scorecard identifies the important metrics to assess the competencies and leadership behaviors that contribute to the organization's strategic and talent objectives. Measures such as the internal bench strength of talent for key positions, retention of *A* players, and the percentage of *B* players with *A* potential can give insight into the achievement of the talent strategy.

REWARDS STRATEGY AND SYSTEMS

The rewards strategy should follow from the organization's strategy, driven by the external and internal environment.

> The business strategy must be communicated and implemented in a way that offers guidance for aligning the organization's structure of work, pay philosophy, and reward policies and programs. The reward strategy should specify how the organization's employees and its management can achieve and sustain a competitive advantage. (Scott et al., 2009, pp. 45–46)

It should also consist of core principles that explain the organization's approach to designing the rewards system, as a statement of the philosophy or rewards design criteria that will reflect the organization's approach. Only at that point can decisions be made about the content of the rewards system. Figure 7.4 illustrates the connection between organizational strategy, rewards strategy, and the structure of the rewards system.

For example, Honeywell's pay objectives state that they aim "to recognize the importance of high-quality work performance, to encourage a career-long commitment to Honeywell, and to encourage growth both on an individual basis and as a participant on a work team" (Lawler, 1990, p. 42). Core pay principles that follow suggest that Honeywell's compensation practice "must be fully competitive in the market" and that "each individual's pay must be fair in relationship to the pay other employees receive" (Lawler, 1990, p. 42). At Dow Chemical, compensation programs "look at total compensation . . . that is appropriately competitive with various industries and employers with whom we compete." They stress that "we will provide compensation that is responsible to, and reflective of, the quality of performance of both our employees and our business" (Lawler, 1990, p. 43).

Following the articulation of core rewards principles, the reward system itself can be created to implement the philosophy. In doing so, rewards system designers must decide on the basis for rewards and the types of rewards to grant.

Basis for Rewards

There are a multitude of ways that rewards systems can be designed and implemented. As we reviewed at the outset of this chapter, a strategic rewards system is generally performance based versus hierarchy based. It rewards achievement

Figure 7.4 A Model for Strategic Reward Management

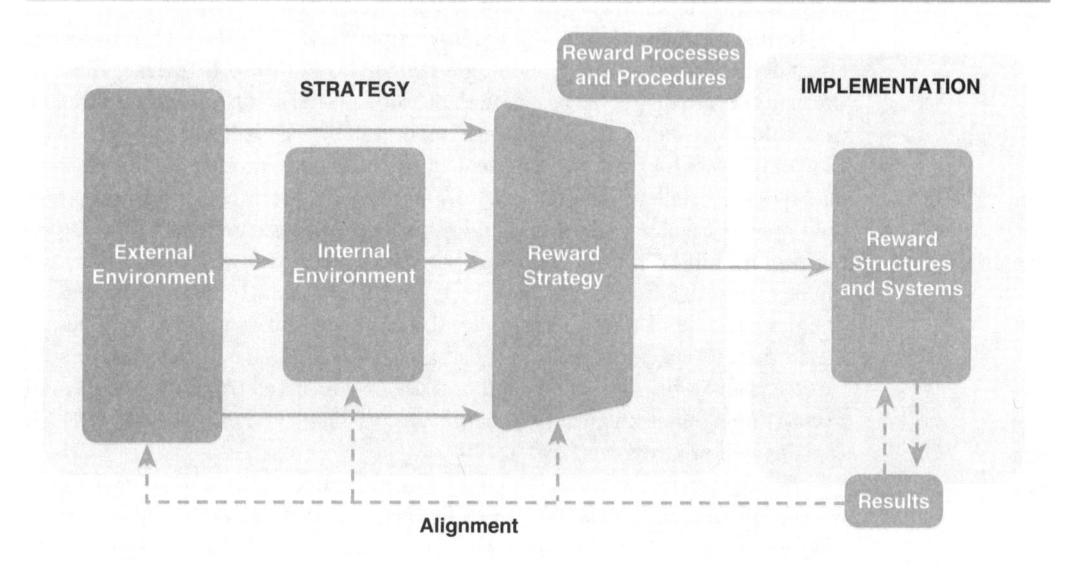

Source: Baeten, X., & Verwaeren, B. (2012). Flexible rewards from a strategic rewards perspective. *Compensation & Benefits Review*, 44(1), pp. 40–49.

of goals versus rank or tenure. However, performance-based pay must consider multiple types of performance and may choose to reward individual performance, team performance, organizational performance, or some combination.

Pay for individual performance. Two widely used methods for paying for individual performance are *incentive plans* and *merit pay*.

Incentive plans, commonly granted for piecework and salespeople, pay based on the completion of a defined set of work or achievement of a sales quota. Pay is variable depending on the achievement of a specific task or outcome. Incentive plans are popular because there is generally a clear line of sight in incentive plans from the individual's behavior and results to the reward. However, as we have seen, incentive plans can produce undesirable behaviors as well. A salesperson who earns a sales commission may ignore a customer needing assistance because the customer has already spoken to a peer who would earn the sales credit. Because it can produce competitive behavior, an incentive plan is best for situations that do not require close cooperation or where other sufficient lateral mechanisms can overcome the competition (Lawler & Jenkins, 1990). Lawler (2000) concludes that two factors must be present for this type of plan to be effective: It must be connected to work that is measurable and completed independently, and it is most effective for individuals who desire monetary rewards and seek achievement.

Merit pay plans are annual salary increases based on a supervisor's rating of an individual's performance. They are the most frequent type of individual pay for performance plan, and the least effective in terms of motivating employee performance (Lawler, 2017; Lawler & Worley, 2006b). Unlike incentive plans, which are one-time monetary payments that can be frequently given and are often substantial, merit pay is generally smaller (a few percentage points of a person's salary), granted annually, and generally permanent increases to a person's annual salary. For employees, the annual increase may be seen as disconnected from performance that could have occurred many months earlier, and the difference in pay of a 5 percent increase for top performers and a 3 percent increase for average performers is often not enough to motivate.

Skill-based pay. Generally employers pay based on the job, with a salary range defined for the role depending on an analysis of the job's market rate. An alternative is to pay people based on their value in the market rather than the job they hold. One version of this is skill-based pay. A skill-based pay system recognizes employees for their ongoing growth and development, encouraging them to maintain their skills as the organization's strategy evolves. Strategically important skills are rewarded more highly. Employees are rewarded based on their ability to perform multiple job tasks, increasing the organization's flexibility as employees can be moved to different tasks when required. Rather than hiring two employees, one may be able to move between jobs as required. The employer may design a plan that grants employees rewards based on additional certifications or specialized coursework. The most common use of skill-based pay is in research and development functions where a technical skill "ladder" can be developed that explains skill progression (Lawler, 1990).

Such a system can be challenging to create, which explains some of the early resistance to it. Skill-based pay must fit with the organization's culture, generally working best where employees are highly involved and have some decision-making empowerment. The organization must be clear on the skill profile that is needed today and in the future. There must be a way to measure skill acquisition and decide on a method for pricing which skills will earn how much compensation. There should also be a consideration made for adjusting compensation to reflect unneeded skills that have become obsolete, as in the case of technical skills that are no longer useful.

Interest in skill-based pay has varied over time, having been called a "runaway train" (Zingheim & Schuster, 2002) and a "fad" (Giancola, 2011). Yet there is evidence to support the conclusion that employees will learn new skills and learn them faster when skill-based pay is given (Dierdorff & Surface, 2008). Lawler (2017), a longtime advocate of skill-based pay, notes that today's organizations increasingly require the ability to reward skill development to keep up with the rapid pace of change.

Pay for team performance. Some jobs are individualized and the work activity is done alone; in others, the interdependent nature of the work means that coordination and teaming is required. Where individuals contribute to a team, a team compensation approach makes sense and can reinforce contributions to all types of teams, whether they are self-directed, virtual, or ad hoc teams. Many organizations expect team success but continue to reward individual achievement, but "the sole use of individually-based compensation systems in a team-based environment sends mixed messages—work as a team, but benefit solely from your own efforts" (Zobal, 1999, p. 24).

An effective way to motivate team performance is to create clear measures of team success and grant all team members a reward equally based on the team's results. A team incentive plan can reduce competitive behavior among team members, encourage collaboration, and prompt team members to watch out for poor performance. For example, if a team earns a bonus if it reaches a monthly goal to respond to 95 percent of customer inquiries within 24 hours, team members may be motivated to help colleagues reach the goal together. A combined approach is also possible where team members can be rewarded for the team's success as well as their individual contributions to the team.

Pay for organizational performance. In addition to individual performance and team results, members can also be rewarded for the success of the entire organization. While it is often difficult for an individual to see a direct correlation between their own actions and the organization's results, such plans communicate the importance of collective cooperation. They can also reduce interdepartmental conflict. Lawler and Worley (2006b) argue that when organizational rewards are tied to performance compared to that of competitors, organizational members are more motivated to accept strategic change.

Any of these approaches to pay for performance in isolation may have unintended consequences. Thus, Lawler concludes that "overall, the most generally applicable approach to paying talent for performance is some combination of a budgeted bonus plan that rewards individual performance and a business unit or a corporate performance-funded bonus plan like profit sharing" (Lawler, 2017a, p. 83).

Types of Rewards

The rewards system must also decide on the type of rewards to give. Today, many organizations consider a broad range of rewards as a holistic package granted to employees, called a "total rewards" or "rewards mix" approach. Definitions can range from narrow (meaning financial compensation only) to broad (meaning anything that an employee finds valuable, from flexible hours to a casual dress policy to onsite dry cleaning services). WorldatWork, the former name for the American Compensation Association, defines *total rewards* to include compensation, benefits, work–life (such as time off, dependent care, and well-being programs), performance and recognition, and development and career opportunities (WorldatWork, 2007). The most common financial rewards given for individual, team, and organizational performance are the following:

1. **Bonus systems**. Bonuses given at the completion of major milestones or accomplishments (e.g., a product release) can demonstrate a direct relationship between performance and rewards. They can be very flexible in adapting to the magnitude of the performance and can be granted at any time, from weekly to monthly to annually. Generally they are one-time cash rewards and do not increase base pay like a merit increase, permitting rewards to be both direct and potentially substantial.

2. **Profit-sharing plans**. Similarly, profit-sharing plans can be equally flexible and based on the financial success of the company, generally after a threshold goal is met at the organizational level. Employees can be given the same amount or a percentage of their salary.

3. **Stock ownership plans**. Stock plans come in many forms. They can grant employees stock in the company outright, they can give employees the right to purchase company stock at a discount, or they can grant options to purchase stock at a specified price (Lawler, 2000). Stock plans may have a weak effect on motivation because there are many factors that can change the stock price. However, they can contribute to an increased feeling of psychological concern for the organization.

In administering any of these types of rewards and considering the basis for the rewards described above, the rewards system design must consider whether it will be applicable to every part of the organization (centralized) or allowed to differ based on division or geography (decentralized). The use of centralized rewards makes sense to create a broad feeling of internal fairness and justice within the organization, but this also tends to allow units less flexibility. A decentralized approach allows units to decide on the rewards approach that makes sense for the unit, which may be preferred when units are highly differentiated (e.g., one unit supports products in an established, stable market where another acts as an entrepreneurial start-up). Different rewards practices may be necessary based on the strategy of the unit, necessary skills, and goals.

One option that began in the 1970s is to design a rewards program that is individualized and flexible for employees. Most organizations grant the same rewards to similar profiles of employees (e.g., top executives, hourly workers) (Lawler, 2011). "Cafeteria-style" or "flexible-benefit" plans allow employees to choose the mix of rewards that they value the most. Flexible plans allow trades so that employees could choose more money or more vacation time, a choice of a company car or a transportation budget, cash or additional medical coverage, cash rewards or stock rewards (Baeten & Verwaeren, 2012; Lawler, 2011). D. Brown (2014) argues that organizations should move to a "smart rewards" focus "with a more balanced approach that aims to make it easy for employees to engage with and understand their rewards and facilitate them to take action, so as to maximize the value of the package for their own needs" (p. 150). Such plans can be difficult to administer but this approach can also allow employees to receive the benefits they find most valuable, thus maximizing the motivational potential for the rewards.

Designing a Rewards System That Works

To summarize many of the best rewards practices reviewed in this chapter, Aguinis, Joo, and Gottfredson (2013, pp. 243–246) offer five best practice recommendations on how to use rewards effectively.

1. **Define and measure performance accurately**. Begin with the strategy, and identify the outcomes expected by the strategy, defining key metrics using a system such as the balanced scorecard, at the organizational, unit, and team levels. Consider what employees are expected to do (or avoid) in contributing to performance, listing both desirable and undesirable behaviors.

2. **Make rewards contingent on performance**. "Incentives should link performance to pay and should link performance to standards. Rewards should relate directly to the nature of performance required at each level of the organization. Rewards should be linked to objectives that are within the group's or individual's power to control" (Nadler & Tushman, 1997, p. 107). There should be a clear line of sight from an employee's actions to the rewards given.

3. **Reward employees in a timely manner**. "Incentive plans should match measurement periods for rewards to relevant performance periods" (Nadler & Tushman, 1997, p. 107). When given in a timely manner close to the performance being recognized, rewards are more likely to reinforce the connection between performance, results, and rewards.

4. **Maintain justice in the rewards systems.** Consider the principles of distributive and procedural justice in both outcomes and administrative processes of rewards.

5. **Use monetary and nonmonetary rewards.** Informal recognition, praise, and public acknowledgment, along with other nonmonetary rewards, are often not used enough and can be powerful motivators (Galbraith, 2014a).

Many experts recommend involving employees in the design of the rewards system. When employees are involved in the design, they can make recommendations about what they value. They are knowledgeable about potential unintended consequences of metrics and can explain how other employees might respond to a rewards design (Lawler, 2000). Moreover, no rewards system design should remain static, so during a change in the rewards system, employees who are involved in the redesign can help to communicate and sell the design to their peers. Communication to employees is also a critical part of managing the rewards system, but most organizations communicate about rewards only about once per year (D. Brown, 2014). Transparency about the rewards system is also advisable, since many employees can easily locate comparison points with other employees or companies. Openness about rewards practices increases employee trust (Lawler, 2000).

Rewards, Strategy, and Other STAR Points

As we have seen, the rewards design can support or inhibit progress in the rest of the design. Hambrick and Snow (1988) explain that different strategies require different rewards systems. Prospectors, as we saw in Chapter 3, seek growth and entry into new markets. Compensation systems in these organizations should reinforce growth in market share, new product introductions, and new sales channels. The reward system must be flexible to respond to dynamic shifts in the business, and rewards should be delivered frequently. Defenders, on the other hand, with a more mature and stable business strategy, should have a stable reward system. There will likely be a smaller proportion of variable or incentive pay in the rewards mix. Rewards should emphasize long-term growth and stability, and rewards for cost management or quality improvements to processes and products.

Rewards can support the structure point of the star when members of the same division or unit are measured and rewarded similarly based on performance. In these cases, the unit may see increased collaboration and teaming among members who see themselves sharing a common destiny. Such an approach may contradict the processes and lateral capability point of the star, however. If members of one unit believe that they are competing with another unit, they will be less likely to engage in cross-unit coordination (Lawler & Jenkins, 1990). Consider a compensation plan where product revenue is the basis for a quarterly bonus plan. Those who work in product A may feel competitive with those in product B, even in front of the same customer. Including a measure of organizational performance in the reward system (or bonus for solution-based, integrated sales) can temper this competitive behavior. Burton, Obel, and Håkonsson (2015) write that matrix organizations can benefit from profit-sharing rewards to encourage collaboration across the lines of the matrix and discourage competition.

Rewards can contribute to a shift to a customer-centric versus a product-centric approach. At a product-centric company, bonuses are given to salespeople as a commission based on a percentage of the sale. At a customer-centric company, compensation is granted based on the customer's satisfaction with the purchase, encouraging long-term customer relationships (Galbraith, 2005).

In another example of how rewards can support structure as well as lateral capability, Galbraith (2000) writes that rewards systems can encourage a teaming strategy to sell to global customers. Self-organizing teams that are composed of product line employees and geography-based employees may come together to make a customer sale. An incentive system rewards cooperation and not competition by allocating the revenue flexibly across the multiple product lines and geographies. In addition to financial results, customer satisfaction metrics contribute to a total score which determines the bonuses allocated to each member of the team.

Similarly, Schuster and Kesler (2011) offer examples of how the rewards point can support lateral capability. Key account managers who must integrate across product lines to provide one point of contact for customers can be measured on bundled sales rather than for one product line. Functional managers who work within product lines can be measured on functional performance but also product line performance to reinforce both product innovation and functional excellence. See the box below for examples of how rewards can change based on the global context.

GLOBAL CONSIDERATIONS IN REWARDS

There is some research support for the idea that certain rewards practices, such as pay for performance, differ in effectiveness based on the cultural context.

Allen, White, Takeda, and Helms (2004) compared reward practices in the United States and Japan. They point out that rewards are more effective when they are culturally appropriate. In Japan, where employees value collectivism and have a long-term orientation, team-based rewards have been prevalent. Regular salary increases and annual bonuses given equally reward loyalty and long-term commitment. In their study, individual pay for performance plans in Japan were less effective than they were among the American workers studied. Praise and manager appreciation, team-based rewards, and feedback from customers to encourage continuous personal improvement were all valued among the Japanese employees.

Chang and Hahn (2006) studied pay for performance systems in Korea, where rewards have traditionally been granted based on seniority. They found support among employees for pay for individual performance systems, particularly when the reward approach was accompanied by supervisor feedback that gave a clear explanation for the pay decision.

In another study done in a collectivist culture, China, Zhou and Martocchio (2001) found that Chinese and American managers made reward and recognition decisions based on different criteria. Chinese managers tended to place more emphasis on personal need and circumstance in the allocation of financial rewards than American managers. However, both Chinese and American managers placed individual performance as the primary criterion for rewards.

Among Russian and U.S. managers, one study found that both groups used performance as the basis for distributing rewards equitably, but the Russian managers were slightly more likely to take need into account (Giacobbe-Miller, Miller, & Victorov, 1998).

As Gerhart and Fang (2014) explain, there are differences in rewards system effectiveness but they are generally small. They conclude that "country and/or national culture differences are less of a contingency variable than expected" (p. 50).

SUMMARY

An effective design of the rewards point of the star should support the rest of the organization's design. By aligning individual goals with organizational goals, rewards are intended to motivate employees to engage in the actions and behaviors that support the strategy. When improperly created, poor rewards can drive unintended consequences, including unethical behavior, counterproductive behavior, and conflict. Expectancy theory and other supporting research suggests that employees will be motivated when they perceive a reward as valuable, they trust that performance will lead to rewards, and they feel that they can achieve the result through their own control. Motivation can be both intrinsic and extrinsic, and jobs can be designed to maximize intrinsic motivation even while extrinsic rewards are given. Metrics are another important component of the rewards point of the star, because measuring results precedes any granting of rewards. A tool such as the balanced scorecard can help to communicate goals, set future direction, and measure past results. Importantly, a strategic approach to rewards should be to reward based on performance, which can be measured at the individual, team, and organization-wide levels using any number of forms of rewards.

QUESTIONS FOR DISCUSSION

1. Have you ever seen unintended consequences of rewards at work? How so? How could this unintended consequence have been avoided?
2. Consider what motivates you at work or in your leisure time. What intrinsic and extrinsic motivators drive you to act in both circumstances?
3. What rewards mix matters most for you? Are you motivated more by financial compensation, stock, time off, or benefits? How can a different mix of rewards support different organization designs?

FOR FURTHER READING

Kaplan, R. S., & Norton, D. P. (1996). *The balanced scorecard: Translating strategy into action.* Boston, MA: Harvard Business.

Kaplan, R. S., & Norton, D. P. (2001). *The strategy-focused organization.* Boston, MA: Harvard Business.

Lawler, E. E., III. (1990). *Strategic pay: Aligning organizational strategies and pay systems.* San Francisco, CA: Jossey-Bass.

Lawler, E. E., III. (2000). *Rewarding excellence.* San Francisco, CA: Jossey-Bass.

Schuster, M., & Kesler, G. (2011). Aligning rewards systems in organization design: How to activate the orphan star point. *People & Strategy, 34*(4), 38–45.

EXERCISES

1. Continue with Part III of the organization design simulation activity. In Part III, you will complete the star for your organization design by addressing the talent issues we have discussed in Chapters 6 and 7, exploring people and rewards practices for your fictional organization. Turn to the Appendix for further instructions.
2. Based on what you now know about rewards, use the table below to identify how you might design the rewards point

of the star to support the other four star points. Consider whether you would use merit pay, incentive pay, skill-based pay, pay for team performance, and/or pay for organizational performance. Would you grant bonuses, profit-sharing, stock ownership, or a mix of these? What potential problems can you identify with your reward approach?

Feature of Organization Design	How Would You Design the Rewards Point of the Star?	What Could Go Wrong? What Might Be Unintended Consequences?
Functional organization with communities of practice who share information across geographies		
Geographic organization where project managers are integrators across functions		
Product organization where engineering teams collaborate on core technologies		
Matrix organization with product and geography lines		
Front–back organization where account managers bundle solutions from different product units		
Customer organization where customer service representatives work together to share solutions to common customer problems		
Pivot roles include key account managers for the company's top 50 customer accounts		
Service technician role is changing to a generalist (service all products) instead of specialist (service only one product type) model		

CASE STUDY 3: A TALENT AND REWARDS STRATEGY AT EZP CONSULTING

Discussion Questions

1. What is the strategy of EZP Consulting, and how is it changing? What is driving the change in the strategy?
2. How are the current people and rewards practices out of alignment with the changing strategy? How do the existing roles need to change? What will be the important changes to the people and rewards aspects of the organization design?

3. What recommendations will you make to Sam in your next meeting to describe the job requirements of the two new roles? How will you define rewards for these roles?

* * *

"Here's the conundrum I have been investigating. How can we complete 96 percent of our consulting projects with our clients on time and below budget, and yet also have just a 66 percent client satisfaction rate?" Sam Warner was pacing the room, deep in thought. It seemed to Desiree Morris, the talent management consultant at EZP Consulting, that Sam's question was expressed as half rhetorical, half in disbelief. The two were meeting in a glass-walled conference room on the 23rd floor of the downtown office building that comprised EZP Consulting headquarters.

EZP Consulting is a small boutique professional services consulting firm. It is much smaller than the Accentures or Deloittes in the management consulting industry, but has generally been well-respected until a recent downturn. They specialize in implementing video collaboration software for medium-size global businesses that have a virtual workforce and need the ability to connect employees via video streaming in major office locations. EZP works with clients on projects to install video software and equipment and to manage the complex information technology requirements of the implementation. EZP Consulting does not design or sell the video equipment. Clients turn to EZP after they have bought the equipment from the original manufacturer and they need a third-party professional firm to install it.

Not long after Sam arrived 6 months ago he made an immediate impact. Unlike many other senior vice presidents that had come before him in his role, Sam managed several consulting projects on his own as a way of understanding EZP's processes, infrastructure, products, and talent. After the first few of these projects were completed, Sam began making changes to his organization. He streamlined the standard implementation protocol, eliminating unnecessary bureaucracy. He reduced the number of approvals required on client project change orders to put more control in the hands of the implementation team. Recently, he also restructured the organization into four functional departments: client partnerships, project management, technology engineering, and change management.

"I've made some important discoveries in my work on actual project teams," Sam continued. "I found that project managers are burdened by red tape in our outdated processes. A minor change request that added only 6 to 8 hours of project time came all the way to me for approval, frustrating our teams and delaying the project. They should have the authority to make those changes on their own. We added three layers of quality checks on every step of the process, even when there had never been an error requiring so much infrastructure on the project. We would fly someone from Denver to Charlotte just to check that basic cables were plugged in correctly," Sam said, exasperated.

"That sounds time consuming and expensive," Desiree agreed.

"It is, but to be truthful, those were practices that only affected us. Clients did not really notice. Our profits were impacted by the increased expenses on our consulting projects. No, what causes client dissatisfaction is our inability to establish an effective client partnership and help them improve their business practices. We approach our consulting projects as technology implementations. We install, plug in, test, verify. We make sure the video equipment is functioning. When we leave, the power is on and a clear video image shows up on the screen," Sam began. "That is all important. But it cannot be enough."

"Back in the days when video equipment was extremely complicated, the average client required our help. It wasn't like putting together an IKEA bookcase with easy to read written instructions. There were software bugs and a maze of cords and cables to run. But today things have changed. Our clients are more sophisticated and knowledgeable. The products are more intuitive and easier to use. The projects are still complicated, and clients do want our help," Sam added, "but they also expect us to help them use the products they have purchased to improve collaboration in their organizations."

"In addition, one trend I see is that more of our clients are renting equipment instead of owning it. Part of this trend is because they do not want the huge initial expense of a large equipment purchase, but the bigger benefit to them is that they also gain the ability to upgrade the equipment much more easily. When they do that, ideally they will call us back to help them with the upgrade. We get repeat customers. We also want to expand our services into other kinds of technology implementations beyond video, but we can't continue to grow our business unless we have customers who are loyal and turn to us again and again," Sam offered. "They will only do this if they are highly satisfied with their experience with us."

"Our organization was designed for a kind of project that was focused on one thing—a quick and inexpensive technology implementation—but our organization in the future needs to be focused on customer satisfaction and a client-partnership mentality that encourages repeat business. We need to instill this mindset in our project teams, and today we have defined the project work on just a small part of what the teams need to do. All of the work today stops after the implementation is completed. We leave the client site and they never hear from us again because we don't follow up with clients to answer questions or resolve any problems that have come up." Sam paused. "The reason we have such low client satisfaction scores is because we are only meeting a small portion of their needs."

Desiree summarized. "You are saying that our project teams are doing what we have asked, but what our clients need and expect from us is starting to change. I can see a ton of implications for how our teams work with our clients and how our project teams are structured and rewarded."

"That's right," Sam continued. "From our clients' perspective, we are missing the point. They want help training their employees and explaining why video collaboration tools will help their employees work together more effectively. Our role should be much more than plugging in equipment."

"Tell me more about how the project teams work," Desiree responded.

"Currently we have only two roles on a project team: the project manager, who maintains the budget and project timeline, and the technology engineers that do the implementation work. The whole team gets a 5 percent salary bonus at the end of the project if they come in under deadline and under budget. This reward system also has to change," Sam answered.

"I created two new departments because I also want to add two new roles to our projects. First is the client partner, who has the responsibility for client satisfaction and the client relationship. That person should be able to identify other ways that we can work with our clients in the future and generate repeat business. The client partner should understand the client's business and advise them. Second, I also want a change management consultant added to the team, to help create training programs and help the client with a rollout plan for their employees. The change consultant will create communication packages so that our clients can effectively use the technology and increase collaboration among employees in their organizations. I still want to provide a bonus plan for the team, and project budgets and timelines are still an important way for us to measure our success, but the bonus plan also needs to be based on client satisfaction. Somehow we also need to reward for ongoing work with a client and growth of future business.

"Here are the job descriptions that we currently have." Sam handed Desiree a sheet of paper with both job roles explained.

Sam summarized, "I need your help in updating these and creating new ones for the new roles on our implementation teams. More than that, however, I need your help in outlining our talent strategy. I want you to develop a talent program that explains changes we need to make in these areas:

1. Write the job descriptions for client partner and change management consultant. Research how other professional services organizations (like Accenture and Deloitte) describe these roles and list the main 5 to 10 activities we should expect them to perform.

Job Description: Project Manager

The project manager maintains the schedule and ensures satisfactory progress on the client project to confirm that the overall project maintains budget and timeline commitments to the client.

Essential Duties

- Manages the project schedule, identifies areas of risk to the schedule, and communicates to the client and internal management when project completion is at risk
- Maintains the project scope and requirements and negotiates schedule and scope changes with the client
- Documents all steps and work breakdown tasks for each project
- Prepares project budget
- Communicates with project team members to clarify duties and coordinate activities

Metrics

- Percentage of tasks completed on time
- Project budget meets client commitment
- Overall project timeline meets client commitment

Job Description: Technology Engineer

The technology engineer is responsible for the technical implementation for the client. The team member maintains up-to-date knowledge of all aspects of the relevant technology to ensure a successful technical implementation on the project.

Essential Duties

- Installs and tests video equipment at client site and ensures that the equipment is working properly
- Troubleshoots and initiates corrective actions as required when errors or problems arise
- Works with other team members and the project manager to ensure that activities are completed according to client commitments and overall project timeline
- Communicates with project manager to explain unforeseen situations that may compromise the project timeline or budget

Metrics

- Completion of tasks within project timeline
- Completion of tasks within budget

2. How should we revise our talent management and performance evaluation practices? How should we evaluate the four roles on our implementation teams to know if they are successful?
3. How should we reward our talent? How should we change our reward and recognition programs to reflect what we are evaluating in our team members?"

"Any other thoughts you have about our people and talent strategy would be welcome. We need our organization design to match what our clients expect from us, so I'm counting on you to help us redefine that for the new EZP Consulting teams," Sam emphasized. "I'll put a meeting on our schedules for one week from today. I look forward to seeing your ideas then."

CHAPTER 8

REORGANIZING, MANAGING CHANGE, AND TRANSITIONS

Learning Objectives

In this chapter you will learn

- How concerns about managing change and resistance to change impact the design transition.
- What factors to attend to as a designer manages a redesign, including staffing, pace, scope, communication, and feedback.
- The function of organizational culture and its impact on the design effort.
- The role of leadership in organization design.

Let's look at how one organization conducted a redesign. The organization design of the Valves and Controls business unit of Tyco Flow Control had outlived its time. The company decided to focus its attention on its core customer groups and to organize by the key industry segments of customers that purchased its products, such as the oil and gas, mining, and water and chemical industries. The challenge was to develop an integrated global organization that could work together across significant geographic boundaries rather than relying on a distant headquarters organization to make all decisions. With 8,000 employees in more than 300 global locations, this was no small feat. A core team was identified (including HR, organization development, strategy, and line leadership) to manage the organization design process, and a broader expanded team was created to make design decisions. The expanded team members represented a diverse group of skills and backgrounds as well as layers across the hierarchy. This decision to include broad involvement in the design was intended to role model what was expected out of the organization in the end, namely the ability to work in a collaborative and matrixed environment. The expanded team made several early foundational design decisions and decided to increase involvement even more.

In a 3-day organization design workshop, 75 employees debated design alternatives and models. They discussed sensitive subjects of authority, power, and control while avoiding moving forward with decisions that might be politically attractive but wrong for the company. New leaders were identified for the new units, and the units were staffed through an open process over the following months that matched employees to the skill needs of the roles rather than the leaders' personal preferences or friendships. Six months into the new design, leaders came together to share problems and challenges with the actual versus the imagined design. This allowed leaders to work out problems of power and governance between regional and global roles and to assess and adjust the design as appropriate.

Several significant results were achieved in the 3 years since the initial design discussions took place. An important customer that had wanted a global contract for 5 years (but had never been able to get Tyco to accommodate them) finally was able to negotiate a global agreement. A global product roadmap was created. The new global manufacturing operations saw increased efficiencies in facilities usage. Perhaps the most lasting impact was the development of the leaders that participated in the design work. Through a collaborative process, leaders were involved in changes that affected them as they learned how to engage in the process of strategic redesign (Rice & Nash, 2011).

* * *

To this point, we have focused on designing organizations from scratch. Beginning with the strategy and the design criteria, we have discussed how the designer works out the choices in each point of the STAR model. These choices involve making trade-offs and being conscious of implications of each point on other design decisions to ensure alignment.

The reality, however, is that designing a brand new organization from a blank sheet of paper is rare. Most leaders seek to change a current design rather than invent new organizations. They know that employees work within today's structures and existing processes, and that some aspects of these familiar structures, processes, skills, or systems will need to change. Thus, most designers must face the even more difficult task of reorganizing, or working to transition an existing design to a new one. They integrate newly acquired companies, divide departments to focus on new product lines, downsize, and divest businesses. They must take into account the history and previous designs of the existing organization. Leaders and designers must confront the practical realities of disrupting comfortable routines, resistance from organizational members at all levels, and the significant investment of resources it takes to accomplish a design change. They are faced with the difficulty captured in the adage of "changing the tires on a moving car."

In examining organizational transitions, we must also keep in mind that organizational life is like a movie and not a photograph. As several authors have noted,

> The conventional design framework is largely static, and while it can be very useful to managers as a conceptual device for constructing a new organization, it does not offer the managers of ongoing organizations the specific practical guidance they need to keep their organizations aligned with changing environmental conditions. (Snow, Miles, & Miles, 2006, pp. 12–13)

With the STAR model we have temporarily frozen the design elements for purpose of analysis and decision making, but we also know that people are continually refining their designs and making changes to them.

In this respect, we must be reminded that the popular metaphor of an organization design as a blueprint or concrete building framework can be taken too far. An organization design cannot exist without the people that bring the design to life and turn abstract decisions into real-world action. Making a design change is more complex than redrawing part of a blueprint, since people must be involved in adopting the necessary changes. Organization design must involve both the "hard" abstract and conceptual issues involved in the STAR model as well as the "soft" issues of people, change, and transition (Bate, Khan, & Pyle, 2000).

In this chapter, we will discuss the challenges in organization design change and transition. We will look at how to understand the mechanics of personal change and resistance and turn to some of the practical issues of staffing changes, pace and timing, scope and sequencing, communicating, and evaluating and modifying the design as changes take shape. Next, we will turn our attention to the relationship of organizational culture and design and conclude with a discussion of the role of leadership in organization design.

CHANGE AND RESISTANCE

Design changes require a conscious attention to managing change and resistance from organizational members. As if it was not challenging enough to build momentum to kick off the design project and make the design choices, the design itself must now be put into place. "Now your troubles begin," write Senge et al. (1999):

> As your original "seedlings" begin taking root, they come into contact with new features of their environment, such as predators, rivals, and other life-forms that will resist the presence of a new entity. Your task is now to sustain life, not just over a few months, but over a period of years. (p. 240)

Indeed, once people try out aspects of the new design, they may find the changes exceedingly difficult to maintain. For example, the new team roles may not feel as comfortable as the old roles, and members may long for the past despite the fact that the old roles did not work well. The new structure for the division might cause confusion and mistakes as people wonder who is responsible for which decisions.

To understand how to create a transition plan at an organizational level, we must first understand the nature of change at a very personal level. An important part of how people think at work is through *schemas*. Schemas are the familiar cognitive concepts and beliefs that govern how we approach our lives and work environments (George & Jones, 2001). Schemas help us develop familiar patterns that aid us in interpreting what is happening to make sense of our work. We develop schemas so that we know how to make sense of and act on information, so we know what to do when a rush order comes in or the production line is shut down due to an equipment malfunction. Schemas help organizational members organize not only the work itself but also how that work relates to other schemas they have developed about the organization, coworkers, the physical environment, and more.

Change threatens these existing schemas and requires the development of new ones, forcing us to question what was once familiar, known, and comfortable. The termination of a product line, an acquisition and integration of a new company, or a new competitive threat are all disruptive events to familiar patterns.

Design changes are among these disruptive events, requiring the adoption of new roles, coordination mechanisms, and learning new skills.

It is the discrepancy and inconsistency between existing, known schemas and new, unfamiliar ones that first prompts individuals to consider how change affects them (George & Jones, 2001). This is also the time when individuals may resist change as they recognize the need to shed old schemas and adopt new ones.

Personal Transitions

It is a truism that people respond to change in different ways. Some are energized by learning new skills or experiencing a different environment, perhaps motivated by the possibilities of a brighter future. Others may be frustrated or anxious when faced with the unknown, perhaps uncertain how to adapt to change, or sad that an enjoyable current state is about to end. Many have mixed emotions. Whatever the emotions, personal change is very often an affective process as individuals go through stages of transitions that Bridges (1980) calls *endings*, *the neutral zone*, and *new beginnings*.

Endings. All transitions begin with endings, or the recognition and liberation of the past. Endings can prompt confusion and fear. Change can require letting go of past processes, beliefs, and ways of working, but change can also mean letting go of relationships and familiar places. It can also mean changes to one's personal identity, which may happen when career transitions prompt people to rethink who they have been and the meaning that their work has for them personally. The comfortable identity I have developed of myself as a good administrator, police officer, teacher, marketing representative, or book editor is now threatened, and an important piece of my identity may feel lost. Endings are experiences of loss, and people naturally "grieve" during this process, experiencing emotions of shock and denial when confronted with change.

The Neutral Zone. The neutral zone is a time when "neither the old nor the new ways work properly" (Holbeche, 2006, p. 74). It can be frustrating and confusing to recognize that a change is taking place, without the comfort of established routines and practices. People can feel bombarded and overwhelmed by new information and may not know how to evaluate or interpret all of it. It can feel uncomfortable and risky to try new things without the knowledge of what may happen next. It may feel as if the transition is taking forever without a clear sense of when the confusion will end.

New Beginnings. Beginnings may occur with stops and starts as people transition to new ways, perhaps experiencing personal setbacks, frustration, or failure as they attempt to change but find it difficult. Disappointment may set in if the new beginning is not all that it was anticipated to be. "It is unrealistic," Bridges (1980) writes, "to expect someone to make a beginning like a sprinter coming out of the starting blocks" (p. 148). Gradually the new beginning may itself become as familiar and comfortable as the old way.

The implication is that "if people are to positively embrace the change, it is important to create safe opportunities for people to come to terms with the change and adjust" (Holbeche, 2006, p. 71). Many managers trying to promote change in organizations, however, take the perspective that employees need to "get on with it," "get over it," or "just deal with it." As Bridges (1980) puts it, "Treating ourselves like appliances that can be unplugged and plugged in again" is an ineffective method for personal change, and we need methods for "making sense out of the lostness and the confusion that we encounter when we have gone through disengagement or disenchantment or disidentification" (p. 130).

A Change and Transition Planning Framework

Kurt Lewin (1951) offered a three-phase model of organizational change in which he described change as a process of (1) unfreezing, (2) moving, and (3) refreezing. Current organizational practices need to be released (or unfrozen) to be changed. Once they are changed, they need to be refrozen as newly adopted regular practices. Lewin pointed out that two forces worked together to maintain equilibrium in an organization: forces promoting a change and forces promoting the status quo. Change can occur only when forces of change are greater than forces maintaining the status quo. This can happen in two ways: if forces promoting change are increased or forces maintaining the status quo are decreased.

For example, imagine that a company is going to introduce a new financial software system. Forces supporting the change might be that (1) the new system will permit a more sophisticated analysis of the company's financial results, (2) the new system will be more accurate than the current system, and (3) the system can be integrated into the current contracts and manufacturing systems. Forces resisting the change might be (1) the need for extensive employee training, (2) the cost of implementing the system, and (3) the reluctance on the part of employees who have had a bad experience with similar implementations. Lewin's model points out that change will not occur if the training, cost, and resistance are greater than the benefits that the system offers (see Figure 8.1).

Consistent with this same philosophy about transitions, Marks (2006) offers an instructive typology to help guide transitions during downsizings or reorganizing initiatives. Broadly speaking, transition plans should accomplish two tasks:

1. Weaken the forces for maintaining the old
2. Strengthen the forces for developing the new (p. 387)

In other words, transition plans should support employees in realizing the endings and leaving them behind while simultaneously moving toward the new

Figure 8.1 Lewin's Force Field Analysis

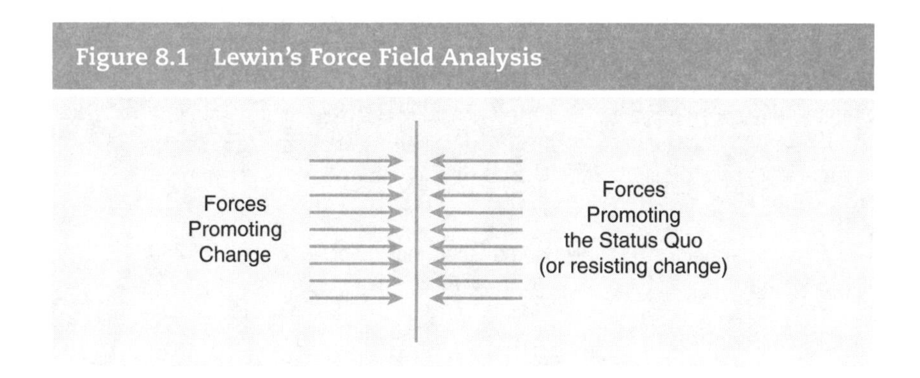

beginnings and encouraging them in that effort. Transition plans must also support employees at two levels. From one perspective, the transition must address the emotional realities involved in the ending stage, letting go of past meanings and relationships that will no longer exist in the new organization, but also adopting the new activities and relationships that are now needed. Emotions may include negative ones such as frustration, anger, and cynicism, or positive ones such as eagerness and anticipation. In addition, the transition must address the business imperatives or the real work that needs to be accomplished for the organization to succeed. Here, too, past activities (as well as processes, reports, goals, and skills) must be discarded and new ones adopted. Integrating the two tasks with the two levels results in the four categories of transition activity depicted in Figure 8.2.

For each of the four categories of the transition to address, a variety of actions can support the transition, as displayed in Table 8.1. This simple framework of activities can remind leaders and design teams that employees need support in

Figure 8.2 A Framework for Facilitating Workplace Recovery After Transitions

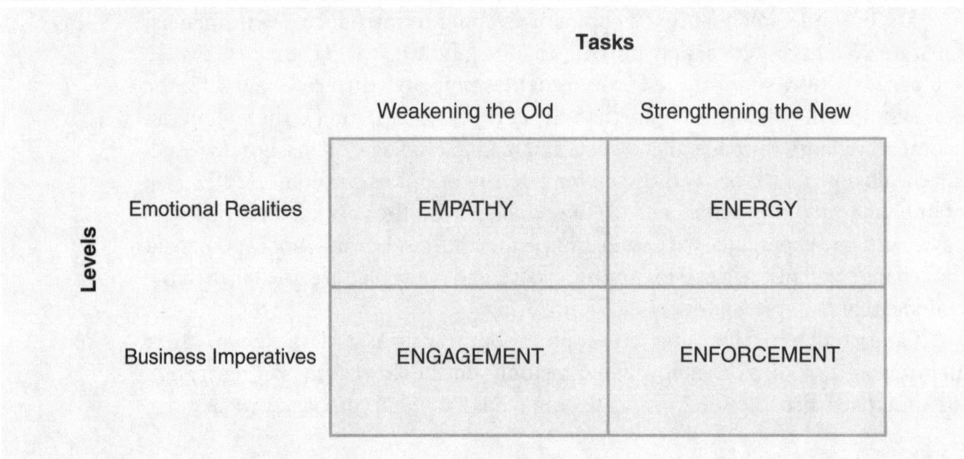

		Tasks	
		Weakening the Old	Strengthening the New
Levels	Emotional Realities	EMPATHY	ENERGY
	Business Imperatives	ENGAGEMENT	ENFORCEMENT

Source: Marks, M. L. (2006). Workplace recovery after mergers, acquisitions, and downsizings: Facilitating individual adaptation to major organizational transitions. *Organizational Dynamics*, 35, pp. 384–399.

Table 8.1 Transition Action Planning

	Purpose	Actions
Empathy	Letting people know that leadership acknowledges that things have been difficult and, for at least awhile longer, will continue to be difficult	• Acknowledging realities and difficulties of transition and adaptation • Offering workshops to raise awareness of transition dynamics and the adaptation process • Using symbols, ceremonies, and forums to end the old
Engagement	Creating understanding of and support for the need to end the old and accept new organizational realities	• Communicating and providing opportunities for involvement • Helping people prioritize their work and get it done • Diagnosing and eliminating barriers to adaptation

Energy	Getting people excited about the new organizational realities and supporting them in realizing them	• Clarifying a vision of a new and better organization • Creating a learning environment and opportunities for short-term wins • Connecting with people and providing support while accepting confusion and backsliding
Enforcement	Solidifying perceptions, expectations, and behaviors that are congruent with the desired posttransition organization	• Involving people in bringing the vision to life • Aligning systems and operating standards with new organizational realities • Tracking the development of the desired posttransition organization

Source: Adapted from Marks, M. L. (2006). Workplace recovery after mergers, acquisitions, and downsizings: Facilitating individual adaptation to major organizational transitions. *Organizational Dynamics*, 35, p. 391.

intentionally adopting the new design. Leaders can personally display empathy for the challenges of change while building energy for the future. They can engage employees in addressing problems with old design practices while enforcing the requirements of the new design.

Resistance

Transitioning out of the endings, through the neutral zone, and into new beginnings can mean encountering resistance. Indeed, Kotter and Schlesinger (2008) write that "organizational change efforts often run into some form of human resistance" (p. 131), and the causes they cite include parochial self-interest, misunderstanding and lack of trust, different assessments of the costs or benefits of the change, and low tolerance for change. O'Toole (1995) provides a list of 33 reasons that lie at the heart of resistance to change, including fear of the unknown, fatigue over too much change, cynicism that change is possible, and a desire to keep the status quo and one's comfortable habits. Resistance is a natural, common, and expected reaction to most change programs.

Dent and Goldberg (1999) reviewed the evolution of resistance since its inception, noting that "the phrase *overcoming resistance to change* implicitly suggests that the source of the problem is solely within the subordinates and that the supervisor or more senior executive must overcome this unnatural reaction" (p. 37). The connotation we have of resistance to change is of a recalcitrant, disobedient, and irrational employee audience actively or passively working to oppose the justified, beneficial, and helpful actions of a rational leader trying to help. Resistance is seen as existing only in "them," not as a function of any actions of the leader, and it is almost universally seen as negative.

As a result, we often try to bypass or push through resistance with force, which often causes even more resistance. In this respect, leaders and design practitioners may be contributing to the very resistance we are trying to avoid, through misrepresentation, inauthentic behavior, or ambivalence of our own. We may ignore the dual advantages and disadvantages of a change and promote only the positives, offering an intentional or unintended misrepresentation of the change. When leaders hide or avoid discussing a change in order to avoid eliciting resistance from organizational members (or avoid discussing resistance itself), they may unwittingly encourage resistance from members who see through the inauthentic behavior.

Leaders who are later asked to account for the failure of a change program will "take credit for successful changes and blame other factors, such as resistance, for problems and failures" (Ford, Ford, & D'Amelio, 2008, p. 364). This justification not only minimizes the leader's responsibility but serves to reinforce commonly held notions that change failures are due to resistance. Consequently, it may be more valuable to set aside the label and instead approach interactions with employees as an opportunity to engage them in a conversation.

Rethinking resistance and seeing it in a different light can offer a number of benefits. When resistance is sought as a continuing part of the change conversation, it can provide useful data. By "listening keenly to comments, complaints, and criticisms for cues to adjust the pace, scope or sequencing of change and/or its implementation" (Ford et al., 2008, p. 369), recipients' feedback, positive and negative, can be taken into account to create a better solution. The negative impacts of resistance can be minimized by considering the transition plans in the framework above, and the communication practices described in the next section.

REORGANIZING AND TRANSITION PLANNING

As you recall from Chapter 1, many organizations have failed with redesign initiatives (see box). They engage in "empty restructuring, in which regular and repeated restructuring takes precedence over the more challenging issues" (Bate et al., 2000, p. 449). Failed redesign can be due to poor design choices, but it can also be due to neglected attention to transition work. "Even the best designs can be derailed by ill-planned, poorly executed implementation" (Nadler & Tushman, 1997, p. 230), particularly when leaders assume that a mass communication or organizational announcement will suffice in moving a design from concept to implementation.

Getting the transition plan right can help to minimize some of the major costs in redesign that include disruption to employees and customers, stress, skepticism and cynicism among employees, a feeling of chronic instability, and distracted managers and employees (Nadler & Tushman, 1997, pp. 218–219). The transition plan should consider how roles in the new organization design will be staffed,

WHY REORGANIZATIONS FAIL

A McKinsey study revealed the top seven reasons why organization design changes fail (Heidari-Robinson & Heywood, 2016a, p. 89):

1. Employees actively resist the changes.
2. Insufficient resources—people, time, money—are devoted to the effort.
3. Employees are distracted from their day-to-day activities, and individual productivity declines.
4. Leaders actively resist the changes.
5. The organizational chart changes, but the way people work stays the same.
6. Employees leave because of the reorganization.
7. Unplanned activities, such as an unforeseen need to change IT systems or to communicate the changes in multiple languages, disrupt implementation.

the pace and timing of the change, the scope and sequence of the changes, how changes will be communicated, and how feedback will be obtained and ongoing adaptations will be made.

Structure, Reporting Relationships, and Staffing

Once an organization redesign initiative is announced, it will often be accompanied by a high degree of anxiety and worry among employees who will wonder how the changes will affect them. During the design planning an organizational structure has been identified, perhaps down to a few levels of detail. There may be fewer employees in the new organization, there may be different leaders or teams, and there may be different jobs to be done requiring different skills. Thus, the transition plan must consider how the organization will be staffed.

The staffing process for the new design can take a number of forms depending on the complexity of the design change and how much openness or choice is desired.

An open process: Generally involves employees bidding or interviewing for roles in the new organization. At the extreme, all roles in the new organization are open for bidding regardless of who may already be in the role. The design team would do the following:

- "Publish full job descriptions, criteria, and person specifications together with the vision, the new organization chart, the mission, and goals."
- Invite employees to consider the published jobs in relation to their career development plans, their match to the criteria, their skills, and abilities.
- "Hold 1:1 manager–employee discussions on options and possibilities" (Stanford, 2005, p. 233).

A slotting or appointment process: Generally involves selecting candidates for the job through a less open process than above, which might involve the following:

- Appointing candidates to fill roles as the organization is designed, ensuring that they have the opportunity to participate in subsequent design decisions relevant to their function
- Retaining incumbents in existing jobs
- Offering roles to certain employees based on unique skills or succession plans

Stanford (2005) writes that most staffing plans are likely to use a combination of all of the above mechanisms and that there are advantages and disadvantages with both approaches. A leader with rare skills may be naturally suited to lead a new division and may be selected immediately. In other cases, there may be a dozen entirely new roles and the leaders would like to welcome any candidates who are interested in a challenge or job change. The more openness in the staffing plan, the greater the perception of fairness among employees who appreciate the opportunity to choose the roles they are interested in, although many employees may resent being asked to apply for a role that they already hold. When employees perceive that the process and decisions are fair, they are more likely to accept the design after it is in place. An appointment process may be quick and minimize individual uncertainty for those who are affected, and it may serve to retain top talent who otherwise might be apprehensive about the transition. Yet, it may also be seen as unfair to those who might have been interested and skilled but who were not given the opportunity to express their interest.

Galbraith, Downey, and Kates (2002) offer the advice that senior positions ought to be filled as a priority, to ensure that they can participate in completing the remainder of the staffing of their organization. Staffing decisions should be made rapidly to minimize the pain of uncertainty and speed the adoption of the new roles. Clear criteria for selection and skill requirements for each role should be defined and should drive the staffing decisions instead of politics and playing favorites. Above all, employees should be informed how the staffing process will be conducted.

Pace and Timing

Many leaders are likely to want to rush the implementation process. Indeed, leaders or design teams may have spent months working out complex design decisions and may be eager to get beyond the transition, just as employees may be hearing about it for the first time. With the big decisions completed, many leaders are prone to focus less attention on the postannouncement transition plans and assign those activities to others. The design team commonly begins to struggle with the detailed and unforeseen challenges that arise and require tough decisions, drawing out the process and prompting leaders to slow down to address the details. Heidari-Robinson and Heywood (2016b) observe that one major pitfall of redesign efforts is a "long, sequential planning and evolutionary implementation," pointing out that in their experience, "reorgs that take less than six months to complete the design detailing and implementation are more successful than those that take longer" (pp. 144–145). Galbraith et al. (2002) write that design activities can take 4 to 7.5 months, with another 3 to 9 spent in full implementation. At the same time, 40 percent of design teams "underestimate the effort required" to conduct the transition (Heidari-Robinson & Heywood, 2016b, p. 145) with this timeline.

Table 8.2 Advantages and Disadvantages of Transition Timing

	Rapid Transition ◄———►	A Cautious Pace
Advantages	• Can minimize anxiety and time spent in the transition phase. • Can cause confusion when rapid changes are not communicated or decisions need to be made.	• Employees have time to absorb the changes and be included in decisions. • Details can be worked out and problems solved before they cause major problems.
Disadvantages	• Employees can feel left out. • Can require time or resources that the organization is not prepared to invest.	• Expected results of the design change take longer to realize. • Drawn-out change and longer disruption phase cause fatigue.

What counts as a "rush, big bang" or a "long, drawn-out" implementation is probably a matter of perspective, and there are good arguments for a rapid transition as well as a more conservative pace. The implication is that the design team must evaluate for the unique situation and the magnitude of the change to decide how fast it can be realistically accomplished. Employees may be more or less ready for change. Speed will require enough time, resources, and dedication to address the details, which may also divert attention from day-to-day business issues and customers. A rapid pace may also minimize the time spent in transition. On the other hand, a cautious pace can bring employees along and ensure that they are ready for the changes as they happen, but also will draw out the change effort and its disruption. Table 8.2 summarizes the advantages and disadvantages of the two ends of this continuum.

Cichocki and Irwin (2011, pp. 199–200) offer three questions to consider as the pace and timing of the transition plan are decided:

1. "Does the external environment impose any timescales?" For example, if the organization design change is being made in response to a regulatory requirement, there may be a hard deadline to meet. There may be a looming competitive threat or promise to a major customer that has prompted the design change.
2. "What else is going on in the organization that may influence the timing?" There may be other change initiatives that are equally pressing and result in divided attention. Resources may be unavailable from finance or human resources to help create new financial profit and loss accounts or to map employees to new units.
3. "What constraints or limitations are there?" Members of the organization may be weary of yet another change, there may be high or low levels of resistance, or there may be information technology or other constraints on making a rapid change.

Scope and Sequencing

Another issue to consider in the transition plan is the scope and sequencing of the design change. Some design changes will need to be put in place immediately with a large, global scope. In others, the project can be implemented in phases, starting small and working toward a global implementation. Consider an organization design where a functional organization adding new product groupings would like to move to a matrix structure. The design team may approach this effort in phases, first assigning functional teams to each of the product groups, with the goal of enhancing cross-product teaming at first. Then once those teaming skills are built, the matrix organization could be a logical next step in the organization's evolution. The opposite approach might also be called for, when a design team realizes that "it's sometimes necessary to start out with such a radical redesign that it completely shatters the existing architecture" (Nadler & Tushman, 1997, p. 221). This can send a message that the old design is being transformed in a revolution, not evolution.

Kesler and Kates (2011) recommend using the STAR model as a guide for sequencing the design effort, asking, "Do any of these design pieces have to be implemented first before others can be successful?" (p. 213). For example, it may be the case that training for the skills required in the new organization should come before the structure is changed. It may be easier to change the metrics and rewards system than to restructure an entire division.

There are several options to consider as variations of scope and sequence:

Transition Organization. Imagine that a new manufacturing line is being created which will gradually take more and more of the workload, but is slowly ramping up. There will be a period of time when the new line and the old processes work side by side. There may need to be transition structures (Beckhard & Harris, 1987) put in place where a new manager leads the new process. In some cases, existing management may be able to handle both duties, but in other cases the management work may be quite different from the old ways and the organization would benefit from a transition structure. A transition manager can be appointed to lead a new organization, one who has the clout, respect, and interpersonal skills to manage through the transition (Beckhard & Harris, 1987). Various transition structures exist, including separate formal organizations and a cross-functional team made up of constituencies or departments.

Pilot Organization. Pilot organizations can be a method for trying out the design to see if it works before investing the resources in a full implementation of the design. Moore (2015) writes that in fast-moving industries where innovation is necessary for survival, "incubation zones" can be developed where independent operating units can function without the rules and constraints imposed by the rest of the organization. During the pilot phase, learning can be captured and skills developed that can be used as input to accelerate future pilots or a full implementation. If the pilot is used as a learning opportunity to test the design, then the pilot implementation must be a realistic test case, or it will encourage questioning of the design's logic and effectiveness (Kesler & Kates, 2011).

Global Plan but Local Implementation. The design team should also decide where variations might exist in the implementation of the design. Heidari-Robinson and Heywood (2016b) write of a design effort that encountered significant resistance in Asia, where the local leaders felt the design change would be too disruptive and resource intensive. There, the design team agreed that the Asia organization could be sequenced later in the transition. In another effort, different geographic regions needed flexibility to implement aspects of a design in a way that made sense for their local business needs. In this case, the design team created three documents:

> (1) A description of what the organization should broadly look like when complete; (2) a methodology for how to create the precise answer for any part of the business; and (3) a plan for how to roll out the methodology to over one hundred locations. (Heidari-Robinson & Heywood, 2016b, p. 167)

They called this set of documents the "cookbook" that could be used as the recipe for design changes and taken to local geographies for customization, detailing the required but also variable aspects of the design. The team created a global plan with local implementation guidance.

Communication

Any change plan can be derailed by a poor or absent communication plan, and leaders frequently make several errors in communicating transitions. Leaders often try to keep information secret with the assumption that if employees know about the change effort, it will cause disruption. They push communications activities to others and stay out of the spotlight, making employees wonder why they are not more visible. They provide vague or ambiguous descriptions of what will happen, causing further confusion and questions.

Galpin (1996, pp. 39–41) offers five lessons for leaders in communication during a redesign effort:

1. Messages should be linked to the strategic purpose of the change initiative. Design criteria can be used to explain the rationale for the changes being made, including changes that were considered but not adopted (Galbraith, Downey, & Kates, 2002).
2. Communications should be realistic and honest. Heidari-Robinson and Heywood (2016a) recommend beginning with the basic "who, what, when" questions. Not all answers will be known, and leaders should be transparent about questions that cannot yet be answered.
3. Communications must be proactive rather than reactive. Stanford (2015) advises that "early and adept communications stall the rumor mill and pave the way for building trust that people will be kept informed as the design is shaped" (pp. 100–101).
4. Messages should be repeated consistently through varying channels. Heidari-Robinson and Heywood (2016a) remind leaders to enhance communications beyond simple e-mail cascades to include in-person meetings and smaller team discussions.
5. Avenues of two-way communication are needed to help ensure successful implementation of the changes. At each phase employees should be encouraged to weigh in, ask questions, and guide the change effort.

Different messages are needed across different stages of the design effort. Heidari-Robinson and Heywood (2016a) note that employees are less likely to hear and believe a leader's enthusiasm for the design changes until they are aware of how they personally will be impacted by the design. Table 8.3 lists the phases of the change communication plan and what should be the focus of each phase.

Feedback and Learning

Several principles can aid the transition as the organization tries out the new ways of working specified by the design. Feedback should be gathered so that the organization can learn from how the design is being experienced by employees. Using an approach similar to that described in Chapter 2 (the design assessment), interviews, surveys, and focus groups can provide an evaluation of the organization

Table 8.3 The Four Communication Phases of a Change Effort

Communication Phase	Communication Scope	Communication Purpose
Building awareness ("This is what is happening.")	Organization-wide	• Position change initiatives from a strategic perspective. • Reaffirm organizational principles. • Provide specifics about the process (steering committee, teams, timetable, and so on). • Announce senior management involvement and support.
Giving project status ("This is where we are going.")	Organization-specific	• Demonstrate senior management commitment. • Reaffirm strategic rationale. • Identify management and employee issues. • Gain information from pilot tests. • Provide the big picture for change blueprints.
Rolling out ("This is what it means to you.")	Project-specific	• Continue to show senior management commitment. • Provide specifics on the changes being made. • Share implications of change with those affected. • Provide training for new roles, skills, methods.
Following up ("This is how we will make it work.")	Team-specific	• Continue to show senior management commitment. • Reaffirm organizational principles and strategic focus. • Listen to and act on feedback to make changes successful. • Refine changes to ensure success.

Source: Adapted from Galpin, 1996, p. 46. Republished with permission of John Wiley & Sons, from *The human side of change: A practical guide to organization redesign*, T. J. Galpin, p. 46, © 1996; permission conveyed through Copyright Clearance Center, Inc.

in transition. Metrics and measures can give insight into whether the outcomes sought by the design criteria are being realized (e.g., Are customer orders being produced more quickly? What has been the impact on production costs? Is there greater consistency in advertising due to improved coordination among the marketing organizations globally?).

Throughout the transition process, the design team should be guided by the questions and problems that arise, since no design effort will have anticipated every issue. As Monge (1993) puts it, "Organizational design always takes time, and original conditions may have changed by the time the design is completed and implemented, making it less appropriate than originally anticipated" (p. 343). It may be that an adjustment to the design is needed if "a gap between design and actual use emerges. . . . Use your design principles to guide any changes so that you retain the overall integrity of the project" (Stanford, 2005, p. 218). Heidari-Robinson and Heywood (2016b) note that some complaints about the design may just be growing pains, but it is important to acknowledge that the design is not perfect and listen to suggestions about how to improve the design to deliver the expected results.

Beckhard and Harris (1977) recommend seven practices that can encourage regular maintenance and renewal of a change. They write that these practices can help leaders understand the effectiveness of the change and also provide opportunities for information sharing about the change among members who may only see a certain aspect of the change given the limited view they may have in their individual roles.

1. *Periodic team meetings.* A regular meeting during which team members can come together to share results, perspectives, and opinions about how the change is operating. Beckhard and Harris (1977) write that such meetings invite "members to think through what they have done and what has happened since the last meeting and where they are going in the next intermediate period" (p. 101) in order to encourage members to think about the change as an ongoing process rather than a discrete event.
2. *Organization sensing meetings.* It is useful for top leaders to hear directly from organizational members about how the change is working. Sensing meetings are a process whereby the top leader may meet with groups of employees from various departments throughout the organization. These can be mixed groups of a random sample of employees, or they can include employees with a similar level or role. Provided that these are information-gathering meetings and not used to penalize or discipline anyone, they can be valuable ways of minimizing hierarchy and clarifying the change for both leaders and employees.
3. *Periodic intergroup meetings.* Particularly in intergroup changes where new roles, processes, or relationships are developed, a regular meeting among members of the groups involved can serve as a point to renew and evaluate the changes that have been made.
4. *Renewal conferences.* A renewal conference is a specific event, often held offsite, where organizational leaders or members meet to evaluate and discuss the change.
5. *Goal-directed performance review.* Performance reviews evaluate departments and individuals against specific measurable goals. Having clear and consistent goals, with rewards to support them, provides unambiguous support for the desired change. Documenting these goals and expected results in performance plans helps organizational members to focus on the activities that matter most in support of the change.
6. *Periodic visits from outside consultants.* A return visit from members of the design team who helped to implement the change can encourage the organization to take an objective look at its progress.
7. *Rewards.* As we discussed in Chapter 7, recognition systems should be carefully analyzed for the activities and values that they support.

Rewards should be put into place that "provide recognition to the people who maintain the new and different ways of doing things, especially when under pressure" (Jackson, 2006, p. 184).

ORGANIZATIONAL CULTURE AND DESIGN

Throughout the book, we have occasionally made reference to the organizational culture. If you have been wondering about the place of organizational culture in the STAR model, you are not alone. The relationship of culture to design has been somewhat disputed and controversial. Galbraith (2014a) admits that this is a frequent question, and he responds:

> Leaders cannot directly control the culture. . . . If the strategy is to become more customer-centric, the leaders choose to organize by customer segments, accentuate the customer relationship management process, reward people on the basis of customer satisfaction and customer retention, and hire people who are relationship oriented as opposed to transaction oriented. If the leaders make all those decisions, they're most likely to generate the kind of behavior that then leads to a culture of customer-centricity. (pp. 19–20)

Lorsch and McTague (2016) echo this sentiment, writing that "cultural change is what you get after you've put new processes or structures in place to tackle tough business challenges like reworking an outdated strategy or business model. The culture evolves as you do that important work" (p. 98). They argue that culture is an outcome of other activities, not something that can be addressed straightforwardly.

Others, however, note that organizational culture does have its own influence on the design process. In this view, culture has a reflexive relationship with organization design—it is both an input to and an output of the design. Douglas (1999) commented that

> [W]e view organizational culture as a moderator in the redesign process, affecting the manager's ability to change. . . . Culture is a major influence on the structure of the organization because it provides consistency, order and structure for activity, establishes communication patterns, and determines the nature and use of power. . . . [I]t is a factor in the redesign process over which managers have little or no control. . . . An organization's culture can either assist or derail redesign activities. (p. 622)

Danişman (2010) agrees, based on a study of resistance to an organization design change in a Turkish organization, concluding that "cultural understandings and values seem to restrain alternative design choices" (p. 216). Finally, Schein (2017) pointed out that the relationship of culture and design is more nuanced, perhaps reflecting the maturity of the organization.

> In a young organization, design, structure, architecture, rituals, stories, and formal statements are both culture creators and culture reinforcers. Once an organization has matured and stabilized, these same

> mechanisms come to be constraints on future leaders. . . . Beliefs also vary about how stable a given structure should be, with some leaders seeking a solution and sticking with it while others . . . [are] perpetually redesigning their organization in a search for solutions that better fit the perceived problems of the ever-changing external conditions. (pp. 196–198)

Stanford (2015) explains the surprising lack of attention to culture in organization design by pointing to the fact that much of culture that affects day-to-day behavior is implicit, hidden, and rarely discussed. By contrast, organization design is more likely to be explicit and often purposefully defined. Nonetheless, it makes pragmatic sense for a design leader or team to at least consider the organizational culture as they work on a redesign.

Specifically, the concept of culture can assist designers during the transition time to a new design. Understanding an organization's culture can point to the deep roots behind prior and future design decisions, helping the leadership and design team understand the magnitude of change required in a design transition. An organization where "cover your back" and blame behaviors are common will find it difficult to move to the trusting and collaborative behavior required in a new matrix structure, for example. An organization that prizes differentiation through job titles and status displays may struggle with the new expectation to enhance collaboration through self-managing teams. The greater the perceived inconsistency between the bedrock foundations of culture that existed in the prior design and those expected in the future design, the more challenging it will be to change.

Finally, culture can be a useful lens on the conflicts that occur between people, departments, and organizations (in the case of mergers and acquisitions or joint ventures). It can be useful as an analytic device to explain difficulties that may look like design issues on the surface but could be addressed with another solution (e.g., team building or a cross-department team intervention; see Anderson, 2017).

What Is Culture?

The concept of a "culture" predominantly originates from the field of anthropology and conjures images of social scientists observing distant countries and social groups. Similarly, those who study corporate or organizational cultures have been called "organizational anthropologists" (Smircich, 1985, p. 65), whose task it is to decipher not only "how things are done around here" (a common definition of culture) but also the hidden meanings and assumptions that characterize how organizational members interpret and make sense of what is happening, or "how people think around here."

Culture has been defined in various ways, but most agree that a shorthand definition of culture is "the shared attitudes, values, beliefs, and customs of members of a social unit or organization" (Walter, 1985, p. 301). Schein (2017) provides a more detailed definition of the culture of a group:

> The accumulated shared learning of that group as it solves its problems of external adaptation and internal integration; which has worked well enough to be considered valid and, therefore, to be taught to new members as the correct way to perceive, think, feel, and behave in relation to those problems. The accumulated learning is a pattern or system of

beliefs, values, and behavioral norms that come to be taken for granted as basic assumptions and eventually drop out of awareness. (p. 6)

Basic elements of a culture consist of the following:

- *Language, metaphor, and jargon.* How organizational members speak to one another, using what terms. An example is whether organizational members are referred to as "associates" (some retail stores), "individual contributors" (some corporate environments), or "cast members" (such as at Disneyland). Organizational members develop specialized acronyms and terms that often only they understand.
- *Communication* (patterns and media). Who communicates to whom, on what topics, using which media. In some large organizations, the most senior leaders send e-mail to all employees, while in others, in-person communication is preferred. These choices can be situation or topic dependent as well.
- *Artifacts.* For example, pictures or posters on the wall, lobby decor, or dress style. Some organizations have explicit rules for who is permitted what size office, with what furniture style, or even what model of phone or cell phone calling plan is authorized.
- *Stories, myths, and legends.* What stories from the past resonate with organizational members to recall lessons and learnings from positive or negative events. An organization that has undergone an especially traumatic event, such as a bankruptcy, is likely to have a set of stories and assumptions that are repeated to guide new decisions in order to avoid repeating historical mistakes.
- *Ceremonies, rites, and rituals.* These are formal and informal gatherings or recurring events in which a standard "script" seems to be followed. Examples include a corporate picnic or holiday party, initiation rites such as those in a fraternity or sorority, or even repetitive events such as annual sales conferences, staff meetings, or performance appraisals.
- *Values, ethics, and moral codes.* Doing what is "right" may mean doing it quickly in one organization or doing an exhaustive study of all possible options in another organization. Organizations have espoused values, those that they explicitly articulate, and hidden underlying values, those that guide decision making but about which organizational members are usually less conscious.
- *Decision-making style.* Including what information is needed before a decision is made, who is consulted, whether opinions are freely offered, who makes the final decision, and how it is communicated.

Elements of culture can be visible, such as styles of dress, office spaces, and language choices, and they can also be invisible or hidden, such as the organization's values, ethical beliefs, and preferences. The more deeply held the belief and more tacit the assumption, often the more difficult it is to change. Figure 8.3 illustrates these elements of culture.

Figure 8.3 Elements of Organizational Culture

More Difficult to See and to Change ↓		More Visible and More Easily Changed ↑
	Architecture and office layout	
	Styles of dress	
	Structure and patterns of meetings	
	Language and jargon	
	Decision-making styles	
	Explicitly articulated values and beliefs	
	Underlying philosophies, preferences	
	Hidden assumptions and values	

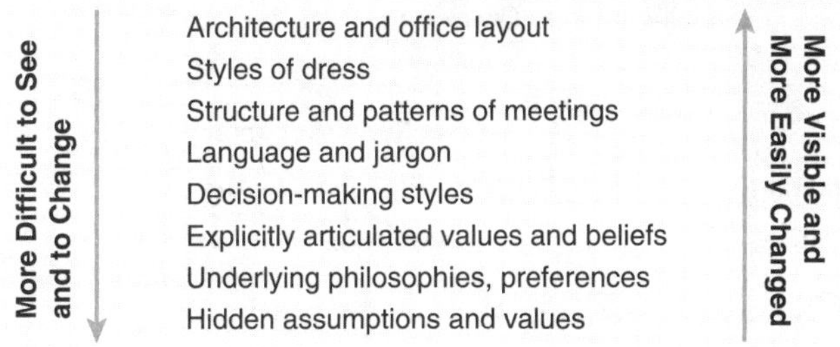

Complicating the notion of culture is that organizations are composed of a number of subgroupings, with different departments and teams that might also exist in different geographies. National cultures and regions have their own cultural attributes as well, so within any given organization there are likely to be many different subcultures operating, changing, and evolving at any given time. Therefore, cultures are not monolithic or singular, and people in the same organization will experience the culture in different ways.

Because of this, culture is likely to be characterized differently by different people in ways that might seem contradictory. An organization might be both collaborative *and* competitive, transparent *and* secretive, bureaucratic *and* permissive, all at different times or in different circumstances (Stanford, 2011).

Understanding Culture: Competing Values Framework

There are many quantitative and qualitative methodologies for studying culture (see Schein, 2017). One of the most widely used frameworks for studying organizational culture is the Competing Values Framework (CVF) developed by Kim Cameron and Robert Quinn. They have developed an Organizational Culture Assessment Instrument (OCAI; Cameron & Quinn, 2011), a quantitative methodology where organizational members complete individual surveys to give change agents insight into the culture. More than 100,000 employees in more than 10,000 organizations have completed the OCAI assessment.

By comparing organizations on dimensions such as internal versus external focus and preferences for flexibility or stability, the "competing values framework" (which is the basis for the OCAI; see Cameron & Freeman, 1991; Cameron & Quinn, 2011; Denison & Spreitzer, 1991) to organizational culture posits four idealized culture types (displayed in Figure 8.4):

- *Clan.* People strongly identify with the group, as in a family, placing a strong emphasis on the team and teamwork. Organizational members are loyal and friendly. Learning and personal development are an important aspect of the organization.
- *Adhocracy.* Innovation is prized, with organizational members having a large amount of independence and autonomy. The organization emphasizes developing cutting-edge products and services and leading

Figure 8.4 The Four Organizational Culture Types

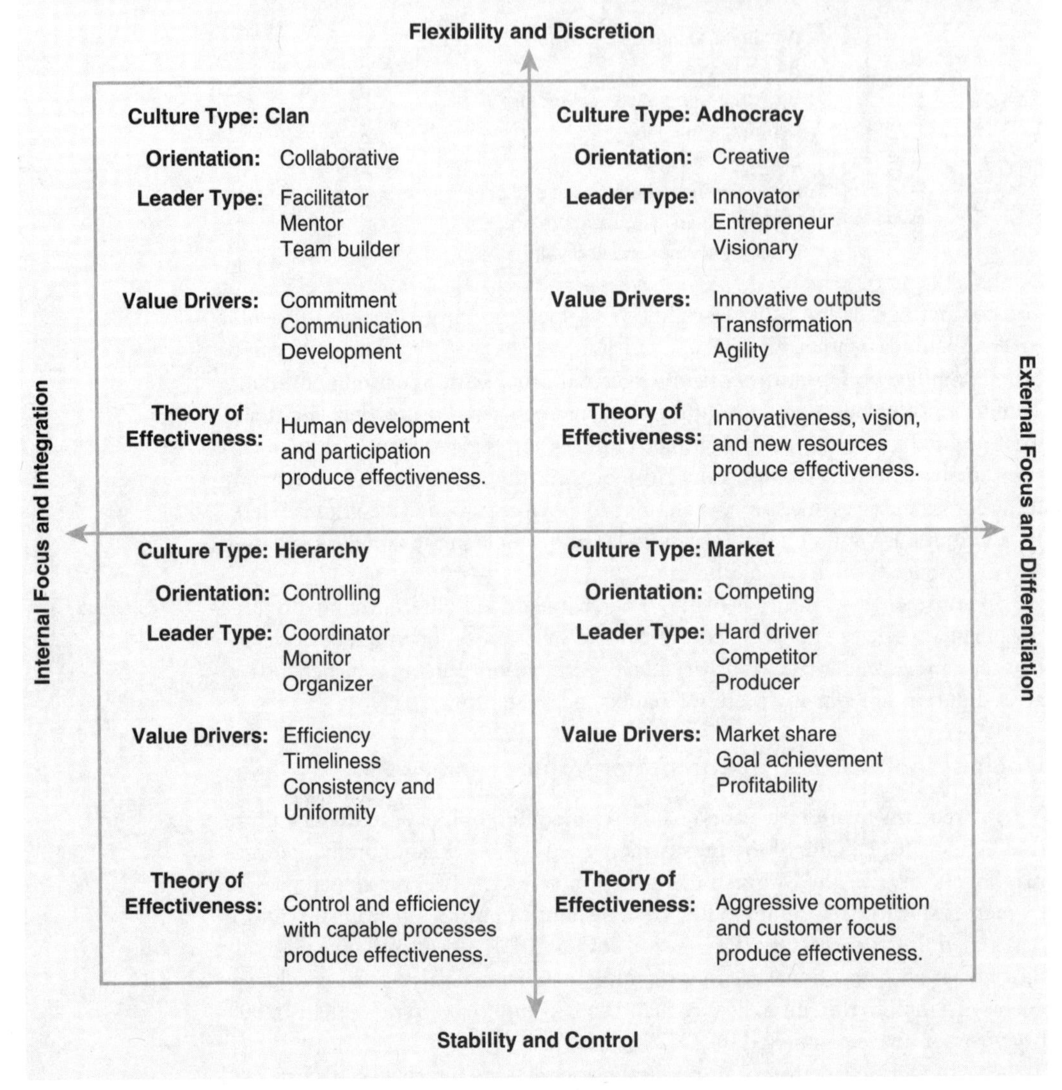

Source: Republished with permission of John Wiley & Sons, from *Diagnosing and changing organizational culture: Based on the competing values framework*, K. S. Cameron, R. E. Quinn, p. 53, © 2011; permission conveyed through Copyright Clearance Center, Inc.

the market, with frequent change. Risk taking, prototypes of changes, and experimentation are common.

- *Hierarchy.* Tradition and formality are dominant values. The emphasis is on stability, rules, and efficient processes. People appreciate security, predictability, and consistency.
- *Market.* Organizational members are competitive, hardworking, and demanding. Productivity and beating the competition are emphasized. Leaders are demanding, pushing people to win through speed and aggressive competitive moves.

It is important to note that every organization contains a blend of all four culture descriptions. Combining the results on the OCAI into a culture plot yields a diagram like that displayed in Figure 8.5. This diagram also happens to be a display of the average culture scores in Cameron and Quinn's database. Different industries also display different culture profiles, as will different subcultures within the same organization.

The CVF suggests that the diagonal dimensions on the grid offer the greatest potential for contradiction in an organization. A hierarchy organization (lower left) that emphasizes consistency, order, and uniformity will find the greatest contradictions with an adhocracy (upper right) organization that emphasizes change and order-disrupting transformation. Clan leaders (upper left) emphasize participation and empowerment (even if decisions are slower) whereas leaders displaying the competing quadrant (lower right) stress speed and urgency (even if people are left behind) (Cameron, Quinn, DeGraff, & Thakor, 2006). The same can be true for different departments in an organization, with production and finance groups tending to display more of the behaviors of the control quadrant, sales and marketing displaying the competitive behaviors of the market quadrant, new product development behavior more like the innovators required in the adhocracy

Figure 8.5 Example Competing Values Culture Plot

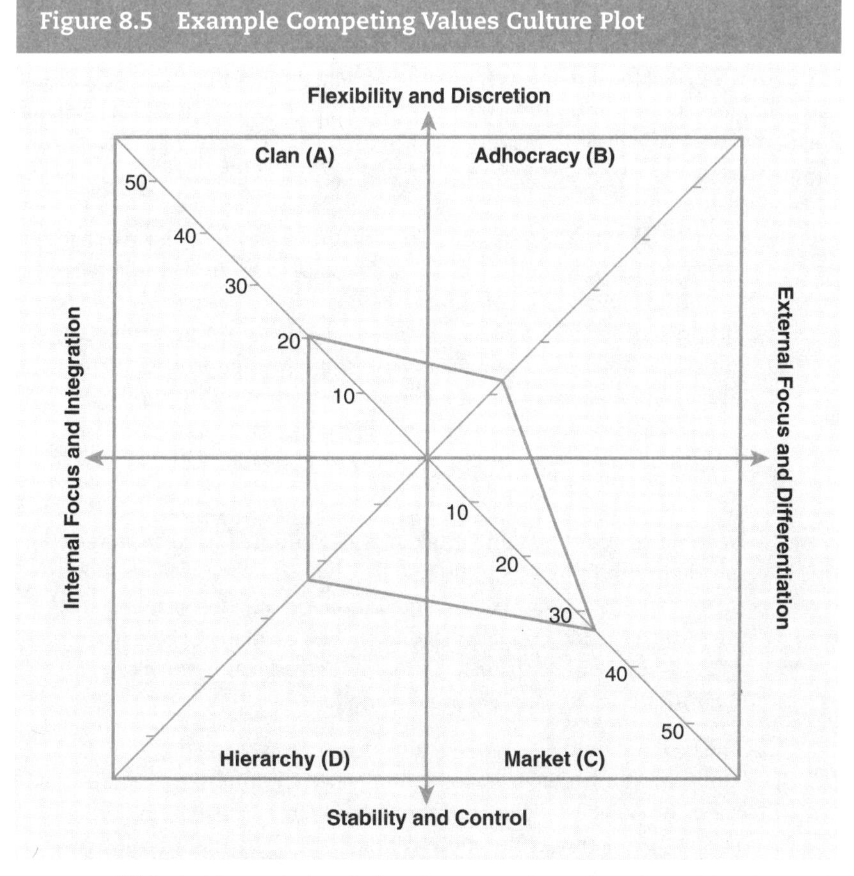

Source: Republished with permission of John Wiley & Sons, from *Diagnosing and changing organizational culture: Based on the competing values framework*, K. S. Cameron, R. E. Quinn, p. 87, © 2011; permission conveyed through Copyright Clearance Center, Inc.

quadrant, and human resources showing the emphasis on people characteristic of the clan quadrant.

Different quadrants have a different mindset about change as well. In the hierarchy quadrant, for example, change is generally approached incrementally, as might happen if the wording on a contract were changed to reflect a new legal phrase. In the adhocracy quadrant, change is likely to be transformational, reengineering the organization's entire approach to contracting. The market quadrant emphasizes changes that are fast to respond to competitive threats, and the clan quadrant seeks change that is long term, involving employees and reaching consensus to ensure that changes stick.

As organizations grow and evolve, they may also emphasize attention to different quadrants. Early in the life of a start-up, new product development and innovation (adhocracy) are likely to be hallmarks of its success. As time goes on and the organization grows in complexity, standard processes are likely to be needed (control). Apple, for example, began as an entrepreneurial company and built camaraderie and cohesiveness (clan) as it grew. Faced with competitive threats from new rival companies, disciplines (hierarchy) and competitive attention (market) became more important (Cameron et al., 2006), explaining the leadership shift from Steve Jobs to John Scully (and back again to Jobs) as these priorities changed throughout the evolution of Apple.

The Competing Values Framework can be used as a way of discussing and creating culture change. Where there is an imbalance from the culture today to the culture needed for the future, the CVF can help leaders and employees articulate what this shift means. Cameron and Quinn (2011) offer a process for changing organizational culture, a process that can usefully accompany an organization design transition:

1. Use the CVF to identify the current culture profile. This can happen with a group of leaders or cross-organization team of employees at multiple levels. The group can reflect on the culture of the past and present, including what key events or decisions have shaped the culture. Schein (2017) advocates a data-gathering process including interviews or focus groups to identify subcultural differences. In this process, group members can help to identify important rites or rituals and underlying assumptions and values that have shaped the culture.
2. Next, the group should identify the organization's future or preferred culture profile. The group can discuss what elements of the culture have been strengths and have contributed to successes, as well as any areas where the organization may need to change or adapt. Schein notes that great insights emerge from a discussion of the group's values and how those may be hindering the organization.
3. The group should discuss what any changes mean and do not mean. A culture profile that reduces hierarchy does not mean that there will be no policies or rules; a culture that increases attention to the market quadrant does not mean ruthlessness or bypassing colleagues' opinions. Greater attention to clan characteristics might mean more involvement from employees at all levels but it does not mean lower performance standards.

4. The group should create an action plan, identifying areas of strength to build on in the existing organization. They can propose immediate changes, even small ones, that can demonstrate the culture change.
5. There should be a discussion of supporting mechanisms for the change such as leadership development, rewards and metrics, and communications throughout the organization.

LEADERSHIP AND ORGANIZATION DESIGN

The work of leadership during an organization design effort includes making design decisions, managing the design project, implementing and carrying out the design change, and aligning leadership actions and behaviors with the expected results of the design and culture of the organization. "Leaders ensure that the design developed is linked to their thinking on the organizational purpose and strategic direction, ensuring sponsorship of the design, obtaining their buy-in and driving the execution of the design" (Cichocki & Irwin, 2011, p. 98). Leaders must be skilled at thinking strategically, considering the external and competitive environment, but also be able to execute that strategy, considering how to carry out the strategy through people and design. Such skills are rare, with only 8 percent of leaders excelling at both strategy and execution, according to one study (Leinwand & Mainardi, 2016). Here we will discuss the leader's role during the design and change processes as well as the posttransition leadership development work needed to ensure that leadership behaviors are consistent with the organization design and cultural transition needed. We will also look at how leaders should work with their new teams.

Leadership's Role During the Design Process

Stanford (2015, pp. 195–201) explains several activities that leaders must do during a design project:

1. "Have a clear grasp of the vision, mission and purpose of the design effort." Leaders must be clear on the rationale for the project and approach it authentically with appropriate expectations.
2. "Determine whether work needs to be reprioritized or resources reallocated," to assist design team members with workload. "Secure resources" for the design team (enough time to dedicate to the work and any financial or people resources required).
3. "Clarify and establish the boundaries of the role" and "establish levels of accountability and responsibility" to ensure that design team members understand the scope of their work.
4. "Mobilize the formal and informal leaders to work together." As the design project reaches an announcement and implementation stage, leaders must involve well-respected informal leaders who have influence throughout the organization, even if they do not hold senior titles.
5. "Build trust quickly by being both credible and competent." Attention will be heightened from employees during an anxious time of redesign,

and employees will look to leaders for consistent behavior to see that actions match words. "Recognize and reduce the fear people may have."

6. "Use power wisely" and "work skillfully with 'followers.'" The leader does not need to rely on position power to make all decisions unilaterally. Decisions can be delegated and input invited in a participative way, increasing the motivation of the organization as "people support what they help create" (Beckhard, 1969, p. 27).
7. "Be conscious of the interests and motivations of other leaders in the program or project." "In most cases there are some leaders who will feel that they will either win or lose from any proposed design and will then act to preserve their own interests at the expense of organizational interests" (Stanford, 2015, p. 201).

The role of leadership in a complex design effort is particularly significant. Complex designs may involve large design teams that need direction, resources, and oversight. There may be multiple stakeholder groups to consider, each of which may be invested or hold a stake in the design and who may support or resist the necessary organizational changes. Design changes with a large scope will also have a tremendous impact on people and their skills and motivation which requires leadership attention.

Leadership's Role During Change

During the change effort, as Galpin (1996) explains, leaders must display six key leadership attributes:

1. **Creativity**, including considering the good ideas that may come from others: Leaders must be open to considering suggestions for innovative solutions, as these may be widely distributed throughout the organization (including frontline employees that witness day-to-day problems).
2. **Team orientation**: The leader cannot make all changes alone and must learn to enlist the influence of others to spread the change message throughout the organization.
3. **Listening skills**: Leaders are prone to relying on one-way communication mechanisms such as e-mails to announce change; they must also equally seek two-way communication methods to gather feedback during the change process, listening to comments, complaints, and suggestions about how the change is working.
4. **Coaching skills**: Leaders must take an active role in helping employees to grow and develop, addressing performance problems, and building confidence throughout the organization to successfully adopt the required changes.
5. **Accountability**: Some leaders have a tendency to announce change and sit back to watch the results. Accountability means being engaged,

participative, taking ownership, and being invested in the change process on a daily basis.

6. **Appreciativeness**: During change, employees may be uncertain about whether they are doing the right things. Leaders should develop a learning culture and express appreciation along the way as employees struggle with change.

Design and Leadership Development

Organization design changes also provide opportunities for leadership development and change. As Kesler and Kates (2011) describe, "When organizations are redesigned, there are almost always new requirements for leader roles and behaviors, often aimed at altering old cultural norms. Those requirements need to be spelled out, and leaders need to be coached and taught to adjust" (p. 168). Leadership alignment to the design and desired culture are critical to ensure consistency in leadership behaviors with the expected design's outcomes. As Stanford (2011) puts it, "Credible leaders who role-model the characteristics they want to see in the organization help reinforce the desired cultural attributes" (p. 187). Cameron, Quinn, DeGraff, and Thakor (2006) describe an individual leadership assessment, using the four-quadrant CVF, to measure leadership competencies required for each quadrant. The assessment presents a leader with feedback on the following competencies:

- **Clan**: Leading through teamwork, leading through interpersonal relationships, leading the development of human capital, leading through cooperation and community, leading through compassion and caring

- **Adhocracy**: Leading through innovation and entrepreneurship, leading the future, leading through improvement and change, leading through creativity, leading through flexibility and agility
- **Market**: Leading through competitiveness, leading through customer relationships, leading through speed, leading with intensity, leading for results
- **Hierarchy**: Leading through rational analysis, leading through information clarity, leading through high reliability, leading through processes, leading through measurement

The assessment can be used not only for individual leadership development activities, but also for the creation of large-scale development programs that can apply throughout the organization to signal the leadership change required. An organization strategy that requires innovativeness in product development may decide to structure according to different product divisions, rewarding key innovators in each division. The culture may need to shift to the adhocracy quadrant, and leaders may need to develop the leadership competencies of leading through innovation and entrepreneurship and leading through creativity. Using these frameworks can guide consistency in messaging and behavior throughout the entire change program, from design to culture shift to leadership competencies.

In addition, the leadership assessment can help leaders see how attention to multiple quadrants is important. For example, while on the surface it may appear contradictory to both lead with intensity and push employees (market) and support organizational members with compassion (clan), it is possible to do both. Leaders may need to learn how to demonstrate "caring confrontation" (Cameron et al., 2006, p. 81), being understanding but also having high expectations. They may need "practical vision" of both the hierarchy (logical and rational analysis) and adhocracy (innovation and flexibility) quadrants.

Leading New Teams

One result of a new organization design is that leaders often have new teams to lead, either because the composition and membership of the team has changed, the mission and goals of the team have changed, or some combination. Watkins (2013) argues that the approach to a new leadership role depends on the business scenario or context for the leader's work. Broadly speaking, there are five of these scenarios, each with a different leadership challenge:

1. **Start-up**: building a new team, initiating a new business, or starting a key strategic initiative. The challenge for start-up situations is creating something from the ground up without a history or framework as a guide. Leaders must often find new team members who will be excited about the opportunity and possibility but be able to cope with the ambiguity that often accompanies the start-up.

2. **Turnaround**: reversing course for a team or department that is not succeeding. Turnaround situations often require quick decisions and swift movement even with incomplete information.
3. **Accelerated growth**: managing a fast-growing organization. Fast growth requires rapid onboarding and hiring new employees and getting them up to speed quickly. Leaders must frequently adjust the infrastructure as the business grows.
4. **Realignment**: similar to turnarounds, but the leader may have more opportunity to make deliberate decisions with a balanced approach between speed and cautiousness.
5. **Sustaining success**: leading a team that has been and is currently successful. The challenge for a new leader can be to motivate people to adopt changes needed to take the organization to another level of success because they may be complacent.

A new leader is likely to encounter a mix of these scenarios depending on the organization. The leader should be clear on the objective, however, as each scenario implies different approaches to change. A start-up team and accelerated growth environment may be highly motivating environments where people are excited to succeed, and their energies need to be channeled appropriately into the right actions and practices to prevent chaos. Turnarounds and realignments may require the leader to find opportunities for small wins and publicize them to build the team's confidence.

Many leaders do not select their team members but inherit them, and team leaders who come to lead intact teams must accomplish three objectives (Watkins, 2016).

1. They must assess team members, through a "mix of one-on-one and team meetings, supplementing with input from key stakeholders such as customers, suppliers, and colleagues outside the team. . . . You'll also look at team members' individual track records and performance evaluations" (p. 63). The leader should evaluate each team member's competence, trustworthiness, energy, people skills, focus, and judgment.
2. They must reshape the team, carefully examining the team's composition and membership to ensure that the right people are in the right roles. The leader must evaluate the team's alignment, clarifying vision, mission, and goals as well as the different roles that members play in accomplishing those objectives. Next, reshaping the team involves evaluating the operating model or the way that the team functions, considering the number, frequency, and purpose of team meetings, for example. The leader must also integrate team members and foster interdependence to ensure that the right coordination is happening where necessary.
3. Finally, the team leader must develop the team, building team dynamics and providing opportunities for learning and growth as a team.

Team start-up meeting interventions (Anderson, 2017) can be an effective way to start teams off quickly. West (2004) writes, "The beginning of a team's life has a significant influence on its later development and effectiveness, especially when crises occur. Start-up interventions can help create team ethos, determine clarity of direction, and shape team working practices" (p. 77). A well-structured team start-up can also do the following:

- Quickly establish agreements and norms so that the team can begin to function more quickly
- Provide opportunities for team member disagreements and misunderstandings to surface earlier rather than later
- Clarify basic team functions such as goals and operating methods
- Allow team members to begin to develop interpersonal relationships
- Provide team members with clear and well-defined roles

An effective start-up meeting begins with a leader's talk, establishing the leader's vision of and expectations for the team and inviting team members to share the same. The team should discuss the team's purpose, vision, goals, and objectives, including major initiatives and activities and their milestones. This is also a time for team members to clarify roles and responsibilities. This topic is particularly important if new team members have joined or team members have left the team in order to establish accountability for ongoing work. Role clarity helps to ensure that members do not waste resources by duplicating work or letting work fall through the cracks due to misunderstandings about responsibilities. The team should discuss operating guidelines and norms such as communication preferences, decision-making patterns, and conflict. Finally, the team start-up meeting should address team meetings to ensure the right meetings with the right purpose, agenda, and attendance are being held.

SUMMARY

As we have seen, most leaders are involved in redesign rather than in designing organizations from scratch. This means that a critical part of organization design is planning and managing change and transitions. The Bridges model of transitions (endings, neutral zone, new beginnings) can shed light into an individual employee's reaction to change. Leaders must help to manage this change by weakening forces for maintaining the old ways of doing things and strengthening the forces for the new, and also addressing both the emotional realities and business imperatives for change. Transition plans must consider staffing plans for the new organization, the pace and timing of change, the scope and sequence of the change, plans for communicating the changes, and opportunities for two-way feedback and learning from the change as it progresses. Organizational culture analysis through a framework such as the Competing Values Framework can be instructive as a lens on the depth and magnitude of change required in adopting a new design, and it can highlight potential areas of struggle or resistance in adopting the principles of a design. Finally, in this chapter we have reviewed the role of leadership in an organization design effort. We have seen the important role that leaders play during the design process, in communicating and reinforcing change, in developing behaviors that align to the design and role modeling what is expected, and in starting new teams.

QUESTIONS FOR DISCUSSION

1. Think of a design change that you have witnessed or researched. Evaluate the pace and timing, scope and sequencing, communication, and feedback and learning in the initiative. What would you change about the transition?
2. Choose one of the quadrants of the Competing Values Framework and describe an organization that you think matches the characteristics of that quadrant. Now choose any other quadrant. What do you think would be the challenges in transitioning an organization to that quadrant? What kinds of organization design changes would support that transition? What design changes would be resisted by members of the organization?
3. Imagine that you are going to hire a new leader to manage an organization design, and you are going to post an online job advertisement for the design leader. What will be some of the most important characteristics you will look for?

FOR FURTHER READING

Cichocki, P., & Irwin, C. (2011). *Organization design: A guide to building effective organizations.* London, England: Kogan Page.

Galpin, T. J. (1996). *The human side of change: A practical guide to organization redesign.* San Francisco, CA: Jossey-Bass.

Heidari-Robinson, S., & Heywood, S. (2016b). *Reorg: How to get it right.* Boston, MA: Harvard Business Preview Press.

Stanford, N. (2015). *Guide to organisation design* (2nd ed.). New York, NY: Public Affairs.

EXERCISE

1. Continue with the final part of the organization design simulation activity. Before you turn to the Appendix, roll your six-sided die one time. Remember your number, and turn to Part IV in the Appendix to learn what has happened with your organization since we left it in Part III.

CASE STUDY 4: REORGANIZING THE FINANCE DEPARTMENT: MANAGING CHANGE AND TRANSITIONS

Read the finance department case and consider the challenges you might anticipate during this reorganization. Develop a transition plan that addresses the following questions:

1. What are the major areas of change from the old design to the new design? What do you think the major concerns will be of employees and managers in the new design? Use the STAR model to identify the transitions at each point of the design.
2. How will you select employees and managers for the roles that need to be filled?

3. How fast will you attempt to implement this change? Will there be milestones and a gradual pace (perhaps a pilot) or will you make a rapid transition?
4. What resistance can you anticipate? On an ongoing basis, how might you continue to support and sustain the change?
5. Imagine that you are preparing to announce this change next week. How will you explain it to employees?

* * *

"Dear Colleagues,

Today marks a major milestone for us as a finance organization. I have an important announcement to share with you about a transition for our department that I believe to be a major step forward to propel us into the next phase of the company.

First, permit me to take you down memory lane.

Some of you remember (or have certainly heard the stories) just 7 short years ago when we started making our specialized organic energy bars for athletes. Our founder, Melissa Waters, used her PhD in nutrition science to develop our proprietary formula for professional athletes after years of experimentation and scientific research. Our production team worked out of Melissa's kitchen and hand-crafted each batch.

We had just one grocery location but we knew we had a unique product when world-renowned athletes started asking us to ship directly to them. The gluten-free bars, combined with our patented packaging, fueled our customers and fueled our growth. As demand grew and our popularity increased, we couldn't keep the bars in stock, especially when we were endorsed by *Professional Triathlete Monthly*. Within 2 years, we were in 23 grocery stores and selling boxes online. We moved into a commercial kitchen.

Much has changed in the past year alone. We have expanded into snack foods. We have begun to sell energy drinks. And with our recent acquisition of AthleteFoodCoach.com, we now provide nutrition coaching for professional and amateur athletes based on scientific research and testing.

Many of these are new and fast-growing business models in a competitive industry space. We have multiple businesses now that are all very different. We sell both products and services, we sell in brick and mortar stores and direct online. We have come under increased profitability pressures in the last year as cheaper competitors have flooded the market. It has become a price war, and while we have had to lower our prices to maintain our market share, that has come at a cost of our profits.

Our business leaders need us as a finance team to support them with the financial knowledge and advice they need to make the right business decisions to expand the company profitably. They need detailed information on pricing strategies for current and new products, unit costs, business case analysis, and much more.

Based on conversations with our senior leaders, I have come to the conclusion that our old finance support model is inadequate for our company's needs. The old model that worked effectively when we were a single product company no longer works adequately, as we have too much complexity now for each of us to know everything about every type of business."

* * *

"And that's all I wrote so far," Heather said.

"It's a great start. I think that reflects everything we discussed to explain the rationale for the redesign," Brad said.

Heather and Brad sat at the long conference room table, reflecting on the debates they had endured during the last 8 weeks. It seemed like yesterday when Heather, the chief financial officer and head of the finance team, tapped Brad to lead the effort. Brad was the first financial analyst she had hired and was most knowledgeable about the organization and industry. She trusted Brad's expertise and knew that he would be a good sounding board for organization design decisions. Heather had told the CEO a few months back that Brad was the highest potential person in the finance organization and should be her eventual successor.

"I agree, and after all of this time, I think we're getting close to communicating," Heather said. "I'm proud of the work that we did, and I'm confident in our choices. I'm concerned about a few points, however, and this is where I need your help before we proceed."

"Let's walk through the whole transition again, so we can clarify what is changing," Heather began. "We currently have a classic functional organizational structure which we have had since the beginning." Heather pulled out her organizational chart.

Old Finance Department Structure

Heather, Chief Financial Officer

Brad, Manager, Planning and Budget	Natasha, Manager, Tax and Investments	Luke, Manager, Purchasing and Procurement	Agnes, Manager, Controller
Budget Analyst	Tax Analyst	Purchasing Analyst	Accountant
Budget Analyst		Purchasing Analyst	Accountant
Budget Analyst		Purchasing Analyst	Accountant
Budget Analyst			
Budget Analyst			

"In our division now, I have 4 managers and 12 financial analysts. Each group works on some area of finance expertise. In your planning and budget team you have five analysts, all responsible for the sales targets for the product areas, annual budgets, and financial reporting. Natasha has the tax and investments area. Since this is smaller, she only has one tax analyst assigned to her, although with the expansion into additional retail stores in new states with new tax regulations, I know this is going to get thornier. Luke has purchasing and procurement, which includes our vendor contracts. Agnes is our controller and maintains our financial records and bank accounts."

"One area where we have always struggled is in cross-functional collaboration," Heather continued. "I have always wanted more teaming between these groups. For example, when we enter into a new retail location, we need a budget plan that includes any tax implications, we need to set up purchasing agreements with the retail chain, and we need to involve Agnes's team if there are new accounts needed."

"That's what we did before we acquired the new coaching business," Brad added. "We pulled together an ad hoc team of the managers plus a few analysts to help us with the business case. We have typically done that informally when a question comes up where we need to coordinate. It's become much more intricate with these new businesses."

"I agree, but it's been a slow process to create ad hoc teams every time we need to coordinate. Everything has increased tenfold in complexity. In the old model, I relied heavily on the management team to be the focus for the business decisions that needed to get made," Heather pointed out. "Now there is too much to know about any one business."

"Right now I have tried to assign two budget analysts to foods, two to drinks, and one to services," Brad admitted. "But the workload on them is tremendous, and the core foods business tends to eat up most of everyone's time."

"Let's look at the major changes in this new model." Heather turned the page over to reveal a different organizational chart.

New Finance Department Structure

Chief Financial Officer

Finance Manager, Foods Unit
Finance Manager, Drinks Unit
Finance Manager, Services
Finance Manager, Online

Finance Analyst
Finance Analyst
Finance Analyst
Finance Analyst
Finance Analyst
Finance Analyst
Finance Analyst
Finance Analyst
Finance Analyst

"I want us to become more business centric and product centric," Heather said. "We will organize the new department by the different product units that we each will work with. All financial reporting, advice, and knowledge will be contained within each finance unit, reporting to me but working closely with the different product leaders. The foods unit general manager will have a finance manager who works with her on everything from planning to tax to accounts to procurement. Same thing for drinks and services. Our nutrition service unit is just one part of services where we think we can grow. I want us to invest our time in helping managers of growth businesses like drinks and services."

"From what we've heard from the general managers when we interviewed them," Brad said, "they are going to appreciate having a single team to handle all of their finance needs. They had been complaining about not knowing who to contact in each finance group; every time they got a report it was inconsistent, because every analyst had a preferred format and methodology for reporting."

"And they complained that the analysts did not understand the business well enough," Heather added. "This way we can focus the whole team's attention on the line of business and coordinate our finance services. And to emphasize how important it is to focus on the needs of the line of business, I want to institute a bonus plan for helping each product area grow as well as customer satisfaction reports from surveys of the business leaders. I also want more generalists, not finance specialists. To provide an integrated finance picture of the business means we need to present one face as a team, not isolated pockets of finance knowledge disconnected from one another."

"I think that makes sense," Brad said cautiously. "But I think it will be a challenge. We all have our specialty areas based on educational background and on comfort level with the established procedures that we are used to."

"Of course," Heather said sympathetically. "We are going to need a training plan. We don't really do much training but I am willing to invest in that. If we have any chance of growing these businesses, we are going to need everyone to come together as a team, learn from one another, and dive in. Look at the current organizational chart. Almost everyone is a specialized 'analyst' of some form, doing one narrow job without a holistic view of the organization. Whether it's planning, tax, procurement, or accounting, everyone must be well-versed in every area. We need flexible and educated utility players, not specialists. If they can't learn or grow or adapt, then maybe this is not the finance team for them." Heather was starting to sound a lot less sympathetic.

"Let's go back to our discussion of the finance manager role for the online business, because that job will still be a direct report to you, but without a team to manage," Brad said.

"Yes. We also heard from the stakeholder interviews of the general managers that we should mirror the rest of the structure in the company. The online business crosses each of the product areas. It's a key growth area for us as a company. While it has always been part of our strategy, we think we can grow 25 percent faster in the online business over the next 2 years. I want someone on my team to focus their attention on that business area, but there must be very close coordination to the other business units. I want one financial analyst from each line of business to also be assigned a dotted line to the online division."

"I guess the elephant in the room has always been the number of boxes on this chart," Brad said quietly. "There are still 4 managers, but only 9 analysts, not 12. We are going to lose three team members."

"I don't have to tell you about the budget for the year," Heather reminded Brad. "Profits are down and we have invested heavily in our expansion. We must tighten our belts for a while. I also have news for you as we consider this transition plan. Natasha has decided to leave the company."

"What? That's a huge blow. She is one of the smartest people I know, an excellent leader, and a sharp business professional. We are going to miss her," Brad said.

"I couldn't agree more," Heather said. "She didn't even know about this transition yet, but she was recruited for a perfect role. She agonized over the decision but finally let me know yesterday."

"So that means a manager opportunity would open up?" Brad asked.

"It certainly could," Heather agreed. "I haven't decided on the placement of the leadership team yet. That brings up another topic I wanted to discuss with you. Brad, I would like for you to consider the manager role for the services unit. It's a growing area of the business where we need your expertise. I also think it would challenge you and grow you as a leader. I've been thinking about tapping Agnes to take on the foods unit and Luke to take on the online unit."

Brad thought for a moment. "Thank you, Heather. I am a little surprised because I assumed I would ask for the foods unit manager role. That's been my entire career here. Can I think about it?"

"Yes, of course," Heather assured him.

"How do you think Agnes and Luke will feel?" Brad asked.

"Agnes knows the foods unit so well, I think it would be a natural fit for her. I also know how much she loves the world of accounting, so I don't know how comfortable she is going to be with the ambiguous world of business cases and planning assumptions. Luke is a born leader and gravitates toward leading his team. I think he would learn a lot in the online role although I think he would miss having a team reporting to him," Heather concluded.

What Brad thought, but did not say, was that he saw Natasha's departure coming. Rumors had been circulating about organizational changes for weeks, and Brad knew that Natasha wanted to stay in a role that allowed her to use her tax expertise. He had a suspicion that Agnes and Luke were looking outside the company for new roles as well. If anyone should take the services job, it should be Agnes, he thought, who had been talking nonstop about the new business since it was acquired. This is going to be only the beginning of disruption, Brad thought, once people found out that a layoff was coming, along with new teams, possibly a new manager, and new jobs.

Heather continued, “We also need to decide on the staffing of the rest of the organization, including the process we will use. We have to decide the pace of the transition and how we will communicate. I want to let people know what we have decided. It’s fair to let them know that we will be downsizing the organization.”

“We have decided so much,” Brad agreed. “And yet there is so much more to do.”

CHAPTER 9

AGILITY

If organizational life is like a movie, then we could say that Chapters 3 through 7 allowed us to press the Pause button momentarily as we analyzed the STAR model and the interrelationships among the five categories of the design. Chapter 8 pressed the Play button, reminding us to see how design changes needed to be implemented in an ongoing organization. There we learned how to implement change and sustain the design over time. Consider, however, that the implicit model of change we have been using assumes that we can take a stable and established organization design, change it, and then return it back to a stable state. In contemporary organizations, the idea of a stable organization where change is the exception does not resonate.

To extend the metaphor, in this chapter, we will hit the Fast Forward button to consider how organization design today requires speed and agility to make more rapid changes in a fast-paced global environment. We will look

Learning Objectives

In this chapter you will learn

- Why agility has become a major concept in organization design.
- How agility impacts every point of the STAR model.
- How organizations are adapting organization designs to become more agile.
- What the elements of learning and leadership agility are.

Source: By permission Steve Breen and Creators Syndicate, Inc.

at how every point of the STAR model must be reconsidered and reimagined to allow the organization to become more agile. We will also examine how agility is a skill for leaders to develop.

WHY AGILITY IS IMPORTANT TODAY

Consider a simple but illustrative example: In 2007 the inexpensive Flip video camera was introduced, a technology that allowed users to take video images with a compact device and transfer the video to their computers via a USB input. It immediately gained significant market share and was popular with consumers, quickly spawning copycat devices from other producers. In 2009, Cisco Systems acquired the parent organization of Flip video. Just over 2 years later, in 2011, the entire operation was shut down. The same video capability, embedded in iPhones and its competitors, made a separate device unnecessary for most users. In just 4 years the company went from a start-up with a major success to virtually nonexistent (Ertel & Solomon, 2014). Cisco may or may not have been aware of the potential for a short leadership position in mobile video devices, but what is notable is the rapid cycle time of a company from inception to nonexistent.

The example is not unusual. Certainly some of the companies in Alfred Chandler's (1962) famous study of strategy and structure, such as DuPont and General Motors, still exist today. Yet consider that over the past decades, more than half of the Fortune 500 companies on the list have disappeared each decade for a myriad of reasons including bankruptcy and acquisition (Worley, Williams, & Lawler, 2014). Reeves and Deimler (2011) note that market leaders used to be able to count on retaining their leadership position, but that in 2008, about one in seven former leaders fell out of the top three for their industry. Market leaders were once strong profitability leaders, rewarded financially for their dominant position. Now that is true in just 7 percent of cases (Reeves & Deimler, 2011). Success and industry position can be tumultuous and provide no guarantee of future success.

Increasing competition and rapid environmental change provide some explanation for these trends. In the 1990s, Harvard business professor Clayton Christensen introduced the theory of disruptive innovation. The idea is that new market entrants usually bring to market a product that is "typically cheaper, simpler, smaller, and, frequently, more convenient to use" (Christensen, 1997, p. xviii). Examples of such disruptive technologies include online retailing, electronic free greeting cards, computer-based distance education, and online stock trading. Higher-end incumbents (full service stock brokerage firms, for example), focusing on a different (often more profitable) market, respond slowly to the upstart competitor while the innovator continues to add enough capabilities to increasingly threaten them (Christensen, Raynor, & McDonald, 2015). Incumbent leaders tend to disregard the smaller upstarts, maintaining confidence in their dominant position and investing in sustaining innovation (gradual product improvements). This is a realistic response when the change occurs slowly, even unnoticeably for quite some time in some industries (Wessel & Christensen, 2012). Eventually the competitor disrupts the incumbent when customers leave, often in a way that renders the original company obsolete (consider digital music and streaming versus music stores, and digital photography versus prints).

In some cases, however, the upstart competitors disrupt quickly from the beginning without a carefully planned evolution in capabilities. Called "big bang disrupters" (Downes & Nunes, 2013), these companies change industries immediately. "We're accustomed to seeing mature products wiped out by new technologies and to ever-shorter product lifecycles. But now entire product lines—whole markets—are being created or destroyed overnight. Disrupters can come out of nowhere and instantly be everywhere" (p. 46). Consumers ask, "Why pay for a product or service when a newly launched smartphone app provides it for free?" which explains the disruption of standalone GPS devices by the Google Maps app (and others like it) available at no charge for most smartphones (Wessel & Christensen, 2012).

Agility becomes a matter of survival in these cases where an organization is required to quickly respond to an unforeseen threat or risk losing the entire business. Among other changes in the business environment making agility a necessity are the rise of new organizational models, the gig economy, and the blurring of industry boundaries.

New Organizational Models. Companies such as Airbnb and Uber provide platforms to connect buyers and sellers, producers, and consumers. These platform businesses gain value from the size of the network that participates in the business, in contrast to pipeline businesses that control the product development process from research and development through supply chain and delivery (Van Alstyne, Parker, & Choudary, 2016). In these businesses, the platform and community itself have a value. Consider that Airbnb announced in 2016 that it would expand through its Trips offering, connecting travelers with local experts or guides that could provide them with new experiences during their vacation, such as cooking classes, truffle hunting in Italy, or a cycling tour through France (Rosenbloom, 2016).

Gig Economy. The majority of large companies have long pursued offshoring or outsourcing arrangements to increase flexibility, and even more use temporary help on a regular basis. Today, dozens of companies connect freelance workers through "human cloud" platforms with those who are willing to pay for help for everything from running errands to complex software coding (TaskRabbit and TopCoder, respectively; Káganer, Carmel, Hirscheim, & Olsen, 2013).

Blurring of Industries. Innovations in technology are blurring industry boundaries as well. Cameras, telephones, and computers were once three separate industries. Now the pervasiveness of mobile video communication (Skype, WhatsApp, FaceTime, and many more) calls into question such neat boundaries and divisions between industries. Amazon, once a start-up Internet bookseller, is estimated to become the world's largest technology company by 2025.

CONTINUOUS DESIGN AND RECONFIGURABLE ORGANIZATIONS

All of these examples demonstrate Galbraith's (1997) observation that "when advantages do not last long, neither do the organizations that execute them. In the past, management crafted a winning business formula and erected barriers to entry to sustain this advantage" (p. 88), creating an organization design to match. Eventually those designs (both product and organization) become copied by competitors and the advantage dissipates. Worse, when an organization aligns itself so strongly around its design and emphasizes organizational stability in the face of a rapidly changing environment, it can inhibit adaptability to future strategic and design changes.

What is required is the capability for continuous design and creating reconfigurable organizations that change frequently to respond to environmental conditions. "We need a new, aligned organizational design in which organizational structures and processes are easily reconfigured and realigned with a constantly changing strategy" (Galbraith, 1997, p. 88). To respond effectively to the rapid changes in the competitive environment, leaders must learn how to make frequent design adaptations. Stanford (2015) writes that today, leaders must

> begin with the view that the design is dynamic, has a life cycle and will change as the context demands, and there will be fewer accusations of design failure and more support from stakeholders. . . . Good designs are not a one-shot effort; they allow for meeting continuous change while simultaneously keeping the business operations running successfully. (pp. 256–257)

This view echoes a point we made in Chapter 1, that organization design is a process, not an event. Many leaders may think that they are always doing design work through annual strategic plans and budget allocations, frequent restructuring, quarterly business reviews, and annual employee performance evaluations and salary reviews. Such practices can, in fact, inhibit agility and rapid adaptation by delaying decisions until the next regular cycle. As we will see, however, agility is not only a matter of speed, but it is also about changing the content of these practices.

The point is that once familiar notions, strategies, industries, business models, and employment relationships are quickly changing. If organization design is one way of achieving a competitive advantage, and today's competitive advantages are being disrupted, then bedrock concepts of organization design may need to adapt to keep pace with the changing environment. "Agile organizations have designs that can adapt quickly in response to internal and external pressures for change or shifts in strategic intent. Adaptable designs have structures, processes, people, and rewards" that can flex to changes in strategy (Worley & Lawler, 2010, p. 195). This means that organizations of the future may look very different from the ones we have become accustomed to, as we will explore.

WHAT AGILITY MEANS

Agility "captures an organization's ability to develop and quickly apply flexible, nimble and dynamic capabilities" (Holbeche, 2015, p. 11). It is also the "capability to make timely, effective, and sustained organization changes" (Worley et al., 2014, p. 26). Importantly, agility is also an organization design capability "that can sense the need for change from both internal and external sources, carry out those changes routinely, and sustain above-average performance" (Worley & Lawler,

2010, p. 194). These definitions stress three key characteristics of agility (Horney, Pasmore, & O'Shea, 2010):

- **Fast**: Agile organizations operate with speed, making rapid decisions and moving quickly.
- **Flexible**: Agile organizations pivot as needed to take advantage of opportunities as they sense them.
- **Focused**: Being fast and flexible is a recipe for whiplash and chaos unless the organization is also focused. Agile organizations do not pursue every idea, they "do a better job of selecting the ones that will deliver on environmental demands" (Worley et al., 2014, pp. 26–27).

These characteristics are enabled by two additional capabilities in agile organizations: a "change-friendly" identity and an ability to sense when change is needed. What many agile organizations have in common is the ability to recognize the need to change based on knowledge of the external environment. They maintain an identity less rooted in specific products and more in lasting values and beliefs. They also hold to a curiosity about the external environment and are regularly seeking new knowledge.

"Change-Friendly" Identity

Agile companies have an ability to invent and reinvent themselves in dynamic ways. Netflix, once the innovator of rental DVDs by mail, evolved to provide streaming services when the technical capabilities and consumer preferences moved in that direction. Its next evolution was to produce its own content. Remaining stuck to the purpose of being a "DVD rental business" would have inhibited Netflix from this very successful path.

Yet despite the reinvention that gets played out in pursuing different activities, agile organizations also maintain an enduring identity that paradoxically allows for such change. Frequent change is accepted in organizations that prepare members for it. As Lawler and Worley (2006a) describe in their analysis of organizations that are "built to change,"

> [A]n organization that prides itself on legendary customer service is in a good position to identify strategic adjustments that enhance its service. . . . When organization members know that announced or intended changes honor the firm's identity, they find it easier to support and commit to new structures and new processes or to building new capabilities. (p. 63)

They point out that an organization's culture and history contribute to its "change-friendly" identity which endures even when the tactics of the strategy change. In some organizations, the leadership team is uncertain whether the company is product or customer driven or whether it values long-term innovation or short-term revenue. As a result, frequent change feels unfocused to employees and customers alike. But when the organization's identity is clear and provides an underlying logic to change, such changes seem consistent and are likely to result in less confusion and resistance.

Sensing Change

One critical capability for agility is to sense that the need for change is coming. "In this environment, competitive advantage comes from reading and responding to signals faster than your rivals do, adapting quickly to change, or capitalizing on technological leadership to influence how demand and competition evolve" (Reeves, Love, & Tillmanns, 2012, p. 76). Doz and Kosonen (2008) note that this involves "early and keen awareness of incipient trends and converging forces with real-time sense-making in strategic situations as they develop and evolve" (p. 96). Agile organizations are carefully attuned to the marketplace, monitoring changes that other organizations miss, ignore, or misinterpret.

Doz and Kosonen's (2008) analysis of Nokia's rise and fall points out that in the late 1980s and early 1990s, Nokia foresaw the rise of mobile telephony. The company sensed a number of trends coming together, including the rise of digital networks and potential mass market interest in a well-designed user interface for a mobile phone (as witnessed in Apple's Mac computers). "Given the history of the company and their own personal experiences, Nokia's executives could perceive and frame, largely in real time, the nature and magnitude of the huge opportunity its competitors failed to see until much later" (Doz & Kosonen, 2008, p. 101). This allowed Nokia to invest in the growth area and organize resources to exploit the potential new market opportunity. However, the same sensing capability, when lost, also explains Nokia's decline. Later in the 1990s, Nokia maintained a focus on third-generation telephony (3G) for too long. The authors explain, "A winning strategy (as celebrated by Nokia when it wrestled worldwide industry market leadership from Motorola in 1998) turns into principles and beliefs, which are then treated as truth and are no longer challenged" (p. 109). Losing attention to the external environment (or failing to question prevailing interpretations) means failing to see the truth until it is too late to act.

Worley, Williams, and Lawler (2014) call this ability of agile organizations to accurately interpret the change in their environments a "perceiving routine." Agile organizations are able to sense the environment, communicate information to decision makers, and interpret environmental signals (p. 67). In typical organizations, it may be the job of the CEO, senior management team, competitive intelligence department, or marketing function to watch industry trends and read the latest predictions. By seeing themselves as the source of external knowledge and interpretation, they miss trends and important sources of data located inside their own organizations. By contrast, agile organizations "maximize the 'surface area' of the firm. As many employees as possible are near to or have direct contact with regulators, suppliers, the local community, watchdog groups and, most important, customers" (Worley & Lawler, 2010, p. 196). Employees who observe trends about customer preferences or complaints, who see unique and interesting uses of products, or who receive requests from customers for product enhancements, can pass along this information internally. This can be a source of valuable knowledge, but only if the organization develops rapid lines of communication that allow the information to be accurately passed along to the right place.

Once the need for change is felt, the organization must be able to adopt an agile organization design, requiring change in every aspect of the STAR model. In the next sections we will explore the principles of agility that alter each point.

AGILE STRATEGY

Agile organizations that maintain an identity that is conducive to change and who engage in regular sensing of the environment also tend to strategize differently. In agile organizations, strategy takes on a different meaning. Rather than an annual strategic plan formalized in a binder that articulates the pursuit of a long-lasting success, agile organizations see the planning process as organic. They have a process for monitoring and evaluating the strategy on a regular basis and communicating strategic information throughout the organization. Most importantly, they are committed to a mindset that sees strategic advantage as temporary.

In Chapter 2, we defined organizational capabilities as the unique and differentiated skills and abilities that give an organization a competitive advantage. In agile organizations, strategy is driven by regularly adapting these to the new needs of the environment through dynamic capabilities. "A dynamic capability is the firm's potential to systematically solve problems, formed by its propensity to sense opportunities and threats, to make timely and market-oriented decisions, and to change its resource base" (Barreto, 2010, p. 271). Agile organizations recognize the need to add new capabilities, combine some, or jettison others. Developing dynamic capabilities in marketing, innovation, product development, supply chain management, and other organizational routines allows rapid environmental adaptation.

Zara and Transient Advantages

> Agile Principle 1: Agile organizations exploit transient advantages.

Recall that in Chapter 3 we reviewed the seminal work of Michael Porter and the example of Southwest Airlines. You will recall that Porter (1996) used Southwest to illustrate the idea that a strategy consists of a number of interlocking activities, all supporting the same strategy of low cost, differentiation, or focus. When those activities support and reinforce one another, a strategy is difficult to copy, and it results in what Porter defined as a strategy—a sustainable competitive advantage.

Yet as we have seen, based on the rapid changes in business models, globalization, and technology, the length of a "sustainable" advantage is questionable. McGrath (2013b) argues that "sustainable competitive advantage is now the exception, not the rule. Transient advantage is the new normal" (p. 64). If strategy is no longer defined as a sustainable competitive advantage but instead as a series of temporary advantages that are quickly exploited, then another model of strategy might be appropriate. Fashion company Zara provides one such example.

Zara is an apparel company based in Spain and one of a number of companies that are now referred to as being in the business of "fast fashion," including H&M, Uniqlo, and Forever21. With revenues of more than €15 billion, Zara is the dominant brand within a €23 billion conglomerate known as Inditex. While Zara has been expanding, opening stores in new markets and witnessing rising profits, competitors have suffered (Egan, 2015). One major Zara competitor, Gap, Inc., announced in 2015 that it would close 675 retail stores over the next several years (Tabuchi & Stout, 2015).

Zara has more than 2,000 stores worldwide in dozens of countries, each receiving shipments twice a week. Zara owns its own factories, allowing it to be responsive to customer demands. Certainly Zara's vertically integrated supply chain provides a major strategic advantage and has been the focus of a number of articles (for example, see Ferdows, Lewis, & Machuca, 2004). But we can also view Zara through the lens of agility to understand how Zara's strategy is based on rapid change and adaptability as its advantage.

There are several ways that Zara acts with much more agility than its competitors. Zara produces 11,000 items each year compared with the 2,000 to 4,000 that competitors are able to produce. A design can be created from a sketch to a physical sample in a matter of hours, which takes weeks for competitors. New orders can be produced and stocked in stores within 4 to 5 weeks, or in as little as 2 weeks for common items, a process that might take 6 to 9 months for Zara's competitors. What is more remarkable is that up to 85 percent of Zara's stocking decisions are made within the current season, reacting immediately to customer trends. By comparison, competitors must make design and purchasing decisions up to a year in advance (Ghemawat & Nueno, 2006). Limited supplies of each item and merciless removal of items that are not selling well means that the stores are always stocked with the latest fashions. Items that sell well can be restocked, and when items do not sell, store managers ask customers for input, returning the items to the factory with feedback about what customers would prefer. Returned items can even be redyed or altered and returned to store shelves.

Zara provides a more appropriate example of strategy today because the company is able to exploit transient advantages, reacting to the latest fashion trends immediately. They are not stuck with risky fashion design decisions for a long period of time, as their competitors are, perhaps missing the window to profit from a fast-moving trend. They can monitor competitive moves and fads on social media, and make quick decisions about how fads affect shifting customer preferences. Systems and processes are designed for agility and to maximize communication from the store level and local customer input to designers at headquarters. For Zara, change is the advantage.

McGrath (2013b) dissects the five waves of a transient advantage, or a common life cycle that occurs for any product or service.

1. First, the product or service goes through a *launch* process to initiate the idea or innovation. The company dedicates resources to bringing the idea to life, trying different versions or formulations until the idea is ready to be brought to customers.

2. The second phase, *ramp-up*, describes the process of bringing the innovation to scale and making it available widely beyond initial trials or pilots.

3. In the third phase, the organization enters an *exploitation* phase to gain market share and profitability as the innovation succeeds. The goal is to assume a leadership position and earn the financial rewards for having gained an advantage over competitors. The hope for most companies is that this phase lasts for as long as possible so the advantage can be as financially rewarding as possible.

4. Eventually the advantage erodes when competitors catch up or customers move on. This prompts a necessary fourth phase of *reconfiguration*, perhaps prompting a new business model.

5. Finally, the fifth phase of *disengagement* results in the difficult decision to discontinue, exit, and dispose of the assets. Here is where resources dedicated to the advantage are reassigned, ideally to a next innovation or idea.

The point is that today's advantages, fleeting and transient, move through this process with a faster cycle time. As the exploitation phase shortens, leaders must recognize when it is time to make the difficult choices to reconfigure before the financial results decline to an unhealthy point. "To stay ahead, they need to constantly start new strategic initiatives, building and exploiting many transient competitive advantages at once" (McGrath, 2013b, p. 64). Thus, at any point in time, agile companies have many transient advantages throughout this pipeline, launching some new ideas while others are discontinued.

Typical companies pay too much attention to the exploitation phase, hanging on to a declining product for too long. As Worley et al. (2014) explain, "[T]he cruel joke is that in attempting to preserve their source of advantage, organizations can overcommit to institutionalization, making them more inert and vulnerable to environmental shifts" (p. 29). Agile organizations acknowledge the important decisions that must be made in each phase of the life cycle of a competitive advantage. They know that recognizing the signs of when to engage in reconfiguration and disengagement is an important competency to remaining agile. According to one study, only 22 percent of leaders indicate that their organizations exit declining businesses effectively. The study's authors concluded that "top executives devote a disproportionate amount of time and attention to businesses with limited upside and send in talented managers who often burn themselves out trying to save businesses that should have been shut down or sold years earlier" (Sull, Homkes, & Sull, 2015, p. 62).

Rapid Prototyping and Experimentation

> Agile Principle 2: Agile organizations engage in rapid prototyping and embrace a "fail fast" mentality.

Zara's small batches of new designs also provide an example of a second characteristic of strategy in agile organizations—prototyping and experimentation. By producing some designs to see if they will be popular with customers and then restocking fast selling products, Zara can test the waters with customers without a large and risky financial consequence. Similarly, agile organizations are not afraid to introduce a trial product to see what might happen. Coughlan and Prokopoff (2004) of the design firm IDEO write that rapid prototyping can give a rough approximation of a product or service so that a potential customer can experience it and offer helpful feedback. Multiple prototypes offer a lower-risk method for pursuing options and learning what aspects of the prototype are successful and which are not.

As McGrath (2013a) describes, these organizations

> share an options-oriented pattern to exploring new opportunities. The essence of this approach is that they make small initial investments to explore opportunities, following up later with more substantial investments as the opportunity warrants. They are also willing to abandon a particular initiative if it doesn't appear to be developing effectively. (p. 47)

Companies that are the "growth outliers" for their industries are willing to place small investments in new markets, technologies, or acquisitions. They diversify their initial bets and then follow up on those that turn out to be promising (McGrath, 2012). Yet in many organizations, an unsuccessful product introduction often results in people losing their jobs and being marked with the shame of failure. Such responses make others risk averse which can squelch innovation.

Agile organizations develop cultures that support appropriate (but not reckless) risk taking. This can be achieved by encouraging "intelligent failures" and an "experimental orientation" (McGrath, 2013a, p. 102). Agile organizations have a "testing routine" that maintains a disciplined approach to project management, budgeting, and ongoing operational reviews to set goals for the test (for example, a small-scale pilot introduction of a new product line in one geography) and evaluate the results. Everyone involved in the experiment knows that "failure is accepted as a legitimate test outcome and a vehicle for learning" (Worley et al., 2014, p. 87). When failure occurs, learning can be used to inform future trials, improving the likelihood of success next time.

Research and development-oriented companies such as pharmaceuticals know that trials, tests, and failure are a part of their business, as do many organizations. But for agile organizations, the ability to experiment rapidly and frequently does not only refer to products and services but also concerns the organization's business models and processes. IKEA, for example, having realized that local real estate prices went up every time they opened a store, began investing in local real estate as well, now earning more profit in some geographies from real estate than the retail store (Reeves & Deimler, 2011).

AGILE STRUCTURE

Agile Principle 3: Agile organizations rethink traditional organizational structures.

Typical organizational structures—hierarchies—are, in some respects, the very antithesis of agility. They tend to exist as stabilizing opportunities, centralizing power and authority, and specifying the scope of responsibilities of departments, teams, and individuals. We observed some of the dangers of too much structure in Chapter 5, noting that too much hierarchy inhibits information sharing and slows down decision making. Kotter (2014) puts it bluntly: "Hierarchies with great management processes and good leaders on top are not built for leaping into a creative future. . . . Management-driven hierarchies are built to minimize risk and keep people in their boxes and silos" (p. 15). Indeed, in today's organizations, "action on the front lines is moving so fast that there simply isn't time to get enough rich information back and forth to senior-level decision makers before the opportunity vanishes" (McGrath, 2013a, p. 148). Our solution to the challenge of vertical structure in Chapter 5 was to create linking opportunities that included networks, shared goals, teams, and more to allow collaboration to occur across the hierarchy.

In agile organizations such dualities between structure and lateral capability are blurred. At the extreme, it might be said that the two points become one. Agile organizations create fluid structures, teams, and decision rights practices that allow for flexibility in strategy execution. Leading adaptive businesses use their organization designs to their advantage and learn how to become "shape shifters" (McGrath, 2013a, p. 27), reconfiguring and morphing themselves as the opportunities require. They avoid a painful and expensive annual restructuring because their structures exist "with permeable boundaries between functions, units and departments that allow for cooperation patterns and strategic collaboration to get established" (Holbeche, 2015, p. 62). Whereas in the past the structure point of the star may have been the foreground, and lateral capability helped to enable the structure, in agile organizations the structure seems to fade into the background, and opportunities for collaboration across the organization become foregrounded.

Two versions of a more agile structure are Kotter's "dual operating system" model and holacracy.

Structure and the "Dual Operating System"

Kotter (2012, 2014) argues that most start-up organizations act like networks. Small, agile, interconnected teams are often driven by the vision of a single entrepreneur. With a smaller organization, a flat hierarchy, and everyone-knows-everyone network, decision making can be nimble. As we saw in Chapter 8 when examining organizational culture, eventually as many organizations evolve, so do the rules and bureaucracies that control the work. The hierarchy that helps to organize and control resources begins to act in opposition to agility by creating reliable and efficient processes and minimizing risk taking. The old agile network dissipates in favor of formalized reporting relationships and hierarchical communication. Kotter (2012) is clear to remind us that hierarchy has its place, and that we have learned how to master hierarchical organizations and their predictable operations such as budgeting, staffing, and monitoring results and efficiency.

Agile organizations have learned how to add a second "operating system," a network model, to enhance the hierarchical organization. In this model, the hierarchy maintains its familiar objectives, "making incremental changes to further improve efficiency, and handling the small initiatives that help a company deal with predictable adjustments such as routine IT upgrades" (Kotter, 2012, p. 50). Alongside the hierarchy is a strategy network, operating in a dynamic way where initiatives form and dissolve as required. It is made up of members throughout the organization without hierarchy or siloes to inhibit communication. Kotter (2014, pp. 23–25) writes that this new operating system has five core principles:

1. **Many people driving important change, and from everywhere, not just the usual few appointees**: Kotter notes that 5 percent to 10 percent of the organization will participate in this "Accelerator network" made up of all levels in the organization.

2. **A "get-to" mindset, not a "have-to" one**: A "volunteer army" forms the network, and while members must have the sponsorship of senior management, they are not a separate group hired specifically and paid solely for their network participation.
3. **Action that is head and heart driven, not just head driven**: The purpose of the network must be compelling and appeal to the emotional interest of participants who want to make a difference.
4. **Much more leadership, not just more management**: "The game is about vision, opportunity, agility, inspired action, passion, innovation, and celebration—not just project management, budget reviews, reporting relationships, compensation, and accountability to a plan" (Kotter, 2014, p. 25).
5. **An inseparable partnership between the hierarchy and the network, not just an enhanced network**: The two systems work together. Every member of the network has a job in the hierarchy, but the network does not function as a layer or department in the hierarchy.

When the network feels a "sense of urgency around a Big opportunity" (p. 27), members of the network work together to share information and voluntarily address it. If someone in the network learns that customers are complaining about a bureaucratic runaround, he or she will put out a call for volunteers to understand the complaint and its causes and put a solution in place, using contacts and practices already well established in the hierarchy (such as budgeting or IT systems). The volunteer army, eager, agile, and not committed to the status quo or sacred cows, also knows how to get work done through the established channels.

Holacracy

By contrast to Kotter's dual operating systems, a second model advocates getting rid of the hierarchy altogether. The Internet retailer Zappos.com made headlines in recent years when CEO Tony Hsieh announced that the company was "banning the boss." A *New York Times* article on the company described it this way: "At Zappos, this means traditional corporate hierarchy is gone. Managers no longer exist. The company's 1,500 employees define their own jobs. Anyone can set the agenda for a meeting" (Gelles, 2015, p. BU1). Companies such as W. L. Gore and Associates and Morning Star are also known for having implemented a holacracy organizational model.

Holacracy relies on process rather than hierarchical power for a group to make decisions and organize its work (Robertson, 2015). Traditional hierarchies with a single leader rely on that leader to empower others, granting the ability of individuals to make decisions, usually within a well-prescribed set of boundaries. As an alternative design, holacracy grants individuals that freedom at the outset. Governance processes substitute shared decision making for the authority formerly granted to the highest-level leader or executive team. Instead of generic and outdated job descriptions used in many organizations, in a holacracy, each person and role has a purpose, a set of tasks or activities for which they are held accountable, and decision authority. If the job description in a holacracy seems to conflict with the responsibilities of another person, either person could raise it to a governance discussion to clarify the roles. In this way, jobs are not fixed at all but continually evolving as the members experience them, as members grow their capabilities or change their interests, and as the organization's needs change. Accountability in a holacracy is not fixed to the hierarchy, so that people are accountable to their managers, but instead every employee is accountable to the expectations of many different colleagues. The holacracy governance process helps to clarify what those expectations are for every person.

Robertson (2015) explains that holacracy contains four practices:

- A constitution, which sets out the "rules of the game" and redistributes authority (an example is available at holacracy.org/constitution)
- A new way to structure an organization and define people's roles and spheres of authority within it
- A unique decision-making process for updating those roles and authorities
- A meeting process for keeping teams in sync and getting work done together (p. 12)

Instead of a traditional pyramid hierarchy, holacracies consist of circles of responsibility. There may be a marketing circle comprising people who work in advertising, social media, and corporate events, and any of those might be characterized as subcircles if there are multiple people working on those areas. Circles are connected to one another through liaison roles called lead links, integrating the work of the marketing circle with that of the sales circle or product development circle, for example. Rep links connect subcircles to the larger circle. Each of the link roles has the responsibility of maintaining the purpose of the circle and raising tensions between that circle's work and the work of others. Governance meetings provide the forum to discuss and resolve the tensions.

Robertson (2015) likens the governance practices of holacracy to the rules of a sport. Most sports proceed without discussion of the rules, known to all participants, until the rules are broken. When that happens, coaches, referees, and players all call attention to the broken rule and disciplinary actions are taken—penalty minutes, yards, points. Like learning the rules of a new sport, learning the practices of holacracy seem foreign at first but eventually become natural after enough practice. Van Vugt (2017) points out that the self-organizing teams in a holacracy have their roots in evolutionary psychology and the tribal behavior of ancestral human societies.

Video game company Valve provides another example of a company that has moved successfully to holacracy. In a detailed account of how Valve employees work in a non-hierarchical organizational model, Puranam and Håkonsson (2015) write,

> There are no job titles, no job descriptions, and no employees called "bosses" in Valve. Instead, employees are encouraged to work on "what interests them and what brings value to Valve." Employees are free to choose how to use their time and talents. Every employee can initiate projects and choose which projects to work on. . . . Projects perceived as

risky may not be able to attract talent and thus may not be adequately staffed. . . . Employees are empowered to the extent that they can "ship" their own projects (provided two or more other employees agree). . . . It is up to the individual employees to talk to others in the company to find out what is happening. To coordinate with each other, employees simply move their wheeled workstations to be physically proximate to team members. (pp. 2–3)

Some have observed that these nonhierarchical models work more effectively in smaller organizations that already have a propensity to a network form of organizing (Birkinshaw, 2015). Others point out that some organizational activities (such as software development work at Valve) are more conducive to self-managed designs (Von Krogh & Geilinger, 2015). Even in the global banking company ING, however, a move to a less hierarchical organization that uses tribes, squads, and chapters instead of traditional hierarchy to organize work has been successful in introducing more agility (Barton, Carey, & Charan, 2018; see https://www.mckinsey.com/industries/financial-services/our-insights/ings-agile-transformation).

It is a myth about holacracy that it has no organizational structure or hierarchy, but the structure of a holacratic organization simply looks different from a traditional pyramid (Bernstein, Bunch, Canner, & Lee, 2016). There remain defined job roles (although they change and evolve), teams that have responsibilities and that organize the work, and results to be accomplished and expected performance measures. The process is open and often more democratic than in a traditional management hierarchy, and the team has the ability to define, redefine, assign, and reassign work as it sees fit. Holacracy assumes that the team, closer to the work, will know best how to organize itself. The structure of the team's processes substitutes for the more familiar functional or geographic structures that we reviewed in Chapter 4.

Whether holacracy is a passing fad or a lasting trend remains to be seen. GitHub, a California-based software company founded in 2007, operated without a traditional hierarchy. It allowed employees to adopt their own job titles, initiate and join projects as they saw fit, and encouraged self-management on the part of individuals and teams. By 2014, with the introduction of a new CEO, the company introduced more processes and procedures to coordinate employees. A hierarchy with formal titles was instituted and projects began to be assigned through a formal process. Studies of "boss-less" organizations and their evolution continue to contribute to our knowledge about whether (or under what circumstances) holacratic forms are successful (Burton et al., 2017).

Critics of holacracy point out that it requires a lot of communication and coordination. Since employees can participate on multiple circles and each circle holds a circle meeting, governance meetings, and other tactical meetings, employees complain that they spend an excessive amount of time in meetings (Gelles, 2015). Some doubt whether the holacracy approach is conducive to organizational strategies that require an overarching global perspective when small local teams may not see the bigger picture (Bernstein et al., 2016). Finally, holacracy offers challenges to talent practices such as hiring and compensation; when roles evolve frequently it can be difficult to manage skill requirements, assignments to new teams, and rewards for accomplishments.

AGILE PROCESSES AND LATERAL CAPABILITY

As we have seen, agile organizations seek to dissolve the strong divisions between hierarchical divisions and foster connections across groups. These practices play out in several ways that agile organizations seek to enhance lateral capability: through agile teams, global collaborative designs, and external networks and partnerships.

Agile Teams

> Agile Principle 4: Agile organizations form and re-form teams as needed to capitalize on opportunities quickly.

McGrath (2012) observes that in many organizations, strategic opportunities are wedged into the existing structure, sometimes inappropriately. Resources (budgets and people) are allocated to different business departments that have a parochial interest in using resources for their own benefit rather than the overarching benefit of the strategy. Rather than push strategic opportunities on an existing (perhaps unwilling) structure, agile organizations "configure the organization to the opportunity, not the other way around" (p. 88). Sometimes this means reconfiguring the organization (rather than pursuing a large restructuring) by combining or splitting organizational units. Another way agile organizations do this is through agile teams, or "disposable" organizational forms that allow members to quickly come together, address a problem or opportunity, and then disband when the work is done (McGrath, 2013a).

Visa's marketing organization moved from a functional structure to a project-based team approach, collaborating with product development and operations for new marketing programs as they arise. The team might include a variety of skills such as social media and online marketing, digital content, marketing operations, and marketing data analytics, allowing team members to quickly move on to other relevant projects with speed (Kane, Palmer, Phillips, Kiron, & Buckley, 2016).

These agile teams are unlike the stereotypical model of a sports or military team, executing a well-practiced set of plays (P. Meyer, 2015). Instead, agile teams should be thought of more like ad hoc, improvisational comedy troupes or jazz bands (Barrett, 2012). Less structured environments like these often exhibit some of the principles explained earlier, such as experimentation, prototyping, and self-management. In addition, an underlying set of values and shared beliefs about the nature of the team seems to characterize these improv teams. They are "often thrown together at a moment's notice without time for lengthy introductions. There is no chance to find out where everyone went to school, to swap resumes, or to discover each person's particular talent or behavioral style" (P. Meyer, 2015, p. 70). Meyer identifies four characteristics of improv teams that also apply to agile business teams (pp. 71–74):

1. **Identify your givens.** "At each opportunity, check that your team is working with the same understanding of the givens." The team must identify the who, what, and where of the team (who is participating, what the team needs to accomplish, what is the setting or context for the

work). Agile teams are defined by the ability to rapidly start up, assess the situation, and decide who will do what.

2. **Agree to agree**. "Once you have identified your givens, agree to them to speed your response and innovation rate." Teams can accelerate their work when they agree to build on the contributions of team members and accept one another as teammates, forming a powerful foundation of trust at the outset. Like successful improv teams that learn how to say "Yes, and" in order to support teammates, agile teams must also accept that speed comes from building, not tearing down, another teammate.
3. **Practice gift giving**. "Be intentional in the gifts you give as a team member, and recognize and reward those gifts that are particularly valuable to the collaboration." Agile teams respect and benefit from the unique contributions of team members.
4. **Find the game**. "Practice finding the game in your agile team by identifying and amplifying patterns of interaction as you play." Like children inventing a game on the fly, agile teams live "in the dynamic present," interpreting and making sense of new information as it comes in. They are not bound to what happened previously.

Certainly the characteristics of effective teams we discussed in Chapter 5 are applicable to agile teams as well. Yet a rapidly changing environment and the need for a rapid team response makes team formation and high performance even more challenging for today's teams. Team members must become comfortable with rapidly shifting roles, members that leave or join on a regular basis, and a constant flow of new information that alters the scope and progress of the team.

Unfortunately, the agile movement of resources and ability to engage in the rapid trust building required in cross-functional agile teams is not a skill common to most organizations. In a study of almost 8,000 managers, Sull, Homkes, and Sull (2015) found that only 20 percent of leaders reported that their organizations were skilled at assigning people in agile ways to strategic opportunities. While 84 percent of respondents reported that they could trust their manager or direct reports, only 59 percent felt that they could trust colleagues in other departments (only slightly more than those who felt they could trust external partners).

Global Collaboration

Agile Principle 5: Agile organizations employ designs that enable rapid global collaboration.

In Chapter 4, we learned that one design choice about organizational structure is whether to centralize or decentralize certain activities. We learned that decentralization and specialization often require lateral capability to reintegrate what had been divided. When the marketing department is decentralized to manage advertisements at a local level, there will need to be some cross-geography team or matrix organization established to ensure that the company's brand messages remain consistent with a common message. We learned that the lateral capability can take various forms, from the establishment of networks to teams to a matrix.

Kesler and Kates (2016) argue that the foundational principle of centralization or decentralization does not need to be an either-or dichotomy. They point out that most centralization or decentralization decisions confuse the need for coordination with the act of control and decision-making ownership. Leaders often mistakenly centralize decisions for control, when coordination is the real objective. For example, when a centralized group at headquarters controls all activity and decisions in a geography (in a "hub and spoke" model), the organization is burdened with slow decision making. Headquarters may not be aware of local nuances or complexity, and thus makes decisions that are disconnected from the reality in the local area. As a result, "one-size-fits-none" (Kesler & Kates, 2016, p. 71). But if every region makes its own decisions with no overarching coordination, the result is a chaotic jumble of disconnected activity. Ultimately both local responsiveness and speed are needed in addition to umbrella global principles like brand messages, large investments requiring economies of scale, and strategy. Coordination is required to integrate divisions, but centralized control is not necessarily the goal.

Global collaboration can be more agile with a "center-led" model, where a centralized group may oversee consistent principles but with local implementation within a set of boundary conditions. As Kesler and Kates (2016) write,

> The goal should be to gain high degrees of integration without high degrees of control for work that must deliver both scale and speed. Some work and decisions—risk management, brand standards, big investments—should be centralized at the corporate level. Other work and decisions are so local, such as translations and local promotions, that no value can be added from people outside a given market and are best left fully decentralized. (p. 55)

To gain the benefits of both centralization and decentralization, agile organizations develop a center that has a unique set of value-added responsibilities but ensure that those responsibilities do not interrupt local agility and responsiveness. The central group takes the responsibility of developing global strategy and direction. They develop guardrails or boundaries within which the local groups can customize to local requirements. They maintain a close contact with regions, connecting different regions that may not have shared their own best practices and innovations with one another. Local regions are free to experiment and adapt as needed, but within reason, with a responsibility to share their learnings with other regions.

The center-led function has four responsibilities: listen and connect, build infrastructure, align and empower, and model collaborative leadership (Kesler & Kates, 2016, p. 69). The result is a global collaboration that avoids the extremes of centralization and decentralization and finds a middle ground where the benefits of both can be achieved.

Partnerships and Collaborative Networks

Another way that agile organizations enable global collaboration is that they do not see organizational divisions as the boundaries for collaboration. Instead, they consider external partnerships as an integral part of the organization's network of capabilities. A key to the reconfigurable organization, writes Galbraith (1997), is the capability to engage in "external networking with partners to expand capabilities that can be combined to create new advantages" (p. 97). Similarly, Reeves and Deimler

(2011) argue that one capability that fosters rapid adaptation and agility is "the ability to manage complex and interconnected systems of multiple stakeholders" (p. 137). In this respect, an industry can be more appropriately thought of as "competing webs or ecosystems of codependent companies than as a handful of competitors producing similar goods and services" (Reeves & Deimler, 2011, p. 139).

In Chapter 4, we reviewed the network structure, an organization structure with a fluid mix of external organizations that enhance the components of a company's existing value chain. The use of external networks has several advantages for an organization: (1) They can enable the external provider to focus its attention on doing a narrow set of tasks extremely well (such as manufacturing or shipping); (2) the external provider can often serve multiple clients, thus reducing their costs and the cost for any given client; and (3) the provider can often react more quickly to market changes and demands than could a company (Huber, 2016). Nike is a good example of a company that recognized that its expertise lay more in design than manufacturing, and outsourced much of this work to external providers.

The Boeing 787 Dreamliner aircraft provides another example of how a collaborative network can work together to design a major innovation. With more than 50 members of the network in 130 countries, the network was organized by Boeing with each partner designing a major aspect of the plane (displayed in Figure 9.2), from the engines designed by Rolls-Royce in the United Kingdom

Figure 9.2 The Boeing 787 Dreamliner Organizational Network

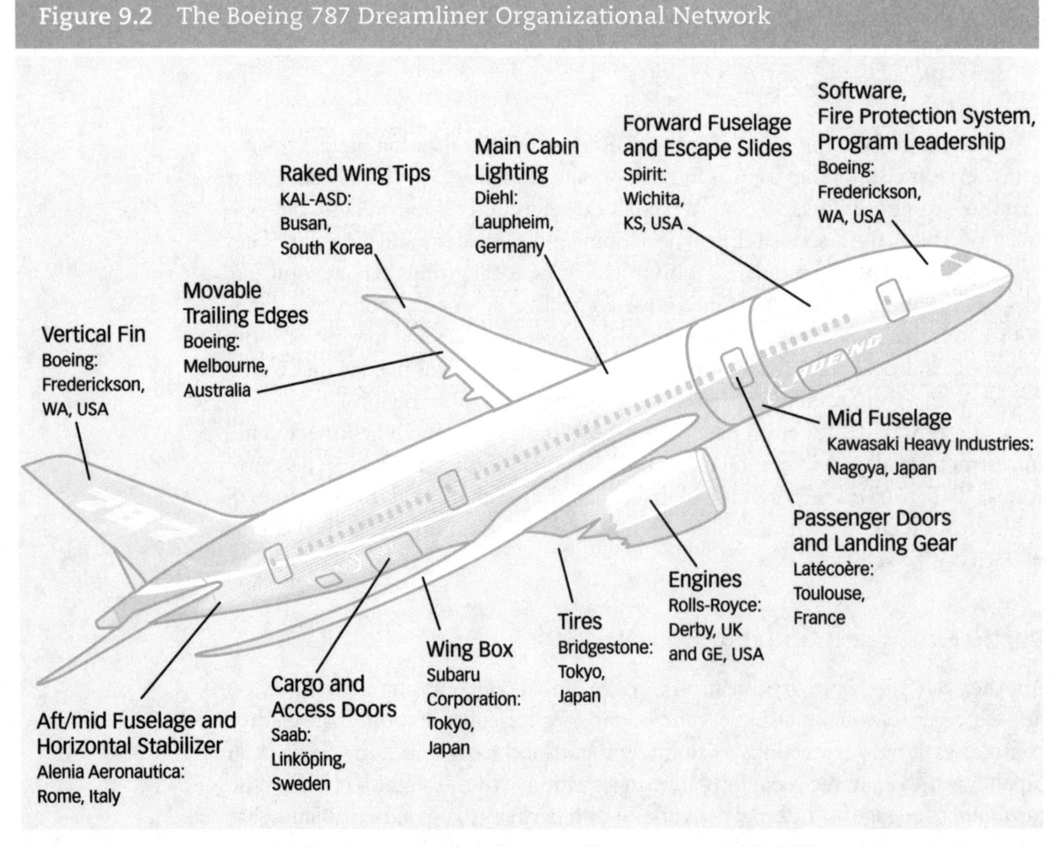

Source: Chambliss, William J., Eglitis, Daina, S. (2015). *Discover sociology, 2nd ed.* Thousand Oaks, CA: SAGE, p. 399.

and GE in the United States to the cargo doors designed by Saab in Sweden. Instead of Boeing designing and manufacturing everything, the network had significant ownership of the designs for their own parts, speeding time to market and reducing manufacturing assembly time. This shifted Boeing's role to an integrator of the work of others (Shuman & Twombly, 2010).

These partnerships have various names or configurations: alliances, outsourcing, offshoring, "hollow," "modular," and "virtual" organizations (Anand & Daft, 2007). Such networks require a choreographer who has the responsibility of bringing the network members together. Whether they are suppliers, distributors, outsourced providers, or joint ventures, the ability to rapidly adapt requires a coordination and communication capability. Companies that lack this capability often make several mistakes with their networks: They fail to consider the partnership in a strategic sense and only seek cost reductions, they keep partners at arm's length and treat them like all other vendors, and they fail to organize in a trusting and collaborative relationship and understand how the partnership requires different skills of their existing staff (Shuman & Twombly, 2010).

AGILE PEOPLE

As we have seen, more and more companies are sourcing talent through the *gig economy*, a term to describe contingent workers often linked to the company through a technology platform that enables the connection (such as Uber and Lyft). These and similar agile organizations "travel light" with the ability to "acquire and discard talent as needed" (Worley et al., 2014, p. 100). They may have irregular talent needs and require workers for only a short period of time. Some estimate that as much as 20 percent to 30 percent of the U.S. workforce is engaged in the gig economy or works outside a typical full time permanent job (Younger & Smallwood, 2016).

Agile people practices are not limited to contingent workers, however. Recall that in Chapter 6, we hinted at ways that more agile companies rethink traditional talent management, redefining careers as a multidimensional career lattice rather than a single vertical path. There we also discussed a "tour of duty" model of careers, with adaptable job assignments that allow employees to learn and employers to benefit from an employees' diverse background and contributions as they move from role to role, inside and outside the company. Indeed, McGrath (2013a) writes that agile organizations demonstrate "fluidity in allocation of talent" (p. 28), building a capability to "reallocate resources flexibly and on an ongoing basis, rather than going through sudden divestitures or restructurings" (p. 41).

To achieve this fluidity in talent, two key characteristics of an agile people design are learning agility and leadership agility.

Learning Agility

> Agile Principle 6: Agile organizations pursue learning agility.

Rapid movement of talent requires an agile approach to employee development. "To build a multiskilled workforce, instead of hiring new people with a narrow skill set to meet a temporary need, leading companies strengthen their existing employees with additional skills" (Holbeche, 2015, p. 63). This is only true, however, when the development can occur at a rapid enough pace to keep up with the shifting skill needs and changing strategy. "In a world of transient advantage, it isn't always possible to know what kind of people you are going to need, so being able to reconfigure the people that you have can be very helpful" (McGrath, 2013a, p. 151). The central competency required to achieve this is the ability for employees to quickly learn new skills and adapt to a changing direction, or learning agility. Like Netflix that reinvented itself with new capabilities, individuals need to be able to rapidly acquire needed skills and reinvent themselves for the demands of the shifting strategy.

Learning agility has four components:

> *People Agility*—describes people who know themselves well, learn from experience, treat others constructively, and are cool and resilient under the pressures of change.
>
> *Results Agility*—describes people who get results under tough conditions, inspire others to perform beyond normal, and exhibit the sort of presence that builds confidence in others.
>
> *Mental Agility*—describes people who think through problems from a fresh point of view and are comfortable with complexity, ambiguity, and explaining their thinking to others.
>
> *Change Agility*—describes people who are curious, have a passion for ideas, like to experiment with test cases, and engage in skill-building activities. (Lombardo & Eichinger, 2000, p. 324)

While researchers debate the exact items that form learning agility (see DeRue, Ashford, & Meyers, 2012), there is agreement that the ability to learn from experience and to rapidly adapt may be more important than any specific skill an employee could possess. Hiring learning agile employees means looking for more than today's skills; it means looking for the characteristics that could make a candidate successful as the organization's skill needs change. Hiring managers and recruiters can ask themselves these questions about a job candidate:

- What characteristics does a promising employee bring to the challenge?
- How do they manage an unfamiliar situation? Do they get excited by matching their attributes against the demands of a task?
- What is the individual's likely career path—the type of positions and highest level in the organization that they can attain? (Holbeche, 2015, p. 174).

Agile organizations are highly reflective about both their successes and failures. In an environment of rapid prototyping and experimentation, agile organizations must capture this learning and communicate it throughout the organization. Technology can enable a UPS driver to receive instant updates on a mobile device, and supervisors conduct 3-minute morning briefings with news, tips, and reminders. Regular reflection as a standard practice (versus period or ad hoc reflection) allows organizations to sustain learnings and remain agile. Moore

(2015) advises organizations to set up an "incubation zone, . . . a domain where learning is the prime objective and fast failure is actually a form of success" (p. 91). To encourage reflection on both successes and failures, leaders and teams should be habitually returning to these three questions:

- What is happening (or has happened)?
- What new information or guidance can we draw from our experience?
- How can we incorporate this new information or guidance into our attitudes, beliefs, and actions going forward? (Meyer, 2015, p. 47)

To summarize, improving performance in an agile organization means more than mastering a new skill or knowledge. "Learning and development for agility requires whole-person engagement to prepare the learner to be effective in unpredictable, ambiguous, unfamiliar, and often changing contexts" (P. Meyer, 2015, p. 131). Typical behavioral learning practices (such as training programs) provide knowledge and look for evidence of it (passing a test, being able to perform a predefined task). In agile organizations, the shifting context and surprising conditions mean that employees must perform tasks in unfamiliar circumstances that were not part of the training curriculum. They will have to adapt previous knowledge to new circumstances, evaluating the situation, and making real-time decisions about what to do. They must learn on the job, through experience or in unexpected ways that do not look like the typical training courses. Performance feedback cannot wait for an annual discussion; immediate feedback to acknowledge successes and evaluate improvement opportunities is critical for agile learning.

Leadership Agility

> Agile Principle 7: Agile organizations consider agility to be a leadership competency.

Perhaps unsurprisingly, in an environment of less hierarchy, more cross-functional teaming and an emphasis on coordination, not only do employee roles change in agile organizations, but so does the definition of leadership. "It is unrealistic to expect that top leaders will have all the answers, especially in knowledge-based organizations, and old-style hierarchical approaches are of limited use" (Holbeche, 2015, p. 247). In their study of leadership agility, Joiner and Josephs (2007) write that 90 percent of leaders follow a traditional "heroic" leadership mindset, maintaining power, control, and authority. They alone set strategic direction, assign and coordinate activities of subordinate staff, and measure and monitor performance. By contrast, only 10 percent of leaders can be called "post-heroic" leaders. Post-heroic leaders

- develop a vision that inspires and aligns the team;
- promote a highly participative and empowering team work environment;
- seek out and learn from a broad range of diverse viewpoints;

- express empathy;
- develop collaboration on their teams;
- seek feedback; and
- can adapt their leadership style, recognizing when it is important to take charge or take a supporting role.

Leadership in an agile organization is much more likely to be distributed and collective than concentrated in a single person at the top of the pyramid. Agile leaders tend to see leadership as a process of engaging employees in a participative conversation rather than the responsibility to exercise power. They tend to view organization as a process or verb rather than a noun, with the leader's responsibility being to connect and engage employees as the organization changes and evolves. Agile leaders "encourage naysayers, positive deviants, and rabble-rousers to challenge the status quo" (Worley et al., 2014, p. 66). They inspire openness and even dissent, so that healthy debates result in the best solution.

One model of leadership agility skills uses the word AGILE to identify the important characteristics of agile leadership (Horney et al., 2010):

- **Anticipate Change.** Agile leaders develop mechanisms for sensing the environment. They monitor the organization's performance and future trends to predict when changes might be needed, and align the vision and value proposition of the organization.
- **Generate Confidence.** Agile leaders ensure that employees understand how the work they do every day results in an outcome for a stakeholder or customer. They align the organization's objectives, goals, and priorities with the vision and values. They encourage employees to learn something new to build confidence in transferring knowledge to new and unfamiliar circumstances.
- **Initiate Action.** Agile leaders hold a predisposition for action. They develop a culture of urgency and achievement. Agile leaders model collaborative decision making, empowering employees to make decisions themselves rather than wait for permission and miss an opportunity. They connect people and teams across the organization with an action-oriented mindset.
- **Liberate Thinking.** Agile leaders value diversity, are inclusive, and value input from every contributor. They focus relentlessly on customers and how the organization can best serve them. Agile leaders encourage and expect that everyone will contribute to innovations and suggestions for improvement.
- **Evaluate Results.** Agile leaders maintain high standards for performance with measurable outcomes. They ensure that employees understand priorities and are given real-time feedback with consistent metrics.

To these characteristics Joiner and Josephs (2007) add four complementary competencies of agile leaders:

- *Context-setting agility* refers to the ability of a leader to have situational awareness, seeing the big picture. Agile leaders develop a long-term sense of purpose that transcends any individual project or meeting.
- *Stakeholder agility* refers to the leader's ability to connect with stakeholders to see an issue from another person's perspective. They engage others in dialogue even when the leader's perspective is in conflict, with the belief that respectful engagement among people with different beliefs will result in a better outcome.
- *Creative agility* involves developing novel solutions to complex problems that the leader may not have seen before. Conventional wisdom and past solutions inform but do not inhibit current approaches.
- *Self-leadership agility* involves self-awareness and the pursuit of personal and professional development. Agile leaders seek feedback about their own strengths and weaknesses, are conscious about their leadership identity, and experiment with behavior change with a growth mindset.

Four practices encourage a culture of agile leadership: individual and team coaching, creating an agile executive leadership team, enhancing the organization's competency models with agility characteristics, and creating action learning programs (Joiner, 2009). Developing leadership agility involves more than another leadership training course, but instead centers the leader on building a capacity for reflection (Joiner & Josephs, 2007). Leaders should reflect on the situation and assess it before taking action. They should clarify their intent and the outcomes they are trying to reach, building self-awareness about any assumptions or feelings that might be preventing them from taking a different course. Such a shift to inquiry, instead of jumping into reactive behavior, encourages leaders to become more conscious of the choices they are making and their underlying rationale. These capabilities are effectively built through 360-degree feedback programs and leadership coaching that enhance workshops and simulations where leaders can experiment with new behaviors and reflect on their own effectiveness.

AGILE REWARDS

Agile Principle 8: Agile organizations create flexible rewards practices.

We know from our discussion of rewards in Chapter 7 that organizations that use annual raises based on seniority tend to be less adaptable to change. Tenure and seniority pay does not reward success but endurance, which rewards complacency rather than adaptability. We emphasized how the design of the rewards system should be based on the strategy, such as entry into new markets, development of new products, or efficiencies and cost management. In a rapidly changing environment, with its transient advantages, sticking to well-established rewards systems can be a hindrance to agility. Typical organizations are loath to change rewards systems, but "there is no substitute for changing a reward system if it is not contributing to dynamic alignment. . . . Failure to revise the reward system will create a failure to change" (Lawler & Worley, 2006a, pp. 252–253).

In agile organizations, jobs and their associated performance metrics may change frequently. Consequently, the use of bonus systems, such as those given at the end of a performance cycle or completion of a successful project, can flexibly tailor the reward to changing circumstances. A bonus can be allocated to individuals or members of a project team after completion of a customer project that is on time and on budget. When work tasks change frequently, person-based (versus job-based) pay systems can reward people for achievement of tasks and learning new skills. "This reinforces a culture that values growth and personal development; the result is a highly talented workforce that is receptive to change" (Worley & Lawler, 2010, p. 196).

Lawler and Worley (2006) identify two other features of rewards systems in agile, built to change organizations to support the principles of agility that we have already discussed. First, agile organizations provide rewards for risk taking and innovation. Google, for example, created a "Founders' Award" to offer significant stock compensation for employees who developed innovations. In other organizations, employees are provided with bonuses for suggestions or idea innovations that grow the business and support customers. Second, they reward "good" failures that provide useful insights and opportunities for the organization to learn from experiments that did not work out. Organizations that punish all failed experiments will find themselves with a risk-averse population. Instead, they can reward appropriate risk taking by rewarding the learning that is captured and spread throughout the organization.

SUMMARY OF AGILITY PRINCIPLES

1. Agile organizations exploit transient advantages.
2. Agile organizations engage in rapid prototyping and embrace a "fail fast" mentality.
3. Agile organizations rethink traditional organizational structures.
4. Agile organizations form and re-form teams as needed to capitalize on opportunities quickly.
5. Agile organizations employ designs that enable rapid global collaboration.
6. Agile organizations pursue learning agility.
7. Agile organizations consider agility to be a leadership competency.
8. Agile organizations create flexible rewards practices.

AGILITY AND STABILITY

A surprising finding about agile organizations is that they also place an emphasis on stability. "People are not very effective when facing extreme uncertainty—it tends to be paralyzing" (McGrath, 2013a, p. 34). Too much change is chaotic, as we have observed. Recall that in Chapter 1, we learned about the classic Burns and Stalker (1961) study that characterized organizations as either mechanistic or organic. In agile organizations, which tend to display more of the characteristics of organic structures, there remain some mechanistic or formal elements.

> Organizations making the agility shift are finding a dynamic middle ground upon which to centralize or create hubs for many key management functions. . . . At the same time they are flattening out and networking across other projects and services. When structuring for agility, fluidity and stability are not competing values. (P. Meyer, 2015, pp. 95–96)

Consistent and predictable routines can provide efficiency and agility as long as those routines continue to provide value and do not inhibit necessary adaptation. Some aspects of agile organizations remain remarkably consistent, such as identity, culture, and values. (Indeed some organizations such as insurance companies and financial institutions count on their reputations for stable and consistent operations.) McGrath (2012, 2013a) finds that agile organizations also maintain consistent strategy statements, leadership teams, employee populations, and client and partner relationships. Thus, agility and stability are not contradictions but work hand in hand. Employees can innovate and work in regularly reconfigured project teams but against a backdrop of a foundational mission, key relationships, and cultural values that are commonly shared across the organization.

Some organizations emphasize the functional organization structure as a "home base" for employees. Even though employees may be assigned regularly to projects with colleagues outside their immediate management structure, the functions can hold a long-term perspective on the capabilities and skills needed in the future. The functional structure can monitor professional trends and pursue knowledge depth, for example, in technical or scientific areas (Galbraith, 1997). Galbraith (2010) writes that in reconfigurable organizations

> the first stable part is the basic structure, and the second stable part is the set of common business processes. As people move from one team assignment to another, the processes are common and stay the same. . . . The variable parts of the organization are the teams that form and reform, and the management decision-making groups that allocate resources and determine priorities. (p. 119)

Innovation practices in agile organizations maintain an unconfined process for free thinking and experimentation, but such practices are also controlled to ensure that experiments take place within a relatively bounded domain consistent with the organization's purpose and identity (Holbeche, 2015).

SUMMARY

The reconfigurable organization, continuous design, and "disposable" organizational form all describe the idea that an organization's design today must become agile and adaptable. Agile organizations are fast, flexible, and focused, with a change-friendly identity and the capability to sense when change is needed. The shift to agility impacts every aspect of the STAR model of organization design that we have studied. Strategy today has become a series of transient competitive advantages that must be continually pursued. Agile organizations engage in prototyping and experimentation with a belief that failures can provide opportunities for rapid learning. Agile organizations rethink organizational structures and in some cases eliminate the emphasis on hierarchy, substituting instead an emphasis on collaborative practices and teaming. People practices in such organizations stress learning agility and leadership agility, seeking employees that can learn quickly and apply knowledge to new and changing contexts. The role of leadership changes in agile organizations to a distributed model, where leaders develop the capacity for collaboration across the organization and encourage the agile practices that form the other elements of the star. Rewards practices in agile organizations, commonly bonus or performance-based rewards, are equally dynamic to support the rest of the organization's agile practices. Finally, agility and stability are not contradictory, but instead work interdependently to provide employees with consistency at the same time as the organization pursues change.

QUESTIONS FOR DISCUSSION

1. What recent innovations or disruptions can you identify that make agile organization designs a necessity? Compare a recent disruption to one from a decade ago. How do the two situations differ?
2. Would you like to work in an organization that is pursuing a holacracy? Why or why not? What other agile practices covered in this chapter would make an organization a more attractive employer to you? What practices would make that organization a less attractive place to work?
3. Consider an organization that you are familiar with or have researched, and describe the balance between agility and stability in that organization. Are there practices that were too agile or too frequently changing? Are there practices that were too stable and that inhibited the organization from making the changes necessary to remain competitive? What lessons from agile organizations that we have reviewed in this chapter could have helped that organization?

FOR FURTHER READING

Holbeche, L. (2015). *The agile organization.* London, England: Kogan Page.

McGrath, R. G. (2013). *The end of competitive advantage.* Boston, MA: Harvard Business Review Press.

Meyer, P. (2015). *The agility shift.* Brookline, MA: Bibliomotion.

Worley, C. G., & Lawler, E. E., III. (2010). Agility and organization design: A diagnostic framework. *Organizational Dynamics, 39*(2), 194–204.

Worley, C. G., Williams, T., & Lawler, E. E., III. (2014). *The agility factor.* San Francisco, CA: Jossey-Bass.

CHAPTER 10

FUTURE DIRECTIONS OF ORGANIZATION DESIGN

In Chapter 9, we explored how trends such as the move to agility are changing organization design. Indeed, throughout the book we have hinted at ways that our social environment is changing organizational strategies and thus organization designs. In this chapter, we take a deeper look at some of these issues and how they may be shaping the next movements in organization design. We will also look at the skills that it takes to be an effective organization design practitioner.

Learning Objectives

In this chapter you will learn

- Emerging trends that are changing the field of organization design.
- How trends such as big data and sustainability will affect organization design.
- What skills make an effective organization design practitioner.

EMERGING BELIEFS ABOUT ORGANIZATIONS AND DESIGN

Futurist and thought leader Jacob Morgan's book *The Future of Work* (2014) outlines five trends shaping the world of work, which we touched on briefly in Chapter 1:

1. **New behaviors driven by social media:** People connect on Facebook and read and contribute to reviews of products and services on Yelp. They connect with current, past, and prospective coworkers on LinkedIn and start up side businesses on Etsy. The expectation to be able to connect to anyone at any time changes traditional notions and expectations for how connections happen in the workplace. Communication spreads throughout an organization in ways that do not follow hierarchical lines.
2. **Technologies:** Cloud technologies allow for rapid technology deployments by almost anyone in a democratic way inside organizations (e.g., virtually no IT department chose Google as a search engine—employees simply started using it). Collaboration platforms provide new ways for employees to connect and coordinate their work.

3. **Millennial workforce:** Millennials (those born roughly between the early 1980s and the late 1990s and early 2000s) are rapidly becoming the majority of the workforce. The millennial generation that has grown up with technology and social connections brings expectations to work about how technology and collaboration should operate.
4. **Mobility:** Smartphones are ubiquitous. Employees can complete their work with an Internet connection on a train or while waiting for a flight at the airport. Employers like Cisco and IBM count a significant population as having no fixed office.
5. **Globalization:** Teams and talent work together independent of location, and an employee's home office matters little.

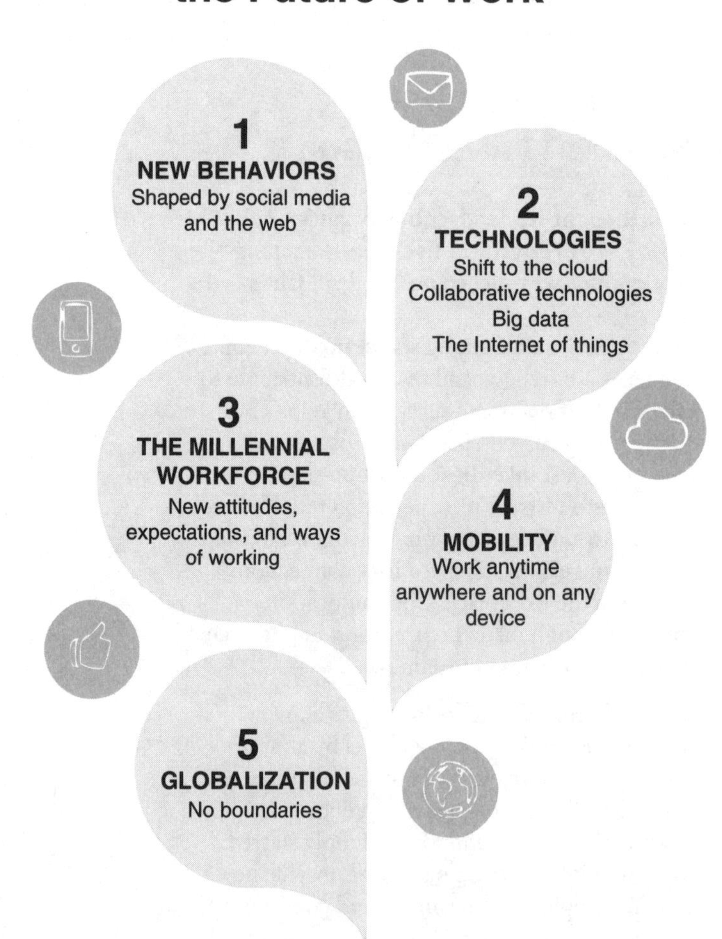

Source: https://www.ie.edu/corporate-relations/insights/the-five-trends-shaping-the-future-of-work/

CHARACTERISTICS OF THE ORGANIZATION OF THE FUTURE

Morgan predicts that the organization of the future has 14 characteristics:

1. Is globally distributed with smaller teams
2. Has a connected workforce
3. Is intrapreneurial
4. Operates like a small company
5. Focuses on creating a place of "want" instead of a place of "need"
6. Adapts to change faster
7. Innovates anywhere
8. Runs in the cloud
9. Sees more women in senior management roles
10. Operates with a flatter structure
11. Tells stories
12. Democratizes learning
13. Shifts from profit to prosperity
14. Adapts to the future employee and the future manager (Morgan, 2014, p. 146)

Work Trends Create Design Challenges

Morgan's five trends will influence how organizations operate (see box). They will also influence organization designs in several ways, including the following.

Rapidly Changing Strategy. We have already seen how "transient advantage" has become commonplace. Organizations continue to increase in complexity, adding new market segments and geographies that must be managed internally, with new departments, divisions, regional offices, product lines, and so on to handle the work.

The Organization as Ecosystem. We have also seen how organizational boundaries are blurring, with an increasing number of collaborative relationships that are no longer minor partnership arrangements but instead are integral to an organization's work (Burton, 2013). Organizations are part of elaborate ecosystems rather than neatly self-contained entities. In retail stores, store management can now manage their own stock levels and inventory on a supplier's website, and the supplier has access to stocking the store shelves themselves. Thus, organization design can no longer stop at the boundary of the organization.

Rapid Collaboration Is Required. Not surprisingly, the emergence of new technologies has a major effect on collaboration inside organizations, allowing "members of an organization to self-organize and thereby avoid the delays, distortions, and other damaging effects of hierarchically organized systems" (Snow, Fjeldstad, & Langer, 2017, p. 1). Jordan (2017) contends that we are witnessing a "period of lag between the uptake of tools that improve coordination and the birth of organizational forms capable of utilizing the benefits" (p. 6), suggesting that the coming years will prompt significant organizational changes as companies increasingly come to terms with the implications of technology on design.

New Types of Teams. In Chapter 9 we discussed how organizations are adapting teams to be more ad hoc and episodic than long lasting or permanent. They operate more like Hollywood movie teams with actors, directors, cinematographers, and support staff that complete a project together in a short period of time and then disband. They must learn to build trust immediately, determine goals, roles, and responsibilities, and then perform.

The "Gig Economy" Means That Organizations Engage New Types of Workers on a Contingent or Project Basis. An unstable talent base becomes the norm and organizations must regularly seek to attract new talent and retain current talent. One study estimated that as much as 94 percent of the net employment growth from 2005 to 2015 occurred as a result of alternative work arrangements, including temporary and contract work (L. Katz & Krueger, 2016).

Virtual Is the Rule, not the Exception. Design work must enable collaborative mechanisms to address the increasing coordination needed globally. Many of these connections now need to happen virtually, enabled by technology.

Analytics Will Have a Role to Play in Design. In Chapter 5, we discussed the trend of social network analysis (also called organizational network analysis) to understand patterns of interaction and collaborative behavior. Once the domain of academic social scientists, social network analysis can now be used by design practitioners. It can provide insight into employee collaboration to improve the strength of social ties in internal and external networks. Talent analytics can give insight into which team members with which skills would be the ideal group to solve a problem based on the combination of competencies needed. We will look at further examples of analytics such as the impact of big data in the next section.

Leadership Behaviors Change in This Environment. The shift away from episodic, large-scale massive restructurings means that leaders must regularly engage in adaptive changes, small and large. A leader's role in design must shift to scanning the external environment and diagnosis to observe how design can be improved. The leader's job is ongoing alignment with strategy and the rest of the design in a "continuous design" mindset. In an adaptive organization, leaders must also become career coaches to retain employees and empower decision making to encourage responsiveness.

Organizational Cultural Challenges Impact Acceptance of These New Ways of Working and New Designs. Leaders and designers must work to create an environment of adaptability and resilience in the face of constant change. Pressures for innovation require an entrepreneurial, start-up mentality even in large organizations. Organizations must develop a continuous learning mindset to encourage employees to engage in regular skill development.

Global Cultural Differences may become more paramount on teams where employees work across geographic lines in different time zones with different cultural norms about power differences, collective versus individual values, and long-term or short-term orientation (Hofstede, 2001; Hofstede, Hofstede, & Minkov, 2010). Employees need to collaborate in an environment of greater workplace diversity.

Design Challenges Shape Design Process

The organization design process must also adapt based on these design trends, as many organizations will have little patience for extended design efforts that take months or years to realize any results. Alan Meyer (2013) proposes five emerging assumptions that should impact the work of design:

1. Instead of an overt focus on "fit" and "congruence," designers must recognize the complex environment of organizations. "Organizations face multiple environments and these environments evolve continuously. Designers should avoid rigid configurations of components and tight alignments with environmental elements" (p. 17). Designs can be evaluated for agility rather than fit (Alberts, 2012).
2. Instead of a focus on hierarchy and structure to guide behavior of organizational members, "organization designs should emerge from 'design thinking' by invoking principles that generate empathy with users, identify related worlds, and test new ideas via rapid prototyping" (A. Meyer, 2013, p. 17). They can pilot design efforts on a smaller scale before bringing them throughout the organization.
3. Instead of a focus on design to control behavior and contribute to stability, designs should be emergent. "Organization designs should propel organizations away from equilibrium for that is where self-organizing processes can occur. Designs should set in motion novel actions in pursuit of novel goals" (A. Meyer, 2013, p. 17).
4. Instead of developing designs to fit with an existing environment, "designers may seek to change environments to render them more munificent for and receptive to organizations" (A. Meyer, 2013, p. 17).
5. Instead of designs being abstract and theoretical ideas, "design principles can be elicited by behavioral simulations in the laboratory and discovered by acting within 3D virtual environments" such as with avatars in virtual worlds where designs can be tested (A. Meyer, 2013, p. 17).

Many of these assumptions and recommendations for the future of design call into question the established design knowledge that we have reviewed in this book. Yet as organizations change in practice, the field of organization design must change as well. The field of organization design has generally lagged behind practice, with researchers studying and examining design changes after they have taken shape among practitioners. The opportunity for future research in organization design is to become forward looking in order to "build and test prototypes of new organizations that are needed for the future, to speed up the process of their development" (according to Snow, described in Håkonsson, 2015, p. 51). In addition, researchers must prioritize translating theory and academic jargon into action and practice that is useful knowledge to managers and designers. Finally, the research field of organization design will need to "learn more about how to organize large-scale, multi-party collaborative processes" (Håkonsson, 2015, p. 51), internal and external to organizations. Along these lines, Alberts (2012) proposes that organization design has a role to play in large-scale complex enterprises at a global scale (such as global financial crises, climate change, and natural disasters).

FUTURE TRENDS IN ORGANIZATION DESIGN THEORY AND PRACTICE

In addition to the trend toward agility that we reviewed in Chapter 9, three specific areas where these trends in organizations are affecting organization design are (1) big data, (2) digital technology, and (3) the move to create more sustainable organizations.

Big Data

Organizations have long had the capability to extract insights from data. What is new about big data is that the data sets themselves are extremely large so that organizations can actually analyze every data point rather than a smaller sample (e.g., every credit card transaction, every job applicant, every click on a website). Moreover, algorithms to analyze the data can now do so in real time. Credit card processing companies can identify potential fraudulent transactions while the transaction is being processed, either confirming the questionable transaction with a text to the purchaser, or alerting the authorities to detain the person making the fraudulent purchase (Galbraith, 2014a). Real-time analysis of Twitter or Facebook postings can give immediate feedback about customer opinions before focus groups and Internet surveys can (Gabel & Tokarski, 2014). Stores can stock additional merchandise based on analysis of weather patterns, ordering snow shovels, jackets, or umbrellas when the weather is likely to be poor. Amusement parks can quickly respond to fluctuations in attendance by directing more staff to handle larger crowds (Slinger & Morrison, 2014). Sales data that used to be analyzed on a regular interval (monthly, quarterly) can now be updated in real time. The volume of data, variety of data, and real-time intelligence that can be gained from big data bring new insights to organizational decision making (Galbraith, 2014a). It is such a monumental change that Galbraith (2012) has called it "the next strategic emphasis of the future enterprise organization" (p. 4).

Organization design is impacted by big data in two ways (Galbraith, 2014a).

First, the organization is likely to experience a shift in the power base from executive or senior-level decision makers who reside at the top of a hierarchy to experts and data scientists who generate insights based on the data analysis. "The location of decisions will change, for example, as [executives] find that they need to allow their judgment-based decisions-making to be modified, and at times overruled, by data-driven insights" (Slinger & Morrison, 2014, p. 18). The successful use of big data will depend on whether the power base in the organization is supportive or resistant to it. Some organizations see benefits in the establishment of a chief digital officer (CDO) whose responsibilities include the use of big data. The CDO brings together the many different data points that exist in pockets throughout the organization. Data analytics functions often occur throughout the organization, such as in finance, human resources, and marketing, each often owning its own data set and technologies. The CDO role has the authority to mediate disputes that arise between divisions. In an organization like Proctor & Gamble that relies heavily on data analytics, the chief information officer (CIO) can assume this role, but in organizations where resistance is likely, the CDO role may need to be granted additional power and authority by reporting to the CEO.

Second, not only is the power base shifted, but big data challenges the speed of decision-making practices. Advertising and supply chain management are two areas where companies have seen significant benefits from big data. In contrast to the traditional "campaign" model of advertising, where ads were developed and tested with focus groups over a long period, modern advertising has adopted a "newsroom" model. Multiple ads can be created and shown not only on television, but YouTube, Facebook, and Twitter. Based on the real-time analysis of social media response to an ad, modifications can be made to future advertising strategy. This was the case in the 2013 Super Bowl in which Coca-Cola set up a response team to monitor response to ads shown early in the game. "Even before the first ad was finished playing, the teams were planning and making modifications to their second ads. . . . In order to respond in real time, these fast-response teams had to be supported by analytics to sift through all of the social media responses and make sense of them" (Galbraith, 2104b, p. 6). The rapid cycle time required in these situations means that the team does not have the luxury to engage in lengthy meetings and run every decision up the hierarchy. Similarly, when Nike launched the Nike+ shoe sensor and app, it created an online community where users upload running routes and interact with other runners. That data provides a tremendous amount of useful insights that can be used for product development and other initiatives. A Nike team monitors the online community for positive and negative customer feedback and can quickly pass along information about developing trends. In addition, supply chain management provides another application of rapid response using big data. At Proctor & Gamble, a "control tower" provides information on dozens of video screens about stock and inventory levels, manufacturing capability, and logistics and shipping capacity across the supply chain (Galbraith, 2014a).

Companies need to be restructured to deal with big data, because "resource allocation becomes much more flexible. . . . With visibility of demand levels and supply volumes, they find it easier to move people, capital, and other resources across sites, functions, roles, and positions" (Slinger & Morrison, 2014, p. 18). The insights and capabilities enabled by big data can enhance the speed of decision making and also allow a company to make better products and understand its customers more deeply. As we have seen, however, organizations must pursue flexible enough organization designs that they can take advantage of the new insights by redirecting resources to the appropriate areas.

An organization has a choice to make about how to structure its digital strategy. In some companies, a digital function is placed in the product development function and in the digital marketing function, each with like-minded software and hardware engineers. Another alternative is to create a separate digital division, which Galbraith argues has greater benefits because it allows the unit to operate at a faster pace. The unit cannot be completely independent, however, since it will need to be closely connected to the product development and marketing functions (Galbraith, 2014b).

In the end, big data affects every point of the STAR model. The strategy shift to creating digitally enabled businesses prompts questions about whether they should exist as separate structural units or whether that digital capability should be integrated into existing units. Processes such as advertising or supply chain management need to operate cross-functionally to take advantage of the real-time feedback that big data provides. The organization needs to hire people with technology skills and reward the development of those competencies and the cross-functional teamwork that is required.

Digital Technologies, Platforms, and Business Models

Technology increasingly allows employees to self-mobilize, "aimed at getting the right numbers of the right types of participants in the right places at the right times doing the right things right" (Dyer & Ericksen, 2010, p. 448). In other words, digital technologies provide platforms that enable employees to collaborate more effectively with one another, reducing hierarchy and providing the means for self-organizing. Organization design researchers have proposed an "actor-oriented" organization design model based on "shared access to information and other resources as well as the protocols and infrastructures by which actors connect and collaborate" (Snow, Fjeldstad, & Langer, 2017, p. 8). Shared purposes and norms guide organizing in ways that used to be the responsibility of management. Organizations increasingly consist of both human actors and digital or technology agents that work together, with some jobs being performed in part by the human actor in collaboration with a robotic or digital actor using artificial intelligence and algorithms. This makes technology increasingly part of an organization's design. James March has been researching organizational behavior for more than 60 years and has observed the current impacts of technology on organization design.

> I think students of organizations need to explore the implications of contemporary efforts to take the humans out of human organizations. Insofar as robots perform the physical tasks of organization and artificial intelligence performs the management tasks, organizations will still exist and their design will still be critical; but the issues and their resolution will be somewhat different. (Dong, March, & Workiewicz, 2017, p. 17)

Digital technologies have encouraged the proliferation of new business models with platform businesses such as eBay, Uber, and Airbnb, where the business exists to connect suppliers and consumers. The model for these businesses calls into question basic assumptions about starting a business, namely that it requires a tremendous amount of initial capital to acquire the necessary supplies and inventory. Uber drivers are not employees and they own their own vehicles that they elect to use whenever they wish to work. An Uber driver has no (human) manager, instead earning feedback from riders, and operational algorithms control much of the Uber organization. Much of the innovative aspects of these business models are not addressed by current organization design theory or concepts.

Jordan (2017) points out that the influence of digital technologies and new organizational models prompts fundamental questions which also challenge prevailing assumptions about organization design:

- What is a boss? What constitutes seniority or superiority in an organization? How will Millennials (informed via social media about salary, perks, and other discrepancies within or among organizations) adapt to assumptions of structural inferiority at work?
- How will organizational design accommodate new modes of coordination that do not depend on concurrent physical presence in a factory, office, clinic, or other structure?
- How will organizations adapt to new limits to institutional authority, whether logistical (the contractor status of Uber drivers), geopolitical

(globalized workforces outside a direct chain of command), or cultural (the resistance to received wisdom by Internet populations)?

- How will formal organizations respond to competition, for both customers and talent, from new kinds of social assemblages?
- How will organizations that previously held a monopoly on certain kinds of information, such as salary data, respond when social networks routinely make that information (in this example, offers and raises) visible?
- How will traditional organizational models accommodate new behaviors—some previously unimagined or culturally unacceptable, such as trolling—of people alone and in groups?
- How can organizational design react to these changes in something close to real time rather than on the timetables of academic research and HR practice that have historically been measured in years or even decades?
- How will organizations balance the timeless tension between efficient centralization and responsive decentralization given the speed and reach of large-scale digital organizations? (pp. 8–9)

Future research and practice will likely develop answers to many of these questions. It is also likely that as new technologies evolve and new organizational models are created to take advantage of them, organization designers will find additional questions to ask.

Sustainability and the Triple Bottom Line

In recent years, there has been a growing interest and acknowledgment that the move to create sustainable organizations and communities also impacts organization design. The issue is how to design an organization to embrace a "triple bottom line" of social, economic, and environmental responsibility (or people, profit, and planet). How can organizations minimize their impact on the planet? How can they go even further to proactively contribute to a healthier environment and community? Responding to these questions is a major challenge, due in no small part to the diverse beliefs and opinions about the problem itself.

> At one extreme are those contesting the scientific consensus that global warming is occurring and/or that human activity has contributed to it. They tend to deny corporate accountability for remedying the situation or any other ills caused by toxicity, pollution, or social injustice. At the other end of the continuum are firms that have made a fundamental commitment to build a more sustainable future, and see it as the right business model to bring us out of this mess. (S. A. Mohrman & Worley, 2010, p. 289)

Laszlo and Laszlo (2011) explain that many organizations begin their work toward sustainability by first complying with mandated regulations in a "business as usual" capacity, for example, to recycle, reduce their emissions and pollution into the atmosphere, or eliminate certain environmentally toxic or hazardous materials in their products. This reactive compliance to reduce the ecological damage the organization inflicts can be contrasted with organizations that intend to proactively create healthy ecosystems. Laszlo and Laszlo call this a "sustainability as usual" capacity where sustainable practices become a systemic part of the organization.

Many organization design and development practitioners who are already attuned to the interconnected nature of systems and experienced at the implementation of large-scale change are drawn to this important cause that makes use of several skills:

> Our systems thinking skills are going to be sorely needed. Our planning, conflict, creativity, large group intervention, and many other capabilities are all needed in many quarters already. Resource depletion and economic limits may call us to work towards greater local self-sufficiency. There is much work to do. (Adams, Royal, & Church, 2011, p. 1)

Socially responsible and sustainable organizations have a unique organization design challenge. They are often neither fully for-profit enterprises nor nonprofit charities, but can have a component of both. SOLO Eyewear, for example, produces sunglasses with a portion of the profits from each sale dedicated to eye care such as glasses and eye surgeries for people in need around the world (Schroeder & Denoble, 2014). Socially responsible organizations differentiate themselves with a vision that draws customers and contribute to a meaningful brand. They require leaders who can articulate that vision for the organization and inspire loyalty and commitment among employees.

Traditional organization design, some argue, cannot fully respond to the challenges of a sustainable enterprise, as it sees organizations through a very rational and economic lens trying to reduce costs and maximize benefits. In a socially responsible organization, some of the costs are also benefits (Parrish, 2010). Proceeds may be redirected away from reducing costs in the supply chain or designing new product innovations, for example, and those funds used to fulfill the organization's mission. Profits are put toward beneficiaries that had nothing to do with the profit-generation part of the business (e.g., the original sale of eyewear). Santos, Pache, and Birkholz (2015) argue that the potential conflicts and trade-offs presented are significant challenges, and that this type of business is among the most complex social enterprises to manage. To accomplish these trade-offs, one study found that social businesses "employed a skillful mix of alternative design principles to achieve organizational effectiveness and efficiency" (Parrish, 2010, p. 521), with a shifting mix of stakeholders who were all worthy and necessary beneficiaries of the organization's efforts. This can be achieved, some argue, by structuring the organization according to its commercial and social value chains (Santos, Pache, & Birkholz, 2015), allowing the two different divisions to pursue two different objectives.

Changes in Organization Design Practice: A Case Study of Royal Dutch Shell

The oil and energy company Royal Dutch Shell has long been a pioneer of scenario planning. Scenario planning was developed as a management methodology in the late 1960s and 1970s at Shell to better plan for the possible economic and oil demand conditions of the mid-1970s. By using a process of defining and elaborating on various alternative scenarios, they could prepare for what they saw as (and what turned out to be) an eventual oil crisis (Wack, 1985a, 1985b).

Shell's 2050 scenario considers that energy demands are increasing and supply is unlikely to keep pace to match. Globalization is seen as a continuing trend along with increasing global and government regulation, with pressures on energy producers to increase cost efficiencies and security. Organizations will need to be increasingly transparent and pressured to operate in socially responsible and sustainable ways in the production of energy. Based on the scenario plan, the company asked, "[W]hat might those factors suggest with regard to the need for changed organization design elements to effectively respond to them?" (Steinmetz, Bennett, & Håkonsson, 2012, p. 8).

In the past, design efforts had been led by a decentralized team, lacking a coherent vision or integrated process. Leaders tended to be short-term focused and would lose energy as the demands of the business distracted from the work of design. The practice of organization design at Shell has moved to become the responsibility of the human resources organization. The HR business partner works with leaders to integrate organization design, talent management, and people-related consulting efforts. Whereas organization design efforts in the past were piecemeal and evolutionary, having HR involved in design decisions provides a more strategic, long-term solution.

The evolution of organization design at Shell provides insights about pressures of the field of organization design (Steinmetz et al., 2012):

- Considering the trend of continued globalization, design efforts involve people from around the world, so projects must now "fully accommodate multiple diverse cultures" (p. 9).
- Given the company's emphasis on sustainability, design itself must follow suit. "Design processes themselves must be more sustainable, organic, and ongoing, and less mechanistic and short term, with assurances built into the processes" (p. 9).
- The company now prefers a strategic organization design process, conducting diagnostic assessments and clarifying strategy.
- The company's interest in globalization but local adaptation means that "some organization design projects will be owned at the global rather than local level. Global standard operating models will apply in certain areas, and design will allow for less variation and choice locally" (p. 9).
- The demands for transparency and consumer interest in a company's environmental practices will prompt more open and participative organization design work with stakeholders.
- The increase in global government regulations means that governance practices and compliance must be built into the organization design.

THE ORGANIZATION DESIGN PRACTITIONER ROLE AND SKILLS

We began the book with the point that design is a leadership competency, but that many leaders have not had formal opportunities to learn the process and concepts of design. Much of the time leaders are assisted in the design effort by external consultants, or increasingly, by internal human resources or organization development consultants. HR and organization development consultants can help to diagnose challenges with the current design, facilitate leadership discussions of design options, ensure the alignment of people and rewards strategies including new skills required in the design, and promote cultural values in line with the new organization's form. HR leaders who understand how to manage change and transitions can help to create plans to manage transitions to a new design.

Yet HR is often not consulted on design efforts. As one study pointed out, "Perhaps HR should play a leading role in organization design, but in practice we find this is not always the case. . . . Organization design is a complex and difficult discipline requiring strategic insight, business understanding, and intellectual rigor, which does not always play to HR's strengths" (Corporate Research Forum, 2013, p. 80). The study concluded that organization design "is a potential area for HR to excel, but requires the highest level of skills. A blend of strategic, organizational effectiveness and interpersonal skills is required, but this is a rare combination and difficult to develop" (p. 85). In addition, leading an organization design project requires the HR practitioner to consult with line leaders with a strong partnership, developing a trusting and collaborative relationship.

Stanford (2005, pp. 25–26) outlines the different roles that managers and HR practitioners play at various stages of the design effort (see Table 10.1).

Table 10.1 Manager and HR Practitioner Activity During the Design Effort

Design Phase	Manager Activity	HR Practitioner Activity
Preparing for Change	Deciding that change is necessary to achieve business outcomes (including assessing the drivers for change) Assessing various options for making the change Evaluating the chosen route (organization design or not) in order to feel confident about the way forward Ensuring the sponsor is supportive of the way forward	Coaching the manager to decide (or not) to change Providing information and support to the manager to help him or her make the right choices Probing and challenging to ensure the manager is on solid ground in his or her decision
Choosing to Redesign	Determining the scope and boundaries of the project Getting sponsors and stakeholders on board Identifying potential project team leaders and members for the high-level and detailed-level teams	Drafting the high-level scope document Following up with sponsors and stakeholders Guiding and suggesting on potential project team leaders and members
Creating the High-Level Design and the Detailed Design	Initiating the design process Keeping a firm grip on its progress via the high-level and detailed-level teams	Helping manager and project team define and agree • Core business purpose • Unique selling point

	Intervening and stepping back appropriately Keeping the day-to-day business running	• Vision, mission, objectives • Principles • Boundary statements • Critical success factors • Measures of success • Target areas—processes, systems, technologies, facilities, skills, culture, people Working with the project manager to manage the assignment including creating the project structure and plan, process mapping, identifying issues and opportunities for improvement
Handling the Transition	Leading the transition process Motivating people to work with the changes Projecting confidence and optimism Adjusting plan appropriately	Surveying responses to change and relaying to manager Recommending actions as needed to maintain progress Supporting and guiding people into new state
Reviewing the Design	Commissioning a postimplementation review about 8 weeks after project closure Assessing the findings against the intended project outcomes Taking action to address issues and concerns to ensure benefits of change are delivered Transferring knowledge, skills, and learning gained in the OD project	Ensuring postimplementation review is thorough and reliable Guiding and supporting manager to understanding, communicating, and acting on the findings Following through on the agreed actions and recommending a second review about 6 months after project closure

Source: Stanford, N. (2005). *Organization design: The collaborative approach*. Amsterdam, Netherlands: Elsevier.

The work of design requires a diversity of interdisciplinary skills, and there have been several inventories of skills required for organization design practitioners (Cichocki & Irwin, 2011; Kates, 2009; Kesler & Kates, 2011; Stanford, 2005). Like the field of organization development, there is no single agreed-upon certification or skill set required to be an organization design practitioner (Anderson, 2017). Table 10.2 lists skills that are helpful in organization design, but this list is not all-inclusive. Some of the skill areas are content oriented (knowledge of finance or job design) whereas others describe interpersonal skills (dealing with conflict, listening, communicating diplomatically). This list emphasizes the challenge for HR practitioners as the skills of design require both strategic business acumen and the interpersonal ability to build a partnership with line executives in what can be a tension-filled and ambiguous process. Mastering the skills of organization design also provides HR with a tremendous opportunity to build its organizational influence and play a major role in the execution of the organization's strategy.

Table 10.2 Skills Required for an Organization Design Practitioner

Skill Area	Description
Business and Management Acumen	• Understanding how organizations function, how the enterprise makes money or serves its customers, fundamentals of business strategy, accounting, business risk management, financial budgeting and planning, management practices, procedures and controls, mergers and acquisitions. • Knowing information systems, sales and marketing, supply chain operations.
Human Resources Acumen	• Knowing the processes of hiring, termination, HR law, training and development, compensation and rewards, job design, performance management.
Diagnosis and Assessment	• Gathering data about the current state of the organization through interviews, focus groups, surveys, observations, or documents. • Being comfortable with both qualitative and quantitative data analysis. • Understanding root causes versus surface-level symptoms. • Identifying the most appropriate levels that will have lasting results and address the root causes.
Project Management	• Planning and organizing the steps of the design effort, sequencing activities, clarifying scope and objectives, measuring progress and project achievement.
Design Mindset	• Being able to anticipate impacts of design choices on the organization's practices and its members. • Acknowledging that "Designers—whether of organizations, buildings, information technology systems, or functional objects—share a common ability to conceive of and articulate how their designs will work" (Kates, 2009, p. 454). • Having intellectual curiosity about systems and how the design works in reality. • Translating design theory or thinking into practical, actionable steps.
Systems Thinking	• Understanding that organization designers must see the interrelationships, the whole as well as the parts. "It is important to be able to see an organization as more than a collection of individuals and to be able to discern the interconnected political, social, and information networks that have formed" (Kates, 2009, p. 454).
Process Orientation	• Analyzing process effectiveness or inefficiencies, process mapping, process design.
Evaluation and Measurement	• Identifying key performance indicators for a process or organization, designing an appropriate evaluation methodology. • Researching design skills, statistical analysis techniques, comfortable with spreadsheets.
Organizational Change	• Understanding fundamentals of change and transition, how to communicate and implement changes, impacts of change programs on people and teams, the psychology of personal and team transitions.

Consulting and Facilitation	• Establishing trusting partnerships with leaders, contracting, data gathering, giving feedback, facilitating meetings, dealing with conflict, gaining agreement. • Having confidence to surface disagreements, play devil's advocate, and test ideas with a senior leadership team.
Problem Solving and Creativity	• Being able to frame a problem and see it from multiple points of view, asking guiding questions to arrive at a thoughtful answer. • Thinking imaginatively but realistically and practical as well when required.
Communication and Presentation	• Having verbal and written communication ability to express ideas in a variety of forms including presentations, documents, e-mail, and more. • Collaborating with others with tact and diplomacy.
Stakeholder Management	• Being aware of organizational politics and power dynamics. • Listening actively to the concerns of multiple stakeholders. • Persuading or negotiating with individuals and groups to take action. • Building rapport, commitment, and involvement.
Flexibility and Adaptability	• Being able to manage through multiple and competing priorities, being comfortable moving forward in ambiguous situations and where a path or a right answer is not known.

SUMMARY

The nature of organizations is changing, and organization designs are changing with them. Driven by factors such as technology, globalization, social media, mobility, and the new behaviors that come with them, organizations are witnessing major changes that impact design. These design changes include blurring organizational boundaries through the creation of business ecosystems, rapidly changing strategies, and an increased need for and ability to collaborate internally and externally. Ad hoc teams form and disband quickly to address immediate problems, and organizational members may be transient workers who move on to their next opportunity after a project is completed. Virtual workers and global colleagues mean that teams can be composed of workers anywhere. The role of leadership changes in the new organization from hierarchical command to a monitor of organizational adaptation. Big data, digital transformation, and sustainability are three trends for practitioners to be knowledgeable about as they design organizations for the future. Organization design theory will need to catch up with organization design practice to be able to provide insights and new design forms for practitioners to prototype. Design work requires both content knowledge and interpersonal effectiveness. This is a potential area for human resources and organization development practitioners to play a role in helping organizations execute their strategies, by facilitating design efforts.

QUESTIONS FOR DISCUSSION

1. In what ways have you seen the changes reviewed in this chapter impact your own workplace (or an organization that you have researched)?
2. Identify an opportunity to use big data in an organization that you are familiar with. How might the insights from big data be used? What do you think the acceptance or resistance would be to the power shift in decision making that comes from insights generated by algorithms versus the leadership team?
3. Examine the list of skills in Table 10.2 again. Which of these skill areas are strengths that you possess, and which are areas that you need to further develop? How might your strengths help you lead an organization design effort? How could you develop the areas in which you are weaker?

FOR FURTHER READING

Burton, R. M. (2013). The future of organization design: An interpretative synthesis in three themes. *Journal of Organization Design*, *2*(1), 42–44.

Galbraith, J. R. (2014b). Organization design challenges resulting from big data. *Journal of Organization Design*, *3*(1), 2–13.

Meyer, A. (2013). Emerging assumptions about organization design, knowledge and action. *Journal of Organization Design*, *2*(3), 16–22.

Morgan, J. (2014). *The future of work*. Hoboken, NJ: Wiley.

APPENDIX

ORGANIZATION DESIGN SIMULATION ACTIVITY

Part I: Strategy

In this four-part simulation activity, you will have the opportunity to design a fictional organization using the principles from the chapters. In essence, you'll be creating your own case study. You will face real-life constraints on your design work, which have already started with your dice rolls (see the instructions at the end of Chapter 3 if you did not start there). You can be as inventive as you want, as long as your choices remain consistent within your constraints.

The scenario: You are the right-hand chief of staff to the top leader of the organization. The leader considers you to be the consultant to the top management team about all matters related to organization design. Your task will be to design an organization using the STAR model that fits the profile you have been given, according to concepts and ideas that we have learned about thus far in the book.

Your Profile

What kind of organization are you? To find out, refer to Figure A.1 and the dice rolls that you conducted. Your organizational profile will be based on the numbers you rolled.

For example, if you roll a 6 for your third roll (cash), it means that your organization has a very high amount of cash on hand and a good financial situation. If you roll a 3 for people, your organization has between 1,001 and 5,000 employees. If you have a 2 for global reach, your organization is regionally based (e.g., southwest United States or Eastern Europe). "Capability" means your organization's current skill and performance level at product development, operations, or sales and marketing (definitions noted in Figure A.1 on the next page).

On the surface, some of these characteristics may look inconsistent. For example, it might seem counterintuitive to have low operations capability but a major global presence. In this case, it's likely that your organization does not manufacture its own products for global customers, but uses outsourced manufacturing. (Maybe it doesn't manufacture anything?) If you have a low number of employees but a lot of cash, perhaps you're a small investment firm. Be creative! Consider nonprofits, educational institutions, governments and their agencies, health care organizations, consortiums and alliances, and for-profit companies. You can invent flying cars or sell missions to Mars. You can choose whatever you want, but **the key is consistency and good design practice.**

Your Mission: Create an Organization and Explain Its Strategy

Using your organization's profile numbers, create a fictional organization and design it according to this organizational profile, focusing on the strategy of your organization as we learned about in Chapter 3. Give your organization a name and tell us everything you can about it.

Figure A.1 Dice Roll Definitions

Roll 1: Global Reach and Locations	Roll 2: People	Roll 3: Cash and Financial Position	Roll 4: Product Development Capability (R&D innovation)	Roll 5: Operations Capability (manufacturing, shipping, logistics, information technology, customer support)	Roll 6: Sales and Marketing Capability (getting new customers, retaining customers)
1. Local only (city/state)	1. 50–500 employees	1. Significant debt, very poor financial position	1. Very low capability	1. Very low capability	1. Very low capability
2. Regional	2. 501–1,000 employees	2. No cash, poor financial position	2. Low capability	2. Low capability	2. Low capability
3. Nationwide	3. 1,001–5,000 employees	3. Low cash, fair financial position	3. Low to moderate capability	3. Low to moderate capability	3. Low to moderate capability
4. Minor global presence	4. 5,001–25,000 employees	4. Medium cash, good financial position	4. Moderate to high capability	4. Moderate to high capability	4. Moderate to high capability
5. Moderate global presence	5. 25,001–100,000 employees	5. High cash, very good financial position	5. High capability	5. High capability	5. High capability
6. Major global presence	6. 100,001–500,000 employees	6. Very high cash, excellent financial position	6. Very high capability	6. Very high capability	6. Very high capability

Answer the following questions about your organization:

1. What does your organization do? Write the five design criteria for your organization (refer to Chapter 2 for guidance).
2. What does it produce, if anything, and in what market(s) does the organization participate? Who are your "customers"?
3. Where is the organization located?
4. Who are your organization's competitors, and what is your strategy—your source of competitive advantage? Research the strategy of at least one real organization that competes with your organization and note how your organization is different. Apply concepts that we discussed in Chapter 3, such as the generic strategy models, Porter's Five Forces, or blue ocean strategy.

Part II: Structure and Processes and Lateral Capability

Now that you have created your fictional organization and described its strategy, you can begin to work on the next two elements of the organization design: structure, and processes and lateral capability.

Structure

Using the concepts we learned about in Chapter 4, create an organizational structure to fit this strategy. How does the structure follow from the strategy? What are the major divisions of your organization and what are they responsible for? How many employees work in each division, and how are divisions structured? To answer these questions, it may be helpful to create an organizational chart for your organization.

In addition to describing how you have organized your departments, consider these other important elements of organization structure:

1. Centralization and decentralization: What functions should be centralized? Where should decision making be decentralized? Why?
2. Span of control: Will your organization have a wide or narrow span of control? Why? How many management and leadership roles do you anticipate for your organization?
3. Division of labor: What jobs require deep specialization? Which require low specialization?

What are the advantages and disadvantages of this structure? Knowing what we have learned about various structure types and their advantages and disadvantages, what potential problems can you anticipate from this structure?

Processes and Lateral Capability

Given your chosen structure and the flaws you identified in it, what lateral capabilities are required for your organization? Describe where you would implement less formal mechanisms (i.e., low lateral capability) or where you would choose more formal mechanisms (i.e., high lateral capability).

Consider, for example, the types of lateral capability we studied in Chapter 5:

- What informal networks would you foster and how would you do that?
- What are the organization's major cross-functional processes, opportunities for shared goals, or what technology coordination mechanisms you would implement?
- Where might teams be required, if at all?
- Would you have any integrative roles? Why, and what would those roles accomplish?
- Would a matrix organization be appropriate? Why or why not? What dimensions of the matrix would you select?

Finally, why did you select these lateral coordinating mechanisms? What disadvantages of the structure are solved here? How are these consistent with the rest of the star?

Part III: People and Rewards

In Part III, you will complete the remaining two points of the star for your organization design.

People Practices

Explain the unique people practices of your organization that set you apart from your competitors and give you a strategic advantage. What special capabilities are required in your organization, and how have you defined your people practices to take those into consideration? How are these consistent with the rest of the star? (As we read in Chapter 6, it is insufficient to state that "our people are our biggest asset" and leave it at generalities such as that. State specifically why your people strategy is unique to your organization and why it supports other components of your organization design). How are your people practices unique to supporting the strategic agenda of your organization, and why will they give you a competitive advantage?

Consider these important people-related considerations that we discussed in Chapter 6:

- Where does your organization require talent that is better than your competitors? What are your organization's pivot roles or strategic "A" positions?
- How will you identify and treat high-potential employees?
- What career development programs exist in your organization?
- How will you conduct performance appraisals? How will you ensure that you realize the benefits and not the negative consequences of performance management?
- What learning and development programs will be critical to your success?

Reward Practices

As we have learned, rewards practices can have negative unintended consequences. Here you will explain what rewards programs will drive motivation for your employees to achieve goals that are aligned with the strategy. Consider these topics covered in Chapter 7:

- What goals, scorecards, and metrics will you create? Specifically what metrics will the organization use to know that it is achieving the strategy?
- What values and behaviors are important in your organization?
- How will organization members be rewarded? What types of rewards will you give? How will you match compensation and rewards practices to fit the needs of your design? How are these consistent with the rest of the star?

Part IV: Reorganizing

With the star complete, your organization is humming along. However, as we know from our readings, organization design cannot remain static. Strategies change, structures change, and the rest of the star must change along with it. What kinds of changes are occurring in your organization? That's what this activity is all about: reorganizing and redesigning to change.

The executive management staff recently took a 5-day retreat. After an extensive review of the past year's operations and a strategic planning session to plan the future direction of the organization, the team made some important decisions. They now need your help revisiting the design because some major changes are about to take place.

To find out what's happened in your organization, refer to Figure A.2 and your dice roll.

Figure A.2 Reorganization Dice Roll Descriptions

Dice Roll = 1 The leadership team has decided to innovate. A new division has been formed to expand on the previous work of the organization, but the team has determined that no additional employees can be added. Instead, the division will be staffed with employees from existing divisions.	**Dice Roll = 2** The executive team has concluded that the organization is struggling and has decided to refocus its strategic priorities. They have decided to divest the organization of one or more of its current offerings (products or services) or outsource an existing division. In addition, they want to reduce the population by 10 percent to 20 percent.	**Dice Roll = 3** A key partnership or alliance has been identified. The executive team has concluded that based on current capabilities, it makes sense to work on a joint venture. Depending on the company's cash position, either a new division will be added (if your old cash roll was 4 to 6) or an existing division (old cash roll 1 to 3) will be given the role of working on the partnership. No new employees can be added.
Dice Roll = 4 Based on success with recent pilot projects in new regions, the executive team has decided to expand. Two new offices will be opened in two new countries. Add 10 percent to your employee population.	**Dice Roll = 5** An acquisition! The executive team has purchased a competitor and now needs to integrate those capabilities and employees into its current operations. Expand the strategy and add up to 15 percent of your employee population.	**Dice Roll = 6** Rising real estate prices and challenges in some geographies have prompted the executive team to cut back the number of offices or locations. Reduce your previous dice roll for global reach in half, and downsize your employee population by 10 percent.

How does the executive team's decision fit with your current strategy and design? Such strategic choices often look inconsistent on the surface but are in response to competitive or market trends. Consider what larger trends might have prompted these decisions, and how they might have implications on your organization design.

It is now time to examine what effect these changes have on the strategy, structure, processes and lateral capability, people, and rewards choices that you have made. Describe what changes to the organization design you need to make, and what new advantages and disadvantages the changes now hold for you. Consider the following:

- **Strategy**: What are the implications to your organization's strategy based on these changes? Do you have a different competitive position than you had before? What might have changed in the organization's strategy?

- **Structure**: Do you have a different structure type now? Which one? What does it look like? What are its advantages and disadvantages? Do you have more/fewer employees? Plans to hire or downsize? Where and why?
- **Processes and Lateral Capability**: What new lateral capabilities are required, if any? Why? How will you implement these?
- **People**: What implications are there for your people and talent strategy? Consider changes you may need to make to career development, learning and development, and performance management practices.
- **Rewards**: What implications are there to the organization's rewards practices? What goals and metrics will now be important, and how have these changed? What new values and behaviors will you seek to encourage through your rewards practices? How will compensation and other nonmonetary recognition be affected?
- **Reorganizing and managing transitions**: What will be some of the major challenges in transitioning to this new design? Who might resist the change to the new structure? What departments will likely face the biggest transition? How will you choose to implement the new design? Will you proceed with a rapid transition or at a more cautious pace? Will you pilot changes or sequence them before a larger implementation? How will you communicate the changes?

REFERENCES

Adams, J., Royal, C., & Church, A. (2011). OD and sustainability. *OD Practitioner, 43*(4), 1–2.

Aguinis, H., Joo, H., & Gottfredson, R. K. (2013). What monetary rewards can and cannot do: How to show employees the money. *Business Horizons, 56*, 241–249.

Al Ariss, A. (2014) (Ed.). *Global talent management: Challenges, strategies, and opportunities*. New York, NY: Springer.

Alberts, D. S. (2012). Rethinking organizational design for complex endeavors. *Journal of Organization Design, 1*(1), 14–17.

Allen, R. S., White, C. S., Takeda, M. B., & Helms, M. M. (2004). Rewards and organizational performance in Japan and the United States: A comparison. *Compensation & Benefits Review, 36*(1), 7–14.

Anand, N., & Daft, R. L. (2007). What is the right organization design? *Organizational Dynamics, 36*, 329–344.

Anderson, D. L. (2017). *Organization development: The process of leading organizational change* (4th ed.). Thousand Oaks, CA: Sage.

Angelo, C., Alessandro, M., Massimo, S., & Davide, S. (2010). Building a process-based organization: The design roadmap at Superjet International. *Knowledge and Process Management, 17*(2), 49–61.

Ansoff, I. (1965). *Corporate strategy*. London, England: McGraw-Hill.

Arthur, M. B., & Rousseau, D. M. (Eds.). (1996). *The boundaryless career*. New York, NY: Oxford University Press.

Ashby, W. (1956). *An introduction to cybernetics*. New York, NY: Wiley.

Ashkenas, R., Ulrich, D., Jick, T., & Kerr, S. (2002). *The boundaryless organization*. San Francisco, CA: Jossey-Bass.

Baeten, X., & Verwaeren, B. (2012). Flexible rewards from a strategic rewards perspective. *Compensation & Benefits Review, 44*(1), 40–49.

Bahrami, H. (1992). The emerging flexible organization: Perspectives from Silicon Valley. *California Management Review, 34*, 33–52.

Barkema, H. G., & Schijven, M. (2008). Towards unlocking the full potential of acquisitions: The role of organizational restructuring. *Academy of Management Journal, 51*, 496–722.

Barnard, C. I. (1938/1968). *The functions of the executive*. Cambridge, MA: Harvard University Press.

Barreto, I. (2010). Dynamic capabilities: A review of past research and an agenda for the future. *Journal of Management, 36*(1), 256–280.

Barrett, F. J. (2012). *Yes to the mess: Surprising leadership lessons from jazz*. Boston, MA: Harvard Business Review Press.

Bartlett, C. A. (1986). Building and managing the transnational: The new organizational challenge. In M. E. Porter (Ed.), *Competition in global industries* (pp. 367–401). Boston, MA: Harvard Business.

Bartlett, C. A., & Ghoshal, S. (2002). Building competitive advantage through people. *MIT Sloan Management Review, 43*(2), 34–41.

Barton, D., Carey, D., & Charan, R. (2018). One bank's agile team experiment. *Harvard Business Review, 96*(2), 59–61.

Bate, P., Khan, R., & Pyle, A. J. (2000). Culturally sensitive structuring: An action research-based approach to organization development and design. *Public Administration Quarterly, 23*, 445–470.

Beatty, R. W., & Schneier, C. E. (1997). New HR roles to impact organizational performance: From "partners" to "players." *Human Resource Management, 36*, 29–37.

Becker, B. E., & Huselid, M. A. (1998). High performance work systems and firm performance. *Research in Personnel and Human Resources Management, 16*, 53–101.

Becker, B. E., & Huselid, M. A. (2010). Strategic human resources management: Where do we go from here? In A. Wilkinson, N. Bacon, T. Redman, & S. Snell (Eds.), *The SAGE handbook of human resource management* (pp. 351–376). London, England: Sage.

Becker, B. E., Huselid, M. A., Beatty, R. W. (2009). *The differentiated workforce*. Boston, MA: Harvard Business.

Beckhard, R. (1969). *Organization development: Strategies and models.* Reading, MA: Addison-Wesley.

Beckhard, R., & Harris, R. (1977). *Organizational transitions.* Reading, MA: Addison-Wesley.

Beckhard, R., & Harris, R. (1987). *Organizational transitions* (2nd ed.). Reading, MA: Addison-Wesley.

Beckman, S. L. (2009). Introduction to a symposium on organizational design. *California Management Review, 51*(4), 6–10.

Benko, C., & Anderson, M. (2010). *The corporate lattice.* Boston, MA: Harvard Business Review Press.

Bernoff, J., & Schadler, T. (2010). Empowered. *Harvard Business Review, 88*(7/8), 95–101.

Bernstein, E., Bunch, J., Canner, N., & Lee, M. (2016). Beyond the holacracy hype. *Harvard Business Review, 94*(7/8), 38–49.

Birkinshaw, J. (2015). What lessons should we learn from Valve's innovative management model? *Journal of Organization Design, 4*(2), 8–9.

Bolstorff, P., & Rosenbaum, R. (2012). *Supply chain excellence.* New York, NY: AMACOM.

Boudreau, J. W., & Lawler, E. E., III. (2014). The strategic role of HR in the United States and China: Relationships with HR outcomes and effects of management approaches. In P. Sparrow, H. Scullion, & I. Tarique (Eds.), *Strategic talent management* (pp. 197–223). Cambridge, England: Cambridge University Press.

Boudreau, J. W., & Ramstead, P. M. (2007). *Beyond HR: The new science of human capital.* Boston, MA: Harvard Business.

Brickley, J. A., Smith, C. W., Jr., Zimmerman, J. L., & Willett, J. (2003). *Designing organizations to create value: From structure to strategy.* New York, NY: McGraw-Hill.

Bridges, W. (1980). *Transitions.* Reading, MA: Addison-Wesley.

Brown, D. (2014). The future of reward management: From total reward strategies to smart rewards. *Compensation & Benefits Review, 46*(3), 147–151.

Brown, S. L., & Eisenhardt, K. M. (1998). *Competing on the edge: Strategy as structured chaos.* Boston, MA: Harvard Business Review Press.

Bryan, L. L., & Joyce, C. I. (2007). *Mobilizing minds: Creating wealth from talent in the 21st-century organization.* New York, NY: McGraw-Hill.

Bryant, A. (1995, April 14). Continental is dropping "Lite" service. *New York Times*, D1.

Buchanan, D., & Badham, R. (2008). *Power, politics, and organizational change.* London, England: Sage.

Buckingham, M., & Goodall, A. (2015). Reinventing performance management. *Harvard Business Review, 93*(4), 40–50.

Burns, T., & Stalker, G. M. (1961). *The management of innovation.* London, England: Tavistock.

Burström, T., & Jacobsson, M. (2011). The role and importance of "glue people" in projects. *The IUP Journal of Soft Skills, 5*(1), 7–15.

Burton, R. M. (2013). The future of organization design: An interpretative synthesis in three themes. *Journal of Organization Design, 2*(1), 42–44.

Burton, R. M., Håkonsson, D. D., Nickerson, J., Puranam, P., Workiewicz, M., & Zenger, T. (2017). GitHub: Exploring the space between boss-less and hierarchical forms of organizing. *Journal of Organization Design, 6*(10): 1–19.

Burton, R. M., Obel, B., & Håkonsson, D. D. (2015). How to get the matrix organization to work. *Journal of Organization Design, 4*(3), 37–45.

Cameron, K. S., & Freeman, S. J. (1991). Cultural congruence, strength, and type: Relationships to effectiveness. *Research in Organizational Change and Development, 5*, 23–58.

Cameron, K. S., & Quinn, R. E. (2011). *Diagnosing and changing organizational culture: Based on the Competing Values Framework.* San Francisco, CA: Jossey-Bass.

Cameron, K. S., Quinn, R. E., DeGraff, J., & Thakor, A. V. (2006). *Competing values leadership: Creating values in organizations.* Cheltenham, England: Edward Elgar.

Campbell-Hunt, C. (2000). What have we learned about generic competitive strategy? A meta-analysis. *Strategic Management Journal, 21*, 127–154.

Camuffo, A., & Wilhelm, M. (2016). Complementarities and organizational (Mis)fit: A retrospective analysis of the Toyota recall crisis. *Journal of Organization Design, 5(4):* 1–13.

Cappelli, P. (2008a). Talent management for the twenty-first century. *Harvard Business Review, 86*(3), 74–81.

Cappelli, P. (2008b). *Talent on demand.* Boston, MA: Harvard Business.

Cappelli, P. (2009). A supply chain approach to workforce planning. *Organizational Dynamics, 38*(1), 8–15.

Cerasoli, C. P., Nicklin, J. M., & Ford, M. T. (2014). Intrinsic motivation and extrinsic incentives jointly predict performance: A 40-year meta-analysis. *Psychological Bulletin, 140*, 980–1008.

Chandler, A. D., Jr. (1962). *Strategy and structure: Chapters in the history of the industrial enterprise.* Cambridge, MA: MIT Press.

Chang, E., & Hahn, J. (2006). Does pay-for-performance enhance perceived distributive justice for collectivistic employees? *Personnel Review, 35*(4), 397–412.

Chappell, L. (2015, January 15). Industry 'can't give up on EVs': Despite cheap gas, developers press on. *Automotive News, 89*(6654).

Charan, R. (1991). How networks reshape organizations—for results. *Harvard Business Review, 69*(5), 94–115.

Chen, B. X. (2014, August 11). Simplifying the bull: How Picasso helps to teach Apple's style. *New York Times*, A1.

Chermack, T. J., & Lynham, S. A. (2002). Definitions and outcome variables of scenario planning. *Human Resource Development Review, 1*, 366–383.

Cherns, A. B. (1977). Can behavioral science help design organizations? *Organizational Dynamics, 5*(4), 44–64.

Child, J. (1977). Organization design and performance: Contingency theory and beyond. In E. H. Burack & A. R. Negandhi (Eds.), *Organization design: Theoretical perspectives and empirical findings* (pp. 169–183). Kent, OH: Comparative Administration Research Institute.

Christensen, C. M. (1997). *The innovator's dilemma.* New York, NY: Harper Business.

Christensen, C. M., Raynor, M., & McDonald, R. (2015). What is disruptive innovation? *Harvard Business Review, 93*(12), 44–53.

Cichocki, P., & Irwin, C. (2011). *Organization design: A guide to building effective organizations.* London, England: Kogan Page.

Cohn, M. (2010). *Succeeding with agile.* Upper Saddle River, NJ: Addison-Wesley.

Collings, D. G., & Mellahi, K. (2009). Strategic talent management: A review and research agenda. *Human Resource Management Review, 19*, 304–313.

Collis, D. J., & Rukstad, M. G. (2008). Can you say what your strategy is? *Harvard Business Review, 86*(4), 82–90.

Colvin, G. (2017, June 15). Can Wells Fargo get well? *Fortune, 175*(8), 138–146.

Corporate Research Forum. (2013). *Emerging approaches to organization design.* London, England: Author.

Coughlan, P., & Prokopoff, I. (2004). Managing change, by design. In R. J. Boland, Jr., & F. Collopy (Eds.), *Managing as designing* (pp. 188–192). Stanford, CA: Stanford University Press.

Cross, R., Dowling, C., Gerbasi, A., Gulas, V., & Thomas, R. J. (2010). How organizational network analysis facilitated transition from a regional to a global IT function. *MIS Quarterly Executive, 9*(3), 133–145.

Cross, R., & Gray, J. (2013). Where has the time gone? Addressing collaboration overload in a networked economy. *California Management Review, 56*(1), 50–66.

Cross, R., Kase, R., Kilduff, M., & King, Z. (2013). Bridging the gap between research and practice in organizational network analysis: A conversation between Rob Cross and Martin Kilduff. *Human Resource Management, 52*(4), 627–644.

Cross, R., Rebele, R., & Grant, A. (2016). Collaborative overload. *Harvard Business Review, 94*(1/2), 74–79.

Danişman, A. (2010). Good intentions and failed implementations: Understanding culture-based resistance to organizational change. *European Journal of Work and Organizational Psychology, 19*, 200–220.

D'Aveni, R. (1994). *Hypercompetition.* New York, NY: The Free Press.

Davis, S. M., & Lawrence, P. R. (1977). *Matrix.* Reading, MA: Addison-Wesley.

Davison, B. (2003). Management span of control: How wide is too wide? *Journal of Business Strategy, 24*(4), 22–29.

De Kluyver, C. A., & Pearce, J. A. (2003). *Strategy: A view from the top.* Upper Saddle River, NJ: Prentice Hall.

Deci, E. J., Koestner, R., & Ryan, R. M. (1999). A meta-analytic review of experiments examining the effects of extrinsic rewards on intrinsic motivation. *Psychological Bulletin, 125*, 627–668.

Denison, D. R., & Spreitzer, G. M. (1991). Organizational culture and organizational development: A competing values approach. *Research in Organizational Change and Development, 5*, 1–21.

Dent, E. B., & Goldberg, S. G. (1999). Challenging "resistance to change." *Journal of Applied Behavioral Science, 35*(1), 25–41.

DeRue, D. S., Ashford, S. J., & Myers, C. G. (2012). Learning agility: In search of conceptual clarity and theoretical grounding. *Industrial and Organizational Psychology, 5*, 258–279.

Dhillon, I., & Gupta, S. (2015). Organizational restructuring and collaborative creativity: The case of

Microsoft and Sony. *The IUP Journal of Business Strategy, 12*(1), 53–65.

Dierdorff, E. C., & Surface, E. A. (2008). If you pay for skills, will they learn? Skill change and maintenance under a skill-based pay system. *Journal of Management, 34*(4), 721–743.

Doh, J., Smith, R., Stumpf, S., & Tymon, W. G., Jr. (2014). Emerging markets and regional patterns in talent management: The challenge of India and China. In P. Sparrow, H. Scullion, & I. Tarique (Eds.), *Strategic talent management* (pp. 224–253). Cambridge, England: Cambridge University Press.

Donaldson, L. (2001). *The contingency theory of organizations.* Thousand Oaks, CA: Sage.

Donaldson, L., & Joffe, G. (2014). Fit: The key to organizational design. *Journal of Organization Design, 3*(3), 38–45.

Dong, J., March, J. G., & Workiewicz, M. (2017). On organizing: An interview with James G. March. *Journal of Organization Design, 6*(14), 1–19.

Donovan, J., & Benko, C. (2016). AT&T's talent overhaul. *Harvard Business Review, 94*(10), 69–73.

Douglas, C. (1999). Organization redesign: The current state and projected trends. *Management Decision, 37*(8), 621–627.

Dowell, B. E. (2010). Managing leadership talent pools. In R. Silzer & B. E. Dowell (Eds.), *Strategy-driven talent management* (pp. 399–438). San Francisco, CA: Jossey-Bass.

Downes, L., & Nunes, P. F. (2013). Big-bang disruption. *Harvard Business Review, 91*(3), 44–56.

Doz, Y., & Konsonen, M. (2008). The dynamics of strategic agility: Nokia's rollercoaster experience. *California Management Review, 50*(3), 95–118.

Drucker, P. (1964). *Managing for results.* New York, NY: Harper.

Dyer, L., & Ericksen, J. (2010). Complexity-based agile enterprises: Putting self-organizing emergence to work. In A. Wilkinson, N. Bacon, T. Redman, & S. Snell (Eds.), *The SAGE handbook of human resource management* (pp. 438–459). London, England: Sage.

Egan, M. (2015). *How Banana Republic is getting killed by fast fashion.* Retrieved from http://money.cnn.com/2015/11/10/investing/banana-republic-gap-fast-fashion/index.html

Eriksen, B. (2006). Organization design constraints on strategy and performance. In R. M. Burton, B. Eriksen, D. D. Håkonsson, & C. C Snow (Eds.), *Organization design: The evolving state-of-the-art* (pp. 165–180). New York, NY: Springer.

Ertel, C., & Solomon, L. K. (2014). *Moments of impact: How to design strategic conversations that accelerate change.* New York, NY: Simon & Schuster.

Faulkner, D., & Bowman, C. (1992). Generic strategies and congruent organisational structures: Some suggestions. *European Management Journal, 10*(4), 494–500.

Fayard, A., & Weeks, J. (2011). Who moved my cube? *Harvard Business Review, 89*(7/8), 103–110.

Ferdows, K., Lewis, M. A., & Machuca, J. A. D. (2004). Rapid fire fulfillment. *Harvard Business Review, 82*(11), 104–110.

Fernández-Aráoz, C. (2014). 21st century talent spotting. *Harvard Business Review, 92*(6), 46–56.

Fjelstad, O. D., Snow, C. C., Miles, R. E., & Lettl, C. (2012). The architecture of collaboration. *Strategic Management Journal, 33*, 734–750.

Ford, J. D., Ford, L. W., & D'Amelio, A. (2008). Resistance to change: The rest of the story. *Academy of Management Review, 33*, 362–377.

Freedman, A. (2013). *Strategy: A history.* New York, NY: Oxford.

Friedman, T. L. (2007). *The world is flat.* New York, NY: Farrar, Straus and Giroux.

Gabel, T. J., & Tokarski, C. (2014). Big data and organization design: Key challenges await the survey research firm. *Journal of Organization Design, 3*(1), 37–45.

Galbraith, J. R. (1971). Matrix organization designs. *Business Horizons, 14*(1), 29–40.

Galbraith, J. R. (1973). *Designing complex organizations.* Reading, MA: Addison-Wesley.

Galbraith, J. R. (1977). *Organization design.* Reading, MA: Addison-Wesley.

Galbraith, J. R. (1991). Structural responses to competitive strategies. In R. H. Kilmann, I. Kilmann, & Associates (Eds.), *Making organizations competitive* (pp. 51–75). San Francisco, CA: Jossey-Bass.

Galbraith, J. R. (1994). *Competing with flexible lateral organizations* (2nd ed.). Reading, MA: Addison-Wesley.

Galbraith, J. R. (1995). *Designing organizations: An executive briefing on strategy, structure, and process.* San Francisco, CA: Jossey-Bass.

Galbraith, J. R. (1997). The reconfigurable organization. In F. Hesselbein, M. Goldsmith, & R. Beckhard

(Eds.), *The organization of the future* (pp. 87–97). San Francisco, CA: Jossey-Bass.

Galbraith, J. R. (2000). *Designing the global corporation.* San Francisco, CA: Jossey-Bass.

Galbraith, J. R. (2002). *Designing organizations: An executive guide to strategy, structure, and process.* San Francisco, CA: Jossey-Bass.

Galbraith, J. R. (2005). *Designing the customer-centric organization.* San Francisco, CA: Jossey-Bass.

Galbraith, J. R. (2008). Organization design. In T. G. Cummings (Ed.), *Handbook of organization development* (pp. 325–352). Thousand Oaks, CA: Sage.

Galbraith, J. R. (2009). *Designing matrix organizations that actually work.* San Francisco, CA: Jossey-Bass.

Galbraith, J. R. (2010). The multi-dimensional and reconfigurable organization. *Organizational Dynamics, 39*(2), 115–125.

Galbraith, J. R. (2012). The evolution of enterprise organization designs. *Journal of Organization Design, 1*(2), 1–13.

Galbraith, J. R. (2014a). *Designing organizations: Strategy, structure, and process at the business unit and enterprise levels* (3rd ed.). San Francisco, CA: Jossey-Bass.

Galbraith, J. R. (2014b). Organization design challenges resulting from big data. *Journal of Organization Design, 3(1)*, 2–13.

Galbraith, J. R., Downey, D., & Kates, A. (2002). *Designing dynamic organizations.* New York, NY: AMACOM.

Galbraith, J. R., & Lawler, E. E., III. (1998). The challenge of change: Organizing for competitive advantage. In S. A. Mohrman, J. R. Galbraith, E. E. Lawler III, & Associates (Eds.), *Tomorrow's organization: Crafting winning capabilities in a dynamic world* (pp. 1–20). San Francisco, CA: Jossey-Bass.

Galpin, T. J. (1996). *The human side of change: A practical guide to organization redesign.* San Francisco, CA: Jossey-Bass.

Galpin, T., & Herndon, M. (2008). Merger repair: When M&As go wrong. *Journal of Business Strategy, 29*(1), 4–12.

Gardner, H. K. (2016). *Smart collaboration.* Boston, MA: Harvard Business Review Press.

Gelles, D. (2015, July 19). Pushing shoes and a vision. *New York Times*, BU1, 6.

George, J. M., & Jones, G. R. (2001). Towards a process model of individual change in organizations. *Human Relations, 54*, 419–444.

Gerhart, B. (2010). Compensation. In A. Wilkinson, N. Bacon, T. Redman, & S. Snell, *The SAGE handbook of human resource management* (pp. 210–230). London, England: Sage.

Gerhart, B., & Fang, M. (2014). Pay for (individual) performance: Issues, claims, evidence, and the role of sorting effects. *Human Resource Management Review, 24*, 41–52.

Ghemawat, P., & Nueno, J. L. (2006). *Zara: Fast fashion.* Harvard Business Cases 9–703–497.

Giacobbe-Miller, J. K., Miller, D. J., & Victorov, V. I. (1998). A comparison of Russian and U.S. pay allocation decisions, distributive justice judgments, and productivity under different payment conditions. *Personnel Psychology, 51*, 137–163.

Giancola, F. L. (2011). Skill-based pay: Fad or classic? *Compensation & Benefits Review, 43*(4), 220–226.

Golembiewski, R. T. (2000). Role analysis technique. In R. T. Golembiewski (Ed.), *Handbook of organizational consultation* (2nd ed., pp. 507–508). New York, NY: Marcel Dekker.

Goold, M., & Campbell, A. (2002a). *Designing effective organizations.* San Francisco, CA: Jossey-Bass.

Goold, M., & Campbell, A. (2002b). Do you have a well-designed organization? *Harvard Business Review, 80*(3), 117–124.

Gramling, A. A., Hermanson, D. R., Hermanson, H. M., & Ye, Z. (2010). Addressing problems with the segregation of duties in smaller companies. *CPA Journal, 80*(7), 30–34.

Gratton, L. (2011). Workplace 2025—What will it look like? *Organizational Dynamics, 40*, 246–254.

Greenwood, R., & Miller, D. (2010). Tackling design anew: Getting back to the heart of organizational theory. *Academy of Management Perspectives, 24*, 78–88.

Greiner, L. E. (1998). Evolution and revolution as organizations grow. *Harvard Business Review, 76*(3), 55–68.

Gutteridge, T. G., Leibowitz, Z. B., & Shore, J. E. (1993). *Organizational career development.* San Francisco, CA: Jossey-Bass.

Hackman, J. R., & Oldham, G. R. (1976). Motivation through the design of work: Test of a theory. *Organizational behavior and human performance, 16*, 250–279.

Hackman, J. R., & Oldham, G. R. (1980). *Work redesign.* Reading, MA: Addison-Wesley.

Håkonsson, D. D. (2015). Resume of interview with Professor Charles Snow. *Journal of Organization Design, 4*(1), 50–51.

Hambrick, D. C., & Fredrickson, J. W. (2001). Are you sure you have a strategy? *Academy of Management Executive, 15*(4), 48–59.

Hambrick, D. C., & Snow, C. C. (1988). Strategic reward systems. In C. C. Snow (Ed.), *Strategy, organization design, and human resource management* (pp. 333–368). Greenwich, CT: JAI Press.

Hamel, G. (2011). First, let's fire all the managers. *Harvard Business Review, 89*(12), 48–60.

Hamel, G., & Prahalad, C. K. (1994). *Competing for the future.* Boston, MA: Harvard Business Review Press.

Hammer, M., & Champy, J. (1993). *Reengineering the corporation: A manifesto for business revolution.* New York, NY: Harper Business.

Heckman, F. (1996). The participative design approach. *Journal for Quality and Participation, 19*, 48–51.

Heidari-Robinson, S., & Heywood, S. (2016a, November). Getting reorgs right. *Harvard Business Review,* 84–89.

Heidari-Robinson, S., & Heywood, S. (2016b). *Reorg: How to get it right.* Boston, MA: Harvard Business Preview Press.

Hemp, P. (2002). My week as a room service waiter at the Ritz. *Harvard Business Review, 80*(6), 50–62.

Herzberg, F. (1993). Introduction to the Transaction edition. In F. Herzberg, B. Mausner, & B. B. Snyderman, *The motivation to work* (pp. xi–xviii). New Brunswick, NJ: Transaction.

Herzberg, F., Mausner, B., & Snyderman, B. B. (1959). *The motivation to work.* New York, NY: Wiley.

Hirschhorn, L., & Gilmore, T. (1992). The new boundaries of the "boundaryless" company. *Harvard Business Review, 70*, 104–115.

Hodges J. (2009, December 31). Office (and beanbag) sharing among strangers. *Wall Street Journal*, p. D3.

Hoffman, N. P. (2000). An examination of the "sustainable competitive advantage" concept: Past, present, and future. *Academy of Marketing Science Review, 2000*, 1–14.

Hoffman, R., Casnocha, B., & Yeh, C. (2013). Tours of duty: The new employer-employee contract. *Harvard Business Review, 91*(6), 49–56.

Hofstede, G. (2001). *Culture's consequences.* Thousand Oaks, CA: Sage.

Hofstede, G., Hofstede, G. J., & Minkov, M. (2010). *Cultures and organizations: Software of the mind.* New York, NY: McGraw-Hill.

Holbeche, L. (2006). *Understanding change.* Amsterdam, Netherlands: Elsevier.

Holbeche, L. (2015). *The agile organization.* London, England: Kogan Page.

Horney, N., Pasmore, B., & O'Shea, T. (2010). Leadership agility: A business imperative for a VUCA world. *People & Strategy, 33*(4), 32–38.

Hrebiniak, L. G., Joyce, W. F., & Snow, C. C. (1988). Strategy, structure, and performance: Past and future research. In C. C. Snow (Ed.), *Strategy, organization design, and human resource management* (pp. 3–54). Greenwich, CT: JAI Press.

Huber, G. (2016). Changes in the structures of U.S. companies: Action implications for executives and researchers. *Journal of Organization Design, 5*(8), 1–8.

Hunt, S. T. (2014). *Commonsense talent management.* San Francisco, CA: Wiley.

Huselid, M. A., Beatty, R. W., & Becker, B. E. (2005). "A players" or "A positions"? The strategic logic of workforce management. *Harvard Business Review, 83*(12), 110–117.

Huselid, M. A., & Becker, B. E. (2011). Bridging micro and macro domains: Workforce differentiation and strategic human resource management. *Journal of Management, 37*(2), 421–428.

Huselid, M. A., Becker, B. E., & Beatty, R. W. (2005). *The workforce scorecard.* Boston, MA: Harvard Business.

Inkpen, A., & Ramaswamy, K. (2005). *Global strategy: Creating and sustaining advantage across borders.* New York, NY: Oxford University Press.

Jackson, J. C. (2006). *Organization development.* Lanham, MD: University Press.

Jargon, J. (2014, Oct. 30). McDonald's plans to change U.S. structure. *Wall Street Journal (Online).* Retrieved from https://www.wsj.com/articles/mcdonalds-to-change-u-s-structure-1414695278

Johns, T., & Gratton, L. (2013). The third wave of virtual work. *Harvard Business Review, 91*(1), 66–73.

Johnson, D. W., & Lewicki, R. J. (1969). The initiation of superordinate goals. *Journal of Applied Behavioral Science, 5*, 9–24.

Joiner, B. (2009). Creating a culture of agile leaders: A developmental approach. *People & Strategy, 32*(4), 28–35.

Joiner, B., & Josephs, S. (2007). *Leadership agility: Five levels of mastery for anticipating and initiating change*. San Francisco, CA: Jossey-Bass.

Jordan, J. M. (2017). Challenges to large-scale digital organization: The case of Uber. *Journal of Organization Design*, *6*(11), 1–12.

Joyce, W. F., McGee, V. E., & Slocum, J. W., Jr. (1997). Designing lateral organizations: An analysis of the benefits, costs, and enablers of nonhierarchical organizational forms. *Decision Sciences*, *28*(1), 1–25.

Káganer, E., Carmel, E., Hirscheim, R., & Olsen, T. (2013). Managing the human cloud. *MIT Sloan Management Review*, *54*(2), 23–32.

Kane, G. C., Palmer, D., Phillips, A. N., Kiron, D., & Buckley, N. (2016, Summer). Aligning the organization for its digital future. *MIT Sloan Management Review*, *58*(1), 1–28.

Kaplan, R. S., & Norton, D. P. (1992). The balanced scorecard—Measures that drive performance. *Harvard Business Review*, *70*, 71–79.

Kaplan, R. S., & Norton, D. P. (1993). Putting the balanced scorecard to work. *Harvard Business Review*, *71*, 134–147.

Kaplan, R. S., & Norton, D. P. (1996). *The balanced scorecard: Translating strategy into action*. Boston, MA: Harvard Business Review Press.

Kaplan, R. S., & Norton, D. P. (2001). *The strategy-focused organization*. Boston, MA: Harvard Business Review Press.

Kast, F. E., & Rosenzweig, J. E. (1972). General systems theory: Applications for organization and management. *Academy of Management Journal*, *15*, 447–465.

Kates, A. (2009). Organization design. In W. J. Rothwell, J. M. Stavros, R. L. Sullivan, & A. Sullivan (Eds.), *Practicing organization development* (pp. 446–456). Hoboken, NJ: Wiley.

Kates, A. (2011). Organization design: An interview with Jay Galbraith. *People & Strategy*, *34*(4), 14–17.

Kates, A., & Galbraith, J. R. (2007). *Designing your organization: Using the star model to solve 5 critical design challenges*. San Francisco, CA: Jossey-Bass.

Katz, D., & Kahn, R. L. (1966). *The social psychology of organizations*. New York, NY: Wiley.

Katz, L., & Krueger, A. B. (2016). *The rise and nature of alternative work* (National Bureau of Economic Research Working Paper 22667). Retrieved from https://krueger.princeton.edu/sites/default/files/akrueger/files/katz_krueger_cws_-_march_29_20165.pdf

Keller, J. R., & Cappelli, P. (2014). A supply-chain approach to talent management. In P. Sparrow, H. Scullion, & I. Tarique (Eds.), *Strategic talent management* (pp. 117–150). Cambridge, England: Cambridge University Press.

Keren, M., & Levhari, D. (1979). The optimum span of control in a pure hierarchy. *Management Science*, *25*, 1162–1173.

Kerr, J., & Slocum, J. W., Jr. (1987). Managing corporate culture through rewards systems. *Academy of Management Executive*, *1*, 99–108.

Kerr, S. (1975). On the folly of rewarding "A," while hoping for "B." *Academy of Management Journal*, *18*, 769–783.

Kesler, G. (2008). How Coke's CEO aligned strategy and people to re-charge growth: An interview with Neville Isdell. *People & Strategy*, *31*(2), 18–21.

Kesler, G., & Kates, A. (2011). *Leading organization design*. San Francisco, CA: Jossey-Bass.

Kesler, G., & Kates, A. (2016). *Bridging organization design and performance: 5 ways to activate a global operating model*. Hoboken, NJ: Wiley.

Kesler, G., Kates, A., & Oberg, T. (2016). Design smart decision-making into the organization (and forget RACI). *People & Strategy*, *39*(3), 36–40.

Kilmann, R. H., & McKelvey, B. (1975). The MAPS route to better organization design. *California Management Review*, *17*(3), 23–31.

Kim, W. C., & Mauborgne, R. (2009). How strategy shapes structure. *Harvard Business Review*, *87*(9), 72–80).

Kim, W. C., & Mauborgne, R. (2015). *Blue ocean strategy*. Boston, MA: Harvard Business Review Press.

Kimberly, J. R. (1984). The anatomy of organizational design. *Journal of Management*, *10*(1), 109–126.

Kohn, A. (1993a). *Punished by rewards*. Boston, MA: Houghton Mifflin.

Kohn, A. (1993b). Why incentive plans cannot work. *Harvard Business Review*, *74*(5), 54–63.

Kotter, J. (2012). Accelerate. *Harvard Business Review*, *90*(11), 44–58.

Kotter, J. (2014). *Accelerate*. Boston, MA: Harvard Business Review Press.

Kotter, J. P., & Schlesinger, L. A. (2008). Choosing strategies for change. *Harvard Business Review*, *86*(7–8), 130–139.

Kunisch, S., Müller-Stewens, G., & Campbell, A. (2014). Why corporate functions stumble. *Harvard Business Review, 92*(12), 111–117.

Lancaster, L. C., & Stillman, D. (2010). *The M-factor: How the millennial generation is rocking the workplace.* New York, NY: HarperCollins.

Larson, C. E., & LaFasto, F. M. J. (1989). *TeamWork: What must go right/what can go wrong.* Newbury Park, CA: Sage.

Laszlo, A., & Laszlo, K. C. (2011). Systemic sustainability in OD practice: Bottom line and top line reasoning. *OD Practitioner, 43*(4), 10–16.

Latham, G. P., & Locke, E. A. (2008). Employee motivation. In J. Barling & C. L. Cooper (Eds.), *The SAGE handbook of organizational behavior (Vol. 1)* (pp. 318–333). Los Angeles, CA: Sage.

Lawler, E. E., III. (1990). *Strategic pay: Aligning organizational strategies and pay systems.* San Francisco, CA: Jossey-Bass.

Lawler, E. E., III. (2000). *Rewarding excellence.* San Francisco, CA: Jossey-Bass.

Lawler, E. E., III. (2008). *Talent: Making people your competitive advantage.* San Francisco, CA: Jossey-Bass.

Lawler, E. E., III. (2011). Creating a new employment deal: Total rewards and the new workforce. *Organizational Dynamics, 40,* 302–309.

Lawler, E. E., III. (2017). *Reinventing talent management.* Oakland, CA: Berrett-Koehler.

Lawler, E. E., III, & Boudreau, J. W. (2015). *Global trends in human resource management: A twenty-year analysis.* Stanford, CA: Stanford Business Books.

Lawler, E. E., III, & Jenkins, G. D., Jr. (1990). Strategic reward systems. In M. D. Dunnette & L. M. Hough (Eds.), *Handbook of industrial and organizational psychology, Vol. 3* (2nd ed., pp. 1009–1055). Palo Alto, CA: Consulting Psychologists Press.

Lawler, E. E., III, & Worley, C. G. (2006a). *Built to change.* San Francisco, CA: Jossey-Bass.

Lawler, E. E., III, & Worley, C. G. (2006b, March/April). Winning support for organizational change: Designing employee reward systems that keep on working. *Ivey Business Journal,* 1–5.

Lawrence, P. R., & Lorsch, J. W. (1967a). New management job: The integrator. *Harvard Business Review, 45*(6), 142–151.

Lawrence, P. R., & Lorsch, J. W. (1967b). *Organization and environment: Managing differentiation and integration.* Boston, MA: Harvard Business Review Press.

Lawrence, P. R., & Lorsch, J. W. (1969). *Developing organizations: Diagnosis and action.* Reading, MA: Addison-Wesley.

Ledford, G. E., Jr. (2014). The changing landscape of employee rewards: Observations and prescriptions. *Organizational Dynamics, 43,* 168–179.

Ledford, G. E., Jr., Gerhart, B., & Fang, M. (2013). Negative effects of extrinsic rewards on intrinsic motivation: More smoke than fire. *WorldatWork Journal, 22*(2), 17–29.

Leinwand, P., & Mainardi, C. (2016). *Strategy that works.* Boston, MA: Harvard Business Review Press.

Lewin, K. (1951). *Field theory in social science.* New York, NY: Harper & Brothers.

Locke, E. A., & Latham, G. P. (2002). Building a practically useful theory of goal setting and task motivation: A 35-year odyssey. *American Psychologist, 57,* 705–717.

Lombardo, M. M., & Eichinger, R. W. (2000). High potentials as high learners. *Human Resource Management, 39,* 321–330.

Lorsch, J. W., & McTague, E. (2016). Culture is not the culprit. *Harvard Business Review, 94*(4), 97–105.

Lytle, W. O. (2002). Accelerating the organization design process. *Reflections, 4*(2), 69–77.

Magretta, J. (2012). *Understanding Michael Porter.* Boston, MA: Harvard Business Review Press.

Mankins, M. C., & Garton, E. (2017). *Time, talent, energy.* Boston, MA: Harvard Business Review Press.

March, J. G. (1994). *A primer on decision making.* New York, NY: The Free Press.

Markides, C. (2004). What is strategy and how do you know if you have one? *Business Strategy Review, 15*(2), 5–12.

Marks, M. L. (2006). Workplace recovery after mergers, acquisitions, and downsizings: Facilitating individual adaptation to major organizational transitions. *Organizational Dynamics, 35,* 384–399.

Martins, L. L., Gilson, L. L., & Maynard, M. T. (2004). Virtual teams: What do we know and where do we go from here? *Journal of Management, 30,* 805–835.

Mattson, M., Torbiörn, I., & Hellgren, I. (2014). Effects of staff bonus systems on safety behaviors. *Human Resource Management Review, 24,* 17–30.

Maxwell, I. (2009). *Managing sustainable innovation.* New York, NY: Springer.

McCann, J., & Galbraith, J. R. (1981). Interdepartmental relations. In P. C. Nystrom & W. H. Starbuck (Eds.),

Handbook of organizational design, vol. 1 (pp. 60–84). Oxford, England: Oxford University Press.

McGrath, R. G. (2012). How the growth outliers do it. *Harvard Business Review, 90*(1–2), 111–116.

McGrath, R. G. (2013a). *The end of competitive advantage.* Boston, MA: Harvard Business.

McGrath, R. G. (2013b). Transient advantage. *Harvard Business Review, 91*(6), 62–70.

Meyer, A. (2013). Emerging assumptions about organization design, knowledge and action. *Journal of Organization Design, 2*(3), 16–22.

Meyer, M. W. (2002). *Rethinking performance measurement.* Cambridge, England: Cambridge University Press.

Meyer, P. (2015). *The agility shift.* Brookline, MA: Bibliomotion.

Michaels, E., Handfield-Jones, H., & Axelrod, B. (2001). *The war for talent.* Boston, MA: Harvard Business.

Miles, R. E., Coleman, H. J., Jr., & Creed, W. E. D. (1995). Keys to success in corporate redesign. *California Management Review, 37*(3), 128–145.

Miles, R. E., & Snow, C. C. (1978). *Organizational strategy, structure, and process.* New York, NY: McGraw-Hill.

Miles, R. E., & Snow, C. C. (1984). Designing strategic human resources management systems. *Organizational Dynamics, 13*(1), 36–52.

Miles, R. E., & Snow, C. C. (1986). Organizations: New concepts for new forms. *California Management Review, 28*, 62–73.

Miles, R. E., & Snow, C. C. (1992). Causes of failure in network organizations. *California Management Review, 34*, 53–72.

Miles, R. E., Snow, C. C., Fjeldstad, Ø. D., Miles, G., & Lettl, C. (2010). Designing organizations to meet 21st-century opportunities and challenges. *Organizational Dynamics, 39*, 93–103.

Milgrom, P., & Roberts, J. (1995). Complementarities and fit: Strategy, structure, and organizational change in manufacturing. *Journal of Accounting and Economics, 19*, 179–208.

Miller, D. (1987). Strategy making and structure: Analysis and implications for performance. *Academy of Management Journal, 30*, 7–32.

Miller, D. (1992). The generic strategy trap. *The Journal of Business Strategy, 13*(1), 37–41.

Mintzberg, H. (1979). *The structuring of organizations.* Englewood Cliffs, NJ: Prentice-Hall.

Mintzberg, H. (1987). Five Ps for strategy. *California Management Review, 30*(1), 11–24.

Mintzberg, H., Ahlstrand, B., & Lampel, J. (1998). *Strategy safari.* New York, NY: The Free Press.

Miozza, M. L., & Wyld, D. C. (2002). The carrot or the soft stick? The perspective of American safety professionals on behavior and incentive-based protection programmes. *Management Research News, 25*(11), 23–41.

Mohrman, A. M., Jr., Resnick-West, S. M., Lawler, E. E., III. (1989). *Designing performance appraisal systems.* San Francisco, CA: Jossey-Bass.

Mohrman, S., & Pillans, G. (2013). *Emerging approaches to organisation design.* London, England: Corporate Research Forum.

Mohrman, S. A., & Worley, C. G. (2010). The organizational sustainability journey: Introduction to the special issue. *Organizational Dynamics, 39*, 289–294.

Monge, P. R. (1993). (Re)Designing dynamic organizations. In G. P. Huber & W. H. Glick (Eds.), *Organizational change and redesign* (pp. 323–345). Oxford, England: Oxford University Press.

Moore, G. A. (2015). *Zone to win: Organizing in an age of disruption.* New York, NY: Diversion Books.

Morgan, J. (2014). *The future of work.* Hoboken, NJ: Wiley.

Morrison, R. (2015). *Data-driven organization design.* London, England: Kogan Page.

Nadler, D. (1977). *Feedback and organization development: Using data-based methods.* Reading, MA: Addison-Wesley.

Nadler, D. A., & Tushman, M. L. (1983). A general diagnostic model for organizational behavior: Applying a congruence perspective. In J. R. Hackman, E. E. Lawler III, & L. W. Porter (Eds.), *Perspectives on behavior in organizations* (2nd ed., pp. 112–124). New York, NY: McGraw-Hill.

Nadler, D., & Tushman, M. (1988). *Strategic organization design.* Glenview, IL: Scott, Foresman and Company.

Nadler, D. A., & Tushman, M. L. (1992). Designing organizations that have good fit: A framework for understanding new architectures. In D. A. Nadler, M. S. Gerstein, R. B. Shaw, & Associates (Eds.), *Organizational architecture: Designs for changing organizations* (pp. 39–56). San Francisco, CA: Jossey-Bass.

Nadler, D. A., & Tushman, M. L. (1997). *Competing by design: The power of organizational architecture* (2nd ed.). New York, NY: Oxford University Press.

Nesheim, T. (2011). Balancing process ownership and line management in a matrix-like organization. *Knowledge and Process Management, 18*(2), 109–119.

Niles, S. G. (2005). *Career development interventions in the 21st century*. Upper Saddle River, NJ: Pearson.

Nissen, M. (2014). Organization design for dynamic fit. *Journal of Organization Design*, *3*, 30–42.

Niven, P. (2014). *Balanced scorecard evolution: A dynamic approach to strategy execution*. Hoboken, NJ: Wiley.

Noe, R. A., Clarke, A. D. M., & Klein, H. J. (2014). Learning in the twenty-first century workplace. *Annual Review of Organizational Psychology and Organizational Behavior*, *1*, 245–275.

Noonan, M. C., & Glass, J. L. (2012, June). The hard truth about telecommuting. *Monthly Labor Review*, *1*(35), 38–45.

Oldham, G. R., & Hackman, J. R. (2010). Not what it was and not what it will be: The future of job design research. *Journal of Organizational Behavior*, *31*, 463–479.

Osterwalder, A., & Pigneur, T. (2010). *Business model generation*. Hoboken, NJ: Wiley.

Ostroff, F. (1999). *The horizontal organization*. New York, NY: Oxford University Press.

O'Toole, J. (1995). *Leading change: Overcoming the ideology of comfort and the tyranny of custom*. San Francisco, CA: Jossey-Bass.

Ouchi, W. G. (2006). Power to the principals: Decentralization in three large school districts. *Organization Science*, *17*, 298–307.

Parker, G. M. (1994). *Cross-functional teams*. San Francisco, CA: Jossey-Bass.

Parnell, J. A. (1997). New evidence in the generic strategy and business performance debate: A research note. *British Journal of Management*, *8*, 175–181.

Parnell, J. A. (2006). Generic strategies after two decades: A reconceptualization of competitive strategy. *Management Decision*, *44*, 1139–1154.

Parnell, J. A., & Wright, P. (1993). Generic strategy and performance: An empirical test of the Miles and Snow typology. *British Journal of Management*, *4*, 29–36.

Parrish, B. D. (2010). Sustainability-driven entrepreneurship: Principles of organization design. *Journal of Business Venturing*, *25*, 510–523.

Pasmore, W. A. (1988). *Designing effective organizations*. New York, NY: Wiley.

Paulson, M. (2016, June 9). "Hamilton" raises prices to thwart scalpers: Premium seats now at $849. *New York Times*, A19.

Penrose, E. (1959). *The theory of the growth of the firm*. New York, NY: Oxford.

Pfeffer, J. (2007). *What were they thinking? Unconventional wisdom about management*. Boston, MA: Harvard Business Review Press.

Pink, D. H. (2010). *Drive*. New York, NY: Riverhead.

Porter, M. E. (1979). How competitive forces shape strategy. *Harvard Business Review*, *57*(2), 137–145.

Porter, M. E. (1980). *Competitive strategy*. New York, NY: The Free Press.

Porter, M. E. (1985). *Competitive advantage*. New York, NY: The Free Press.

Porter, M. E. (1986). Competition in global industries: A conceptual framework. In M. E. Porter (Ed.), *Competition in global industries* (pp. 15–60). Boston, MA: Harvard Business.

Porter, M. E. (1987). From competitive advantage to corporate strategy. *Harvard Business Review*, *65*(3), 43–59.

Porter, M. E. (1996). What is strategy? *Harvard Business Review*, *74*(6), 61–78.

Porter, M. E. (2001). Strategy and the Internet. *Harvard Business Review*, *79*(3), 62–78.

Porter, M. E. (2008). The five competitive forces that shape strategy. *Harvard Business Review*, *86*(1), 78–93.

Prahalad, C. K., & Hamel, G. (1990). The core competence of the corporation. *Harvard Business Review*, *68*(3), 79–90.

Proehl, R. A. (1996). Enhancing the effectiveness of cross-functional teams. *Leadership & Organization Development Journal*, *17*, 3–10.

Proposal to Create the Department of Homeland Security. (2002). Retrieved from https://www.dhs.gov/sites/default/files/publications/book_0.pdf

Puranam, P., & Håkonsson, D. D. (2015). Valve's way. *Journal of Organization Design*, *4*(2), 2–4.

Ready, D. A., Hill, L. A., & Thomas, R. J. (2014). Building a game-changing talent strategy. *Harvard Business Review*, *92*(1/2), 63–68.

Reckard, E. S. (2013, December 22). Wells Fargo sales quotas come at a cost. *Los Angeles Times*, p. A1.

Reeves, M., & Deimler, M. (2011). Adaptability: The new competitive advantage. *Harvard Business Review*, *89*(7/8), 135–141.

Reeves, M., Love, C., & Tillmanns, P. (2012). Your strategy needs a strategy. *Harvard Business Review, 90*(9), 76–83.

Regenold, S. (2009, February 5). Working away. *New York Times*, pp. D1, D4.

Reingold, J. (2016). Can P&G find its aim again? *Fortune, 173*(8), 172–180.

Rice, J., & Nash, M. (2011). Lessons learned from a global organization redesign. *People & Strategy, 34*(4), 56–68.

Robertson, B. J. (2015). *Holacracy: The new management system for a rapidly changing world*. New York, NY: Henry Holt.

Rogers, P., & Blenko, M. (2006). Who has the D? *Harvard Business Review, 84*(1), 52–61.

Ronda-Pupo, G. A. & Guerras-Martin, L. A. (2012). Dynamics of the evolution of the strategy concept 1962–2008: A co-word analysis. *Strategic Management Journal, 33*, 162–188.

Rosenbloom, S. (2016, December 4). Navigating the new and expanded Airbnb. *New York Times*, p. 3.

Roth, W. F. (2014). Evaluation and reward systems: The key shapers of organization culture. *Performance Improvement, 53*(8), 24–29.

Ruddy, T., & Anand, P. (2010). Managing talent in global organizations. In R. Silzer & B. E. Dowell (Eds.), *Strategy-driven talent management* (pp. 549–593). San Francisco, CA: Jossey-Bass.

Rugman, A., & Verbeke, A. (1993). Generic strategies in global competition. In A. M. Rugman & A. Verbeke (Eds.), *Research in global strategic management*, Vol. 4. *Global competition: Beyond the three generics* (pp. 3–15). Greenwich, CT: JAI Press.

Rugman, A., & Verbeke, A. (2006). Strategies for multinational enterprises. In A. Campbell & D. O. Faulkner (Eds.), *The Oxford handbook of strategy* (pp. 675–697). Oxford, England: Oxford University Press.

Salavou, H. E. (2015). Competitive strategies and their shift to the future. *European Business Review, 27*(1), 80–99.

Samnani, A., & Singh, P. (2014). Performance-enhancing compensation practices and employee productivity: The role of workplace bullying. *Human Resource Management Review, 24*, 5–16.

Santos, F., Pache, A., & Birkholz, C. (2015). Making hybrids work: Aligning business models and organizational design for social enterprises. *California Management Review, 57*(3), 36–58.

Schein, E. H. (1978). *Career dynamics: Managing individual and organizational needs*. Reading, MA: Addison-Wesley.

Schein, E. H. (2017). *Organizational culture and leadership* (5th ed.). Hoboken, NJ: Wiley.

Schroeder, B., & Denoble, A. (2014). How to design a triple bottom line organization. *Journal of Organization Design, 3*(2), 48–57.

Schuster, M., & Kesler, G. (2011). Aligning rewards systems in organization design: How to activate the orphan star point. *People & Strategy, 34*(4), 38–45.

Scott, D., McMullen, T. D., Shields, J., & Bowbin, B. (2009). Reward alignment: High hopes and hard facts. *WorldAtWork Journal, Fourth Quarter*, 32–47.

Senge, P. M. (1990). *The fifth discipline*. New York, NY: Doubleday/Currency.

Senge, P., Kleiner, A., Roberts, C., Ross, R., Roth, G., & Smith, B. (1999). *The dance of change*. New York, NY: Doubleday.

Shamir, B. (1999). Leadership in boundaryless organizations: Disposable or indispensable? *European Journal of Work and Organizational Psychology, 8*, 49–71.

Shapiro, B. P., Rangan, V. K., & Sviokla, J. (1992). Staple yourself to an order. *Harvard Business Review, 70*(4), 113–122.

Shaw, J. D., & Gupta, N. (2015). Let the evidence speak again! Financial incentives are more effective than we thought. *Human Resource Management Journal, 25*, 281–293.

Sherif, M. (1979). Superordinate goals in the reduction of intergroup conflict: An experimental evaluation. In W. G. Austin & S. Worchel (Eds.), *The social psychology of intergroup relations* (pp. 257–261). Belmont, CA: Wadsworth.

Sherman, J. D., & Keller, R. T. (2011). Suboptimal assessment of interunit task interdependence: Modes of integration and information processing for coordination performance. *Organization Science, 22*(1), 245–261.

Shields, J., & Kaine, S. (2016). Performance and reward basics. In J. Shields, M. Brown, S. Kaine, C. Dolle-Samuel, A. North-Samardzic, P. McLean, . . . & J. Robinson (Eds.), *Managing employee performance and reward: Concepts, practices, strategies* (2nd ed.) (pp. 3–17). Cambridge, England: Cambridge University Press.

Shuman, J., & Twombly, J. (2010). Collaborative networks are the organization: An innovation in organization design and management. *Vikalpa, 35*(1), 1–13.

Silzer, R., & Church, A. H. (2010). Identifying and assessing high-potential talent. In R. Silzer & B. E. Dowell (Eds.), *Strategy-driven talent management* (pp. 213–279). San Francisco, CA: Jossey-Bass.

Silzer, R., & Dowell, B. E. (2010). Strategic talent management matters. In R. Silzer & B. E. Dowell (Eds.), *Strategy-driven talent management* (pp. 3–72). San Francisco, CA: Jossey-Bass.

Simons, R. (2005). *Levers of organization design.* Boston, MA: Harvard Business.

Slinger, G., & Morrison, R. (2014). Will organization design be affected by big data? *Journal of Organization Design, 3*(3), 17–26.

Smart, B. D. (1999). *Topgrading.* Paramus, NJ: Prentice Hall.

Smircich, L. (1985). Is the concept of culture a paradigm for understanding organizations and ourselves? In P. J. Frost, L. F. Moore, M. R. Louis, C. C. Lundberg, & J. Martin (Eds.), *Organizational culture* (pp. 55–72). Beverly Hills, CA: Sage.

Smith, C. H. (2012). How to build an ACO. *Trustee, 65*(2), 26–27.

Snow, C. C. (2015). Organizing in the age of competition, cooperation, and collaboration. *Journal of Leadership & Organizational Studies, 22*, 433–442.

Snow, C. C., Fjeldstad, O. D., & Langer, A. M. (2017). Designing the digital organization. *Journal of Organization Design, 6*(7), 1–13.

Snow, C. C., Miles, R. E., & Miles, G. (2006). The configurational approach to organization design: Four recommended initiatives. In R. M. Burton, B. Eriksen, D. D. Håkonsson, & C. C Snow (Eds.), *Organization design: The evolving state-of-the-art* (pp. 3–18). New York, NY: Springer.

Som, A. (2008). *Organization redesign and innovative HRM.* New Delhi, India: Oxford University Press.

Sparrow, P., Farndale, E., & Scullion, H. (2014). Globalizing the HR architecture: The challenges facing corporate HQ and international-mobility functions. In P. Sparrow, H. Scullion, & I. Tarique (Eds.), *Strategic talent management* (pp. 254–277). Cambridge, England: Cambridge University Press.

Sparrow, P., Scullion, H., & Tarique, I. (2014). Multiple lenses on talent management: Definitions and contours of the field. In P. Sparrow, H. Scullion, & I. Tarique (Eds.), *Strategic talent management* (pp. 36–69). Cambridge, England: Cambridge University Press.

Staats, B. R., & Gino, F. (2012). Specialization and variety in repetitive tasks: Evidence from a Japanese bank. *Management Science, 58*(6), 1141–1159.

Stahl, G. K., Bjorkman, I., Farndale, E., Morris, S. S., Paauwe, J., Stiles, P., . . . & Wright, P. (2012). Six principles of effective global talent management. *MIT Sloan Management Review, 53*(2), 25–32.

Stalk, G., Evans, P., & Shulman, L. E. (1992). Competing on capabilities: The new rules of corporate strategy. *Harvard Business Review, 70*(2), 57–69.

Stanford, N. (2005). *Organization design: The collaborative approach.* Amsterdam, Netherlands: Elsevier.

Stanford, N. (2007). *Guide to organisation design.* London, England: The Economist.

Stanford, N. (2011). *Corporate culture: Getting it right.* Hoboken, NJ: Wiley.

Stanford, N. (2015). *Guide to organisation design* (2nd ed.). New York, NY: Public Affairs.

Starbuck, W. H., & Nystrom, P. C. (1981). Designing and understanding organizations. In P. C. Nystrom & W. H. Starbuck (Eds.), *Handbook of organizational design, vol. 1* (pp. ix–xxii). Oxford, England: Oxford University Press.

Stebbins, M. W., & Shani, A. B. (1989). Organization design: Beyond the "Mafia" model. *Organizational Dynamics, 17*(3), 18–30.

Steers, R. M., Mowday, R. T., & Shapiro, D. L. (2004). The future of work motivation theory. *Academy of Management Review, 29*, 379–387.

Steil, G., Jr., & Gibbons-Carr, M. (2005). Large group scenario planning: Scenario planning with the whole system in the room. *Journal of Applied Behavioral Science, 41*, 15–29.

Steinmetz, J., Bennett, C., & Håkonsson, D. D. (2012). A practitioner's view of the future of organization design: Future trends and implications for Royal Dutch Shell. *Journal of Organization Design, 1*(1), 7–12.

Stevens, L. (2014, September 12). At UPS, e-commerce boom proves a heavy lift. *Wall Street Journal, 264*(62), A1, A10.

Sull, D., Homkes, R., & Sull, C. (2015). Why strategy execution unravels—and what to do about it. *Harvard Business Review, 93*(3), 58–66.

Sullivan, S. E. (1999). The changing nature of careers: A review and research agenda. *Journal of Management, 25*, 457–484.

Tabuchi, H., & Stout, H. (2015, June 15). *Gap's fashion-backward moment.* Retrieved from https://www.nytimes.com/2015/06/21/business/gaps-fashion-backward-moment.html? emc=eta1&_r=0

Tarique, I., & Schuler, R. (2014). A typology of talent-management strategies. In P. Sparrow, H. Scullion, & I. Tarique (Eds.), *Strategic talent management* (pp. 177–193). Cambridge, England: Cambridge University Press.

Taylor, A. (2006, November 13). Ford's student driver takes the wheel. *Fortune, 154*(10), 96–100.

Taylor, F. W. (1911). *The principles of scientific management.* New York, NY: Harper & Row.

Tett, G. (2015). *The silo effect.* New York, NY: Simon & Schuster.

Thompson, A. A., Jr., Strickland III, A. J., & Gamble, J. E. (2008). *Crafting and executing strategy: The quest for competitive advantage* (16th ed.). Boston, MA: McGraw-Hill.

Thompson, J. D. (1967). *Organizations in action.* New York, NY: McGraw-Hill.

Tichy, N., & Fombrun, C. (1979). Network analysis in organizational settings. *Human Relations, 32*, 923–965.

Tolchinsky, P. D., & Wenzl, L. (2014). High engagement organization design. *People & Strategy, 37*(1), 34–38.

Topp, K., & Desjardins, J. H. (2011). Span of control. In Wolf, J. A., Hanson, H., & Moir, M. J (Eds.), *Organization development in health care* (pp. 211–230). Charlotte, NJ: Information Age.

Tosi, H. L., Jr., & Slocum, J. W., Jr. (1984). Contingency theory: Some suggested directions. *Journal of Management, 10*, 9–26.

Treacy, M., & Wiersema, F. (1993). Customer intimacy and other value disciplines. *Harvard Business Review, 71*(1), 84–93.

Treacy, M., & Wiersema, F. (1995). *The discipline of market leaders.* New York, NY: Basic Books.

Trost, A. (2014). *Talent relationship management.* New York, NY: Springer.

Tushman, M. L., & Nadler, D. A. (1978). Information processing as an integrating concept in organizational design. *Academy of Management Review, 3*, 613–624.

Urwick, L. F. (1956). The manager's span of control. *Harvard Business Review, 34*(3), 39–47.

Van Alstyne, M. W., Parker, G. G., & Choudary, S. P. (2016). Pipelines, platforms, and the new rules of strategy. *Harvard Business Review, 94*(4), 54–62.

Van de Ven, A. H., Delbecq, A. L., & Koenig, R. Jr. (1976). Determinants of coordination modes within organizations. *American Sociological Review, 41*, 322–338.

Van de Ven, A. H., & Joyce, W. F. (1981). Overview of perspectives on organization design and behavior. In A. H. Van de Ven & W. F. Joyce (Eds.), *Perspectives on organization design and behavior* (pp. 1–16). New York, NY: Wiley.

Van Vugt, M. (2017). Evolutionary psychology: Theoretical foundations for the study of organizations. *Journal of Organization Design, 6*(9), 1–16.

Visscher, K., & Fisscher, O. A. M. (2009). Cycles and diamonds: How management consultants diverge and converge in organization design processes. *Creativity and Innovation Management, 18*(2), 121–131.

Von Krogh, G., & Geilinger, N. (2015). Valve's organization: Opportunities and open questions. *Journal of Organization Design, 4*(2), 18–19.

Vroom, V. H. (1964). *Work and motivation.* New York, NY: Wiley.

Vroom, V. H. (2013). Expectancy theory. In E. H. Kessler (Ed.), *Encyclopedia of management theory* (pp. 271–276). Thousand Oaks, CA: Sage.

Wack, P. (1985a). Scenarios: Shooting the rapids. *Harvard Business Review, 63*(6), 139–150.

Wack, P. (1985b). Scenarios: Unchartered waters ahead. *Harvard Business Review, 63*(5), 73–89.

Walker, A. H., & Lorsch, J. W. (1968). Organizational choice: Product vs. function. *Harvard Business Review, 46*(6), 129–138.

Walter, G. A. (1985). Culture collisions in mergers and acquisitions. In P. J. Frost, L. F. Moore, M. R. Louis, C. C. Lundberg, & J. Martin (Eds.), *Organizational culture* (pp. 301–314). Beverly Hills, CA: Sage.

Watkins, M. D. (2013). *The first 90 days.* Boston, MA: Harvard Business Review Press.

Watkins, M. D. (2016). Leading the team you inherit. *Harvard Business Review, 94*(6), 61–67.

Watts, S. (2001). *The Magic Kingdom: Walt Disney and the American way of life.* Columbia: University of Missouri Press.

Webb, E. J., Campbell, D. T., Schwartz, R. D., & Sechrest, L. (1966). *Unobtrusive measures: Nonreactive research in the social sciences*. Chicago, IL: Rand McNally.

Webb, E., & Weick, K. E. (1979). Unobtrusive measures in organizational theory: A reminder. *Administrative Science Quarterly, 24*, 650–659.

Webber, S. S. (2002). Leadership and trust facilitating cross-functional team success. *Journal of Management Development, 21*, 201–214.

Weibel, A., & Rota, S. (2002). Fairness as a motivator. In B. S. Grey & M. Osterloh (Eds.), *Successful management by motivation* (pp. 171–189). Berlin, Germany: Springer.

Weick, K. E. (1993). Organizational design as improvisation. In G. P. Huber & W. H. Glick (Eds.), *Organizational change and redesign* (pp. 346–379). Oxford, England: Oxford University Press.

Weick, K. E. (2004). Rethinking organizational design. In R. J. Boland, Jr., & F. Collopy (Eds.), *Managing as designing* (pp. 36–53). Stanford, CA: Stanford University Press.

Weick, K. E., & Quinn, R. E. (1999). Organizational change and development. *Annual Review of Psychology, 50*, 361–386.

Wenger, E. C., McDermott, R., & Snyder, W. M. (2002). *Cultivating communities of practice*. Boston, MA: Harvard Business.

Wenger, E. C., & Snyder, W. M. (2000). Communities of practice: The organizational frontier. *Harvard Business Review, 78*(1), 139–145.

Wessel, M., & Christensen, C. M. (2012). Surviving disruption. *Harvard Business Review, 90*(12), 56–64.

West, M. A. (2004). *Effective teamwork: Practical lessons from organizational research* (2nd ed.). Malden, MA: Blackwell.

Whittington, R., Pettigrew, A., Peck, S., Fenton, E., & Conyon, M. (1999). Change and complementarities in the new competitive landscape: A European panel study, 1992–1996. *Organization Science, 10*, 583–600.

Wiener-Bronner, D., & Sanicola, L. (2018, January 11). *Sam's Club store closings are a PR mess on Walmart's big day*. Retrieved from http://money.cnn.com/2018/01/11/news/companies/walmart-sams-club-pr-mess/index.html

Womack, J. P., Jones, D. T., & Roos, D. (1990). *The machine that changed the world*. New York, NY: Simon & Schuster.

Woodman, R. W., & Pasmore, W. A. (2002). The heart of it all: Group- and team-based interventions in organization development. In J. Waclawski & A. H. Church (Eds.), *Organization development: A data-driven approach to organizational change* (pp. 164–176). San Francisco, CA: Jossey-Bass.

WorldatWork. (2007). *The WorldatWork handbook of compensation, benefits & total rewards*. Hoboken, NJ: Wiley.

Worley, C. G., & Lawler, E. E., III. (2010). Agility and organization design: A diagnostic framework. *Organizational Dynamics, 39*(2), 194–204.

Worley, C. G., Williams, T., & Lawler, E. E., III. (2014). *The agility factor*. San Francisco, CA: Jossey-Bass.

Worren, N. (2011). Hitting the sweet spot between separation and integration in organization design. *People & Strategy, 34*(4), 24–30.

Yoo, Y., Boland, R. J., Jr., & Lyytinen, K. (2006). From organization design to organization designing. *Organization Science, 17*, 215–229.

Yost, P. R., & Plunkett, M. M. (2010). Developing leadership talent through experience. In R. Silzer & B. E. Dowell (Eds.), *Strategy-driven talent management* (pp. 313–348). San Francisco, CA: Jossey-Bass.

Younger, J., & Smallwood, N. (2016). *Agile talent: How to source and manage outside experts*. Boston, MA: Harvard Business Review Press.

Zeffane, R. (1992). Organizational structures: Design in the nineties. *Leadership & Organization Development Journal, 13*(6), 18–23.

Zhou, J., & Martocchio, J. J. (2001). Chinese and American managers' compensation award decisions: A comparative policy-capturing study. *Personnel Psychology, 54*(1), 115–145.

Zingheim, P. K., & Schuster, J. R. (2002). Reassessing the value of skill-based pay: Getting the runaway train back on track. *WorldatWork Journal, 11*(3), 1–7.

Zobal, C. (1999). The "ideal" team compensation system—An overview, part II. *Team Performance Management, 5*(1), 23–45.

INDEX